My respect for Linda Sommer as ar [...]
hearts together. We have a common interest [...] knowing Jesus and making him
known. I encourage you to take this daily journey with Linda through God's
Word and be challenged to apply God's Word to your daily life.

—BABBIE MASON
PRESIDENT
BABBIE MASON MINISTRIES

A life-giving and joyful prescription for success is a daily dose of God's Word.
As Linda Sommer proves, the best part is that no matter where you are on the
journey, you can take it with you.

—DR. MARK RUTLAND
PRESIDENT
SOUTHEASTERN COLLEGE

Linda Sommer, in both of her devotional books, *Around the Word in 365 Days*
and *You Can Take It With You*, has crafted two practical hands-on tools that
will greatly enrich your reading of the Bible. Her daily devotionals provide
clarity, encouragement, and real-life applications of key passages throughout
the Scriptures.

—DR. KENNETH BOA
PRESIDENT
REFLECTIONS MINISTRIES

A DAILY DEVOTIONAL GUIDE FOR DOING GOD'S WORD

YOU CAN TAKE IT
WITH YOU

"...lay up for yourselves
treasures in heaven..."
(Matthew 6:20a)

LINDA SOMMER

Blessings,

Linda Sommer

CREATION
HOUSE PRESS

*Dear Bob &
Barbara,*

*May the
Lord bless you.
The joy of the
Lord is your
strength.*

Phil. 2:13

You Can Take It With You by Linda Sommer
Published by Creation House Press
A Strang Company
600 Rinehart Road
Lake Mary, Florida 32746
www.creationhouse.com

Unless otherwise noted, Scripture quotations are from the New King James
Version of the Bible. Copyright © 1979, 1980, 1982 by Thomas Nelson, Inc.,
publishers. Used by permission.

Scripture quotations marked KJV are from the King James Version of the Bible.

Cover design by Ededron J. Hernandez

Library of Congress Control Number: 2004102755
International Standard Book Number: 1-59185-562-4

04 05 06 07 08 — 987654321
Printed in the United States of America

I dedicate this book to my three sons,
Russell, Ronald, and Raymond,
who will be part of the inheritance my husband, Tom, and I
will leave when we see Jesus face to face.
As we look at the eight grandchildren our sons have,
we rejoice because we know they will be trained
in the fear of the Lord and will be
laborers in this last great harvest.

David wrote, "Praise the LORD! Blessed is the man
who fears the LORD, who delights greatly
in His commandments. His descendants will be mighty
on earth; the generation of the upright will be blessed"
(Psalm 112:1–2). Tom and I may not live to see
our grandchildren graduate from college,
but we will be present to see them
receive their spiritual diplomas
(heavenly rewards).

Acknowledgments

My loving appreciation to...

The Three in One: My loving heavenly Father, who revealed through His Word the many treasures we can take with us to heaven. Jesus Christ, the lover of my soul, who made it possible for me to be co-heir with Him. Because of His sacrifice, I can enjoy the inheritance of His kingdom here on earth and in heaven. The Holy Spirit, who helped me to discover new ways to glorify Jesus in my daily life.

Tyndale House, who published the One Year Bible that has so blessed me over the years.

Allen Quain, manager of Creation House Press, and his editors and staff who put the final touches on this book.

Gail Deel and Sara Dixon for the early editing.

David Provost for the picture on the back cover.

Fred Kelly for writing the Foreword.

My Monday night prayer group, who prayed many effective prayers for this book.

My husband, Tom, for his loving support throughout this project.

Contents

Foreword

B ooks offer us the chance to explore familiar topics with a new insight. Many books have been written about the Bible with unique perspectives and a diversity of viewpoints to help us make our study of the Word more effective. Authors with years of study can communicate truth in ways we might never grasp. Indeed, writers with any kind of special experiences can make a connection to the Truth that is powerful and effective. This is that sort of book.

To read the Word of God is a Christian imperative, yet it seems many Christians do not. That is a pity since the blessing attendant to its reading makes the Bible a treasure of greatest value. But since reading a book about The Book can whet one's appetite, much as a fragrant aroma calls one to hurry to one's dinner, all is not lost. Even lifelong procrastinators can read this work of daily devotionals and be encouraged to crack open the Word to see for themselves what these studies from life reveal.

Linda Sommer's daily insights into the Word of God are accompanied by some very delightful anecdotes. After a lifetime of marriage and parenting, she has a million stories about life going wrong, going sideways, and going wonderfully right. Moments of sheer ecstasy, moments of pain and grief, and a monumental faith mark these pages.

I have known Linda for nearly thirty years and have been hearing her laughter up and down the corridors of our church all of that time. This woman knows something about life, and love, and family, and her greatest love has always been Jesus.

Come explore the pages of God's Book with a woman of verve, a woman of style. Here is the antidote to the boring ritual of morning devotions, and I promise you will learn to love The Book more than ever as you read this book, and that is the greatest desire of the author. She wants us to love The Book with the intensity she loves it, to feel its power with her same passion, and to discover its endless answers to life's perplexities. Happy reading!

—REVEREND FRED KELLY
SENIOR PASTOR
LANDMARK CHURCH

Introduction

As I enter my golden years, investments take on a new meaning. I realize I will leave behind all my monetary investments when I exit this earth. What will I be able to invest in now that will add to my heavenly bank account? Is it too late for me to start making eternal investments that will have an effect upon my eternal rewards in heaven?

Jesus tells us not to lay up treasures on this earth where moth and rust corrupt and where thieves break in and steal; instead, we are to lay up for ourselves treasures in heaven where moth and rust will not corrupt, and where thieves will not break through to steal. (See Matthew 6:19–20.) What we treasure is what we give our hearts and souls to keep.

This exhortation of Jesus caused me to examine my own life and ask myself these questions:

- Where is my treasure?
- Is it on earth?
- Or is it in heaven?

I discovered the answer to these questions when I was touring Israel. Our tour was at Megiddo, and we were observing the twenty or more layers of civilization. Each civilization was reduced to less than one foot of ash. As I looked at this amazing phenomenon, the Lord spoke this to my heart: *"Why do you spend so much time taking care of ashes?"*

I realized how much of my time is spent tending to earthly things that will ultimately burn. At that moment, I was challenged to invest my life into three eternal things–faith, hope, and love. I have come to see that these three things will last forever. Why? Because they represent the eternal soul of Jesus—His mind, His emotions and His will. Jesus' mind was filled with faith, His emotions were anchored in hope, and His will was motivated by His love for His heavenly Father.

When I invest in growing in faith, hope, and love, I am laying up for myself treasures in heaven. When I go to heaven there are only a few things I will be able to take with me. I will take my soul and spirit, the Word of God I have hidden in my heart, the fear of the Lord, the praise and worship of the Lord, the prayers I have prayed on earth, my thoughts, and words about the Lord. These glorious treasures will increase in the exact measure that I increase in faith, hope, and love.

After writing *Around the Word in 365 Days*, a devotional companion book to the *One Year Bible* published by Tyndale House, I was challenged to write a book of devotions that would emphasize the eternal treasures we can invest in as we prepare ourselves for eternity. Moses exhorted us to teach ourselves to number our days so that we can apply our hearts to wisdom. (See Psalm 90:12.)

When we are young, we think we will live forever. We have plenty of time to make commitments, keep promises, and think about our eternal destination. If you are like me, I was often less than wise in the decisions I made in my youth. I was more interested in having fun and friends each day because I knew I had many tomorrows. When our tomorrows on this earth begin to grow fewer, we want to redeem the time.

Instead of wasting it, *You Can Take It With You* is written to challenge us all to make eternal investments while we are still living.

One of the investments I want to make while I am still alive is to write a devotional on every passage listed in the One Year Bible. For over thirty years I have read the Bible through each year. My annual journey through the Bible became much more exciting when I began to use the One Year Bible plan of reading scriptures. The daily readings are divided into passages from the Old Testament, the New Testament, Psalms, and Proverbs. I feel like I am getting a complete meal of spiritual food as I use this method of reading the Bible.

My previous book, *Around the Word in 365 Days*, highlighted one of the four passages listed for the day in the *One Year Bible*. The devotions in *You Can Take it With You* are based on passages that were not highlighted in my first devotional book. As we journey this year through the Bible, we will make stops along the way that will cause us to look and listen to God's Word with spiritual eyes and ears tuned to the things eternal.

This devotional book is not only written for seniors, but also for those of any age who recognize that their days may be short on this earth. I believe we are in the End Times. The Lord could come at any time. This should give us all an urgency to make every day count and to daily add to our heavenly bank accounts.

The investment lessons at the end of each devotional will help us change our way of thinking. Repentance is a change of our minds—a turn-around in our thinking. Repentance is a gift from God in response to a heart that cries out for change. True repentance is not just asking for forgiveness and saying we are sorry. It is receiving the power of God to turn away from our sins. The turnaround in our thinking is demonstrated by a change in our behavior.

It is never too late in life for us to change the way we think and the way we behave. The changes we make as we number our days will affect our rewards in heaven. I pray my own soul will grow daily to be more like the soul of Jesus. I want my mind to be renewed to think with faith. I want my emotions to be anchored in the hope built on nothing less than Jesus Christ and His righteousness. I want my will to be motivated by love for my heavenly Father just as Jesus' will was moved with compassion.

According to a recent Gallup poll, 87 percent of professing Christians admit that they do not read the Bible regularly. *You Can Take It With You* will inspire you to read through the Bible in a year. If you have never had a regular program for reading the Bible through in a year, *You Can Take It With You* will encourage you to be consistent in the daily discipline of Bible reading. Join me as I daily journey through the Bible this year. We will make a stop daily to deposit something eternal into our heavenly bank account!

Don't Forget the "Begets"
Matthew 1:1–2:12

As I read through the Bible each year, I usually use the "*Reader's Digest* Method," after the publication that condenses novels into a capsulated form. I read this morning's reading in Matthew 1. After reading the first two names listed, I skipped over the rest of the names. Then I remembered the testimony of a completed Jew whose whole life was changed when he read Matthew 1.

His name was Abraham, and he lived in Jerusalem. Abraham had been taking guitar lessons for one year when his teacher gave every student a special gift. As he presented the same gift to each student, the teacher said, "Don't open this until you are alone and quiet." Abraham hurried from his teacher's home eager to find that quiet spot where he could open his new treasure. He found a quiet street and sat on the curb. He tore into this package and to his horror discovered his gift was a small black book entitled *The New Testament*. Abraham immediately threw the gift in the gutter because, as an Orthodox Jew, he was forbidden to read the New Testament.

Abraham continued to take guitar lessons, but now he knew his teacher wanted him to learn more than how to play the guitar. Several weeks passed when his teacher asked, "Abraham, how did you like my gift?" Abraham quickly responded, "Oh, I lost it." "We can fix that," the teacher said. "Here is another one. I trust you will enjoy it."

Abraham left with the gift, but this time the temptation was too great. "It won't hurt if I just read the first page," Abraham thought as he began to read. He had not even finished reading the first chapter of Matthew, when Abraham's eyes were opened. As he read the lineage of Jesus and how Jesus descended from David, he knew Jesus was the Messiah. He knew Messiah had to come from the house of David. Abraham became a believer through reading the "begets." Abraham was begotten (born into the kingdom of God) by the "begets." Every word in God's Word has the power to change lives. Treasure each word and don't skip the "begets."

> *Father, Your Word never returns void. Help me to treasure every Word*
> *as I read through the Bible this year.*

Daily Deposit: We need to pray about the gifts we give to others. One gift could change a life for eternity. One of the joys in my life has been the privilege of giving my book, *Around the Word in 365 Days*, to people, as the Lord leads me. Any gift that presents God's Word has the potential of changing a life. God's Word always performs what it is sent out to do, and it never returns void. God's Word is an eternal treasure that we can share with people here and now.

Can Anything Good Come From Nazareth?
Matthew 2:13–3:6

When my husband and I lead tours to Israel, we tell the bus driver not to go to Nazareth. The driver usually thanks us for leaving this city out of our itinerary because Nazareth today is filled with traffic confined to extremely narrow roads.

The Nazareth where Jesus grew into manhood, however, was quite different. Nazareth was a peaceful little village set on a hillside. On our last visit to Israel, we decided to go to Nazareth because one of the couples in the tour group expressed a great desire to visit this city. Our tour leader led us to the home of Mary and Joseph. Archeologists exposed the foundation of what was believed to be the actual home where Jesus grew in wisdom, stature, and favor with God and man.

In our reading today, Matthew tells us that when Joseph and Mary returned to Israel after Herod died, they settled in the town of Nazareth. When Jesus began His earthly ministry, many Jews doubted His claim to be the Son of God because they knew prophets had declared that the Messiah would be from Bethlehem.

When Philip found Nathaniel and told him they had found the One the law and the prophets wrote about (Jesus of Nazareth, the son of Joseph), Nathaniel responded, "Can anything good come out of Nazareth?" To those living in the time of Jesus, Nazareth was considered a "nothing town." Even though it was prophesied that Messiah would be called a Nazarene, the minds of many were closed to the truth that Jesus was both their Messiah and the Son of God. During Jesus' ministry, He returned to Nazareth. He was met there by such unbelief that no mighty miracles could take place. The citizens of Nazareth remembered Jesus only as the son of Joseph, the carpenter. "How could He be the Son of God?" they questioned.

What would Jesus' response be to the question, "Can anything good come out of Nazareth?" I believe His response would be the same response He gave to the rich young ruler. When this rich young man called Jesus good, He responded, "Why do you call Me good? No one is good but God." When Jesus said this, He was acknowledging the truth that He was not only the Son of God, but also the Son of Man. Jesus, the Son of Man, as a human being was subject to the very same temptations we are. Only His total dependency upon God the Father and His Word gave Him the power to overcome Satan. Are you totally dependent upon God's goodness and His good Word to deliver you today?

Jesus, let Your goodness flow through me today.

Daily Deposit: Sometimes we feel like we have too many wasted years as we review our lives, but one act of goodness in faith today can redeem the wasted years.

More "Begets"
Genesis 5:1–7:24

The passage today lists the descendents of Adam from the birth of Seth to the birth of Noah's three sons, Shem, Ham and Japeth. There is no mention of Cain. Cain was Adam's firstborn who received a curse because he killed his brother Abel. After Abel's murder, God gave Adam a son after his own likeness. His name was Seth.

God's desire has always been to raise up a people after His own likeness. This is one of the reasons He created man. Remember the words, "Let Us create man in Our image, according to our likeness" (Gen. 1:26). Who was the "us" in this statement? God is a triune God–God the Father, God the Son, and God the Holy Spirit. The great "Three in One" created man in His image. God spoke His Word (Jesus Christ is the living Word of God) and then He breathed into man (the Holy Spirit was breathed into man), and man became a living soul created in the image of God, according to His likeness.

God is love. God designed man to be the physical manifestation of His love. God is a Spirit, and at the time of creation Jesus still had not been born on earth as a man. Earth was created of matter–something that could be touched and seen. To manifest Himself on earth, God needed a physical body to display His love.

God created man, but sin entered after Adam and Eve ate from the tree of knowledge of good and evil. This delayed God's plan to display His love in human form. Mankind did not grow more like God, but instead grew more like the devil. God had no other choice but to begin again. All mankind, but eight people (Noah, his wife, his sons and their wives) were destroyed in the great flood. Then Noah's son, Ham, saw his father's nakedness, and, once again, man was cursed. Ham's son Caanan was cursed. God said that Caanan and all of his descendents would be servants of servants to their brethren.

Would there ever be a people who would display God's love to all the earth? Thank God, we know the rest of the story. All the curses placed upon man because of his disobedience were reversed on the cross by the only perfect, righteous human being. His name is Jesus Christ, King of Kings and Lord of Lords. Because of the blood Jesus shed as God's perfect sacrifice for sin, we now are made righteous in the sight of God. We now, as Christ's body on earth, have the great privilege to display God's love to all mankind. Have you displayed God's love today to someone?

Father, thank You for sending Your Son as a gift of Your love.

Daily Deposit: Right now, as you sit in your chair, you can display God's love by praying for your children, grandchildren, and generations to come to all become vessels of God's love on earth. The witness of your descendents will continue after you are gone.

The Symbol of Peace
Genesis 8:1–10:32

The rains came and lasted for forty days. I'm sure Noah wondered if the storm would ever cease. It took one hundred and fifty days before the waters began to decrease. How would Noah know when it was safe to venture once again upon land? After ten months had passed, Noah sent a raven out from the ark in hopes that it would return. He also sent a dove from the ark as a test. The raven continued to go to and fro on the earth and found no resting place, never returning to the ark. The dove also found no resting place for the sole of her foot, but she returned to the ark. Noah drew the dove back into the ark and waited. Once again he sent the dove out from the ark after waiting for seven days. This time the dove returned in the same evening with a fresh olive leaf in her beak. Noah then knew the waters had receded from the earth. Seven days later he sent the dove out again, but this time the dove did not return.

The international sign for peace is the dove with an olive leaf in its beak. You see this sign on Christmas cards and on many other documents. The dove with the olive leaf expresses that the storms are over and it is now safe. Peace at last reigns. The dove with the olive leaf, however, has a much deeper meaning. We know when the Holy Spirit descended upon Jesus at His baptism the Holy Spirit was in the form of a dove. The oil from the olive tree was what the priests used to light the candlestick in the temple. The candlestick represents the fire of the Holy Spirit. Each of the seven branches of the candlestick represents an empowerment or anointing of the Holy Spirit. If we look at Isaiah 11:2, we see these words, "The Spirit of the Lord shall rest upon Him, the Spirit of wisdom and understanding, the Spirit of counsel and might, the Spirit of knowledge and of the fear of the Lord." The dove with the olive leaf can also represent the powerful anointing of the Holy Spirit.

When will we experience peace in the midst of every storm in our lives? When will it be safe to venture out and possess the land? The answer to these questions is found in the symbol of peace (the dove with the olive leaf). Only when God's anointing rests upon us, and His power ignites us will we be empowered to experience peace, no matter what stormy trials we face. This inspires me to ask today for the anointing of God's Holy Spirit. Will you join me as I pray?

> *Lord, only You know what storms I may face today. I need Your Spirit*
> *to anoint me anew and afresh.*

Daily Deposit: One of the fruits of love is peace. This fruit is a peace that only Jesus can give us. It is the peace that comes in the midst of the storm. He left His peace to us as our inheritance. We can give the peace of Jesus as an inheritance to our children and grandchildren. This is an inheritance that will never be foolishly spent.

January 5

Read: Genesis 11:1–13:4; Matthew 5:1–26, Psalm 5:1–12, Proverbs 1:24–28

The Divided Tongue
Genesis 11:1–13:4

Proverbs has so much to say about the power of the tongue. We read in Proverbs 18:21, "Death and life are in the power of the tongue, And those who love it will eat its fruit." We have all heard the expression: "You may have to eat those words." This expression is a good summary of Proverbs 18:21. We also read in Proverbs 21:6, "Getting treasures by a lying tongue is the fleeting fantasy of those who seek death." Proverbs 12:19 says, "The truthful lip shall be established forever, But a lying tongue is but for a moment."

In our passage today we see what power the tongue can wield. Yesterday we talked about the peace that can come in the midst of the storms in our lives if we will operate in the anointing of the Holy Spirit. When we operate in the anointing of the Holy Spirit, our tongues will be used to dispense life, not death to others. A lying tongue can cause death, but a wholesome tongue is a tree of life. (See Proverbs 15:4.)

After the flood, all of mankind spoke the same language. We might ask the question, "Why wouldn't this be great?" My husband and I have had many foreign students stay in our home. We had a Chinese daughter live with us for five years, a Russian son lived with us for seven years, and a Hungarian young man stayed with us for nine months. We were able to communicate our love freely to the Chinese girl and the Russian young man because they spoke English well. This is why they became like a son and daughter to us. However, we experienced great difficulty as we tried to express love to this Hungarian young man. He knew very little English. How we longed to reach out to him in love, but often our attempts were misunderstood because of the language barrier. I often prayed, "Lord, it would be so easy to communicate with Gabor if we spoke the same language."

In our passage today, we see how God divided the languages of every nation. Why did He do such a thing? We forget that God knows our hearts, and He knew that pride was ruling in the hearts of men. He knew if they continued to speak the same language, pride would be their destruction. Pride is the source of all contention. To prevent strife, He confused their language and scattered the nations abroad. Perhaps over history, wars have been prevented because people did not speak the same language. God knew that men's hearts were wicked, and if they all spoke the same language, even more wickedness would come upon the earth.

Lord, help me to speak life, not death today.

Daily Deposit: The words we speak have the power to bring life or death to those we talk to today. Words about Jesus always bring life to others, and they are recorded in a book in heaven. (See Malachi 3:16.)

Be Perfect
Matthew 5:27–48

"Therefore you shall be perfect just as your Father in heaven is perfect." This exhortation comes in the middle of what we call the *Sermon on the Mount.* After the delivery of all the beatitudes, Jesus exhorts us to "be" as perfect as our heavenly Father. Our natural response to this exhortation is, "Lord, there is no way I can be as perfect as God the Father!" All the commandments and exhortations in the *Sermon on the Mount* are impossible to man.

As human beings we are plagued with three lusts: the lust of the flesh (seeking to fulfill our five senses in an indulgent or addictive way); the lust of the eyes (fantasies, greedy longings in our minds and covetousness), and the lust called "the pride of life" (trusting in our own resources and personal ability rather than trusting in God's provision and grace). We are stuck with these lusts until we die. Jesus knew this was our condition when He delivered the *Sermon on the Mount.* Jesus was expressing that it is the attitude of the heart that counts with God. The religious Jews in Jesus' day sought to establish their own righteousness by obeying the law. Jesus was making it clear that keeping the law was impossible. We may look obedient to God by our outward actions. However, if our heart motivation is to earn righteousness through outward obedience, our actions are not pleasing to God.

Jesus overcame the world with all of its lusts, and He is our only hope to overcome our own fleshly lusts. The only way we can be perfect in the sight of God is to give our lives to the only perfect human being who ever lived on earth. His name is Jesus. He can cleanse and heal our hearts and enable us by His grace to walk in the ways of God. My life verse is Philippians 2:13, "For it is God who works in you both to will and to do for His good pleasure." Jesus is God in the flesh. On the cross He conquered sin and death.

Jesus satisfied God's requirement of a blood sacrifice for sin. Without the shedding of blood there is no remission of sin. When we receive Jesus as our Lord and Savior, by faith believing that He lived to give us abundant life and that He died and was resurrected to give us eternal life, He comes to dwell within us. No longer are we dependent upon our own ability. We now can respond to the ability of Jesus, the Perfect One, to empower us to live a life that pleases God. Only the life of Jesus can please the Father, and only Jesus' life within us can enable us to live a life that is pleasing to God. Have you received the Perfect One who can help you be more like God the Father?

> *Father, I know I am not perfect. Thank You for sending the Perfect One, Jesus Christ, to live His life through me.*

Daily Deposit: Any work done through Christ (the Perfect One) will last eternally. Our own works done in our own power will be burned. (See 1 Corinthians 3:12–15.)

The Blessings of Obedience
Genesis 16:1–18:19

Yesterday we talked about being perfect as the Father in heaven is perfect. The conclusion was that none of us is perfect, but Jesus Christ is the only Perfect One. Through His life within us we can obey the Father.

The story in Genesis clearly shows the consequences of disobedience and the rewards of obedience. Abraham had a heart that wanted to obey the Lord, but He was just like us. He was not perfect. Many years prior to that, God had promised Him that he would have a son. Abraham got tired of waiting. He was now eighty-six years old, and Sarah was past her child-bearing years. The thought of impregnating his wife at her age seemed impossible. Abraham was led astray by the lust called the *pride of life*. In a weak moment Abraham listened to his wife's suggestion that he take her handmaiden, Hagar, and impregnate her. Hagar gave birth to Ishmael. The angel told Hagar that Ishmael would be as a wild man. His hand would be against every man's hand and every man's hand would be against him, and he would dwell in the presence of his brethren. Through this conception the Arab nation was birthed and the Jewish-Arab conflict was also born.

One moment of impatience created a problem that is with us to this day. Generations were affected by Abraham's going ahead of what God promised. Yet, Abraham is still called the father of our faith. Abraham believed God at the moment that the promise of a son was given to him, and the Lord accounted his faith to him for righteousness. However, Abraham failed to wait with patience for the promise. It is through patience that we inherit the promises of God. God did not give up on Abraham. He exhorted him to walk before him and to be perfect. This time Abraham obeyed God, and even though Sarah laughed at the possibility of having a child at ninety-nine, by faith, Abraham acted upon this promise. He impregnated Sarah when she was ninety-nine and he was one hundred years old. Now that took faith!

The obedience of Abraham this time resulted in the birth of Isaac through whom the Jewish nation was birthed. This time Abraham refused to look at what appeared impossible in the natural. He considered not his own body or Sarah's, but, instead, believed God would deliver what He had promised. This is the secret of fruitful faith. For faith to be born in our hearts, we must look to God, not to ourselves. Through Abraham's seed (Jesus Christ was a descendent of Abraham) all nations have been blessed. Are there promises God has made to you that you have yet to see fulfilled? The story of Abraham should encourage us all not to go ahead of God's promises. God has an appointed time of fulfillment, and, until that time, we must wait with patience.

Lord, forgive me for my impatience. Give me faith to wait upon You.

Daily Deposit: One act of impatience today can rob you of a blessing in eternity.

January 8

What Will I Wear?
Matthew 6:25–7:14

As my oldest son played his guitar and sang the song, "Seek Ye First the Kingdom of God" at my youngest son's wedding, I was thinking about what I would wear the next day after the wedding was over. In our passage today Jesus exhorts us to take no thought about what we will wear. However, throughout most of my life I have had a constant battle with thoughts about clothes. Often I find myself planning my total outfit for the next day in the middle of worship. Has this ever happened to you?

My youngest son requested this song, "Seek Ye First the Kingdom of God," because he has experienced God's faithful provision of food and clothes in his life. He and his wife are still experiencing God's faithful provision of their daily needs in Hungary where they are missionaries. I, too, have seen God's faithfulness in meeting the daily needs of clothing and food. I know He will provide what I need to wear, but I still am absorbed with thoughts about what I will wear.

After much prayer, I have finally come to the conclusion that the obsession in my mind about clothes comes from a lust for clothes. To be honest, I love clothes, and I love to look attractive. I guess that is vanity. I have tried to convince my husband that I have a clothes ministry. I have had people tell me on many occasions how my clothes make them happy or lift them up and brighten their day. I like to wear bright clothes. Just the other day I asked my husband for more money for my clothes ministry. I told him that maybe he could take a tax deduction for this ministry.

Slowly the Lord is setting me free from this lust. First He set me free from condemning myself for such thoughts. One day while I was worshiping the Lord, the thought of what I would wear that evening invaded my mind. I was really getting under condemnation when I heard this exhortation in my spirit: "Linda, do not condemn yourself for these thoughts. I am into clothes Myself. Remember your teaching last week on the priestly garments." I knew the Lord was speaking to me. Sometimes the condemnation we place on ourselves when we sin is worse than the sin itself. God wants us to confess our sins to Him instead of condemning ourselves for them.

Are you experiencing nagging thoughts in your mind that take your focus off of the Lord? I heard someone say once that whatever we think about more than we think about God is an idol. Wow! I've got some idol smashing to do! The only way we can keep our mind's eye single upon the Lord as we worship Him is to allow Him to fight such thoughts.

Lord, help! I give You my distracting thoughts.

Daily Deposit: The book of remembrance in heaven records every time we think about Jesus. Take your thoughts captive today to Him. (See Malachi 3:16; 2 Corinthians 10:4–6.)

January 9

The Solid Rock
Matthew 7:15–29

One of my favorite hymns has this verse: "On Christ the solid rock I stand. All other ground is sinking sand." Jesus ends the *Sermon on the Mount* with this exhortation: "Therefore whoever hears these sayings of Mine, and does them, I will liken him to a wise man who built his house on the rock: and the rain descended, the floods came, and the winds blew and beat on that house, and it did not fall for it was founded on the rock."

Jesus is our rock; He is our sure foundation. David, in Psalm 18:46, said, "The Lord lives! Blessed be my rock"! If we build on any other foundation, but Jesus Christ, we cannot expect our spiritual houses to stand. We are the temples of the Holy Spirit. We not only build our house upon Jesus who is the Rock, but Jesus Christ, our Rock, dwells within us. This reality came to me at a time of crisis.

As I crested the hill of a neighborhood street, suddenly what looked like an orange ball hit my car. I slammed on the brakes, and to my horror I saw a small boy in a heap by the curb. It was not a ball; it was a boy! The boy sped down his driveway on his bicycle, and crashed into my car. My heart sinks even today when I remember the sound of my car impacting flesh and bones. I ran to his side, and he was not breathing. All I could do was pray in the spirit and ask God to spare him so he could live to know Jesus. The days that followed were the days when I became aware of the Rock within me.

Each day I went to the hospital to check to see how this eight-year-old boy was doing. His name was Richey. He had massive injuries, and they had to remove his spleen. I'll never forget the morning Richey's condition changed from serious to critical. I felt I was sinking in quicksand when I heard this report from his nurse. She said he had breathing problems in the night. I called everyone I knew and asked them to pray for Richey. One of my prayer partners came to the hospital and asked if she could lay hands on Richey's mother in proxy to pray for Richey's healing. Even though Richey's mother was not a believer, she consented. After kneeling and praying in the intensive care waiting room, my friend and I went to the hospital chapel to pray some more. My friend had to leave after spending a half hour in prayer, and I was left alone with all of my fears. As I rode the elevator to the lower floor to join Richey's mother again, my faith was like sand washing away as the waves of doubt and unbelief crashed in upon me. "Lord, I cried. I believe. Help my unbelief!" In that moment the Rock, Jesus Christ, within me began to strengthen me, my heart stopped pounding and a peace settled over me. The elevator doors opened, and Richey's mom told me the crisis had passed.

Lord, You are the Rock Who will give me sure footing when the waves of trouble try to submerge me.

Daily Deposit: We have the very faith of Jesus Christ (the Rock). Galatians 2:20 tells us we live by the faith of the Son of God. That faith is eternal.

January 10

Sending God's Word
Matthew 8:1–17

There is no time and space with God. In this passage, Jesus honored the faith of the centurion and was able to heal the centurion's servant without personally going to pray for his sick servant. Yesterday, I shared about the healing of the eight-year-old boy who received massive injuries when my car hit him. An intercessor came to the hospital to pray for the boy. Later, I discovered others were praying diligently for Richey.

A Catholic prayer group met every Monday night, and it was on a Monday night that Richey had his breathing problems and almost died. While this prayer group was meeting, someone in the group was impressed to pray for a young boy in a hospital bed.

As this person prayed, a vision unfolded. This prayer warrior shared what he was seeing in the spirit. He saw two strong men come into the hospital room. They lifted the young boy off the bed and as the prayers continued, he saw the men gently lay the boy down on the bed. When I heard about this vision, I knew the two strong men were angels who were ready to take Richey, but the prayers of the saints paved the way for God to intervene. This group sent God's Word of healing to Richey, and his life was spared.

The major vehicle God uses to intervene on earth is prayer. The Bible says the prayer of a righteous man avails much. When Richey was injured that day, I cried out to God to not let Richey die until he knew Jesus in a personal way. Even that prayer was answered later when I had the opportunity to sit with Richey in his home while his mother went to an appointment. I took a simple little book about Jesus to read to Richey. Richey listened attentively. He was still in some pain and had to remain in a rented hospital bed until his broken bones knitted together. Richey had two questions after I read and shared how Jesus would take him to heaven to live with Him forever if he asked Jesus to come into his heart. The questions were: "Are there any cars in heaven?" and, "Are there any doctors in heaven?" After assuring Richey that there was no sickness or pain in heaven, Richey said, "I want to go to heaven." Richey received Jesus into his heart.

We build a highway to heaven every time we pray for someone. Through prayer we can bridge heaven and earth, nations and peoples. This highway is called "Faith" and it is paved with a substance called hope. The Faith Highway leads straight to the throne room. The vehicle that travels this highway is called prayer. Our prayers today can be sent across mountains and oceans to people in need. We have the great privilege of traveling by the vehicle of prayer to distant lands. Is there someone you want to reach today with God's Word through prayer?

Lord, help me to daily build the Faith Highway so my prayers can
travel and affect the lives of people far away.

Daily Deposit: The moment we buy a car, it depreciates. The vehicle of prayer will never depreciate and it lasts eternally.

The Power of the Blood of Jesus
Matthew 8:18–34

Those poor pigs! Every time I read this passage in Matthew, I feel sorry for those demon-possessed pigs that drowned in the sea. It has always been a mystery to me why Jesus did this. Didn't He have the power to bind the demons and tell them to leave without having to send them into pigs?

When I was in prayer one day the mystery was solved. I asked the Lord why He did not bind the demons. The answer I heard in the Spirit made a lot of sense.

> I could not bind the demons because I had not shed My blood on the cross. It is my shed blood that gives my followers not only the power to cast out demons, but also to bind them. I defeated Satan and all his demonic forces on the cross.

This raises another question. What happened to the demons that the disciples cast out before Jesus died on the cross? I believe they remained in their spiritual domain until the time of the cross. If we could have our spiritual eyes opened, we would see that we are surrounded by a great cloud of witnesses, angels, and demonic spirits. God in His mercy has kept us from seeing these demonic forces. Jesus cast the demons into the pigs as a demonstration of His authority over demons. It gives me great comfort to know that He has given us that same authority. We are on the other side of the cross now. We not only have His authority, but we also have the knowledge that Satan and every demonic force was dealt with on the cross, and now we can deal with demons effectively.

The moment Jesus died on the cross, the gates of hell could no longer prevail against the church. Today, the body of Christ has the indwelling Christ, His authority, and His blood. The Bible tells us that we overcome Satan by the blood of the Lamb and by the word of our testimony. (See Revelation 12:11.) When you speak out loud what the Scriptures say about the blood of Jesus, you are using both the sword of the Spirit and the blood of Jesus against Satan. He has to flee. The next time Satan tries to vex you with his demonic forces, speak aloud the following:

> *Because of the blood of Jesus, I am forgiven, made righteous, sanctified, healed, and justified! Because of the blood of Jesus, Satan has no power over me and no place in me!*

Daily Deposit: The reason we do not use the weapons of warfare, mentioned in 2 Corinthians 10:4–6, is that we doubt we have the authority to use them.

January 12

Layers of Lying
Genesis 26:17–27:46

When we travel, we always layer our clothes so, no matter what the weather is, we will be comfortable. When we were in China during January, I was dressed in so many layers that I had difficulty walking. When we bedded down for the night, I dressed in my hat, scarf, boots, and coat. I crawled under three blankets. The next morning I woke up and forgot where I was. I was so covered over with layers of clothing and blankets that I couldn't move. I thought to myself, "Dear Lord, I had a stroke in the night and now I am paralyzed." Then I realized where I was and slowly freed myself from the pounds of layers on my body.

The passage today shares the consequences of lying. One lie leads to another lie, and just as the layer of clothing paralyzed me, lying and covering one lie with either an excuse or another lie will cause us to be unable to walk in the power of the Holy Spirit. We will be paralyzed and unable to move forward in the Lord. One of the major reasons we lie is that we are afraid of what people will think about us or what they might do to us. When we fear men instead of trusting God, we will find ourselves lying to cover up or to escape. In our passage today we see how Jacob lied to Isaac because he wanted to please his mother, and he did not trust God to bless him. The name *Jacob* means "usurper." Jacob successfully deceived Isaac and received the blessing that belonged to Esau.

The pattern of lying continued in Jacob's life. Every time Jacob lied he lost something. When he lied to obtain his father's blessing, he lost his family. He had to flee from his father's house because he feared Esau. You have heard the expression, "Cheaters never win." Another expression that is true is "Liars always lose." In fact, if we live a life of continual lying, we run the risk of being thrown into the lake of fire. That should send chills to all who are tempted to lie. When we lie we will lose our relationship with others and also our fellowship with God.

Have you ever lied in a moment of fear? If we are honest with ourselves, we must confess we have done this. Being honest with ourselves and with God when we lie is the way we can break the pattern of lying in our lives. First we must confess the sin of lying and receive Christ's forgiveness. Then Jesus is able to begin to cleanse us after our honest confession. (See 1 John 1:9.) So often we try to cover our own sins by lying. We may fool others, but we will never fool God. Lies and deception are the devil's game. Honesty and humility are God's plan for our lives.

Lord, I humbly confess the times I have lied.

Daily Deposit: No one on earth may ever know we have lied, but God knows. If we do not confess to Jesus when we lie, these lies will be judged in eternity.

Laboring in the Kingdom
Matthew 9:18–38

When my three boys were young, I began to pray that all three would be used as laborers in the last great harvest of the Lord. God has answered this prayer. There is no greater joy than for a mother and father to see their children walking in God's truth. One son is presently serving in Budapest with his wife and child. They have a coffee house ministry that is reaching out to both secular Jews and Gentiles who need to have a personal relationship with Jesus Christ. Another son served in China as a teacher for three years, and he hopes to return to China with his family where he will teach English as a second language. We do not have to serve in a foreign country, however, to be a laborer in the Lord's vineyard. There is much work to do right where we live. Our other son and his wife are laborers in the vineyard of their local community and church.

Jesus exhorts us in this passage to pray for laborers because the laborers are few, but the harvest is great. Jesus knew the time would come when there would be such a great harvest of souls that every Christian would need to be a laborer. Not all of us can go to a foreign land, but we can reach people thousands of miles away through our prayers of intercession. We can pray that God will raise up laborers in the lands we cannot go to ourselves.

As we look at this passage, Jesus demonstrates to us what laboring in the harvest really entails. First, we notice Jesus never minded being interrupted. He was always available. Second, we see that Jesus met the needs of the people when they came to Him. Jesus did not have to go out looking for ministry. We must remember that the only ministry we have is the "ministry of the moment." Whomever we are talking to on the phone, praying for, or speaking to at this moment is our ministry. Jesus simply walked along the Sea of Galilee and ministered to the people as they came to Him. Third, we see that Jesus' motivation was not to please man, but to please the Father. He loved people, but His major goal was to please the Father because He loved the Father. He only did those things He knew the Father wanted Him to do, and He only said the things that He knew the Father wanted Him to say.

This mode of operation is called "walking in the Spirit." We have to learn as laborers to be led by the Holy Spirit. This will save us from wasting a lot of time doing unfruitful things. God is looking for fruitful laborers in this last great harvest. Are you willing to be interrupted today by someone who needs ministry? Is your goal to please the Father by doing His will instead of our own? I am convicted as I write this.

Lord, forgive me for the times I have looked at others as inconvenient interruptions in my life. Help me to minister in the moment.

Daily Deposit: The ministry we have in the moments can have an eternal effect on the lives we daily encounter.

January 14

The Promise of Persecution
Matthew 10:1–26

We are always quick to claim the promises that God makes, especially the ones that benefit us. There are many promises in the Bible, however, that guarantee hard times and persecution. Remember Jesus' promise of tribulation, "In the world you will have tribulation; but be of good cheer, I have overcome the world" (John 16:33). Today's reading says that people who hate Jesus will also hate us because we are His followers.

If you are an American citizen, perhaps you have not encountered such persecution. Did you know that the saints in some persecuted countries pray for the Christians in America to experience persecution? When I learned this, my first response was, "How dare they pray this way." Then I came to an understanding of how persecution purifies us and reveals our true motivations. I also remembered Jesus' words, "Blessed are those who are persecuted for righteousness' sake, For theirs is the kingdom of heaven" (Matt. 5:10).

Recently I heard the story about some Russian Christians who were gathered to worship in a secret place. This was before the Iron Curtain fell. Suddenly eight uniformed men stormed through the doors. These men lined everyone against the wall and said, "All those who promise never to meet again secretly can leave immediately without punishment." Several people left. Those who remained were still lined against the wall, and they knew they would be beaten and put in jail. Instead of a cruel beating, however, their persecutors wrapped their arms around them and said, "Now we know you are true brothers in Christ." The intruders were Christian imposters who were testing their brothers in Christ.

If we also are true brothers in Christ, the time will come when we will face persecution. We may not have to face a firing line, a whip, or a lead pipe, but we will experience sarcasm, ridicule, and rejection. The question I leave with you is, "Have you experienced some kind of persecution?" Maybe people do not know you are a Christian.

Lord, persecution comes in many forms. I've never been jailed for my faith, but I have experienced ridicule because I am a believer. Help me, Lord, to pass any test in the future when I might be persecuted for righteousness sake. I never want to deny You. Help me also to learn to pray for my persecutors.

Daily Deposit: One of the fruits of love is faithfulness. (See Galatians 5:22.) At the end of time we will be judged on how faithful to Christ we remained while we lived on earth. Faithfulness is truly tested when we are faced with persecution.

January 15

You Are Important to God
Matthew 10:27–11:6

One of the basic needs of every human being is the need for significance. Significance, success, and security are three of the basic needs of mankind. Three key questions people ask are: "Where am I going; why am I here, and what am I doing?" We all want to be indispensable, but the truth is, we are dispensable in the sight of others.

We can receive great comfort, however, in the fact that we are never indispensable to God. We are not only significant to Him, but we are also very precious to Him. Our passage today tells us that His eyes are on the sparrow. He personally attends every sparrow's funeral. Did you know that the sparrow is the only bird that is found in every country in the world? God is present each time one of those sparrows falls. You are more precious to Him than a sparrow. In fact He thinks about you all the time. His thoughts toward you outnumber the sands on every seashore. He even knows the number of hairs on your head.

Psalm 116:15 says, "Precious in the sight of the LORD is the death of His saints." The word *precious* here means "costly." It is costly to God for a saint to die because a living epistle can no longer be read of men, and a shining light has left the earth. Life is so short, but the good news is, that even after our death, our light for Jesus can keep shining. How can this happen? Our prayers for others will have an impact upon generations to come if the Lord tarries. Others can read the words we write down after we are gone. The most precious treasures I found after my mother's death were the high school English papers she wrote. So many of them expressed her faith and her beautiful outlook on life. Today we can even leave videos and tapes that will keep our lights shining on earth.

You are important to God, and what you do, say, and write in your lifetime can affect generations to come. This challenges me to write my thoughts about God on paper and to pray diligently for my children, grandchildren and even their children's children. Today if you submit yourself to the leading of the Holy Spirit, something you say or do can affect the tomorrows for generations. Now that is significant!

> *Lord, forgive me for the times I have been down on myself and felt like You have forgotten me. You have never forgotten me, and You are looking forward to expressing Your glory and love through me to others in the days ahead. Thank You Lord for being the Significant One who gives my life significance.*

Daily Deposit: No one on earth hears our closet prayers, but in eternity we will meet those who have benefited from our prayers for them. No one on earth will know our thoughts if we do not express them on paper.

January 16

Read: Genesis 32:13–34:31; Matthew 11:7–30; Psalm 14:1–7; Proverbs 3:19–20

We Reap What We Sow
Genesis 32:13–34:31

We have already spoken about Jacob and the pattern of lying in his life. We saw how lying will always cause loss in a person's life. One of the main losses a liar encounters is the loss of trust from others. Trust and respect for a person diminishes when he or she continually tells lies. In today's passage we will see the consequences of Jacob's lying.

It was time for Jacob to face the music. He fled from his father's house in fear of what Esau would do to him as a result of stealing Esau's blessing. The same fears that caused him to flee were now stirring once again. He received news that Esau was on the way to meet him. This time his fears did not cause him to flee. On the contrary, the same very tormenting fears drove him to cry out to God. Listen to his appeal to God: "I am not worthy of the least of all the mercies and of all the truth which You have shown Your servant…Deliver me, I pray, from the hand of my brother, from the hand of Esau; for I fear him" (Gen. 32:10–11). Then Jacob reminded God of His promise to make his descendents as the sand of the sea, which cannot be numbered. Jacob was "sweating it out."

In response to Jacob's prayer, God met Jacob and wrestled with him all night long. Jacob would not let go, until God blessed him. God touched Jacob's thigh, and Jacob became lame. I believe God was telling Jacob that his running days were over. It was time to face his sin, repent of it, and begin again. God did bless Jacob early the next morning. He gave Jacob a new name. Jacob's name (usurper or liar) was changed to Israel, which means "Prince." God also prepared Esau's heart to both receive and forgive Jacob.

The consequences of Jacob's sin of lying lasted for several generations. We learn in God's Word that the sins of the fathers are visited upon the children to the third and fourth generation. (See Exodus 34:7.) Jacob's sons, Simeon and Reuben, deceived the sons of Shechem and murdered them. When we confess and repent of our sins, we are forgiven and cleansed, but the consequences of our sin may affect generations to come.

Jacob opened the door to a lying spirit that plagued some of his children. The seed of sin we plant may take years to germinate, but eventually the rotting fruit of sin will be evidenced. Think about this when you are tempted to sin. With the Lord's strength you can overcome every temptation. Remember when you close the door to sin in your life, you are closing that door for your children, their children, and their children's children.

> *Lord, I realize now that when I give in to temptation, I have opened the door to Satan and given him the right to affect future generations. Help me always to send You to answer the door when temptation knocks.*

Daily Deposit: The consequences of our own sins have a ripple effect into eternity.

January 17

Curses Continue
Genesis 35:1–36:43

Genesis is a study of human nature, and throughout its pages every human weakness is exposed. We see the consequences of sin. Our study of Jacob's sin of lying revealed how his sin affected the next generations. Our reading today demonstrates the consequences of a curse. Curses are simply negative words that are spoken over people. Proverbs tells us there is always a cause for a curse. (See Proverbs 26:2.) The cause is our lack of wisdom and our disobedience to God either in word or deed.

Remember the story of Jacob's escape from Laban's home? Jacob left Laban and took all that he thought rightfully belonged to him, including Laban's daughters and his grandchildren. Something else was taken, however, that brought a curse upon his family. Without Jacob's knowledge, Rachel stole her father's idols. Laban came to upbraid Jacob for leaving without even saying goodbye and also to reclaim his stolen idols. Rachel hid the idols under the saddle of her camel.

When Laban told Jacob his gods were stolen, Jacob responded with this curse, "With whomever you find your gods, do not let him live" (Gen. 31:32). Unknowingly Jacob had just placed a curse upon his beloved wife Rachel. Jacob had no idea that Rachel was the one who had stolen the idols. This curse was fulfilled when Rachel died while giving birth to Benjamin. Proverbs tells us death and life are in the power of the tongue. (See Proverbs 18:21.) We see here the power of negative words over a life. I believe if we could have our eyes opened to the spiritual domain surrounding us we would see dark clouds over people who have received judgmental, critical, and negative words spoken against them.

We should be careful whenever we open our mouths to speak. Words once spoken are like bullets fired that cannot be retrieved and they can do damage even to those we love most dearly. The words we speak can plant curses that will bear fruit eventually. The negative words we speak are the very weapons satan uses to harm those we love. The good news is that we can break those curses. We can break them because Jesus became a curse for us so that we can be delivered from every curse. Our inheritance now as servants of the Lord is to declare our deliverance from every curse. We overcome negative curses with positive declarations. We can pray out loud the positive declaration based on Isaiah 54:17. Make this your prayer and proclamation:

> *No weapon formed against me will prosper. I condemn every word of judgment others have spoken over me. My righteousness is of Jesus Christ.*

Daily Deposit: We can free people eternally from all curses when we tell them about Jesus.

Sibling Rivalry

Genesis 37:1–38:30

It is a blessed family that experiences no sibling rivalry. I came from such a family, and God has blessed me with three sons who enjoy and love one another. When one son did well, the other sons rejoiced and were proud of their brother. Of course, the boys would have their little battles, but their battles were not rooted in jealousy or pride.

The Bible tells us that pride is the source of all contention. (See Proverbs 13:10.) It also tells us that if we have bitter envy and self-seeking, we open the door to confusion and every evil thing. (See James 4:14, 16.) Pride and envy are the two main reasons for strife. We also learn that it is our own lusts—the lust of the flesh, the lust of the eyes, and the pride of life—that cause wars. (See James 4:1–2.) When there is sibling rivalry one or all of these three roots of strife—pride, jealousy, and lusts—are in operation.

As parents, our goal is to show no favoritism. This is a tall order, because some children are just more loveable than others. We cannot love all of our children equally, but we can love them specially. One of the secrets to laying a foundation for no sibling rivalry is to spend quality time with each child. Another secret is to never praise one child in front of another child. It is also wise not to compare one child with another. If we do any of these things we set the stage for pride and jealousy that will cause strife between brothers and sisters.

In our passage today we see that Israel blew it with his children. He had two favorite sons, and he was quite open about his feelings. Rachel was Israel's favorite wife, and she bore him two sons, Joseph and Benjamin. He was especially partial to Joseph, and made Joseph a coat of many colors. When Israel did this, he sowed the seeds for strife in his own home. The jealousy that was born through favoritism even led to attempted murder. Jealousy is one of the main causes of murder. The first murder recorded in the Bible occurred when Cain became jealous of his brother Abel.

Whenever we open the door to strife in our home because of jealousy, pride, or our own lusts, we have prepared a haven for satan and all his demonic forces. Demonic spirits feed on strife, and satan wants to keep the atmosphere of strife in our homes.

What strategy can we use to set an atmosphere of peace, instead of strife, in our homes? First, each child needs to feel secure in the love of his parents. Pride has two extremes: superiority or low self-esteem. When a child is secure in his parents' love, neither extreme of pride has an opportunity to blossom. Second, each child should be praised for his character, not his performance. When we praise the performance, rather than the character of a child, that child can become performance oriented.

Lord, help today's parents create an atmosphere of peace, not strife, in their homes.

Daily Deposit: Words can bring strife. Such words will be judged in eternity.

January 19

Read: Genesis 39:1–41:16; Matthew 12:46–13:23; Psalm 17:1–15; Proverbs 3:33–35

Fruitfulness
Matthew 12:46–13:23

The first exhortation God gave to man was, "Be fruitful and multiply" (Gen. 1:22). God loves fruitfulness. He created every living thing to multiply. Physical and spiritual fruitfulness are pleasing to God. Some people cannot have children, but they can have many spiritual children. We want to be fruitful in our Christian walk. We want to display the fruit of the spirit of love that manifests itself in joy, peace, faithfulness, longsuffering, self-control, kindness, goodness, and gentleness. (See Galatians 5:22–23.) We multiply our fruitfulness when we disciple others.

There are two major factors that influence our fruitfulness: hearing the voice of the Lord and obeying His voice. Today's passage is the parable of the sower. This parable tells us how we hear God's Word will determine the fruitfulness of our lives. We hear God's Word with our hearts, not our ears. The heart conditions described in this parable are:

The Callous Heart. This condition is described in Matthew 13:4, 19. This heart cannot even receive the seed of the Word of God. Why? Because the Word cannot penetrate the heart that has been trodden down and made hard by the world with all of its lusts. This person cannot understand God's Word, so now the enemy can quickly snatch it away.

The Careless Heart. This condition is described in Matthew 13:5, 20–21. This heart receives the Word immediately with joy, but the seed of God's Word cannot take root. This heart has stones, such as rejection, willfulness, and other sins, that block the seed from taking root. Sin causes this person to care more about himself and to care less about God. He stumbles when times of testing, trials, and tribulations come.

The Cluttered Heart. This condition is described in Matthew 13:7, 22. This heart receives the Word, but the seed of God's Word is choked by thorns, or the cares of this world. The cares of the world often can be the lust of flesh that causes us to seek our own pleasure rather than God's pleasure, or the deceitfulness of riches, or the lust of the eyes that causes covetousness and greed. This person becomes unfruitful because of the lusts in his soul.

The Clean Heart. This condition is described in Matthew 13:8, 23. This heart receives and understands the Word of God; therefore, the seed of God's Word is able to take root, bear fruit, and produce for some a hundredfold, for some sixty, for some thirty.

Lord, help me to have a hearing heart that always receives Your Word with joy and understanding. Help me to obey Your Word.

Daily Deposit: God's Word is eternal, and how we hear God's Word on earth will determine our rewards in heaven.

A Shared Destiny
Genesis 41:17–42:17

As Christian parents, our greatest desire was to see our children laboring effectively in the kingdom of God when they grew up. We prayed toward this end, but we also shared with them what we felt God had called them to fulfill in their lives. I remember asking the Lord what His calling for each of our three sons was. A calling is not a ministry or a vocation.

A calling is like a golden thread sent from the throne room that gathers together all the aspects of our lives into a spiritual garment that fits us perfectly. You have heard the expression "tailor-made." God has a "tailor-made plan," or call, for each of His children, and we can ask Him to show us what that call is for ourselves and for our children. When I asked the Lord to reveal His call for each of my sons I heard with my spiritual ears the following: "Your oldest son is called to be a bridge between races; your middle son is called to be a bridge between nations, and your youngest son is called to be a bridge between families." We have seen these special callings fulfilled in each of our sons' lives.

To be fruitful in the kingdom of God you need to know what your calling is. Every person needs to have a sense of destiny. Parents need to impart this to their children. We shared with our boys what I heard in prayer from the Lord, and they knew God loved them and had a purpose for their lives. The problem with most teenagers today is that they do not have a sense of destiny. They have lost hope and fear the future.

Joseph was given a sense of destiny when he was a young teenager. God revealed to him in a dream exactly what would happen later in his life. In our passage today we see Joseph's destiny unfold. When Joseph's brothers came to ask Joseph for food, they bowed down before him. Then Joseph remembered the dream God had given him many years before, about his brothers bowing before him. Joseph had experienced betrayal, imprisonment, false accusations, attempted murder, but through it all, Joseph became better, instead of bitter. Because Joseph knew his destiny, what he experienced along the way of his life did not discourage him. He was confident that God's destiny and calling for his life would be fulfilled and it was.

Do you know your calling and destiny? We all will have different callings, but we all share the same destiny. As Christians, we are *predestined to be conformed to the image of Jesus Christ.* Our common destiny is to become more like Christ each day. "Faithful is he that calleth you, who also will do it" (1 Thess. 5:24, KJV).

> *Lord, help me to impart Your destiny to all my physical and spiritual children.*

Daily Deposit: The impartation of God's destiny to my children and grandchildren is a gift that could change their lives for eternity.

Read: Genesis 42:18–43:34; Matthew 13:47–14:13; Psalm 18:16–34; Proverbs 4:7–10

Strongholds That Cause a Snare
Matthew 13:47–14:13

This passage in Matthew speaks about two strongholds that ensnare us as we travel life's journey. A stronghold is a pattern of thinking that will open the door to satan's activity in our lives. These two strongholds are like strong twin brothers who can throw us in to satan's snare if we do not resist them and pull them down. The two strongholds are the "fear of man" and "pleasing man."

Herod was bound by both of these strongholds. Eventually, not only was he ensnared, but he lost his life because of his cooperation with these strong twin brothers. Herod first gave into the fear of man. He did not kill John the Baptist at first because he feared what men would think of him and what men might do to him. His motivation for sparing John was purely selfish. He did not want the people to come against him. This fear kept him from killing John, only for a season.

During our lifetimes we often do things, or don't do things, because we fear what others will think or what others will do. I can remember one incident in my own life which clearly revealed I was bound by the fear of man. My husband was an officer in the Army, and we were invited to the general's home for tea. This was a big event so I studied up on the rules for such an occasion. I discovered that the rulebook said those attending such a function should wear their gloves at all times. I obeyed the rules and wore my gloves, even when I chose certain dainties from the lovely tea table. I chose Chinese cookies, which are round cookies coated with powdered sugar. When I sat down to eat, one of these cookies slipped out of my gloved hands and flew into the center of the general's oriental rug. I was horrified and paralyzed with fear. Then the general's wife graciously whispered in my ear, "Dear, you can take your gloves off while you eat." What a relief!

Those crazy actions were caused by the fear that I would not do things just right and people would laugh at me. As it turned out, I'm sure I gave many present quite a chuckle. We often put ourselves under such pressure when we seek to do everything just right for fear of what others might think.

"Pleasing men" is the second stronghold Herod cooperated with, and this resulted in the death of John the Baptist. At the persuasion of his wife's daughter, Herod had John the Baptist's head cut off. He wanted to please her.

Lord, help me to pull down strongholds.

Daily Deposit: "In the fear of the LORD there is strong confidence" (Prov. 14:26). The fear of the Lord is also the beginning of wisdom. (See Proverbs 1:7.) The fear of the Lord gives us the strength we need to pull down all evil strongholds in our lives and keeps us from doing foolish and unwise things.

The Test
Genesis 44:1–45:28

One of the things I dreaded most when I was in school was test time. Often we would have pop quizzes that were always a challenge, because the performance of these depended on whether or not the student was keeping up with his homework. Life is a learning experience, and throughout our lives we will experience many tests. God never tempts us with evil, but He does test us. Often, we do not know ahead of time when we will encounter these tests. The good news is that God's plan is for us to pass the tests that He gives us, and He never flunks us out of His classroom when we fail a test. If we fail the test the first time, He will always give us a make-up quiz.

In our passage today we see how Joseph's brothers were given a make-up test. When Joseph's brothers sold him into slavery, they thought they would never see Joseph again. Jealousy led to attempted murder, but God's protective hand was upon Joseph. Even though Joseph's brothers gave in to the temptation to get rid of Joseph, God did not give up on them. We see this pattern over and over again in the Bible. Abraham, Isaac, Jacob, David, and Peter all flunked and gave in to temptation, but God did not allow them to flunk totally out of His classroom. God is the Great Redeemer, and He can redeem our failings. He never gives up on us.

Joseph, with God's inspiration, designed a test for his brothers. He placed his silver cup in Benjamin's bag and planned to accuse Benjamin of stealing the cup. Would his brothers abandon Benjamin as they had abandoned him? This time the brothers passed the test. When the cup was found, the brothers stood with Benjamin and returned with him to Joseph. When his brothers appeared before him with their brother Benjamin, Joseph no longer could hide his identity. He told his brothers that he was Joseph.

With hearts pounding, the brothers stood before Joseph in unbelief. *Could this be the brother they sold into slavery? What would he do to them?* Joseph assured his brothers that what they meant for evil, God worked for their good. What a statement! We see a similar statement by Paul, in Romans 8:28, "We know that all things work together for good to those who love God, to those who are the called according to His purpose."

When God allows a test time in our lives, His plan is for us to pass the test. Because we are human and are often subject to our own fleshly desires and willfulness, we may not pass the test the first time. However, God will continue to patiently retest us until the day comes when we pass it.

Lord, help me to pass Your tests the first time.

Daily Deposit: How we perform when we are tested in this life will influence our eternal rewards in heaven. God tests our faith through allowing trials in our lives. Jesus is always praying that our faith not fail. He prayed for Peter this way.

Land of Goshen
Genesis 46:1–47:31

Have you heard the expression, "Well, land of Goshen"? This is a popular expression in the South. When a person says, "Well, land of Goshen," they are declaring God's goodness. It is like saying, "Well, goodness gracious," or, "For heaven's sake." As a southerner, I heard all of these expressions often. All three expressions were used when something good happened to someone.

Something good happened to the children of Israel. They were permitted to dwell in the most fertile part of the land of Rameses. This land was called *Goshen*. They dwelled here in peace and prosperity, as long as Joseph was alive. Later they became slaves when a new pharaoh became ruler of the land. This pharaoh so feared the rapid growth of the children of Israel in the land of Goshen that he ordered the midwives to kill all the boy babies born to the Israelite women.

Four hundred years of bondage passed, but God had not forgotten His promise to Abraham, Isaac, and Jacob. The children of Israel would once again live in the Promised Land. God appointed Moses to deliver the children. During all the plagues sent upon Egypt, the children of Israel were provided for and protected by God from these plagues.

None of the plagues ever were permitted to penetrate the borders of the land of Goshen. The children of Israel had to do something to protect themselves from the last plague when the firstborn of the Egyptians were killed. They had to place the blood of a lamb on their doorposts to protect their own families and their firstborn from dying when the death angel passed over the land.

God has promised protection and provision to those who trust in the blood of Jesus to protect them. One of my daily prayers is: "Father, I place the blood of Jesus on the doorpost of my heart and on all my loved ones today." By faith I am declaring that the blood of Jesus can both cleanse me and protect my family. When I accepted Jesus as my Lord and Savior, I entered the Kingdom of God. Just like the land of Goshen, this kingdom is a place of peace and joy. It is a fertile land filled with God's righteousness through Jesus Christ. When we daily dwell in God's kingdom, we will experience peace of mind, right standing with God and the joy that only the Holy Spirit can give.

Lord, today I place my family and myself under the protection of Your blood. I hide myself under the shelter of Your wings.

Daily Deposit: The blood of Jesus has purchased us the land of Goshen—God's Kingdom here on earth. Are you living in the land of Goshen today?

January 24

Discernment
Matthew 15:29–16:12

"Red sky at night; sailor's delight; red sky in the morning; sailor take warning." When the sky is red at night, or at sunset, this usually means the next day will be bright and sunny. However, if at sunrise the sky is red, the day usually will be stormy. The Pharisees and Sadducees knew this expression well and could discern the weather by the color of the sky at sunset and sunrise. They, however, could not discern the signs of the times. Jesus upbraids them and says, "You know how to discern the face of the sky, but you cannot discern the signs of the times" (Matt. 16:3).

To make the right decisions in life, we need discernment. No living man has perfect discernment at all times; however, the Holy Spirit can give us discernment when we need it, if we ask Him. We are exhorted in the Book of James to ask for wisdom. The promise is given to us that if we do ask for wisdom, God will give it to us and He will not upbraid us. (See James 5:1.) Wisdom is applied knowledge, and in the application of knowledge, we need discernment and prudence. Complete discernment is a gift from God that we can receive from Him when we ask.

Some people turn on the weather channel to find out the weather for the day, before they seek God in prayer about their day. Weather does affect us, but inquiring of the Lord daily is more important than inquiring daily about the weather.

Even the disciples had a problem with discernment. When Jesus warned them to beware of the leaven of the Pharisees, they thought Jesus was talking about physical bread. They thought Jesus was commenting on the fact that they brought no bread with them when they crossed the lake. They had quickly forgotten that Jesus, the very bread of life, had just made provision for over 5,000 people by blessing five loaves of bread.

God has plans and provisions for us every day we live. God longs to share these plans and His provisions with us, but so often we fail to spend time with Him. Time with Him would let us discern what His plans are and how He will provide for us each day. Are God's plans for you more important than your own plans? Do you trust Him for you daily bread?

Lord, forgive me for the times I have not discerned what is the most important thing in my life every day. Forgive me for the times I have been consumed with worry, cares, and concerns. Today I give You my cares with full assurance that You are the best caretaker ever.

Daily Deposit: Jesus is the eternal bread of life. Spend time with Him today.

January 25

Read: Genesis 50:1–Exodus 2:10; Matthew 16:13–17:9; Psalm 21:1–13; Proverbs 5:1–6

Divine Revelation and Declaration
Matthew 16:13–17:9

We could hear the soothing sound of the falls at Banyas, where Caesarea Philippi is located. It was our seventh trip to Israel, and we were standing together at one of my most favorite places in all of Israel. Banyas is Northern Galilee and is where the headwaters of the Jordan River begin. At this very spot, the divine revelation of Jesus, as the Son of the living God, was given to Peter. When Jesus asked the question, "But who do you say that I am?" Peter responded with this good confession, "You are the Christ, the Son of the living God." We looked at the rocky cliff just beyond where we stood and read these words from Matthew 16:17–19:

> Blessed are you, Simon Bar-Jonah, for flesh and blood has not revealed this to you, but My Father who is in heaven. And I also say to you that you are Peter, and on this rock I will build My church, and the gates of Hades shall not prevail against it. And I will give you the keys of the kingdom of heaven, and whatever you bind on earth will be bound in heaven, and whatever you loose on earth will be loosed in heaven.

There have been many interpretations of this passage. Catholics interpret this passage to mean that Peter would be the rock upon which Jesus would build His church, because the Hebrew name for Peter is *rock*. However, a careful analysis of this Scripture reveals that the church would be built upon Peter's declaration that Jesus is the Christ, the Son of the Living God. Many people believe the church was birthed at Pentecost, just fifty days after Jesus ascended to heaven, but I believe the church was birthed on the day this divine revelation was given to Peter.

Those who heard Peter make this bold confession received the keys to the kingdom of heaven. They received the authority in the name of Jesus Christ, the Son of the living God, to bind and loose principalities and powers and demonic forces in the spiritual realm. That day Jesus gave His disciples His own authority to affect things in the spiritual realm. Because of this new authority to bind and loose in Jesus' name, the gates of Hades would never prevail against the church. Everyone who believes on this great name of Jesus and who receives Him as their Lord and Savior can use the same keys to the kingdom that Peter and the disciples used while they ministered on earth.

Lord, thank You for the keys to the kingdom. Help me to use them daily.

Daily Deposit: When we use the keys of the kingdom to do spiritual warfare here on earth, we affect things in the heavenly realm.

January 26

Faith As a Mustard Seed
Matthew 17:10–27

I n the 1950s, when I was in high school, all the girls wore "mustard seed" necklaces to school. This faddish piece of jewelry was a tiny little mustard seed encapsulated in a glass teardrop that hung from a gold chain. Where this fad had its roots I have no idea, but I do know that all through high school, I faithfully wore my precious mustard seed. I recall how tiny the mustard seed was.

Jesus mentions the mustard seed in today's passage. He probably was holding the tiny seed in His hand when He said:

> If you have faith as a mustard seed, you will say to this mountain, "Move from here to there," and it will move; and nothing will be impossible for you.
> —MATTHEW 17:20

What a statement! We do not have to have a lot of faith to do mighty things in the spirit. All it takes is a little faith to accomplish the impossible. There are times in our lives, however, when we feel we cannot even muster up a mustard seed of faith. I had such a time in my life when I hit a little boy with my car. As I shared in the January 10 devotional, the boy was on the critical list at the hospital for days. The days of waiting seemed endless. One day I found I had faith to believe for his healing only to find myself doubting the next day. My constant cry was, "Lord I believe, help my unbelief."

When we have those sinking spells and our faith begins to waiver, we can also call out for the gift of faith. Paul writes:

> I am crucified with Christ: nevertheless I live; yet not I, but Christ liveth in me: and the life which I now live in the flesh I live by the faith of the Son of God, who loved me, and gave himself for me.
> —GALATIANS 2:20, KJV

When we run out of our own faith, we can tap into Jesus' endless supply of faith. Remember Jesus' words to Peter, "Satan has asked for you, that he may sift you as wheat" (Luke 22:31). Jesus told Peter that He would pray for him that his faith not fail. It is comforting to know that every time my faith is tested, Jesus is praying that my faith will not fail. The next time your faith is tested, call out to Jesus. He will supply you with His very own faith that never fails.

Lord, help me not to condemn myself at those times when my own faith seems so weak. Instead, help me to cry out to You.

Daily Deposit: The faith of Jesus is the faith we will carry into heaven. May we depend upon His faith daily.

What's That in Your Hand?

Exodus 4:1–5:21

Yesterday we talked about the faith the size of a mustard seed. The size of our faith is not that important. The release of our faith, however, is essential if we are going to see the mountains that we face in our lives removed. To release our faith we have to speak to the mountain. Faith is always active, and it is never silent. Faith speaks. Paul writes, "'The word is near you, in your mouth and in your heart' (that is the word of faith which we preach): that if you confess with your mouth the Lord Jesus and believe in your heart that God has raised Him from the dead, you will be saved" (Rom. 10:8–9).

Without faith it is impossible to please God. Since we were created for God's pleasure, He has given every child born on earth a measure of faith. Have you ever observed the pure faith a young child displays? The measure of faith given to us can grow or be stifled. Faith comes by hearing and hearing by the Word of God. When we speak in faith to the mountain, we are speaking against the principalities and powers that resist faith. We are also speaking to ourselves, and the hearing of God's Word builds up our faith.

Our reading today illustrates perfectly how faith operates in our lives. The example given is Moses. God asked Moses what was in his hand. Moses responded, "A rod." Then God instructed Moses to cast the rod on the ground. Moses obeyed and the rod became a serpent. Moses fled in fear. Then the Lord instructed Moses to take up the serpent by the tail. Moses obeyed. As his hand caught the tail of the serpent, it became a rod in his hand. It took a lot of faith for Moses to pick up the serpent by its tail because a serpent held in this fashion is able to quickly bite the one holding it.

There were two requirements Moses had to meet in order for faith to be released in his life. First, Moses had to carefully listen to God's instructions and then he had to obey those instructions. To release faith in our lives we must either speak the Word of God out loud or take action when we receive God's instructions. Because Moses was obedient, God was able to demonstrate His power through what Moses held in his hands.

Today God wants to demonstrate His power through what you are holding in your hand. You may be holding a telephone, a pen, a Bible, or someone's hand. While you talk on the phone, you can also listen to God's voice and He will use you to bless the person you are talking to. You may be writing a note to someone. Listen to God's voice and obey the inspiration and instruction He gives. The words you write can stir faith in others. As you hold your Bible, pray and listen for God's voice and God will reveal His power. Lord, help me to have obedient faith.

Lord, help me to have obedient faith.

Daily Deposit: Obedient faith is the faith that speaks and acts. That kind of faith will touch lives for all eternity.

January 28

Persistent Faith
Exodus 5:22–7:25

Perseverance is one of God's characteristics. When God describes Himself in Exodus 34:6 He says, "The LORD, the LORD God, merciful and gracious, longsuffering, and abounding in goodness and truth." Longsuffering is defined as patient, slow and deliberate action.

Longsuffering and forbearance are the roots that bear the fruit of perseverance. Longsuffering is developed as we travel through the long, difficult journey of trials. Forbearance is developed when we have to relate to difficult people. The fruit of perseverance matures as we set our wills to pray and not grow weary in trials and to never give up on people. Aren't you glad God never gave up on you? He suffered with you as you encountered various trials, and Jesus was praying that your faith not fail.

We all have been difficult to deal with at times, but God is always willing to keep relating to us even when we do not want to relate to Him. Jesus had to suffer long through rejection, false accusations, ridicule, misunderstanding, and finally the cross. He had to face people like the Pharisees and Sadducees who were extremely difficult people. Jesus never gave up confronting them. The anger He poured out upon them was righteous anger. His motivation, as He confronted them, was to let them see their own sin with the hope they might repent.

Often God allows trials to continue in our lives so that the fruit of perseverance can be formed in our character. We see in our reading today how God continually hardened Pharaoh's heart. God saw to it that the exit of His children out of Egypt was no piece of cake. He wanted, first, to display His power to the Egyptians, and then He wanted to form perseverance in His chosen people. In fact, God is still working on that project. Throughout history, God's chosen have faced horrific trials. The state of Israel exists today because of the perseverance of a few of God's chosen who never gave up.

Are you going through a trial that seems unending? Are you facing difficult people in your work situation or in your church? God permits these difficulties to form in you perseverance—the determination to do God's will no matter what! As you go through trials, God's will is that your faith will not fail. Every trial is a test of faith. If you persevere, you will pass every test of faith. As you face difficult people, God's will is that you forgive and love them, even as Jesus forgives and loves you. If you persevere and refuse to give up on anyone, you will have the joy of seeing God work His miraculous love and grace in their lives. In fact, you are the very instrument God will use to display His grace and love to them. Perseverance is persistent faith.

Lord, help me to persevere, no matter what trials I experience and no matter what difficult people I encounter.

Daily Deposit: Persistent faith is the faith I can take to heaven.

Entreating the Lord
Exodus 8:1–9:35

As we continue to explore the faith Moses displayed, we see perseverance in prayer. We are exhorted in the Bible to pray and not faint. Moses is an example to us all of perseverance with a mumbling, complaining people who faced one trial after another with a griping attitude rather than a grateful heart. Moses had to both suffer long through the various trials and forbear with a great multitude of people.

At one point Moses began to faint and said, "Just kill me, Lord." He had had it! However, Moses never gave up. His perseverance in prayer for a group of rebellious people is an example to us all of effective intercession. Intercession is standing in the gap for others through persistent prayer. At one point God wanted to wipe out all the children of Israel and start again, but Moses entreated God through intercession. He asked God to wipe his name out of the book of life instead of destroying all the children of Israel. He was willing to lay his life down for the sake of others. Persevering prayer develops in us as we are willing to lay our own lives down for the sake of others. This may mean getting up in the middle of the night to pray for someone or leaving your home to go to pray for the person with a desperate need who telephoned you.

God displayed His power to Pharaoh through Moses' intercession. God has chosen to intervene in our lives through the prayers of faithful people. God is all-powerful and He could have easily stopped every plague, just as He began every plague upon Egypt. But instead, He chose Moses as an intercessor. After every plague, Pharaoh asked Moses to entreat God on behalf of the Egyptians. Moses faithfully did this. Maybe one of the reasons God kept hardening Pharaoh's heart was to help Moses sharpen his intercessory skills. God has chosen us to give His Word as a voice on this earth. If we refuse to do so and have a weak prayer life, we will not be used in the furthering of the kingdom of God on earth. We are commissioned to pray, "Your kingdom come. Your will be done on earth as it is in heaven" (Luke 11:2). This is a daily prayer to be prayed more than just on Sundays.

We have learned that faith always speaks, and faith is always active. As we speak God's Word in prayer and obey His voice, heaven comes down to us, and glory fills our soul. God's kingdom is advanced through the prayers of the saints. What a privilege we have to give God's Word voice on earth. We entreat the Lord when we are persistent in our prayers for others. God hears our prayers and supplications—those prayers that include strong crying. If we make our prayers and supplications known to Him with thanksgiving, we also receive a great benefit. The great benefit is that God will mount guard over our heart and mind with His peace. Doesn't this challenge and encourage you to have a life of intercession while you are on earth?

Lord, help me to daily entreat You in prayer.

Daily Deposit: The persistent prayers we pray now can affect lives for eternity.

Protective Faith
Matthew 20:1–28

We have been taking an in-depth look at faith. God basically sees people in two main categories: those who believe in Him and those who do not believe in Him. Unbelief is the root of all sin, and faith is the main way we can please God. Faith is so important to God, but it is even more important to us. We are unable to receive anything from God if we do not exercise and release our faith. Faith, however, avails nothing unless it is channeled through love. We can have faith to remove mountains, but God's kingdom will not be furthered on earth if our faith is not channeled through love.

Faith works by love. Some of the facts we have learned about faith are:

- Faith is given in measure to every person born. The size of our faith is not important. The release of our faith is extremely important.
- Faith is active. Faith comes by hearing, but it is not released until we act in obedience.
- Faith always speaks. Faith is released when we give God's Word voice.

Today's passage reveals another fact about faith. Faith protects. This passage contains the most verbally repeated story in the whole Bible. It is the story of the Passover. For thousands of years Jewish fathers have told this story as, each year, they celebrate the story of the deliverance of their people from Egypt. God instructed men in Israel to place the blood of a lamb on the doorpost of their homes. He promised them that the death angel would not visit them to kill their firstborn if they obeyed His instructions. History tells us that every man did what was required. The death angel passed over the children of Israel, but the firstborn of the Egyptians were killed. To receive God's protection, the men had to listen to God's voice and obey His instructions.

To release protective faith in our lives, we need to do something—or to use it. Remember faith is to be used. It does two things—it speaks and acts. Based on this story, we see the importance God places upon the blood. We are told that life is in the blood, and without the shedding of blood, there is no remission of sin. The blood of Jesus has protective power. The Bible also tells us that angels hearken to the voice of God's Word. The moment in which we speak God's Word, angels come to attention. They can protect us. The way to release protective faith in your own household is to speak out loud and to declare what the blood of Jesus does for you and your household. You may want to join us as we pray out loud:

Today, I cover my family with the blood of Jesus.

Daily Deposit: Prayers of faith that impart protection may save a life eternally.

January 31

Read: Exodus 12:14–13:16; Matthew 20:29–21:22; Psalm 25:12–22; Prov. 6:12–15

Faith Sees
Exodus 12:14–13:16

We have learned that faith both speaks and acts. Faith also sees. The age-old story of the great deliverance of the children of Israel out of Egypt has been told for generations, every year at the time of Passover. Moses saw this event with his own eyes, making him well-qualified as an eyewitness to this miraculous event. We were not present when this deliverance occurred, but with our faith eyes, we can see the crossing of the Red Sea, the ten plagues the Egyptians experienced, the land of Goshen where the children of Israel found refuge, and the blood of the lamb sprinkled on the doorpost of the homes. Even though we did not see this with our physical eyes, we can close our eyes and, with our divine imagination, we can see these events in all of their glory.

When God created Adam and Eve, He gave them spiritual eyes, as well as physical eyes. They could only see God with their spiritual eyes, because God is a spirit. When Adam and Eve sinned, this ability to see with spiritual eyes was robbed by satan. When man sinned the divine imagination was tainted, and man began to have wicked imaginations.

God created us with the ability to receive images in our minds to help us envision Him as we worship. All worship is based on images in our minds. You have probably noticed that as you worship God, images of Him on the throne, with Jesus seated at His right hand in heaven, usually come to your mind.

Even though satan successfully robbed us of our spiritual eyes and divine imagination, the good news is that all those who are born again have had their spiritual eyesight and divine imagination restored. As I read today's passage, I envisioned the men dipping the hyssop in the blood of the lamb and applying it on their doorposts. Because of this restored spiritual eyesight, we can see things by faith that happened in the past. Faith enables us to experience "in the now" those things that happened in the past. Faith also gives us the ability to see things in the future. This ability of seeing and understanding things is called *revelation*.

The Bible tells us that the Holy Spirit is able to take the things of Jesus Christ and show them to us. Before we read any passage in God's Word, we need to put on our faith glasses. How do we do this? We simply ask the Holy Spirit to take the things of Jesus that we are reading in God's Word and reveal or show them to us. If you will do this today, you will experience a video show in your mind.

Holy Spirit, I ask You to take the things of Jesus and show them to me today. I am excited about what I will see with my faith glasses.

Daily Deposit: What we see now with faith eyes will be revealed fully in heaven.

February 1

Saying One Thing and Doing Another
Matthew 21:23–46

Have you ever heard a person say, "I will not go to church because there are so many hypocrites in the church?" A hypocrite is a person who says one thing and does another. Jesus confronted people like this whenever He went into the temple. The presence of hypocrites, however, never kept Him out of the temple. He was faced daily with the Pharisees, Sadducees, and scribes who knew the scriptures, quoted the scriptures, but did not obey the scriptures.

Before we begin to call anyone a hypocrite, it might be well for us to have an honest look at ourselves. If I am completely honest, I must confess that many times I say I'll do one thing and then end up doing just the opposite. I often fail to follow through on the promises and commitments I have made, especially to the Lord. Daily, I recognize the gentle promptings of the Holy Spirit, but too often I rationalize these promptings away, or I procrastinate until I miss the divine appointment or opportunity the Holy Spirit wanted to provide! I can remember having someone on my heart for several weeks. The Holy Spirit was prompting me to go visit this Jewish lady who lived in the neighborhood. I felt I was to tell her that Jesus was her Messiah. I procrastinated and did not obey this leading of the Spirit immediately. The day came when I saw many cars outside her home, and I later discovered she had died suddenly of a stroke.

In our passage today, Jesus tells the story about two sons. The first son was asked by his father to go into the fields and work, and he said, "I will not." The second son, when asked by his father, said he would go and work in the fields, but he did not. Then the first son regretted his unwillingness to work, and he decided to honor his father's request. He went and worked in the fields. Jesus then asked the chief priests, elders, and people gathered in the temple this question: "Which of the two did the will of his father?" They all said the first son who did what he was asked. Now we must ask ourselves the question, "Am I doing the will of the Father?" Saying is not doing. Maybe in the past you have had a hard time following through when you received the gentle impressions of the Holy Spirit. If you will be honest and confess this, then God will begin to help you break those old habits of procrastination. Let's face it, procrastination is outright disobedience. We need to call it what it is and ask God to forgive us, and then the cleansing process will begin that will change us.

Lord, forgive me for the times I have procrastinated and missed Your divine appointments.

Daily Deposit: Hearing and obeying the Lord's voice will bring both blessings here on earth and eternal rewards in heaven.

February 2

Being Dressed for the Occasion
Matthew 22:1–32

We had the privilege of parenting a Russian young man for seven years. He came to the United States as an exchange student and planned to only stay a year. We immediately saw the potential of this young man. By God's grace and a lot of prayer, we were able to enroll him at Georgia Tech where he graduated with honors five years later. Vladimir had a unique way of expressing many things. Whenever we were going to an event with him, he asked, "Is it official?" This was his way of asking, "Do I need to dress up?"

Today's passage includes the parable of the wedding feast. This wedding feast was definitely official, but one of the guests failed to dress appropriately, and he had to leave the feast. Some restaurants require that men wear a coat and tie. One time my husband forgot to wear a tie to such a restaurant, and the manager quickly supplied him with a tie. This restaurant did not want to lose any business.

The wedding feast, however, is not an event designed to make money. The wedding feast is free for all those who believe in Jesus Christ. The "official" dress for this occasion is a white robe of righteousness. This special robe is provided for us the moment we accept Jesus as our Lord and Savior. Every true believer will have a white robe. Revelation tells us more about this special robe:

> "Let us be glad and rejoice and give Him glory, for the marriage of the Lamb has come, and His wife has made herself ready." And to her it was granted to be arrayed in fine linen, clean and bright, for the fine linen is the righteous acts of the saints.
> —REVELATION 19:7–8

The righteous acts we do daily add threads to the fine linen garment we will wear at the wedding feast. We are the righteousness of God in Christ Jesus. Every time we allow Jesus to have His way in the daily events and relationships we experience on earth, threads are added to our garment in heaven. If we are just trying to establish our own righteousness by looking good on the outside when we are not right on the inside, threads will not be added to our garment.

A good prayer to pray to help us daily do righteous deeds is:

> Lord, there is none righteous, but You. Live Your life through me today, and inspire me not to miss any righteous deed You want to do through me today.

Daily Deposit: Jesus did only those things He saw the Father do. Those righteous deeds we do by the power and the leading of the Holy Spirit will stand the test of fire when our works are judged in heaven. Keep us sensitive to Your Holy Spirit today.

February 3

Who Is Jesus?
Matthew 22:33–23:12

We had just returned from church, only to be greeted by a knock on our door. I peaked through the glass pane to see who our guests were. A young man and girl who looked to be college age were standing with large portfolios in their hands. Immediately I knew who they were. Earlier that year Jewish art students visited us from Israel. They were going door to door trying to sell their artwork to earn money for their art school in Jerusalem. Now the Lord had sent two more of His beloved people to our home. I welcomed them, and my husband and I sat quietly while they showed us many paintings.

For years I have prayed this prayer: "Lord, may those who cross our threshold be saved and filled with Your Spirit. May they leave our home rejoicing and blessed."

Over the years the Lord has sent many to our door with whom we have prayed to have Christ revealed to them. We have a special love for Jewish people, because they are God's precious treasure. We knew it was no accident that the Lord had sent these two lovely Jewish young people to our home. After they finished showing their paintings to us, we began to share a little bit about our faith. I shared with them that we were Christians who had a great love for the Jewish people. Some good seed was sown in their hearts that day, but I wish I had memorized the passage we read today.

In our passage today we find one of the most powerful scriptures that proves the deity of Christ. Jesus was challenged many times by the religious Jews, but He was always one step ahead of them. This time, Jesus challenged the Pharisees with this question, "What do you think about the Christ? Whose Son is He?" They responded immediately, "The Son of David." Then Jesus quoted a scripture and asked them another question. Jesus quoted from Psalm 110:1 which says, "The Lord said to My Lord," Sit at My right hand, till I make Your enemies Your footstool." Then Jesus asked this question: "If David then calls Him 'Lord' how is he his Son?" A holy hush came upon His audience and they never challenged and questioned Jesus again. This one verse in Psalm 110 is proof positive that Jesus is the Son of God. The Pharisees were unable to refute this statement David made in this psalm. They left Jesus in total silence and I do not doubt that some became believers because of this powerful quote from the scriptures.

So often when I am trying to witness to someone I am so challenged by the questions asked that I find myself speechless. When those times occur, I silently ask the Lord to give me a scripture to share with that person.

Lord, help me today to hide Your Word in my heart, so I will be ready to share it with others.

Daily Deposit: Begin today to memorize some key scriptures that will help you witness to others. Lives can be changed for eternity if you will be faithful to do this.

February 4

Read: Exodus 19:16–21:21; Matthew 23:13–39; Psalm 28:1–9; Proverbs 7:1–5

Gazing at God's Glory
Exodus 19:16–21:21

What a dreadful, fearful sight! A huge cloud with thunder and lightning descended upon Mt. Sinai. A trumpet sounded and a mighty voice, like the rush of many waters, came out of the cloud. Awesome, powerful and magnificent God was manifesting His glory in the sight of all. God had to cloak His glory in the cloud, because if the people gathered saw all of His glory, they would have been consumed instantly. Our God is a consuming fire.

Moses was ordered by God to charge the people not to gaze at this sight. If they did, they were in danger of death. God only invited Moses and Aaron to come up to the top of the mountain. The children of Israel were only permitted to glance momentarily at God's glory. They had to keep their distance from God, the King of the Universe.

The Bible tells us to draw near to God, and He will draw near to us. We no longer have to be in fear and dread of the mighty God we serve. We can stand in His presence today with awe and reverence, without condemnation. We are exhorted in the Bible to fear the Lord, but we are not to be afraid of Him. We fear the Lord when we revere, honor, and obey Him. God no longer has to conceal His glory in a cloud. He has revealed His glory through Jesus Christ. Scriptures tell us this: "For it is God who commanded light to shine out of darkness, who has shone in our hearts to give the light of the knowledge of the glory of God in the face of Jesus Christ. But we have this treasure in earthen vessels, that the excellence of the power may be of God and not of us" (2 Cor. 4:6–7).

We cannot see the face of Jesus Christ with our physical eyes, but we can with our spiritual eyes. The Holy Spirit has the charge to take the things of Jesus Christ and show them to us. As we worship God in Spirit and in truth we can see the face of Jesus with our divine imagination. I challenge you right now to close your eyes and think about Jesus. When you do this, immediately a mental image of His face will appear on the screen of your mind.

God has made Himself totally available to us through Jesus Christ. John and others actually saw Jesus in the flesh. He said, "We beheld His glory, the glory as of the only begotten of the Father" (John 1:14). Now we contain the glory of God within us. He has chosen to place His Son Jesus within us so we now can reveal God's glory to others. God contained His glory—His manifest presence—in Jesus Christ, while Jesus walked on earth. Now we are the earthen vessels He has chosen to reveal His glory to men on earth.

Thank You, Father, for putting on an "earth suit."

Daily Deposit: As we daily see Jesus through eyes of faith, His glory will shine through us.

An Attitude of Gratitude
Exodus 21:22–23:13

Our passage today lists so many laws. It is hard to conceive that the children of Israel even kept half of these laws. Thank God we live in the dispensation of grace today.

One of the character traits of God is His grace. The word "grace" comes from the word "gracious." God says in this passage that He is "gracious." He is also merciful. It is His grace and mercy that balances His justice. God has not changed. Some people believe there is a God of the Old Testament and a God of the New Testament. They believe the God of the Old Testament is a God of justice who comes against the enemies of Israel continually, and the God of the New Testament is a God who is faithful, forgiving, and longsuffering. God is God! He is the same today as He was when He ordered the children of Israel to wipe out all of their enemies.

God has always been gracious, merciful, forgiving, and full of truth. God revealed these aspects of His character in Jesus Christ. The Scriptures tell us that grace and truth came by Jesus Christ. (See John 1:17.) The sacrifice of Jesus on the cross and His resurrection placed us in a position to fully receive all of God's grace. Grace is what enables us not only to be accepted by God, but it is also what enables us to display God's glory to others on earth. I heard someone say that the angels stand in awe as they watch grace have its perfect work in the saints. Most of Paul's letters begin, "Grace and peace be unto you through Jesus Christ our Lord."

God's justice was satisfied on the cross. The penalty for sin was paid in full. All those who have received Jesus as Lord and Savior are no longer appointed to God's wrath. Grace through Jesus Christ has bridged the gap between God's holiness and man's sinfulness. Everyday we need to express our gratefulness for God's grace, which was fully revealed and made available through Jesus Christ.

Recently I was at the checkout in a grocery store and a mother with a small child was in front of me. The little girl was crying because her mother would not let her have the candy that was on the shelf. The mother said, "Precious, remember we need to have a 'Jesus attitude'!" We will always display a "Jesus attitude" when we are grateful for what He has done for us on the cross and for what we experience now on this earth because of His great sacrifice of love. A *Jesus attitude* is an "attitude of gratitude." Whenever we display this, God's glory through Jesus Christ shines out of our lives.

> *Lord, forgive me for taking for granted Your great sacrifice on the cross for me. God's grace was given to me through You. Help me to always have a "Jesus attitude."*

Daily Deposit: The grateful attitude I have now can affect people for eternity.

February 6

The Feasts
Exodus 23:14–25:40

A holy hush settled over the thousands gathered at the Western Wall in Jerusalem. Religious Jews stood together with their Torahs opened to the Book of Ruth. We read silently alongside of them. They were celebrating Shavout, the Feast of Harvest. Ruth met Boaz during harvest time. It has been the tradition to read the book of Ruth during the celebration of this same feast that God ordered Moses and the children of Israel to observe.

Our passage today mentions three feasts that God required all males to come to Jerusalem to celebrate. They were the Feast of Unleavened Bread, the Feast of Harvest, and the Feast of Ingathering or the Feast of Tabernacles. It is a sign of God's faithfulness to His Chosen People that Jews today are able to celebrate these feasts in Jerusalem. God is truly gathering His people together unto Him.

The Feast of Unleavened Bread and the Feast of Harvest were usually observed sometime during the period between mid-March and mid-April. The Feast of Ingathering or Tabernacles was celebrated sometime between mid-September and mid-October. I was also privileged to celebrate the Feast of Tabernacles in Jerusalem. I loved seeing the small booths each family built adjacent to their homes. The families eat their meals together in these booths for seven days.

Feasts are very important to the Lord. They are a time of celebration and remembrance of God's faithfulness to His chosen people. The Feast of Unleavened Bread and the Feast of Harvest remind us of God's provision, and the Feast of Tabernacles reminds us of God's presence.

All the feasts observed by the children of Israel will culminate one day with a huge feast. The setting of this feast will be the New Jerusalem. The host will be Jesus Christ Himself. The honored guests will be all those who have received their robes of righteousness through believing and receiving Jesus Christ as their Lord and Savior. This feast is called the Wedding Feast or the Marriage Supper of the Lamb. God's divine purpose on that day will be fulfilled, and Jew and Gentile believers will celebrate this accomplishment together. Ephesians 1:10 reveals this divine purpose, "That in the dispensation of the fullness of the times He might gather together in one all things in Christ, both which are in heaven and which are on earth—in Him." God loves for us to gather together unto Him, and, at that great Wedding Feast, the body of Christ will be joined together with her Bridegroom, Jesus Christ. Have you made yourself ready for this last great feast?

Lord, help me today to extend the invitation to this feast to others.

Daily Deposit: I don't have to wait until heaven to enjoy a feast with the Lord. He has prepared a table before me filled with eternal food, His Word. He bids us, "Eat."

Let Your Light Shine
Exodus 26:1–27:21

The priests were commanded to always keep the candlestick in the Holy Place burning. The candlestick was located in front of the veil that separated the Holy Place from the Holy of Holies. It provided the light for the Holy Place. There was no light in the Holy of Holies, because God's glory provided the lighting in the Holy of Holies.

The candlestick represents God's anointing in our lives. This special anointing is described in Isaiah 11:2 which says, "The Spirit of the LORD shall rest upon Him, the Spirit of wisdom and understanding, the Spirit of counsel and might, the Spirit of knowledge and of the fear of the LORD." A description of this candlestick is found in Exodus 37:18–23. Six branches were joined in the middle by one stem where the oil was poured. Under each branch at the center stem was a knob that separated and supported the branches. At the top of each of these six branches was a bowl shaped like an almond with a knob and an ornamental flower supporting each bowl. The menorah today is a replica of this candlestick. The six branches represent the Spirit of wisdom and understanding, the Spirit of counsel and might, and the Spirit of knowledge and the fear of the Lord.

Every day the priests would check to be sure there was enough oil to keep the candlestick burning continuously. We are called saints in the light, and Jesus called us the light of the world. The world we live in is not a holy place, but by our very presence, we can be lights shining in the midst of a world that is growing darker by the hour. I remember a demonstration in a stadium where a tiny candle was lit in the center of the field. All the stadium lights were turned off and everyone in that stadium was enveloped in darkness. We all were amazed that we could see that small candle burning on the field below us.

Just as the priests checked the candlestick daily to be sure it had enough oil to burn continuously, we need to check to be sure God's anointing is resting upon us so that our lights for Jesus can be bright all the daylong. You may want to join me as I receive that fresh anointing from the Holy Spirit by praying this prayer.

Father, I ask today for the fresh anointing of Your Holy Spirit. I ask for the Spirit of wisdom and understanding, the Spirit of counsel and might, the Spirit of knowledge and the fear of the Lord to rest upon me today. Help me to keep the light of Jesus shining brightly throughout this day.

Daily Deposit: The light of Jesus shining from your face today could change a life eternally. That light intensifies every time you spend time worshiping and praising Jesus.

February 8

Read: Exodus 28:1–43; Matthew 25:31–26:13; Psalm 31:9–18; Proverbs 8:11–13

Sheep and Goats
Matthew 25:31–26:13

As we traveled along the roads of St. Martin Island we saw many sheep and goats. We had great difficulty distinguishing between the sheep and goats because they were the same color and size. The sheep in the West Indies look almost identical to the goats. We were told by the natives that the only way to discern the difference was that the tails of the sheep pointed downward. Of course goats and sheep each have a unique sound, but we were not near enough to hear the difference.

Jesus speaks about separating the sheep from the goats at the last judgment. Jesus is our Good Shepherd, and He often speaks of believers as *His sheep*. We are the sheep of His pasture. This is not a great compliment, however, because sheep are noted for their inability to do anything for themselves. They never know which way to go unless their shepherd shows them the way. They often stray off the path, and the shepherd has to find them. When they are cast down with their backs on the ground and their feet in the air, they cannot right themselves. They would die in this position if the shepherd did not help them to right themselves. Sheep, however, are smart enough to recognize their shepherd's voice. They will only follow when they hear that voice. Another shepherd can try to lead them, but they will not budge, unless they recognize their own shepherd's voice.

Some of these facts about sheep help us understand why our Good Shepherd calls us *His sheep*. Sheep are totally dependent upon the shepherd for everything. They cannot even find green pastures or water unless the shepherd leads them. Jesus wants us to be totally dependent upon Him to meet all of our daily needs, to lead us where we should go, and to right us when we fall down under the load of the cares of this world.

The sheep represent true believers who are dependent upon their Good Shepherd, and the goats represent those who have refused to believe and trust in Jesus Christ. Sheep are usually careful about what they eat, but goats will eat anything that is put in front of them. Non-believers, like goats, devour whatever the world offers them.

The measuring rod Jesus uses to determine which are sheep and which are goats is "the golden rule." (See Mark 12:33.) Those who love Him with all their hearts and love their neighbor as themselves would enjoy green pastures in both this life and the life to come. Those who are selfish and who refuse to follow Jesus will experience everlasting punishment. God does not delight in punishing the wicked. His desire is that none perish. (See 2 Peter 3:9.)

Lord, may all who I love and know enter Your sheepfold.

Daily Deposit: The rewards we will receive in heaven will be in the exact measure we have depended upon Jesus on earth.

February 9

Wake Up
Matthew 26:1446

The scene was set and the play began. The auditorium was filled with people gathered to watch the annual passion play. The only tickets we could purchase were for a Sunday afternoon. I would have to miss my usual Sunday nap. Sunday is called a day of rest, and I take my Sunday naps seriously. I was able to stay alert for the first half of the play, but when the lights dimmed for the garden scene I was a goner. I felt myself sink lower and lower in my seat. I came to semi-consciousness now and then when my neck jerked. Suddenly a loud voice awakened me out of my deep sleep. I heard, "What! Could you not watch with me one hour?" As my eyes focused once again, I realized where I was. The actor playing Jesus was a bit melodramatic, but the message was clear. The disciples fell asleep on the job. They were asked to wait and watch while Jesus prayed. Twice they fell asleep while Jesus was agonizing in prayer.

Our reading today describes that dreadful night when our Lord was betrayed. When Jesus found Peter, James, and John sleeping, He exhorted them to watch and pray so that they would not fall into temptation.

The scene is set. We are in the last days. The stage is this world that grows darker and darker with each hour. Many are falling asleep. We have been chosen as the players in this last day. The exhortation is the same, "Wait, watch, and pray." The last scene of this life is passing before us, but many continue to sleep. Others are alert. Those who are awake are called *watchmen*—those who are praying without ceasing as the days draw near to the Lord's return. The Bible tells us that in the last days, the love of many will wax cold. (See Matthew 24:12.) Many will give in to the temptation of seducing spirits, and they will not be ready when the Lord returns.

> *Lord, don't let me fall asleep on the job at this the darkest of all hours. Help me Holy Spirit to stay awake and alert against the enemy's temptations. Help me not to fall into complacency and even apathy in these vital last days. I am here still on earth to watch and pray. Help me to do that today.*

Daily Deposit: My spiritual alertness today could save someone from being devoured by the devil. The warfare prayers I pray today may save someone for eternity.

February 10

The Kiss of Death
Matthew 26:47–68

"The kiss of death" is a common idiom most of us have heard. Today's reading talks about such a kiss. Jesus knew Judas would betray Him with a kiss. He did not run from Judas, however, when Judas approached Him. Instead, He received the kiss. Even though it is not recorded, I believe Jesus returned the kiss. We just returned from Peru, and it is customary to greet one another with not only one, but two kisses—one on each cheek. Many cultures greet one another this way. Paul exhorts us to greet one another with a holy kiss. The kiss Jesus received on that fateful night was anything but holy, but He never stopped loving Judas. Such love is beyond our human comprehension. But Paul prays that we might know the height, depth, length, and breadth of the love of God. He prays that we might be rooted and grounded in that love. Loving our enemies and blessing those who curse us are tall commands of our Lord. Humanly, no man is capable of such love. Paul writes that the Holy Spirit sheds the love of God abroad in us.

That night in the garden, Jesus did nothing to save Himself. In fact, He rebuked those who tried to rescue Him. Jesus knew that the scriptures must be fulfilled. He knew that He must go to the cross. On the cross Jesus would receive the kiss of death that paved the way for us to receive the kiss of life through His resurrection.

Jesus said, "I have come that that they may have life, and that they may have it more abundantly" (John 10:10). Each day of our lives He desires to greet us with His kiss of life. Has life become humdrum for you? Do you dread getting out of the bed in the morning? Do you feel like you just exist day-by-day, instead of experiencing and tasting what life holds for you? If this is the way you feel today, Jesus wants to kiss you today. He wants to give you the kiss of life. Spend time in His presence, and allow Him to minister to you. The abundant life He has for you includes joy and peace, forgiveness and mercy, righteousness and cleansing. There may be something blocking your fellowship with the Lord. I have discovered what blocks me from fellowshiping with Jesus is my unconfessed sin. Ask the Holy Spirit to reveal to you any bitterness, unforgiveness, resentment, or anger in your life. It could be you have just become cold because you have not released your burdens to the Lord in prayer. Sometimes we can become so overwhelmed with life that we miss the kiss Jesus wants to give us every day. He loves you. Let Him embrace you today and kiss you with His holy kiss that will change you and your day.

Lord, I have been so distant from You lately. Is there anything I need to confess to You? Holy Spirit show me. Search me and reveal to me any sin that is separating me from the presence of the Lord.

Daily Deposit: The time I spend in the presence of Jesus today helps me to experience a taste of heaven now.

February 11

Fear: Satan's Anesthetic
Matthew 26:69–27:14

Jesus warned Peter that he would deny Him three times before the cock crowed twice. He told Peter, "Satan has asked for you, that he may sift you as wheat. But I have prayed for you, that your faith should not fail" (Luke 22:31). Jesus did not remove the temptation Peter would face. The temptation Peter faced is one we often face. Satan continually tempts us to be afraid. Yet Jesus exhorts us to not be afraid. Fear is the anesthetic satan uses to paralyze us so he can do further damaging surgery to our souls. I have been under that wicked anesthetic many times in my life, and the only way to awaken out of that paralyzed state is to ask Jesus for the gift of faith. We face all kinds of fears in our lives–the fear of man, the fear of failure, the fear of hurt, the fear of death, the fear of illness, and the fear of rejection, to name a few. Peter experienced the fear of man. He was so afraid of what men would do to him that he denied Jesus three times. Jesus, however, was praying that Peter's faith would not fail.

Fear puts a wall between God and us. Only the shield of faith can tear down this wall. One night my son, Ron, was paralyzed with fear. A dark presence came into his room as he slept, and he awakened to stark fear. He could not even speak. He was frozen in fear. He wanted to cry out, but he could not break the sound barrier. Silently, he asked the Lord for help. Then he cried with a loud voice, "Jesus help me." At that moment when the evil presence left, he sank into the safety of the arms of Jesus. If we give in to fear, instead of resisting fear with the shield of faith, the enemy will have success with us.

Peter had already had one test of faith, and, even though he failed that test, Jesus was there to save Him. When he walked on the stormy waters of the Sea of Galilee towards Jesus, he had great faith. However, when he took his eyes off Jesus he began to sink. Whatever we focus on in this life is magnified. Peter was distracted by the roaring waves, and he focused on the waves, rather than Jesus.

Fear will always come knocking on our door. The psalmist David knew this when he wrote, "Whenever I am afraid, I will trust in You [the Lord]" (Ps. 56:3). The next time fear comes knocking at your door, speak these same words out loud, "I will trust in the Lord and not be afraid." When you do this, the shield of faith will go up and the wall of fear will be knocked down.

Lord, forgive me for the times I have taken my focus off of You. The waves of the circumstances and trials in this life have distracted me and sometimes even overwhelmed me.

Daily Deposit: When our focus is upon Jesus today, we lift our heads to look heavenward. Suddenly we feel His support through the storms on earth. (See Psalm 3:3.)

February 12

Exchange and Change
Matthew 27:15–34

It was a cold spring morning, but the chill Barabbas felt was not in the air. Barabbas was frozen with fear when he heard the screams of the crowd crying, "Barabbas! Barabbas!" He thought, "My time is come." His legs began to sink under the weight of dread as the guards escorted him to Pilate. The bright light of the sunshine blinded him when he ascended from the darkness of his dungeon cell. Rubbing his eyes, he finally was able to focus on a man dressed in a simple linen garment. Pilate washed his hands and said, "I am innocent of the blood of this just Person. You see to it" (Matt. 27:24). Barabbas saw the guards reach for their whips, when Pilate said, "Scourge him." Barabbas' heart raced in rhythm to his thoughts: "They will whip me, and then crucify me." The unthinkable then happened! With a sigh of exasperation, Pilate placed his hands on Barabbas and pushed him into the crowds of the people. Barabbas was free.

When Pilate washed his hands before the multitude, Pilate was following a Jewish law. According to the law, if a man was found slain in the fields, the elders of the nearest city were required to slay a heifer. Then the elders of that city washed their hands over the heifer. In the presence of a priest, the elders declared, "Our hands have not shed this blood, nor have our eyes seen it. Provide atonement, O LORD, for Your people Israel, whom You have redeemed, and do not lay innocent blood to the charge of Your people Israel" (Deut. 21:7–8). In our account today, a gentile ruler washed his hands publicly and declared the blood of Jesus was not upon his hands. "And all the people answered and said, 'His blood be on us and on our children'" (Matt. 27:25).

Many exchanges took place on that fateful day. Jesus took the place of Barabbas on the cross. Jesus took our place on the cross. Jesus exchanged the curse the people pronounced over themselves for His forgiveness. He said, "Father, forgive them, for they do not know what they do" (Luke 23:34). Jesus became a curse for us so we might receive the blessings of God. Jesus, who knew no sin, also became sin for us that we might be made the righteousness of God in Him.

Lord, thank You for Your willingness to die on the cross to free me from sin and from every curse.

Daily Deposit: The testimony about these liberating exchanges can change lives for all eternity. How will others hear, if you do not tell them?

Light Becomes Darkness
Matthew 27:35–66

On the cross Jesus accomplished many life-changing exchanges. We spoke of three yesterday. He gave His life to purchase life for us. He became a curse to set us free from curses. He became sin to liberate us from sin. Another exchange is expressed in today's passage. Jesus, the light of the world, became darkness to purchase for us the kingdom of light. The account reads:

> Now from the sixth hour there was darkness over all the land unto the ninth hour. And about the ninth hour Jesus cried with a loud voice, saying Eli, Eli, la'ma sabachthani? That is to say, My God, my God, why hast thou forsaken me?
> —MATTHEW 27:45–46, KJV

Most people do not like to be alone in the dark. I know a Jewish man who came to know Jesus as His Messiah because he experienced loneliness on a dark night. One night he was awakened from a deep sleep and sat straight up in bed. His home was in the country, and it was a cloudy night. He was too far from the nearest street to hear any traffic. All he saw was darkness. All he heard was the sound of his own heartbeat. He was only aware of himself. This thought flashed through his mind, "Hell must be like this." "God, I don't want to go to hell!" he cried out loudly. At that moment a light invaded the room, and he felt a calming presence. It was his Messiah. He surrendered his life to Jesus.

On the cross, Jesus experienced total separation from God. The sins of the world were upon Him. His Heavenly Father had to turn away from Him, because He has purer eyes than to behold evil. Jesus cried out to His Father in His loneliness. The whole earth became dark and stayed dark for three hours. The darkness of the sin upon Jesus shut out the glory light of God. Jesus experienced hell—or total separation from God—so we could be translated from the kingdom of darkness into the kingdom of God's light.

Because of this great exchange, we never have to be overwhelmed with loneliness. We never have to be in total darkness. You have probably heard the expression: "It is darkest before the dawn." On that fateful day over 2,000 years ago, it was the darkest before sun down. We have all experienced sundown times in our life, when we dread to face dark nights alone. But the truth is, we are never alone. We are never in total darkness. Jesus promised to never leave us nor forsake us.

Lord, thank You for translating me from the kingdom of darkness into the kingdom of light.

Daily Deposit: The light of the glory of the Lord in you can brighten the darkness in the world. You are the light of the world. Shine for Jesus today and set others free.

February 14

The Brokenhearted
Psalms 34:11–22

This day is a difficult day for those who have no one to send them a card, flowers, or candy. On this day when love is so freely expressed, many experience depression, because they have no "love of their life." However, the scripture reading today gives hope to those who feel all alone.

David wrote Psalm 34 when he felt alone and destitute. In his desperate attempt to escape from the pursuit of his enemy, Saul, he entered the enemy's camp. He pretended to be crazy, and was permitted to stay with the Philistines for a season. Each day David faced two fears. He feared Saul would find him, and he feared the Philistines would discover his true identity and kill him. In his desperation he cried out to the Lord for mercy.

The Lord heard David's cry, and David wrote down all the ways the Lord helped Him in His time of need. The Lord did the following:

- Saved him from all of his troubles (v.6)
- Sent His angels to encamp around him because David feared the Lord (v.7)
- Blessed him because David trusted in the Lord (v. 8)
- Reminded David of His goodness (v. 8)
- Met all of David's needs (v. 9–10)
- Came near to him because David had a broken heart (v. 18)
- Delivered him from every affliction (v. 19)

David ended his psalm with these words, "The Lord redeems the soul of His servants, and none of those who trust in Him shall be condemned" (v. 22). The Lord has no favorites. If you feel lonely, condemned and desolate today, cry out to the Lord. Only Jesus can heal your broken heart. He is standing with His hands outstretched, to manifest His love, His deliverance, and His healing to you right now. Jesus is the "love of your life."

Lord, I give You my broken heart. Thank You for redeeming my troubled mind, my painful memories, my wounded emotions, and all my rejection.

Daily Deposit: Reach out to someone who seems to have no one today, on Valentine's Day. When you share the love of Jesus with them, you will be giving them an eternal Valentine's gift.

February 15

Construction Workers
Exodus 39:1–40:38

Things can always go wrong whenever people undertake the construction of a building. We had the opportunity to help build our church. Every weekend for one year, fathers, mothers, and teenagers gathered to hammer nails, put up drywall and paint. We were not, by any means, skilled workers like the ones God chose to build the tabernacle. But we had willing hearts to do the work! On one of these weekends, my husband was trying to straighten the trusses of the roof of the building, when suddenly the trusses became unbalanced and crashed to the ground. No one was injured, but some of the trusses were damaged. We made many mistakes like this, but the building was finally finished and dedicated.

The completion of the tabernacle was near. It was time to review every detail of the tabernacle to be sure all of God's requirements were met. Moses looked over all the work and gave it his stamp of approval. It took teamwork to build the tabernacle, and Moses blessed all those who participated in birthing this first dwelling place for God. All the furnishings were completed. God gave Moses specific instructions on where to place every holy article in the tabernacle. All the furnishings were anointed with oil after they were placed in the correct position. The priests were dressed in their holy garments and were also anointed with holy oil. There was only one thing missing. The tent had to be erected to cover the furnishings, and to provide shelter for the priests who would do service in the tabernacle.

The big day came, and Moses himself raised up the tabernacle, fastened its sockets, set up its boards, put in its bars, and raised up its pillars. The covering over the tent was placed carefully on top. Then the testimony was put in the ark, and the mercy seat was placed on top of the ark.

God no longer dwells in tents, temples, or church buildings. He dwells in the hearts of those who have received Jesus as their Lord and Savior. The church today is made with living stones. These living stones are people, anointed by God to be *kings* and *priests* in His kingdom. These living stones are now covered with the tent of God's glory. As we join together in teamwork to complete God's dwelling place on earth, we may not do everything just right, but God is the Master Builder and Jesus Christ is His Foreman. The Holy Spirit within each construction worker is able to perform what is needed to complete the work. When God's house is completed and all the living stones are in place, God will tell Jesus to come for His bride.

> *Lord, help me to cooperate with all the laborers who are building Your kingdom on earth.*

Daily Deposit: When you share the Gospel with someone, you have the opportunity to add another living stone to the Father's dwelling place.

February 16

Coming Near
Leviticus 1:1–3:17

Every year as I read through the Bible, I usually try to breeze through *Leviticus* as fast as possible. At first glance, Leviticus seems to be directed only to the Jewish customs concerning the priestly sacrifices, rules and regulations for cleansing, and food laws. However, God is telling us in *Leviticus* how we can draw near to Him. The word *offering* in Hebrew means "coming near." The various offerings in *Leviticus* do relate to us today—and how we can draw near to God.

The Burnt Offering. This offering created a column of smoke with a pleasing aroma. God was attracted to this smell, and He drew near whenever an animal was burned on the altar. We no longer offer animals on an altar, but there is something in our lives we can offer on the spiritual altar to God every day. We can offer our bodies as a living sacrifice to God. (See Romans 12:1.) Daily, we can offer the members of our bodies to be consumed with God's love, righteousness, peace, and joy.

The one member of the physical body God is especially interested in is the tongue. James says the tongue, although a small member, "sets on fire the course of nature; and it is set on fire by hell" (James 3:6). When we offer our tongues daily to God to be used to speak words of wisdom, encouragement and edification, the sweet aroma of the law of kindness on our tongues causes God to draw near to us. The words we speak can bring blessings or curses, life or death to others. Our negative, strife-filled, critical, judgmental words spoken to others will cause God to seem distant from us. The wall of bitterness and rejection created by such words block us from God's very presence.

The Grain Offering. This offering also was burned and provided a sweet aroma that caused God to draw near. We no longer offer grain offerings, but we can offer God's Word to Him. God's Word is our spiritual bread, and God loves to hear His Word declared on earth. Whenever we give God's Word a voice, both God and His holy angels come to attention and draw close to us.

The Peace Offering. The smell of the animal sacrifices required for the peace offering caused God to draw near. I love to smell a good barbecue, and so does God. Before the animal was offered, the blood of the animal was sprinkled on the altar. It is the blood of Jesus sprinkled on the altar of our hearts that gives us immediate access into God's throne room. We no longer have to wait for God to draw near to us. He is available to hear our prayers and give us grace in time of need because of the blood Jesus shed for the remission of our sins.

Thank You for the blood of Jesus. I can enter the throne room boldly because of His blood.

Daily Deposit: The words we speak will go with us to heaven.

47

Read: Leviticus 4:1–5:19; Mark 2:13–3:6; Psalm 36:1–12; Proverbs 10:1–2

A Sickness Unto Death
Mark 2:13–3:6

With the cost of health care skyrocketing, people are thinking twice before they decide to have optional surgery. Physical surgery can be optional, but spiritual surgery is a necessity. Unattended spiritual sickness can cause eternal death. When we recognize how serious our spiritual condition is, we must go to the throne room, instead of the emergency room.

In our passage today, the scribes and Pharisees criticized Jesus for eating and drinking with publicans and sinners. Jesus responded, "Those who are well have no need of a physician, but those who are sick. I did not come to call the righteous, but sinners, to repentance" (Mark 2:17).

The critically ill in the spirit are those who have not repented. If a person has never accepted Jesus Christ as his or her Lord and Savior, their spirit could face eternal death—or total separation from Jesus Christ. The Great Physician can only take care of our spiritual condition if we go to Him. I have had many minor illnesses in my life. One time, however, I knew I was dying. I was hemorrhaging, and I actually felt my life draining out of me. The life is in the blood. My husband rushed me to the emergency room, and they admitted me immediately. The physician was able to stop the bleeding. I remember coming out of surgery, thanking everyone. God's peace never left me during this time, because I knew if I died I would immediately be in the arms of Jesus.

Jesus is a skillful heart surgeon. He is able to perform spiritual heart surgery. Jesus came to heal the brokenhearted; He loves to liberate those who have been bruised and are bleeding because of abuse, rejection, or abandonment. He invites the brokenhearted to come to Him, to cast their burden upon Him and to learn from Him meekness and lowliness of heart. When anyone accepts this invitation, they will find rest for their souls.

Is there someone you know who needs to have spiritual heart surgery? You could be the one to take them to the Great Physician where he or she can receive a new heart or have their heart healed.

Lord, make me aware of those I know who need spiritual surgery.
Help me to take them to the Great Physician who is able to restore
their souls.

Daily Deposit: Today you can pray for someone who has a broken heart. Listen carefully as you pray. Jesus may want you to help them to His operating room. Only He can heal the brokenhearted.

The Physician Chooses Nurses
Mark 3:7–30

Recently I had to undergo testing for abdominal pain. The physician in charge had a nurse who seemed to be his right hand. She was with him most of the time, and also was often with him during surgery. She was his head nurse. This physician's head nurse seemed to be able to anticipate the physician's every move. He did not have to keep giving orders. She knew exactly how to assist the physician with every patient.

Jesus is the Great Physician, and in our passage today, He chooses His head nurses. The twelve disciples were handpicked after Jesus spent much time in prayer to the Father. Although each one had unique temperaments and personalities, they soon became a team Jesus depended upon. They learned by observing what Jesus did, and He taught them well. On many occasions, the disciples did not understand what Jesus did, but they were willing to cast out demons, heal the sick and preach the gospel, simply because they knew what Jesus did *worked.*

When our three boys were in school, I felt I needed to go to work to help my husband save up for the boys' college education. One morning as I sought the Lord about what to do, I read the phrase "as a nurse cares for her children" in one of Paul's letters. The word "nurse" stood out to me, and I just was positive Jesus was calling me to be a nurse.

I immediately enrolled at my former college and was amazed they accepted all of my credits after my twenty-year absence. They told me I could finish a nursing program in two years and become an RN. I was two quarters into school when I realized this was not for me. I quit all my classes and returned home. Later I sought the Lord and asked Him what the nursing verse was all about. I heard in my spirit that I was called to be a spiritual nurse to help Him heal the brokenhearted, bind up the wounds and set at liberty all those who were bruised. I shouted, "Hallelujah!" I did not have to have a degree for this type of nursing. Since that time, I have had the opportunity to pray for many wounded, rejected, and brokenhearted people. Sometimes I tell the Lord the sick ward is full, and I can't take any more patients.

We are all called to be modern-day disciples of Jesus. This means we are to observe what He did when He walked on earth, and we are to do the same in His name. We are also required to come to Him and learn meekness and lowliness of heart. The Great Physician needs able and equipped nurses to give His Word a voice on earth and to train other nurses. Have you received your nursing degree yet?

Lord, there are so many in the world who are brokenhearted, bruised, and abused. Use me as Your able assistant to help heal them.

Daily Deposit: All of the spiritual patients you help on earth will thank you in heaven.

Called to Be Priests
Leviticus 7:28–9:6

Yesterday we learned we are all called to be disciples of Christ. As His disciples, we are to help Him as He heals the brokenhearted, binds up the wounded, and liberates those who are bruised. We perform these duties like a head nurse performs her duties.

Another calling we all share is the calling to be priests. In the book of Leviticus we see careful instructions given to the priests about how they were to do their service to the Lord. Their first duty was to minister to God and then to the people. The word *priest* in Hebrew means "bridge." The priests had the awesome duty to create a bridge between the people and God. They created this bridge through the offerings. The priests had the mammoth job of carrying out to the last detail all the instructions God gave concerning the offerings. Day in and day out they were to keep the fire on the altar burning and offer the various sacrifices according to the laws of the offerings.

As priests of Christ today, we no longer have to offer sacrifices of animals. The bridge between God and the people has already been provided. Jesus created that bridge when He died on the cross for the sins of the whole world. He reconciled us to God, and now we are charged as priests to give this message of reconciliation to others.

The priests were consecrated to God for His service. Blood was placed on their right ear, right thumb, and right toe. This special service set them apart to hear God's Word, to do God's Word, and to walk in God's ways. To be a faithful priest today, we can pray this prayer of dedication:

> *Lord, help me to hear Your voice today as You instruct me through Your Word. Help me to obey Your Word and Your voice today. Help me to walk in Your ways today. Put me in the right place at the right time and do not allow me to miss out on any divine appointments you may have for me to keep today.*

Daily Deposit: The Lord has instructions for you today. Jesus is the High Priest who has provided the bridge between the Father and the people. Those you tell today about how Jesus reconciled mankind to Himself on the cross may also enter the priesthood of Jesus Christ. You will be with these priests of the Lord in heaven.

February 20

Read: Leviticus 9:7—10:20; Mark 4:26—5:20; Psalm 37:29—40; Proverbs 10:6—7

Salvation Is From the Lord
Psalms 37:29—40

As we continue to meditate on our various common callings, we see another calling of God upon our lives in this psalm. We are nurses to help the Great Physician as He heals hearts, and we are priests who share the ministry of reconciliation with others. We are also all called to be postmen.

One of the most exciting parts of our day occurs when we go to the mailbox to see what the postman has delivered to us. We can't wait to see if there is a personal letter, a check for our ministry, or a letter from one of the ministries we support. Postmen have the responsibility to just deliver the mail. They do not open the mail. We see in this psalm that salvation is from the Lord who has the power to save another person. Only the Father in Heaven has the power to draw people to His Son Jesus. However, if this great gift is never delivered, then no one will be able to open it and receive all the benefits from this gift.

When we were in India we had the opportunity to be postmen. We delivered the gift of salvation to many people as we preached the Gospel to them. We went into villages and set up a platform surrounded with fluorescent lights. The only source of electricity in these villages was found in the Hindu temples. We plugged an extension cord into the power source in the Hindu temple. The source of power, however, we had to offer the people was much greater than any power the Hindu temple had to offer. We had the awesome responsibility to offer to those gathered the wonderful gift of salvation!

We preached the Gospel, and many came forward in response to the invitation to accept Jesus Christ as Savior. Others came forward to receive healing. My husband and I prayed for those who needed healing, and our pastor and his wife prayed for those who needed salvation. Our interpreter asked each person as they came forward if they wanted to receive the gift of salvation or healing. The Indian people have an unusual way of nodding their heads in response to questions. We never could tell if they were saying yes or no. Often those who wanted to receive salvation were put in the healing line by mistake. After some confusion, we usually were able to pull those needing salvation out of the healing line so we could pray for them. As we prayed through the interpreter we again presented each person with the gift of salvation, and they left rejoicing when they opened the gift by trusting Jesus to be their Lord and Savior. We also rejoiced with the angels as person after person came to the front of our meetings to receive their priceless gift of salvation.

Lord, I want to be Your postman today.

Daily Deposit: Someone is waiting for their special delivery today. You can be the postman to deliver a gift that is eternal. What are you waiting for?

February 21

The Most Important Call
Mark 5:21–43

There are many common callings we all share as servants and friends of Jesus Christ here on earth. However, we will be able to accomplish all of our callings only as we fulfill one common call. Without this one calling we will be unable to do the works that God has appointed us to do in this life. Early in Jesus' ministry the people asked Jesus this question: "'What shall we do, that we may work the works of God?' Jesus answered and said to them, 'This is the work of God, that you believe in Him whom He sent'" (John 6:28–29).

The one call we must fulfill in order to accomplish the works of God is the call to have faith. Our greatest work on earth is to believe in Jesus. To fulfill all the callings we have in this lifetime, we have to believe that Jesus will work through us. We are only vessels who transmit God's power through Jesus Christ, to heal the sick and brokenhearted, deliver the oppressed, and to preach the kingdom to others. My life verse is "For it is God who works in you both to will and to do for His good pleasure" (Phil. 2:13). Our focus must be on Jesus, not ourselves, as we do the works He calls us to do.

Our reading today in the Gospel of Mark shares two stories about faith. The story of the woman who pressed through the crowds to touch Jesus' garment and the story of Jairus and his daughter reveal the key to faith. The moment the woman with the issue of blood saw Jesus, she forgot about herself. She forgot about her unclean condition. She forgot she was forbidden to be in crowds. As she drug her weak body through the crowds to touch the hem of Jesus' garment, she had only one thought, and she had only one focus. She thought if she could only get to Jesus she would be healed from her infirmity. She never took her eyes off of Jesus. When Jesus discovered who had received His healing virtue, he said, "Daughter, your faith has made you well. Go in peace, and be healed of your affliction" (Mark 5:34). Her faith drew the healing virtue of Jesus into her body, and she was instantly healed.

Just after the woman was healed, Jairus received the report that his daughter was already dead. Jesus told him, "Do not be afraid; only believe" (Mark 5:36). Jairus knew he could not look at this dreadful situation with natural eyes. He had to have eyes of faith. He was careful to keep His eyes focused on Jesus, as they journeyed together to his house. Everything on this earth grew strangely dim as he beheld the light of the glory and grace in the face of Jesus. Jesus honored his faith and raised his daughter from the dead. Everyone was amazed. To have the kind of faith that produces miraculous results, we must keep our focus upon Jesus. We too will be amazed at how the Lord will use us.

Lord, I turn my eyes upon You.

Daily Deposit: Whenever we keep our focus upon Jesus, our faith releases Him to do miracles in our own lives and in the lives of others.

February 22

The Atmosphere of Faith
Mark 6:1–29

When we were preaching the Word in countries like India and Mexico, we stood amazed at the miracles, healings, signs, and wonders that followed the preaching of God's Word. We had never witnessed such miracles and signs in the United States. After reading today's passage, I have a better understanding of why the power of God to heal and deliver often seems to be hindered in the United States.

Jesus was in His own hometown. Everyone in Nazareth knew him as Joseph's son. They knew His brothers and sisters. When they focused their eyes upon Jesus, they only saw a man. They did not believe He was God in the flesh. Jesus could only heal a few people because of the unbelief surrounding Him. When Jesus went to Jairus' home to raise his daughter from the dead, Jesus had everyone leave the room except for Peter, James, and John. Jesus knew if unbelieving people were in the room with Him, He might be hindered from performing this great miracle because of their unbelief.

Miracles, healings, and deliverances travel on a special highway from heaven. That highway is called *Faith*. It is up to those on earth to provide this highway through prayers and actions based on belief, here on earth. Faith is always involved whenever Jesus ministers through us on earth. We can be filled with faith, but if unbelief is in the atmosphere, we will be limited in what Jesus can do through us. Faith has to be present in order for the works of Jesus to be done on earth. That faith can be in the person who prays for others, or it can be in the person who wants to receive some ministry from Jesus. A friend who ministers often in Colombia, South America, had a person come to him for ministry. This person said, "I don't think I have enough faith to receive my healing." My friend said, "That's okay! I have enough faith for us both."

The childlike faith we saw in India and Mexico paved a wide highway for miracles and wonders to travel earthward. People in these third world countries have to trust in Jesus as their Great Physician because they have no other doctor to go to. We need to pray for such faith to be evidenced, not only in our own lives, but in the lives of all those who believe in Jesus. Jesus posed a question to the two blind men who came to Him for healing. Jesus said to them, "Do you believe that I am able to do this?" They said to Him, "Yes, Lord." Then He touched their eyes, saying, "According to your faith let it be to you" (Matt. 9:29).

Lord, increase my faith.

Daily Deposit: When we fulfill the call to have the faith of little children, Jesus will be able to touch others through our lives. The greatest miracle is salvation. The prayers you pray today with faith for the salvation of others will produce eternal miracles.

February 23

How Faith Increases
Psalms 40:1–10

We can ask the Lord to increase our faith. However, He requires us to cooperate with Him as He answers this prayer. Faith does not drop like rain from heaven. I learned in the fourth grade that rain clouds form in the sky when water evaporates on earth. Faith also must come from a very special kind of water on earth. Faith clouds, filled with showers of blessings, begin when we receive the washing of the water of God's Word. God's Word, spoken and acted upon on earth, produces the faith that will rain miracles, healings, and blessings from heaven upon us.

David was a man after God's own heart because his heart was filled with faith. This psalm expresses his faith and trust in the Lord. David's faith never failed him, because he did the following:

- He waited upon the Lord (v. 1).
- He remembered God's delivering power (v. 2).
- He sang praises to God and new songs to Him (v. 3).
- He trusted the Lord and was not deceived (v. 4).
- He knew God's thoughts were upon him (v. 5).
- He delighted to do God's will instead of his own (v. 8).
- He hid God's Word in his heart (v. 8).
- He proclaimed God's Word to others (v. 9).
- He declared God's faithfulness and salvation to others (v. 10).
- He declared God's loving-kindness and truth to others (v. 10).

Our faith will have a firm foundation if we do the things David did. "Faith comes by hearing, and hearing by the Word of God" (Rom. 10:17). The measure of the increase of our faith will depend upon the measure of the Word of God we have received from others, hidden in our hearts and declared on this earth. We answer the call to faith whenever we spend time in God's Word, share God's Word with others, and receive teaching and preaching from God's Word.

Lord, help me to wash myself daily with Your Word.

Daily Deposit: The Word of God is what feeds our faith. Our faith also increases as we share God's Word with others. Whenever we dispense God's Word to others, their faith increases. As a result, eternal change can happen in their lives.

February 24

Atonement
Leviticus 15:1–16:28

The latter portion of our Leviticus reading today gives the exact details Aaron was to follow before he could enter the Holy Place once a year. The high priest was only allowed to make atonement for himself, for his household, and for all the assembly of Israel once a year. Today, the Jewish people still celebrate the Day of Atonement. This highest of holy days is called Yom Kippur. Animal sacrifices are no longer offered for the atonement of the people. Animal sacrifices were no longer instituted after the death of Jesus Christ. Jesus was both our high priest and our perfect sacrifice who purchased eternal atonement for us on the cross. When Jesus shed His blood on the cross for our sins, we were made righteous in the sight of God. Our unrighteousness was exchanged for His righteousness on the cross.

When my son went to Colombia on a missions trip he experienced a vivid illustration of what Jesus did on the cross for us all. Several young people went with a Columbian evangelist to a very dangerous part of Bogotá. This area, called the "Cartuge," was filled with drug addicts, thieves, and murderers. The youth team went to visit a rehabilitation house for drug addicts. As they entered the house, my son was overwhelmed with the humility of the men he met. They all had received deliverance from their addictions. Because they had been forgiven much, they now could love much. My son, Ron, felt led to have a foot washing ceremony. The men had never heard of this ceremony, so Ron shared the example Jesus gave us in the scriptures.

They all agreed to enter into this ceremony. One of Ron's friends had just put on a brand new pair of socks that morning. First, Ron's friend knelt to wash the feet of the man in front of him. The man slipped his filthy socks off, and Ron's friend proceeded to wash his feet. Then Ron's friend took off his brand new socks so the man could wash his feet. After the foot washing, both men began to reach for their socks. Suddenly Ron's friend was inspired to give the man his brand new socks. Then Ron's friend put the man's dirty socks on his own feet.

This is what happened on the cross. Jesus exchanged our dirty sins for His spotless righteousness. Though our sins may be as scarlet, they can become as white as snow. Why? Because Jesus has purchased us snow-white garments of righteousness. Have you received your spotless robe? We become "at one with God" when we believe in our hearts and confess with our mouths that Jesus Christ is Lord and that He was raised from the dead.

Lord, thank You for exchanging the dirty socks of my sin for the clean socks of Your righteousness.

Daily Deposit: When we tell others of this great exchange, we are storing up treasures in heaven.

February 25

Food for All
Mark 7:24–8:9

One of the special events our church holds yearly is a *Unity Feast*. It is a feast usually held during Black History Month. The food is delicious, and the fellowship is outstanding. The message conveyed by this feast is the oneness in spirit we all experience in Christ, even though we come from many different ethnic backgrounds.

When Jesus delivered the Greek woman's daughter, He was making an exception because her faith was strong. She was a Gentile, and Jesus' first assignment was to preach the kingdom to the Jews. She told Jesus she was willing to take the crumbs from under His table. When He was in Decapolis (ten gentile cities), He told those who were healed and delivered to tell no one. Jesus did not want to be distracted from His first call to the Jews. The day would soon come, however, when there would be enough spiritual food for all. When Jesus died on the cross, He died for the whole world. On that fateful day, the whole world was unified. Everyone born after the cross was eligible to receive salvation through believing and receiving Jesus Christ as their Lord and Savior.

At the foot of the cross everyone is equal. Jesus purchased our salvation by shedding His own blood on the cross for our sins. When Jesus died on the cross, the Father counted everyone in the whole world as worthy of the death of His Son. John 3:16-17 says: "For God so loved the world that He gave His only begotten Son, that whoever believes in Him should not perish but have everlasting life. For God did not send His Son into the world to condemn the world, but that the world through Him might be saved." Jesus paid in full the debts of the sins of the whole world. To receive this payment, however, we must believe the debt for our own sin was paid in full. Salvation is a free gift to all who will believe and receive it. We sing the song, "Jesus loves the little children of the world. Red and yellow, black and white, they are precious in His sight." Everyone is considered precious in the sight of God. No matter what our skin color or ethnic background is, we can be totally one with one another when we receive the priceless gift of salvation.

Do you know your worth? Do you know you are worth the same price that was paid for kings and rulers of nations? Have you entered equality by believing and receiving Jesus Christ? There is still room at the cross for you.

Lord, thank You for counting me worthy when You died on the cross.

Daily Deposit: The gift of salvation is free to all who will believe. Someone you meet today may feel worthless. Tell him or her about the great price that was paid for them on the cross. Whenever we share this good news with someone, we open the door of God's treasure house to them, and we add to our own treasures in heaven.

February 26

Read: Leviticus 19:1–20:21; Mark 8:10–38; Psalm 42:1–11; Proverbs 10:17

Death Leads to Life
Mark 8:10–38

Jesus said, "For what will it profit a man if he gains the whole world, and loses his own soul? Or what will a man give in exchange for his soul?" (Mark 8:36–37). Did you know that one out of one people die? We all have our appointment with death, but there is only one death that leads to life. Only those who believe in Jesus Christ and trust in Him for salvation will experience the death that leads to life. Jesus said, "Take up the cross, and follow Me" (Mark 10:21).

He gave this exhortation before He died on the cross. What did He mean? How can we take up our cross daily and follow Him? People have told me when things are not going well in their lives that this is their cross to bear. Nowhere in the Bible do we have the exhortation to bear our cross. Jesus told us to take up our cross and follow Him. We are to give Jesus every burden. He is the One who bears our burdens. Then what does the cross represent? The cross we are to take up daily is our own lives. When Jesus was lifted and nailed to the cross, He died. When He died, we also died with Him. Paul clearly stated what Jesus was saying when He wrote: "I have been crucified with Christ; it is no longer I who live, but Christ lives in me; and the life which I now live in the flesh I live by faith in the Son of God, who loved me and gave Himself for me"(Gal. 2:20).

Even though Jesus had not experienced the cross yet, He knew the day would come when He would bear all the burden of sin for us on the cross, and He knew when He actually would become sin for us, even though He never sinned. The disciples followed Jesus; however, they could not take up their cross and fully follow Jesus until after Jesus died and was resurrected. On the cross the divine exchange took place. Jesus died so He might live through us. Our sinful life was exchanged for His sinless life. Our own self-righteousness was exchanged for His righteousness. When Jesus died, our sinful life died. When Jesus was buried, our old man of sin was buried. When Jesus was raised, we were raised to newness of life in Him. Granted, we still have to deal with the flesh in our lives. This is why we have to reckon ourselves dead to sin and alive to Christ daily. Whenever we do this we are taking up our cross and following Him. Through His death, burial, and resurrection Jesus has given us the death that leads to life. We now have the power to die to sin and to live in newness of life. The glory of the only begotten Son of the Father lives within me. Am I daily allowing Him to live His life through me? Am I daily taking up the cross of my selfish life and following Him?

Lord, thank You for dying so I might live.

Daily Deposit: Whenever I take up my cross and follow Jesus, my life can change other lives for eternity.

The Flag of Faith
Mark 9:1–29

Without faith it is impossible to please God. (See Hebrews 11:6.) God is so pleased whenever we extend our faith towards Him, because then He can do the things He longs to do for us. God can do anything, and all things are possible to Him. But it is usually faith that releases His activity on earth.

A father with a demon-possessed son came to Jesus for help. The son kept throwing himself into the water and fire. Jesus asked the father how long his son had been this way, and the father said he had been like this since childhood. Then Jesus looked the father in the eyes and said, "If you can believe, all things are possible to him who believes." The father exclaimed, "Lord, I believe; help my unbelief" (Mark 9:23–24).

We all have experienced times when our faith was weak. I had such an experience when I prayed earnestly for the Lord to spare a little boy I hit with my car. For the three weeks he was hospitalized my faith waved like a flag on a flagpole. One day my flag of faith would toss wildly with the winds of doubt and unbelief. The next day my flag of faith would settle and blow gently as I kept my focus on Jesus, the Healer. The day came when this small eight-year-old boy was placed on the critical list. He had breathing problems in the night. On that day my flag of faith flew at half-mast. I cried out, "I believe! Help my unbelief!"

I did not have enough strength to raise my flag of faith without help. When I found out this young boy faced possible death that day, I called everyone who I knew could pray. The Lord heard the cry of the body of Christ and my cry for faith. The boy was spared. Whenever our faith is weak, we can call upon the Lord and the body of Christ to help us raise the flag of our faith.

Lord, whenever I lack faith, help me to remember to call on others to help me pray. Others can hold the flag of faith high when my faith begins to waver because of the circumstances I see in the natural.

Daily Deposit: Whenever we ask Jesus to increase our faith or trust the body of Christ to have faith for us, we will always receive the faith needed to change things for eternity.

February 28

Is There a Real Hell?
Mark 9:30–10:12

Death and hell are two things most people do not like to discuss. If a person knows Jesus Christ and has accepted Him as his Lord and Savior, these two subjects will not strike fear or dread in his heart.

We had an opportunity to go to England with our three boys on a Friendship Force Exchange. This was the first of many exchanges others enjoyed over the years when families from different countries would host one another. We stayed in the home of a family who were members of the *Christadelphian* religion. I had never heard of this religion, but we soon found out that *Christadelphians* do not believe there is a real hell and also do not believe there is a real devil. I would love to believe as they do, but I know better. We discussed many scriptures with this family, but we could not convince them that there was a real hell. I wish I had quoted what Jesus said about hell in our reading today. Jesus spoke of hell three times in this reading, and He gave the same description of hell each time He spoke. He said hell was a place of fire where "their worm does not die, and the fire is not quenched" (Mark 9:46).

We can believe Jesus knew what He was talking about. Hell originally was not created for man. It was created for the devil and his angels. However, people who reject Jesus will have to face hell. When Jesus died on the cross, He conquered both death and hell. He accomplished everything needed for those who believe in Him to escape both death and hell. Of course we will all die, but the moment we leave our physical body, we will be in the presence of the Lord. (See 2 Corinthians 5:8.)

We can also look forward to having a resurrected physical body if we receive God's merciful gift of salvation. Death no longer has any sting, and the grave will not be victorious over us. The news of this victory over death and hell needs to be shared with all those who will listen!

Lord, help me to be bold to share the Good News with others.

Daily Deposit: Look for opportunities today to share the good news of how Jesus won the victory over death and hell on the cross. Your sharing may pull someone out of the fire into the light of eternal glory.

March 1

The Faith of a Child
Mark 10:13–31

We discussed faith many times in our February devotions. The vehicle of prayer must travel the highway of faith to reach the final destination of the throne room of God. I have often tried to muster up faith when I needed it. This technique always failed. Faith is not something we create or conjure up on our own. Faith is a gift from God. The statement Jesus made about faith in our passage today should challenge us all. He said, "Assuredly, I say to you, whoever does not receive the kingdom of God as a little child will by no means enter it" (Mark 10:15).

What blocks most people from receiving Jesus Christ is pride and unbelief. We think we know more than God knows. We are too intelligent to receive anything by faith. Yet, when we drive to work every day, we believe we will reach our destination.

A little child has no problem with faith because he has to use his faith daily. The word *child* in the Greek in this passage means *infant*. When I had my first child I was over-whelmed with the responsibility of parenting. This new addition to our family was totally dependent upon me. Without my constant attention, this tiny little being would not survive. We can only operate in complete faith when we are totally dependent upon God. The moment we begin to rationalize with our minds and think we can handle things ourselves, faith is no longer operative.

Every man born on earth has a measure of faith. (See Romans 12:3.) We all have been given enough faith to believe in something beyond ourselves. There is an inborn desire in man to trust in something more powerful than himself. An infant receives great comfort when strong arms cuddle him. With every beat of a mother's heart, the message of her love and protection is conveyed to the infant.

Like a little child, we must trust in our heavenly Father both to protect and provide for us. When our heavenly Father gave His only begotten Son to the world, He provided not only a way to survive in this life, but also the way to enter eternal and abundant life.

Lord, thank You for Your protection and provision.

Daily Deposit: Many in this world have never been challenged to have faith in Jesus Christ. Today you may share with someone who will become as a little child and enter the kingdom of God. Heaven will be filled with little children.

March 2

Read: Leviticus 25:47–27:13; Mark 10:32–52; Psalm 45:1–17; Proverbs 10:22

What Do You Want Jesus to Do for You?
Mark 10:32–52

How would you respond if Jesus asked you, "What do you want me to do for you?" Most of us would probably have to think for a little while before we would be able to pinpoint only one thing we wanted Jesus to do for us. Twice in our passage today Jesus asked the question, "What do you want me to do for you?"

James and John asked Jesus to do something for them. Jesus asked them, "What do you want me to do for you?" They asked Jesus to grant to them the privilege of sitting on His left and right hand when He came into His kingdom. Jesus then explained that whoever wants to be a leader must be a servant first. I can remember quoting this Scripture to my twelve-year-old son. I told Ray that one day we would rule over angels, cities, and nations and we are in training now to do this. Ray responded, "But Mom, I don't want to be a leader of nations." I said, "Those who are leaders will be servants of all. Jesus came to serve us." He immediately exclaimed, "I think I will be able to serve."

We can identify with James and John. They asked Jesus for position and power, but I believe they just wanted to be as close to Jesus as they could be. Jesus revealed the secret to remaining in His presence continually. When we have a servant's heart, we will always be close to Jesus.

Blind Bartimaeus threw off his garment and ran towards the sound of Jesus' voice. Throwing off his garment was a real act of faith for blind Bartimaeus. In the time of Jesus, blind people did not carry white canes to signify their blindness. Instead, blind people wore special garments to declare their condition to others. When Jesus saw the faith of blind Bartimaeus, He asked him, "What do you want me to do for you?" Bartimaeus responded, "Rabboni, that I may receive my sight." Jesus said, "Go your way, your faith has made you well" (Mark 10:51–52).

Jesus desires to do many things in our lives every day. Whether or not we receive those things He wants to do for us depends upon our attitude. If we think we can handle the day on our own without the Holy Spirit's help, Jesus will not be able to accomplish those things in our lives He longs to accomplish. Is our heart to serve Him and serve others? Or are we just looking for the blessings Jesus has for us? The question in our hearts should be, "Jesus, what do you want me to do today for you and for others?"

Lord, thank You for coming to serve me.

Daily Deposit: Whenever we seek to serve rather than rule, we can expect opportunities to serve every day. Whenever we serve others with the right heart motivation, we are adding to our treasures in heaven.

March 3

The River of Life
Psalms 46:1–11

As I write this, the United States is about to enter war with Iraq. Our psalm today has steadied my heart in these troubled times. I must hold on to the truth that God is my refuge, my very present help in troubled times.

This psalm speaks of a river whose streams make glad the city of God. If we could be transported to the New Jerusalem, we would see this beautiful river flowing from God's throne. It is called the *river of life*. Although we cannot see this river with our natural eyes, we can feel the energizing flow of this river as we worship and praise God. Nation can rage against nation, kingdoms can be moved and removed, but the *river of life* never stops flowing. Only God can make wars cease. As the world situation becomes more intense, we need to still ourselves and know that God is the God Who rules the universe. He can span the universe with one of His hands. He can cup all the waters of the earth in the palm of one hand. Those images of God's greatness are expressed in other psalms David wrote. (See Psalm 33:6–11.) Be still and know that the King of the Universe is your personal God who has the hairs on your head numbered. (See Luke 12:7.) He is exalted above the nations and the whole earth. The God of Jacob is our refuge. If God is for us, who can be against us? We need to remind ourselves of God's greatness and His mighty power in these last days.

Things are not going to get better, as far as the world is concerned. However, those who trust in the Lord will get better. The path of the just will grow brighter and brighter as we approach the coming of the Lord. The Lord of Hosts will be glorified in the body of Christ on earth. Just as surely as we live, all the earth will one day be filled with the glory of the Lord.

Lord, help me not to be troubled in these troubled times.

Daily Deposit: People are seeking to know peace in these times. Your inheritance as a servant of the Lord is the very peace of Jesus Christ. Share that inheritance with someone today.

March 4

Fitting In
Numbers 2:1–3:51

The children of Israel were divided into camps by their tribes. Each tribe had a standard or banner. The tribe of Levi's place was near the tabernacle. Their duty was to prepare all the sacrifices and take care of all the furnishings in the tabernacle. God made sure that every tribe knew its position and every priest knew his duty. They all worked together to accomplish all of God's instructions. We read this statement, "The children of Israel did according to all that the LORD commanded Moses" (Num. 2:34).

Everyone had his place. Each person knew his position and duty. There is a great need in the body of Christ today for the members of the body to know their calling and to use their special gifts in the body. Recently, we had a member of our church leave because she simply could not find her place in our local body. We have people drift in and out of our church continually. God has a place for everyone in His body. We need to help those who have not found their place to find their place quickly, because the Lord is coming soon.

How do we discover our calling? How do we find where we fit in? People who have experienced rejection in their lives usually have a real problem fitting in anywhere. They feel they are on the outside looking in. The key to finding our place in the body of Christ is to get rid of any root of rejection in our hearts. Rejection is a wicked illusion by the master magician, satan. He tries to create rejection in many lives. He was rejected by God, and, ever since he was thrown down to earth he has been trying to capture people with the wicked weapon of rejection.

How can rejection be an illusion? The truth is that Jesus bore our rejection on the cross, to purchase for us total acceptance by the Father. Jesus was despised and rejected by men so He could identify with how it feels to be rejected. He knows, however, that rejection is only a feeling. It is not the truth. We are accepted and loved by the Lord. The love God the Father has for His Son Jesus is the very same love He has for us. Do you believe this? It should not take years of counseling to rid ourselves of the root of rejection. The root of rejection can be dealt with in a moment in time. Do you believe Jesus took your rejection on the cross? If you truly believe this then never receive the lies and illusions of the devil again. Say with me today, "No weapon that is formed against me will prosper. Every tongue that rises against me in judgment I condemn. This is my inheritance as a servant of the Lord and my righteousness is of Him." (See Isaiah 54:17.) Your inheritance is liberty from rejection. Your inheritance is the very righteousness of Jesus Christ. Do you believe this? Accept the truth. Reject the lie and you will be healed from rejection.

Lord, thank You for accepting me just the way I am.

Daily Deposit: Give the good news of God's acceptance to someone today.

March 5

Sad You See
Mark 12:18–37

When we were in Israel, we learned a song from our tour guide. The chorus said, "I'm not a Pharisee because they are not fare you see. I'm not a Sadducee because they are sad you see. I'm just a lamb you see." We all enjoyed singing this song as our bus traveled the highways of Israel. Although the song is a little silly, it is accurate in its description of the Pharisees and Sadducees. The Sadducees did not believe in the resurrection. Anyone who does not believe in the resurrection would experience sadness, especially at the loss of a loved one.

The Sadducees tried to entrap Jesus by asking Him who would be the husband in heaven of a wife who was widowed seven times. Jesus responded, "Are you not therefore mistaken, because you do not know the Scriptures nor the power of God?" (v. 24). The Sadducees were not only sad at Jesus' response, but they were also extremely offended.

The Sadducees prided themselves on knowing the scriptures. Jesus explained to them that there would be no marriage in heaven. He also said God was the God of the living, not the dead. Jesus explained that God identified Himself as the God of Abraham, Isaac, and Jacob. God said, "I am their God," not, "I was their God." God is not the God of the dead, but of the living. I had a friend who lost two husbands in private plane crashes. After she lost the first husband, she asked God what her husband was doing in heaven. God gave her a dream. In the dream she saw her husband in heaven, and she ran to embrace him. He explained to her that they were like sister and brother in heaven, not man and wife. Then she asked him what he had been doing. He replied, "I just had a conversation with Abraham." God truly is the God of the living, not the dead. This should give us great joy, especially when we experience the death of a loved one.

Lord, thank You for Your death and resurrection. Now I can look forward to seeing my loved ones who believe in You again.

Daily Deposit: Some of your friends may not know about the resurrection power of God. Why don't you tell them so you can experience their friendship for eternity?

March 6

The Sign of His Coming
Mark 12:38–13:13

With all the wars and rumors of wars, people are discussing when the Lord might return. James, John, and Andrew asked Jesus privately when He would come again and what would be the sign when all of these things will be fulfilled. If we listen carefully to what Jesus told His disciples, we will discover the only sign that must be fulfilled before He comes again.

Jesus enumerated many events in history that would happen before His return. There will be false prophets. Nations will rise against nations, and kingdoms against kingdoms, but this is only the beginning of sorrows. This is not the sign of His coming. He shared that great persecution would fall upon the Christians. Then Jesus gives the sign of His coming. Notice it is not many signs, but one sign. He said, "And the gospel must first be preached to all the nations" (v. 10).

Why hasn't Jesus come yet? The Apostle Paul believed He would come in his lifetime. Jesus is preparing a house for His bride, the church, and Israel. It was customary in the ancient days in Israel to have a period of espousal before couples married. During this period of espousal, the bride-to-be had all the rights a wife enjoys, with the exception of the sexual consummation of their union. This did not usually occur until after one year of espousal. During that year the bridegroom prepared a house for his bride. This house had to pass the inspection of his father. When the father examined the house and found that it was ready, he then gave the word to his son to go and receive his bride. The wedding feast was prepared, and the union was completed.

Only our heavenly Father knows the day and the hour of Christ's coming. We can know the season, but not the hour. When the gospel has been preached to all nations, when all the people whom God knows will turn to Him and believe in Him have entered His Kingdom as little children, then the signal will be given to Jesus to return to earth. The reason Jesus has not come yet is that the gospel has not been shared with every nation. The sharing of the gospel spread from Jerusalem westward. Now the sharing of the gospel has spanned half the globe and is traveling eastward to China and, finally, to Israel.

When the gospel can be shared openly in China and Israel, we had better start looking up, because our redemption is drawing nigh. We have seen the fall of the Iron Curtain and great revival in Russia. Soon we will see the fall of the "Bamboo Curtain." Muslims will be reached, as well, with the gospel. We can hasten the day of the Lord's return by being faithful to share the gospel with those around us and to pray for those in other nations who are sharing the gospel.

Lord, help me to be faithful to share the Gospel.

Daily Deposit: Today I have the privilege to add to God's house.

65

March 7

Fulfillment and Filling Full
Mark 13:14–37

Yesterday, we learned the sign of Jesus' coming. We were challenged to be faithful to share the gospel with others and to pray for those who are laborers in this last great harvest. Everyone has his theory about when the Lord will return. A friend of mine recently shared a theory he had. He based his theory on our passage today. Jesus continued to describe what would happen in the end days. He described the great time of tribulation that would be more horrible than anything we have ever experienced. The Father's decision to shorten these horrific days would make it possible for some to be saved. The sun will be darkened and the moon will not give its light. The stars will fall, and the powers in the heavens will be shaken. Then they will see the coming of Jesus in the clouds with great power and glory. (See vv. 24–26.) After the description of all of these events, Jesus gave the parable of the fig tree. He said when the fig tree becomes tender and puts forth its leaves we know that summer is near. Then Jesus added, "So you also, when you see these things happening, know that it is near-at the doors! Assuredly, I say to you, this generation will by no means pass away till all these things take place" (vv. 29–30).

The fig tree is usually symbolic of Israel. The leaves began to show on the fig tree of Israel when the nation of Israel was birthed on May 14, 1948. My friend's theory is that anyone who saw the birth of Israel has the possibility of also seeing the coming of the Lord. This friend estimates the Lord's return to be sometime between 2003 and 2018. A generation is usually forty or seventy years according to the Bible. If you add seventy years to 1948, you will have the year 2018. I hope my friend is right, because I could be alive when the Lord returns.

Many in the body of Christ believe we will be raptured before the great tribulation. Others believe we will see all of the tribulation, and still others believe we will only experience the first three and one half years of the tribulation. No matter whether or not you are *pre-trib*, *mid-trib*, or *post-trib* in your eschatology, we all need to make sure of one thing. We all need to be sure we are filled with the Spirit on a daily basis. All of the prophesies might be fulfilled today. It is our responsibility to stay full of the Spirit until Jesus comes.

Lord, help me daily to receive a fresh infilling of Your Spirit.

Daily Deposit: Every time we ask the Lord to fill us with His Spirit, we are making an investment for eternity.

March 8

Two Memorials
Mark 14:1–21

Even though I am only sixty-three and hope to live many more years, I have begun to think about how people will remember me. We all want to be remembered as someone who had an impact upon God's work here on earth. Today's passage speaks of two people whose lives will be remembered forever. One person mentioned is always remembered for her selfless act. The other person is remembered for his selfish act.

The first person mentioned is the woman who anointed Jesus' feet with a very precious ointment. Jesus said she had prepared his body for burial. He responded to her selfless act by saying, "Wherever this gospel is preached in the whole world, what this woman has done will also be told as a memorial to her" (v. 9). We learn in John's gospel that the woman was Mary, Lazarus' sister. Some of Jesus' disciples were indignant when Mary anointed Jesus with this precious ointment. They said, "Why was this fragrant oil wasted?" They said the ointment could have been sold for a great price and given to the poor. Jesus responded by saying, "For you have the poor with you always, and whenever you wish you may do them good; but Me you do not have always. She has done what she could" (vv. 7–8).

The second person who left a lasting memorial is Judas, whose name will be remembered forever. The name *Judas* is used to describe anyone who has betrayed another person. His act of betrayal impacted the world. We learn in John's Gospel that Judas was among those who were offended by Mary's actions, and he was the one who said the ointment should have been sold and given to the poor. John explained that Judas said what he said because he was a thief. Judas was in charge of the money box and often stole from it.

How people will remember us when we die depends upon how we have lived our lives. If we have lived our lives in a selfish way, our memorial will be one of disdain, instead of honor. If we have lived our lives in a selfless way, people will remember our good deeds and words. My mother died five years ago, and I remember her both for what she did and what she said. She loved to cook and, after she was widowed, she supplied many widows with home cooked meals. I remember how she taught us to think about others, even when we were very young. She helped us make joke scrapbooks for a children's hospital. We took these scrapbooks and read them to the children and left them for their future reading. I am still finding words and letters of inspiration she wrote to many. Most of her friends and relatives remember her for one main thing in her life. They say, "As long as Frances lived, I never heard her speak evil of anyone." What a lasting memorial! What will be your lasting memorial?

Lord, help me to live a selfless life.

Daily Deposit: What I speak and do today could change a life for eternity.

Meet Me at the Galilee
Mark 14:22–52

The last supper was finished, and when they went out they sang a hymn. One of the hymns many believe Jesus and the disciples sang was Psalm 118. Psalm 118, traditionally, is sung at Passover. "This is the day the Lord has made, I will be glad and rejoice in it" is one of the sentences in this song. For the joy that was set before Jesus He endured the cross. He comforted His disciples by telling them that when He was resurrected He would go before them to the Galilee.

We have had eight opportunities to tour Israel, and truly I would be happy if our tour group just parked at the Sea of Galilee for the duration of the tour. The Sea is actually a large lake shaped like a David's harp. One can see the Golan Heights in the distance. It is a breathtaking sight. The tour guide who led us on our last two tours to Israel heard the very words Jesus spoke to His disciples when he said, "I will go before you to Galilee" (v. 28).

Our guide was raised in a secular Jewish home. His ancestors were fishermen and carpenters who lived on the Sea of Galilee. Dror, our guide, had a beautiful tenor voice and was awarded a scholarship to study opera in Germany. While he was in Germany, he had a dramatic vision. He was not a believer in Jesus, but Jesus revealed Himself to him in a vision. As Dror was singing Handel's Messiah, he saw the Sea of Galilee. In the middle of the Sea was the face of Jesus! He heard these words, "Why are you here? My presence is more where you lived than here. Return to the Galilee and I will meet you there." Dror packed his bags, left school, and returned to the Galilee.

Every day he rode his bike out to the Sea of Galilee to meet with Jesus. On one of these occasions he saw his cousin who is an archaeologist. She was with several of his other relatives. They yelled to Dror, "Come here quick. We are uncovering an ancient boat!"

That year there had been a drought in Israel. The sea level was low enough to reveal an ancient boat. As they raised the boat out of the water, a rainbow extended from the eastern to the western shore of the Sea of Galilee. The boat was later carbon-dated and found to be a boat used in the times of Jesus! The boat was made of twelve kinds of wood. It is preserved now in a museum in Tiberias. You can see it today. On that exciting day, Dror knew Jesus had met Him in a special way.

Jesus wants to meet with us every day in a special way. We do not have to go to the Sea of Galilee to experience His presence. He is with us wherever we go. He says to us today, "Come meet with Me." We do not have to have a sign to know His presence. When joy floods our soul, we know He is near. When we weep, we also know He is near to comfort us. In His presence is fullness of joy. (See Psalm 16:11.)

Lord, help me to meet with You daily.

Daily Deposit: Spending time in the presence of Jesus can change you forever.

March 10

Read: Numbers 14:1–15:16; Mark 14:53–72; Psalm 53:1–6; Proverbs 11:4

Coming in the Clouds
Mark 14:53–72

Jesus came to our tour guide, Dror, at the Sea of Galilee. One day we will all see Him coming in power in the clouds. When Jesus was asked if He was the Christ by the chief priests and council, He responded, "I am. And you will see the Son of Man sitting at the right hand of the Power, and coming with the clouds in heaven" (Mark 14:62). The men to whom He was speaking died centuries ago. We know that Jesus has yet to come in power in the clouds. However, Jesus' statement was accurate. The righteous and wicked will be raised from the dead. This resurrection will happen when Jesus appears in the clouds and breaks the eastern sky like lightning. The dead in Christ will be the first to be raised. Jesus was telling those gathered that the day would come when they would have to face the judgment of God. After Jesus told them He would return in the clouds, the high priest tore his clothes and said, "What further need do we have of witnesses. You have heard the blasphemy! What do you think?" Then they all condemned Him and said He was worthy of death. (See Mark 14:64.)

What a sobering thought! The wicked and just will be raised from the dead and judged for their words and deeds. The righteous will be judged for reward, and the wicked will be judged for punishment. In this passage, Peter denied Jesus three times. The last time he denied him, he cursed and swore as he exclaimed he had never known Jesus. Will Peter's words go with Him into eternity?

The good news is that Jesus forgave Peter for every word he spoke on that fateful day. Peter repented of what he had done when he wept. He was greatly grieved in his spirit, and he was stunned that his flesh was so weak. On the cross, Jesus removed our transgressions, as far as the east is from the west. (See Psalm 103:12.) We must, however, believe and receive Jesus as Lord and Savior to be spared from the judgment of punishment. Jesus was punished, so we do not ever have to fear God's punishment of us. We are not appointed to God's wrath because of God's grace. Glory! This is good news! Have you shared this Good News with someone today?

Lord, give me opportunities today to share this Good News.

Daily Deposit: The message of the cross is almost too good to be true, but it is true. Whenever we share this message with others, and they receive and believe what we have said, those persons have been spared the punishment of God! And we will meet them again in heaven, where we will both get our just rewards.

March 11

Touching God's Anointed
Numbers 15:17–16:40

K orah (son of Izhar, son of Kohath, son of Levi) and several of the offspring of Reuben gathered two hundred and fifty men against Aaron and Moses. They said to Moses and Aaron, "You take too much upon yourselves, for all the congregation is holy, every one of them, and the LORD is among them. Why then do you exalt yourselves above the assembly of the LORD?" (Num. 16:3). When Moses heard this, he fell to his face and challenged these men to gather themselves the next day and God would reveal to them who was holy.

The rebellious two hundred and fifty men came the next morning with their fire pans to the Tent of meeting. The glory of God appeared, and Aaron and Moses were told to separate themselves from the assembly because He planned to kill the whole congregation. Moses appealed to God's mercy and begged Him not to destroy the whole camp because of these men's sins. God heard Moses' prayer and only destroyed the two hundred and fifty men and their families and possessions with an earthquake.

Korah and his gang wanted equal position with Moses and Aaron. When Korah rebelled and accused Moses and Aaron of pride, he was touching God's anointed with his words. It is not wise to touch God's anointed. There is an account recorded where David had the opportunity to touch God's anointed. David had many opportunities to kill Saul, but he never did. Saul was asleep in one of the caves of Egedi. David discovered him and cut off a piece of his garment. Saul asked him later why he did not kill him when he had the chance. David said he could never touch God's anointed. Even though Saul was his enemy, David knew better than to touch Saul, God's anointed king.

Whenever anyone comes against an anointed pastor or even any servant of the Lord, he faces grievous consequences for such a sin. We are called to honor God and respect and give honor to all of His servants. Whoever has spiritual authority over us deserves our respect. God has chosen, anointed, and placed those people in charge of our very souls.

Those in spiritual authority will have to answer to God Himself on the Day of Judgment when God will reveal even the hearts of men. I have learned over the years to be very careful about what I say about those in spiritual authority over me. Some parents have "fried" pastor for lunch after church instead of fried chicken. We cannot expect our children to honor and respect us if we show no respect and honor to our spiritual fathers and mothers. The story of Korah should cause us all to fear the Lord and to stand in awe of His power and presence with obedient hearts.

Lord, help me to honor and pray for all those in authority.

Daily Deposit: The words I speak about those in spiritual authority on earth will be reviewed in heaven.

March 12

The Complaint Department
Numbers 16:41–18:32

After Korah and his gang were killed in the earthquake (the first earthquake ever recorded on earth), the children of Israel complained and said to God, "You have killed the people of the Lord." Because of their complaint, God sent a plague in the midst of them. Many more of the children of Israel died that day. Moses told Aaron to take a censor of incense into the congregation to make atonement for them, because the wrath of God was upon them. The plague was stopped, but 14,700 died, in addition to the 250 who died in the earthquake.

This true story makes me understand how God feels about our making complaints to one another. When we complain to one another we are murmuring, and God hates murmuring. The mistake the children of Israel made continually was to take their complaints to Moses, while continuing to murmur among themselves. There is only one complaint department created for us as servants and priests of the Lord. That complaint department is called the Throne Room of God. God does not mind if we pour out our complaints to Him privately. David learned this secret. He always poured out His complaints to the Lord, and then he asked for God to create within Him a clean heart and a right spirit.

Later, in our reading, God stopped the complaining for a season when He proved to them that Aaron was His anointed high priest. All the leaders of the tribes of the children of Israel were asked to write their names on a rod. The tribe of Levi wrote Aaron's name on their rod. The twelve rods were placed in the tabernacle, and God told them that the rod that budded would indicate the man God had chosen to be their priest. Aaron's rod budded and the children of Israel stopped their complaints for a season. As we know, however, it was not long before they murmured and complained about other issues.

Aaron and his sons were appointed to serve the people and the Lord in His tabernacle. God set the Levites apart to be priests unto Him, and He said they were a gift to the people. God reserved the best portion of the sacrifices and the grain offerings for the priests to eat. The best of the oil, wine, and grain were given to the priests. We are called priests of the Most High God. When we give our best to God through our prayers for others and our sacrifices of praise to Him, God invites us to partake of the best portion of food. Many of us, however, never taste the best portion of God's spiritual food—His Word—because we do not love God with all of our hearts, nor do we love others as we love ourselves. The exhortation from this reading speaks to me loudly and clearly. I hear God saying to me, "Quit your complaining and get on with loving Me and loving others!"

Lord, help me to not complain. Help me to love.

Daily Deposit: All of our complaining words will be judged if we do not repent.

March 13

Doubting God
Luke 1:1–25

We talked yesterday about the consequences of complaining. The root of complaining is always doubt and fear. Whenever we doubt God and His Word, fear greets us and we will usually begin to complain. We begin to fear the future and the unknown. The children of Israel feared their future, and they did not know what was going to happen to them next. Instead of trusting God, they felt by murmuring and complaining that they could project a little control into the situation.

Fearful people are comforted when they take control of situations. They feel if they are in control, nothing bad will happen to them. Doubt and fear are like twin brothers. They go hand-in-hand. The teamwork of these two wicked twins began in the Garden of Eden. First, satan put doubt in Eve's heart about God's goodness. He suggested to her that God was withholding something good from her. She took the bait. Once she ate of the forbidden fruit of the Tree of the Knowledge of Good and Evil, sin entered and fear was born. As long as Adam and Eve trusted in God, there was no room for sin or fear. Once they began to doubt God and acted in doubt rather than faith, they began to fear. Shame and fear overwhelmed them on their first encounter with God after they had sinned. They wanted to hide from God.

This sequence of doubt and fear are spelled out clearly in our passage today. Zacharias was told by an angel that his prayers for a son had been answered. The angel first told Zacharias not to fear. Then the angel continued to share the name of this child and what this child, named John, would do. Zacharias said to the angel, "How shall I know this? For I am an old man, and my wife is well advanced in years" (v. 18). Zacharias doubted that God could perform this miracle, so he asked for a sign. He received a sign, but it was not the one he hoped to receive. The angel said, "But behold, you will be mute and not able to speak until the day these things take place, because you did not believe my words which will be fulfilled in their own time" (v. 20). There are always consequences when we doubt God, and none of them are good. Whenever we doubt God's Word, we open ourselves up to sin. There is only one sin that leads to all others. That sin is unbelief. God has called us to open our mouths and speak words of faith, not doubt. The saying "I believe God said it and therefore He will do it" should be our watchword daily.

Lord, help me to never doubt Your Word.

Daily Deposit: The words of faith I speak today will be applauded in heaven.

Spring Up, O Well
Numbers 21:1–22:20

The children of Israel continued their pattern of murmuring and complaining. They said to Moses, "Why have you brought us up out of Egypt to die in the wilderness? For there is no food and no water, and our soul loathes this worthless bread" (Num. 21:5). Again we see the severe consequences of murmuring. God sent snakes among them. Moses once again interceded for the people and begged for God's mercy. God responded by telling Moses to make a fiery serpent out of bronze and to set it on a pole. Whoever looked at the bronze serpent would not be bitten. This symbol of the serpent on the pole is used to represent healing. We see the symbol on doctors' degrees and signs. This symbol can also represent the cross. Whenever we look at the cross we are protected from the bites of that old wicked serpent, satan, who seeks to devour us.

God was long suffering with the children of Israel and, again, spared them from total destruction. Then He brought them to the border of Moab, where he told Moses to gather the people by the well at Beer. The children of Israel sang, "Spring up, O well! All of you sing to it" (Num. 21:17). The well produced water and the children of Israel were temporarily satisfied.

The phrase, "Spring up, O well!" was unfamiliar to me until God gave me some unusual instructions. Every time I take trips to foreign countries to minister to people, I ask the Lord what He would have me declare over the land and the people when I go. We were about to take our first trip to Russia. When I asked the Lord what I should declare, He gave me this phrase, "Spring up, O well!" I looked the phrase up in the *Strong's Concordance*, and found this phrase in our passage for today. I was faithful to declare this phrase as we rode the Metro and mingled with the people.

It was not until we experienced our first musical festival to reach out to the Jewish population with the gospel in St. Petersburg, that I understood what this phrase meant. People with ashen gray countenances entered the theatre. I saw no smiles. After the concert, these same people who received Jesus as their Messiah left with laughter and dancing. The wells the Lord wanted to spring up in Russia were the wells of joy. The oppression of communism for seventy years had robbed Russia of her joy. The joy of the Lord is our strength, and these Russians needed great strength to face the future.

They were as thirsty for God's living water as the children of Israel were for physical water. That night these thirsty Russians received both God's living water and the belief in the cross of Jesus Christ. They now could receive healing for their troubled souls.

Lord, help me to spread Your living waters wherever I go.

Daily Deposit: The joy of the Lord in your life can strengthen others eternally.

March 15

Read: Numbers 22:21—23:30; Luke 1:57—80; Psalm 58:1—11; Proverbs 11:12—13

Opening the Mouth
Luke 1:57—80

The mouth is an interesting feature of the body. It is used to take in food and to distribute words to others. What people speak out of their mouths reveals what is in their hearts. Zacharias had dispensed words of doubt earlier when the angel told him he would have a son. At that time the angel told him to name his son *John*. For the full term of Elizabeth's pregnancy, Zacharias remained mute.

Now it was the day the baby was to be circumcised. As family gathered, several discussed what the child should be named. Elizabeth decided to name the baby *John*. Some of the relatives exclaimed, "There is no one among your relatives called by this name." They decided to give a writing tablet to Zacharias to see what name he chose. He wrote that the child should be called *John*. The moment he wrote this, his mouth was opened and prophecy flowed out of his mouth, like waters from a dam recently opened. He spoke of *John* as the one to prepare the way for the horn of salvation God raised up from the house of David. Deliverance from fear and everlasting righteousness would come through this horn of salvation (Jesus). Light would shine out of darkness and the shadow of death.

If we trust God with all of our hearts, we can trust Him to fill our mouths with what we need to say to people. Every day I ask the Lord to let the meditations of my heart and the words of my mouth glorify Him. When the meditations of our hearts are upon Jesus, we will speak the words that will glorify Him. I have had the opportunity to prophesy to many people. This is always exciting to me. When I open my mouth to speak over people, I have no idea what will come out. God has never failed to give a word of edification, exhortation, or knowledge to these people. I'm sure all those gathered around Zacharias and Elizabeth that day were electrified by the prophecy he gave.

Lord, when I open my mouth today, give me the words to speak.

Daily Deposit: The words we speak to others today can change their lives forever.

March 16

The Elderly
Luke 2:1–35

It has been my joy recently to minister to the elderly. One morning before the Bible study I teach in a retirement/nursing home, I asked the ladies to tell a little about themselves. One of the ladies shared she was in this home because no one in her family could take her. My heart was grieved for her, and I wondered if this was the situation Anna, the prophetess, found herself in. Our passage today gives a glimpse into the lives of two elderly people.

It was time for the dedication of Jesus in the temple. Mary's days of purification were over, and she and Joseph took their precious new infant into the temple to present Him to the Lord. The firstborn male child, according to the law, was to be given to the Lord. These male children were called *holy* to the Lord. I have three sons. My oldest son has a special place in my heart, because I know God considers him holy unto Him.

As they entered the temple, there was a man named *Simeon*. He was a just and devout man who had the Holy Spirit upon him. The Holy Spirit told him he would not die before he had seen the Lord's Christ. He was led to come into the temple by the Holy Spirit. The moment he saw Jesus, he took Him into his arms and declared excitedly that he could now die in peace. He had been promised by the Spirit to see his Messiah before his death, and now he was holding his Lord and Savior in his arms. He prophesied that Jesus would be a light to bring revelation to the Gentiles and God's glory to Israel. After he had blessed Jesus, he then turned to Mary and prophesied about the destiny of Jesus. He told her Jesus would fall and then rise as a sign to Israel and a sword would pierce her own soul. The very thoughts of many would be revealed.

Upon hearing the loud voices echoing through the temple, Anna ceased her prayers and joined them. Anna lived in the temple and served God with prayers and fastings, night and day. She was probably around 107 years old. She was married at a young age, lost her husband after seven years of marriage, and had been widowed for eighty-four years.

What was the secret of her longevity? I remembered asking a friend who died at 105 years this question. She replied, "Serving the Lord and eating All Bran." I don't think there was any All Bran in Anna's day, but she spent over ninety-one years of her life in the temple serving the Lord. Both Simeon and Anna feared the Lord. Those who fear the Lord are promised a long life. Simeon and Anna served the Lord and waited patiently upon the Lord for His promises to be fulfilled in their lives. They were empowered by the Holy Spirit.

Lord, empower me to live a long and fruitful life.

Daily Deposit: When we stay in the presence of the Lord, His joy strengthens us to live a long life. Today the time spent with Jesus can add years to your life.

The Victory Banner
Psalms 60:1–12

As David wrote this psalm, he was burdened by the hardness of life. He spoke to the Lord and said, "You have shown your people hard things." We all face hard things in life, and there are many reasons for this. One of the main reasons hard things come into our lives is because we live in a fallen world. Our world is in a state of ongoing corruption. Jesus told us we would have tribulation in this world, but He also told us to be of good cheer. Another reason hard things happen in our lives is because we make wrong decisions. Still another reason we experience hardship is because God tests us. God never tempts us, but He does test us, even as He tested Abraham when Abraham was asked to sacrifice his promised son, Isaac. That was a hard thing.

David's somber mood changed when he remembered the Lord's great provision. He said, "You have given a banner to those who fear You, That it may be displayed because of the truth. Selah That your beloved may be delivered" (vv. 4–5). Recently, our church has begun to wave banners and flags, but many do not understand why we do this. However, in the scriptures, we see the importance of banner waving. Something breaks in the spiritual realm when banners are waved. We were taught that the colors of the various banners even have meaning. David's whole mood changed when he remembered that the Lord had given him a banner. He began to rejoice. He ends the song with a great declaration of victory. He says, "Through God we will do valiantly, For it is He who shall tread down our enemies" (v. 12).

The devil hates banner waving. We have two banners we can wave in the face of the devil that makes him flee instantly. Those two banners are "Love" and "The Word of God." Solomon wrote in the Song of Songs that the banner over him was love. Now David, Solomon's father, wrote about the banner of truth. God's Word is truth. I understood fully the power of God's Word as a banner flown in the spirit realm when I read a book about heaven. The book was called *I Saw Heaven*. It was a precious story told by a young boy who had a vision of heaven. One of the scenes he saw was a huge stadium with people cheering loudly. He looked on the field and there was no sport being played. Instead, the people were looking down through a great hole in the clouds. Their eyes were trained upon the earth. They all held colorful banners and were waving them joyfully. He could not see the heads of these people because the banners covered their heads. He interpreted this scene to be the *great cloud of witnesses* spoken of in Hebrews. As the saints watched the victories the saints on earth won, they all waved their banners and cheered.

Lord, thank You for being Jehovah Nissi.

Daily Deposit: You can cover your loved ones with the banner of love and God's Word when you pray for them today. Satan will have to flee. The Lord is your banner!

March 18

Know Your Calling
Luke 3:1–22

A s we draw closer to the coming of the Lord, it is essential for us to find our place in the body of Christ and to know our calling. I have had the opportunity to pray over many people. Often God will reveal their special calling to me. A calling is not a vocation. It is not a ministry. A calling is like a golden thread that gathers all the various areas of your life into one beautiful glory garment tailor-made for you. God's glory is always revealed, as we are faithful to our calling. Our calling can be used in every area of our lives–the workplace, marketplace, family, and church.

One day in prayer, I asked God what my calling was. First, I asked the Lord to reveal to me my place in the body of Christ. (See 1 Corinthians 12.) Was I an eye, a hand, a foot, or some other part? I heard this statement with my spiritual ears: "You are called to be a voice." Then I looked up in *Strong's Concordance* wherever the word *voice* occurred in the scriptures. When I was led to Luke 3, I discovered not only my calling, but also my mission in life.

John the Baptist was filled with the Holy Spirit when he was in his mother's womb. I pray for the babies in the pregnant women I know to be filled with the Spirit, just as John was. John's father, Zacharias, prophesied about the destiny of Jesus, the horn of salvation, on the day John was circumcised. But Isaiah prophesied John's calling years before John's birth. God knows what each of our callings is, even from the foundation of the earth.

John was called to be a voice to declare the way of the Lord. His words would bring people to repentance, to lead them to make their paths straight and the rough places in their lives smooth. He prepared the way for salvation to be revealed to all flesh. When I read of John's calling, I knew I, too, was a voice to prepare the way for the Lord's second coming. I was called to declare God's Word faithfully through writing, teaching, and singing to the body of Christ , as well as to the world.

Do you know your calling? If you have not discovered your calling yet, ask the Lord what part of the body of Christ you are. You may be His hands to be used to serve others or you may be another voice to declare God's Word on earth.

Lord, I ask You today to reveal to me my calling in life.

Daily Deposit: Once we know God's calling on our lives, we can glorify Him through that calling. Today pray for your loved ones to discover their callings.

March 19

Read: Numbers 28:15–29:40; Luke 3:23–38; Psalm 62:1–12; Proverbs 11:18–19

Generations
Luke 3:23–38

The Gospel of Matthew gives us the lineage of Jesus. Matthew begins his list of Jesus' linage with Abraham and continues to the birth of Christ. There are fourteen generations from Abraham to David, fourteen generations from David until the captivity in Babylon, and fourteen generations from the captivity of Babylon to Christ's birth. Matthew traces Jesus' linage through the line of Joseph. Joseph was only the foster father of Jesus. Jesus is the Son of God; however, he inherited a legal right to Israel's throne through his foster father, Joseph.

Earlier I shared about how the lineage of Jesus in Matthew caused a Jewish friend of mine to know Jesus as His Messiah. As an orthodox Jew, Abraham (my friend) was forbidden to read the New Testament. When his guitar teacher in Jerusalem gave him the New Testament, he threw it in the garbage. Later, the Christian guitar teacher asked Abraham how he liked the gift he gave him. Abraham said he lost it. The guitar teacher then proceeded to give him another New Testament. This time Abraham felt it would be safe to just read the first page of the New Testament. As he read the lineage of Jesus recorded in Matthew, he realized that Jesus was truly the Messiah because he came from the house of David. Abraham was saved that day.

Matthew's purpose in tracing the lineage of Jesus through Joseph was to prove Jesus had the right to the Davidic throne. The lineage of Jesus in the Gospel of Luke traces the generations through Mary, the mother of Jesus. Luke's purpose was to reveal the humanity of Jesus. Mary also was from the house of David.

We are exhorted in the Bible not to spend a lot of time on our family history, because faith operates in the now, not in the past. (See 1 Tim. 1:4; Titus 3:9.) However, there is great value in knowing something about the generations past. We may discover generational curses that have been passed down to our generation or generational iniquities (vulnerability to addictions such as alcohol). Recently, I discovered the genealogy on my mother's side. I was delighted to discover there were generations of devout Christians in her lineage.

Lord, past generations can affect me today, but I can break those curses because You became a curse for me on the cross.

Daily Deposit: Remit today the sins of your ancestors by confessing their sin of spiritual idolatry through occult involvement and various lusts. Forgive them for their sins and claim your inheritance as a son or daughter of God, through your belief in Jesus Christ.

March 20

Is God Wrathful?
Numbers 30:1–31:54

I know a man who has not become a believer in God, mainly because he cannot understand how a loving God could destroy people. Throughout the Old Testament we see orders given to the children of Israel to completely destroy their enemies. Our passage today gives such a story.

The last command Moses gave on earth was to take vengeance on the Midianites. God told Moses to gather 1,000 men from each tribe to go against Midian. The children of Israel were successful and killed every male. They spared the women and children and took them captive. Moses was angry because they took the women captive. He reminded them that the females of Midian, at the word of Baalam, seduced the men of Israel and caused them to sin. Moses instructed the men to kill all the male children and every woman who had slept with a man. They were to spare the young virgin girls. They were told to stay outside the camp for seven days after this so they could be purified.

All of the booty was also to be purified, either by fire or by the purification waters. The booty was then divided among the tribes who battled. A portion was reserved for the Levites. An accounting was made of all the animal booty, and it was divided among the tribes. A census was taken, and not one man had perished in the battle. With grateful hearts, the men from the tribes brought the gold they found to Moses and Eleazar, and it was taken to the tent of meeting as a remembrance of the victory.

This historic story does make one question the goodness of God. We have to remember that God sees the big picture. He knew if the Midianites were not destroyed, they would remain as thorns in the sides of the children of Israel. He also knew the wickedness of the Midianites would influence the children of Israel. God commanded Joshua when he entered the Promised Land to destroy all the "ites" including the Caananites, the Moabites, and the Edomites. These three "ites" represent the three lusts that constantly are thorns in our own flesh. (See 1 John 2:15–16.) We are challenged daily to conquer these lusts—the lust of the flesh, the lust of the eyes, and the lust of the pride of life.

Is God wrathful? God is all-knowing, and in His great wisdom, He sees the damage that can be done to righteous men by wicked leaders of nations. God has the power to raise up regimes and to destroy them. Sometimes God allowed the enemies of Israel to come against them to put Israel on the pathway of repentance of its own wickedness. God's wrath was poured out upon Jesus on the cross; those who believe in Him are not appointed to God's wrath.

Lord, thank You for Your Grace.

Daily Deposit: We may have the opportunity to share with others about God's grace through Jesus Christ. We don't want anyone to be appointed to God's wrath.

March 21

The Way to Catch People
Luke 4:31–5:11

Jesus told Simon to "launch out into the deep and let down your nets for a catch" (v. 4). Simon did not believe they could catch anything in those waters because they had fished all night and had caught nothing. At Jesus' Word, however, he let down the net.

Simon could not believe his eyes when he saw the abundance of fish. Jesus said to him, "Do not be afraid. From now on you will catch men" (Luke 5:10). We are privileged to live during the time of the last great harvest before Jesus comes. There are many hungry fish, or people with hungry hearts who need to be brought into our nets of fellowship! Fellowship means fellows in the same boat. Some of us have spent most of our lives in fellowship, but there are multitudes in the world who do not know the Good News, or the Gospel! Jesus is still able to tell us where to catch fish –meaning, people!

As laborers in this End-Time harvest, we have to be alert to the leading of the Holy Spirit. We may hear the Spirit tell us to go and see someone or to call someone on the phone who needs to know about Jesus. I heard an exciting true story about a person who had a desire to witness; however, this person was trapped in his home without a car. He could go nowhere, so he asked Jesus how he could be a daily witness. Jesus told him how to catch some fish (people). He was led of the Spirit to call three people a day on the phone to witness to them. Often he just looked up names in the telephone book and called people he had never met. On one of these occasions he called a person who was about to commit suicide. After he witnessed, this person gave his life to the Lord and later became a well-known Bible teacher.

Before we catch any "fish," we need to throw out the net! How do we do this? We throw out the net every time we preach the kingdom of God. How do we preach the kingdom of God? The kingdom of God is not meat nor drink, but righteousness, peace, and joy in the Holy Spirit. (See Romans 14:17.)

We need to ask people if they want to be right with God and experience peace, even in troubled times. We need to ask them if they would like to receive a special type of joy that can be maintained, even during difficult circumstances. I know very few people who would not be interested in obtaining these three wonderful gifts of righteousness, peace and joy! After we ask them, then we can tell them how to receive these gifts! The key to acquiring all three of these gifts is to receive Jesus Christ as Lord and Savior. We can share about the life, death, burial, and resurrection of Jesus. Then we can tell them that if they will believe in their hearts and confess with their mouths that Jesus Christ is Lord and that He was raised from the dead, they can receive His righteousness, His peace, and His joy. (See Romans 10:4–10.)

Lord, thank You for Your kingdom.

Daily Deposit: Look today for an opportunity to throw out your net.

March 22

Read: Numbers 33:40–35:34; Luke 5:12–28; Psalm 65:1–13; Proverbs 11:23

Three D's
Luke 5:12–28

The Bible tells us that during the End Times many people's love will wax cold and many will fall away from the faith. Even Jesus questioned whether there would be faith on the earth when He returned. Why do people fall away from the faith? Satan is able to tempt us all in the areas of our three lustful desires—the lust of the flesh, the lust of the eyes, and the pride of life. With the entrance of Internet pornography, I have seen many a saint neutralized in their Christian effectiveness because they are doing pornography and have given in to the lust of the eyes.

The Bible says, in the End Times, people will be lovers of pleasure more than lovers of God. The flesh loves to be fed, and the desire for entertainment and vacations are drawing many away from their first love. We live in the age of knowledge. Knowledge puffs up, and some are beginning to lose their faith because of vain reasoning and pride. Satan has been successful in luring many into his net through these three lustful desires.

What will keep us from falling and losing faith in these End Times? The desire to return to our first love, the discipline of continuing in the Word and prayer, and the determination to never give up our faith are the *Three D's* that will help us hold on to our faith. Today's passage speaks of four men who were applauded for their determination and faith. These four men pushed through the crowds to the home where Jesus was ministering. They were carrying their paralyzed friend on a cot. When they reached the home, they realized there was no way to enter the door of the house because of the crowds. They hoisted their paralyzed friend on top of the roof, removed some tiles, and let the man down by ropes to Jesus. "When [Jesus] saw their faith, He said to him, 'Man, your sins are forgiven you'" (v. 20).

Their determination to not give up, no matter what, brought healing to their friend. We are living in desperate times. Our determination to never give up can bring healing to many as we continue in prayer for them and continue to sow God's Word into their lives. Are you determined today not to give up praying for your lost loved ones and friends? Are you willing to keep sowing God's Word into their lives, even if these loved ones resist and reject you? Don't give up!

> *Lord, help me to have the same determination and faith these four friends displayed.*

Daily Deposit: The loved ones and friends you do not give up on now will spend eternity in heaven with you. Keep praying and sowing.

March 23

What Fills You?
Luke 5:29–6:11

Only the Lord can fill the emptiness in our souls. People pursue many ways to fill this God-shaped vacuum. Some attempt to fill it with pleasure. Others attempt to fill it with food. Many even attempt to fill it with drugs and alcohol. Still others seek to fill their empty souls with religion (endless rules to obtain righteousness). What we fill our souls with determines the fulfillment we will experience in this life.

Jesus saw the emptiness in men's souls. He saw the emptiness within the Pharisees and scribes who were bound by their law-filled religion. He saw the emptiness in those he dined and drank with in the home of Levi. The religious scribes questioned why Jesus hung around sinners. His reply was, "Those who are well have no need of a physician, but those who are sick. I have not come to call the righteous, but sinners, to repentance" (Luke 5:31–32).

Those who are self-righteous have already filled the void in their souls with rules and regulations. They are sick. Those who have filled the void in their souls with various addictions are also sick. Then who is well? Those who have repented and received the righteousness of Jesus Christ and who stay filled with the spirit are well.

Jesus gives the parable of the wineskins to the scribes who questioned the company he kept. He said new wine must be put into new wineskins. Those who have been used to drinking old wine sometimes are not willing to try the new because they think the old tastes better. It was the very tradition (the old ways) of the scribes and Pharisees that kept them from being filled with the new wine of the Holy Spirit.

The exhortation is given in Ephesians 5:18 to not be drunk with wine, but to be filled with the Spirit. We have had the privilege of teaching a marriage course and also counseling married couples. Books and tapes are in abundance on how to improve your marriage. My husband and I have come to one conclusion about how couples can have a rich, fulfilling marriage. The bottom line is that both the husband and the wife have to stay filled with the Spirit. Then the question is asked, "How do you stay filled with the Spirit?" This passage in Ephesians gives the answer, "Speak to each other in psalms and hymns and spiritual songs, singing and making melody in your heart to the Lord, giving thanks always for all things in the name of the Lord Jesus Christ, and submitting to one another in the fear of God." Is this a tall order? When we fill this order we will be continually filled with the Holy Spirit.

Lord, help me today to stay filled with Your Spirit.

Daily Deposit: Today will be a fulfilling day if I stay filled with the Holy Spirit.

March 24

Read: Deuteronomy 2:1–3:29; Luke 6:12–38; Psalm 67:1–7; Proverbs 11:27

Trudging or Triumphing
Deuteronomy 2:1–3:29

The children of Israel were about to enter the Promised Land. They had spent forty years in the wilderness. Moses told them, "For the LORD your God has blessed you in all the work of your hand. He knows your trudging through this great wilderness. These forty years the LORD your God has been with you; you have lacked nothing" (Deut. 2:7).

Sometimes we feel like we are just trudging in the wilderness. The only thing that gets us through such times is to know that the Lord is with us. Somehow I feel, however, that the Lord would rather us triumph through the wilderness instead of trudging through it.

The reason why the children of Israel did not triumph in the wilderness was because they had an attitude of ungratefulness, and they were filled with fear, instead of trust. Their fears and ungratefulness were clearly manifested in their grumbling and complaining. If we want to triumph through trials and wilderness experiences, we must have a joy-filled, grateful heart.

Recently I have started corresponding with a woman prisoner in California. She was falsely accused of killing her boyfriend. She is in prison for life without any hope of parole. She has been in prison for five years. During those five years, her precious mother died and she was unable to be with her in her last days. She left a twenty-two-year-old daughter, and two children, ages eight and ten, when she went into prison. If anyone has ever experienced a wilderness experience, she certainly has. Her letters to me have inspired me. They are filled with joyful phrases like, "Glory to God, Wow-OOO-wee! Every day is a gift to worship God for He is the Great I AM!" She shares that only Jesus has the keys to open her physical prison doors, but He has already opened her up to His great love. She shares, "Jesus has the key to every situation and to the future. He knows everything. I just want Him to get all the glory."

"Wow-OOO-wee!" We need to say this the next time we are going through the wilderness. God never failed to provide for the children of Israel in the wilderness, and He will never fail to provide for us through our wilderness experiences. This is why James writes, "My brethren, count it all joy when you fall into various trials, knowing that the testing of your faith produces patience. But let patience have its perfect work, that you may be perfect and complete, lacking nothing" (James 1:2–3). The children of Israel never let God perfect them because they lacked patience. Patience, a grateful heart, and joy of the Lord are the keys that will get us through every wilderness experience.

Lord, thank You for helping me to triumph in trials.

Daily Deposit: Most trials are allowed to test our faith. When we pass these tests on earth, we can present them to Jesus when we see Him face to face. Our fiery trials on earth will be turned into jewels in heaven.

March 25

Diligence
Deuteronomy 4:1–49

S everal days ago we talked about the three *d's* that will help us keep our faith during the End Times. The three *d's* were the desire to return to our first love, the discipline of continuing in the Word and prayer, and the determination never to give up no matter what the circumstances are. In today's passage we see another "d"—diligence.

God spoke to Moses and the children of Israel just before they entered the Promised Land. He told them to be diligent to keep their souls. Then He told them how they could keep their souls with all diligence. He told them not to forget what they had seen in the past, and not to allow their heart to depart from keeping the laws, statutes, and judgments. Through the laws, statutes, and judgments the children of Israel were able to gain wisdom and understanding in abundance beyond any other nation.

The New Testament tells us that Jesus is the Bishop of our souls, and hope is the anchor for our souls. Our souls are our mind, will, and emotions. This is the part of us called *the flesh*. Daily, our souls speak to us like this: I think, I will, I feel. The "I" part of our soul wants to do its own thing. God wants to translate the "I" in our souls to "Thy." We can only make the statement, "Thy will be done in my life," if our souls are totally surrendered to the bishop of our souls, Jesus Christ. The battle we experience daily is the battle of our flesh, or our souls, with the spirit—or the Holy Spirit within us. When the "I" in our souls speaks louder than the "Thy," we are operating in the flesh, rather than the Spirit.

The Bible tells us to possess our souls with patience. We learned earlier that patience is a fruit of the spirit that can only be developed as we go through trials. During the trials in the wilderness, the children of Israel never developed patience because they failed to obey God's Word. What we produce in this life depends upon what we put into our lives. If we put more worldly things into our lives than godly things, our lives will manifest worldliness, not godliness. We will end up operating in the flesh, rather than the Spirit. To guard our souls from worldliness, we have to give God's Word and our relationship to Jesus Christ top priority. Then, when trials come our way, God will be able to work through us, both to will and to do of His good pleasure. Patience will be developed in our lives. This takes daily diligence, because the enemy will do everything he can to draw us away from God's Word and Jesus.

Lord, help me to be diligent to continue in Your Word.

Daily Deposit: As I daily feed myself God's Word and then apply God's Word to my life, my soul will be transformed to be more like Jesus.

March 26

A Critical, Judgmental Attitude
Luke 7:11–35

H ave you ever been around people who, no matter what you do, find something wrong with it? Wherever Jesus went He was faced with critical, judgmental people. In our passage today, Jesus addressed the Pharisees and lawyers about their attitude. The Pharisees and lawyers had refused to be baptized by John. John's baptism was for repentance. God's will is that none perish, but that all come into the knowledge of Jesus Christ. (See 2 Peter 3:9.) The invitation is open to all to repent and turn to Him, but many will reject the will of God for themselves just as the Pharisees and lawyers did.

Jesus talked about a critical, judgmental generation that criticized John the Baptist because he did not eat bread or drink wine. These critical, judgmental people accused John of having a demon. When Jesus came on the scene, they continued to judge and criticize Him. Jesus both ate and drank. They called Him a glutton and a winebibber and a friend of tax collectors and sinners.

People who constantly find fault with others have rejected the will of God, just as the Pharisees and the lawyers rejected the will of God. The will of God is for us to give thanks in all things. The will of God is for us to esteem one another higher than ourselves. The will of God is for us to speak edifying words, not words that tear down others. Critical, judgmental people lack wisdom. Jesus said, "But wisdom is justified by all her children" (Luke 7:35). He was saying that what people say and do will reveal whether or not they are wise people. Wise people say wise things. Critical, judgmental people speak many unwise things. They want to offer their opinion about everything. Solomon wrote that the person who keeps his lips is wise and he is able to keep his soul from trouble. People who constantly judge others will have those very judgments come back upon them. It is not wise to judge others.

What is the root of a critical, judgmental attitude? The root is pride. Pride always resists and rejects doing the will of God. God resists the proud and gives grace to the humble. (See James 4:6.) This challenges me to humble myself daily before God and ask Him to help me speak wise words.

Lord, I humbly ask You to help me to speak wise words, not critical, judgmental words today.

Daily Deposit: The words I speak will be judged in heaven, and the rewards I will receive will be based on my words and deeds. Today I choose to speak wise words.

March 27

God Loves Jewish People
Deuteronomy 7:1–8:20

Every true Christian has a natural love for Jewish people. In our passage today, God tells exactly why He chose Jewish people to be a light to the Gentiles. It all began with Abraham, who was Syrian. Abraham was a faithful man who ruled his household well. God took note of Abraham, and he loved Abraham. He knew Abraham would be faithful to begin what we know as the Jewish nation. The word *Jew* comes from the Hebrew word *yehuda* which means "praise." We all were created for God's glory and praise, but God has always seen the Jewish people as His special treasure. God said in Deuteronomy 7:6–8:

> For you are a holy people to the LORD your God; the LORD your God has chosen you to be a people for Himself, a special treasure above all the peoples on the face of the earth. The LORD did not set His love on you nor choose you because you were more in number than any other people, for you were the least of all peoples; but because the LORD loves you, and because He would keep the oath which He swore to your fathers, the LORD has brought you out with a mighty hand, and redeemed you from the house of bondage, from the hand of Pharaoh king of Egypt.

The Jewish people were chosen to write the Bible, to be the birth race of the Messiah and to be a light to the Gentiles. Most of the early church was Jewish. All of the twelve disciples were Jewish, and they took the Gospel to the world. Saul (Paul) was Jewish, and he wrote most of the New Testament. As far as we know, the only Gentile writer of the Bible was Luke. We owe a great debt to the Jewish people. Without them, we would have no Bible, no Savior, no Old and New Testament, and no church. These facts alone should make us want to hug every Jewish person we meet. Yet, churches are filled today with anti-Semitism.

Our son is trying to pull down the walls of anti-Semitism in Hungarian churches. He teaches these churches about their Jewish roots. Communism brought with it to Hungary a great hatred for Jewish people. During the German occupation there was also anti-Semitism among the Hungarians. In the age in which we live, anti-Semitism is on the rise in every nation. It is time for true Christians to reach out in love to the Jewish people and ask their forgiveness for the great persecution of their people, by people who called themselves Christians. It is time for Christians to stand up and try to pull down the walls of anti-Semitism in churches.

Lord, thank You for Your Jewish people who have given so much to my faith.

Daily Deposit: Look for a person of Jewish faith, and reach out to him or her in love.

March 28

Hearing and Doing
Luke 8:4–21

The January 19 devotional was on the parable of the sower, given in Matthew 12. This January devotional emphasized that we hear with our hearts, as well as our ears. The parable of the sower is given in both Matthew 12 and Luke 8. In this parable, the soil represents our hearts and the seed represents the Word of God. Four conditions of our hearts were described in the parable—the callous heart (the seed that fell on the wayside); the careless heart (the seed that fell on stony ground and never found root); the cluttered heart (the seed that fell among thorns and was choked from bearing much fruit), and the clean heart (the seed that fell on good ground and bore much fruit).

When Jesus finished the parable, someone told Jesus that his mother and brothers were waiting to see him. He responded, "My mother and My brothers are these who hear the word of God and do it" (Luke 8:21). Jesus' response should challenge us all to not only hear God's Word, but also to do it.

The Holy Spirit speaks to us in many ways. When we read the Word of God, the Holy Spirit can speak to us. When we are in prayer, the Holy Spirit can speak to us. When we are just going through the routines of life, our thoughts can be interrupted by a message from the Holy Spirit. The Holy Spirit can speak to us through the voices of others. Everyday of our lives the Holy Spirit is speaking to us, but often we do not have our spiritual ears tuned to hear what He is saying, nor do we obey when we do hear what the Holy Spirit is saying!

People usually have trouble hearing with their physical ears. Why? Often, something is blocking their hearing. They may just have wax in their ears, or they may have a more serious condition, such as a busted ear drum or nerve damage. We also have trouble hearing with our spiritual ears due to something blocking our hearing. Bitterness, unforgiveness, anger, resentment, unconfessed sin, and rejection are *heart conditions* that can block us from hearing the Holy Spirit and receiving God's Word.

However, one of the major blocks to hearing the Holy Spirit is our unwillingness to do what He is telling us to do. We refuse to obey God's Word and the promptings of the Holy Spirit because we fear what others will think of us and fear that God will not equip us to do what He is telling us to do. What is blocking your hearing today?

> *Lord, forgive me for the times I have received Your Word and heard from Your Holy Spirit, but I did not do what You told me to do. Help me to have a listening and obedient heart.*

Daily Deposit: Confess and repent of anything that may be blocking your spiritual ears. Then ask the Lord today to help you to obey as He leads you by His Word and by His Spirit.

March 29

The Latter Rain
Deuteronomy 11:1–12:32

Moses continued his review of all the Lord had done for the Children of Israel. They were about to enter the Promised Land. Their eyes had seen every great act the Lord had done. Moses told them if they were faithful to obey God's commandments and to love Him and serve Him with all their hearts and souls, God would give them both the early rain and the latter rain. The early and latter rains would cause great fruitfulness in their land. One of the signs of this last great harvest of souls is the latter rain. It has only been in the last few years that Israel has been experiencing both spring and fall rains.

Recently, I experienced a supernatural sign that revealed God's latter rain to me. I was preparing the patio table for our lunch when I heard the sound of rain. It was a clear day with an October sky (bright blue without a cloud in the sky). I looked up and, in the clearing of the woods, I saw raindrops coming from the sky. The raindrops looked like diamonds as the sunlight reflected through them. I looked up to see if I had missed a cloud somewhere, and there was no cloud above this rain. I asked the Lord what this meant, and I heard, "This is a sign of the latter rain." Then I looked up in the scriptures to find out all about the latter rain.

Several scriptures speak of the latter rain. Zechariah exhorts us to ask the Lord for rain in the time of the latter rain. He said the Lord will make flashing clouds and will give them showers of rain. (See Zechariah 10:1.) We are in the time of the latter rain. We are in the time of the last great harvest, and the Lord wants us to ask for more souls. Joel said we should rejoice and be glad because the Lord has given both the former and latter rain faithfully. (See Joel 2:23.) Joel also prophesied that in the last days God would pour out His Spirit upon all flesh.

As those diamond raindrops were falling in my backyard, I heard the Lord tell me that He had bottled up all the tears the saints had shed when they cried out for the salvation of their loved ones and friends. Now He was emptying that bottle and pouring those tears down to earth as the latter rain, and these loved ones and friends would be included in this last great harvest.

Lord, send more rain in this time of Your latter rain.

Daily Deposit: Tears shed today as you cry out for the salvation of souls will bring joy in the morning. Keep asking God for more rain in this season of the latter rain.

March 30

The Cursed Thing
Deuteronomy 13:1–15:23

God warned the children of Israel not to take the spoil of their enemies into their possession, because those things were cursed. People often give us gifts as we travel through the world. We are always gracious to receive such gifts. There have been times, however, when I have not felt a peace about taking some of these gifts into our home. I felt some of these gifts had been used in idol worship.

We need to examine those things in our home to be sure they have not been a part of idol worship. I have been in homes where there have been little Buddhas in gardens or rooms. When I see anything I know that has been used in idol worship in the home of a Christian, I share with them the dangers of this. Demonic activity always surrounds any idols. When we were in India, we wanted to avoid as much demonic activity as possible, but it was nearly impossible to do so. In almost every home we saw not one, but several idols. In India, the Hindus worship over 300 million gods. No wonder the land seems to be cursed with so many disasters and droughts. One of the gods they worship is Sheva, the god of destruction. Guess who he really is? We know that satan is the destroyer, and we are not to be afraid of him or try to appease him.

All idols are cursed things. Thank God we had the covering of prayer and the covering of the blood of Jesus while we were in India. We managed to avoid entering any Hindu temples, but on one occasion we did see many idols. A man on the street invited us to enter a museum to see some eleventh century bronzes. We thought this sounded harmless, but when we entered, all of the bronzes were different idols they worshipped. Some were so grotesque in appearance that there was no doubt they were demonically inspired. As we left the museum, our pastor said to this man, "Frankly, we prefer Jehovah Jireh." I don't think the man understood, but we were grateful, so very grateful for the God of Life and Provision we serve!

There may be no cursed things in your home, but anytime we cling to something more than we cling to God, we have set up an idol in our hearts. I am challenged to examine my own heart, to see if there is any cursed thing within me–any idol that separates me from loving the Lord with all of my heart.

Lord, this passage in Deuteronomy is all about keeping our lives clean and free from idols. Show me the idols in my own life.

Daily Deposit: To finish life's race well, I have to cast aside everything that hinders me. The idols I give up in my own life today will cause me to be liberated in the rest of my tomorrows.

Sit Down and Eat
Luke 9:7–27

"Sit down and eat!" I must have said those words thousands of times during my years of motherhood when I had the joy of living with four hungry males. My husband and my three sons seemed to have insatiable appetites. I spent most of the years of my married life in the kitchen. Sometimes I got a little resentful when I was slaving in the kitchen, and my husband and boys were about their various activities. I used to sing this song in the kitchen, "Alone again, all alone again."

I could really feel the tingles of resentment go up and down my spine when we were not even finished with breakfast and the boys asked, "What's for lunch?" On one of these occasions I confessed my resentment to the Lord, and I heard His still small voice say, "I am always delighted to feed My children." Wow! I was convicted of my ungrateful attitude and had to ask the Lord to forgive me. I thought of the times Jesus fed the multitudes. It was His delight and joy to give physical food to the multitudes. It makes Him even more joyful when He is able to deliver spiritual food to us daily. Few, however, take the time to sit down and eat.

The Lord gave me a promise from Scripture during those days, and I have clung to that promise. He promised me that the day would come when all four of my wonderful men would consider His Word more important than their necessary food. I have seen this come true in the lives of my sons and husband. Jesus told us we do not live by bread alone, but by every Word that proceeds from the mouth of the Father. (See Luke 4:4.)

It was late in the day when the thousands gathered to hear Jesus when Jesus gave the command to His disciples to give those gathered something to eat. They responded, "We have no more than five loaves and two fish, unless we go and buy food for all these people" (Luke 9:13). Jesus took what was available, blessed it, and it was multiplied. Everyone was fed and there were even twelve baskets of food left over. No doubt the disciples ate that.

Jesus is still feeding the multitudes. He is still taking what you have to offer Him, blessing and multiplying it. Do you daily come to His table and partake of the spiritual bread He has prepared just for you? When I was a child, we had the sweet custom of kissing the cook after a meal. As we kissed our mother on the cheek, we told her how much we had enjoyed the meal. Today, after you finish the delicious spiritual meal Jesus has prepared for you, why don't you kiss and thank Him through your worship and praise?

Lord, thank You for continually feeding me Your Word.

Daily Deposit: The Word of God supplies food that will last into eternity.

April 1

Read: Deuteronomy 18:1–20:20; Luke 9:28–50; Psalm 73:1–28; Proverbs 12:10

A Mountaintop Experience
Luke 9:28–50

Often when I return from a retreat I say, "I had a mountaintop experience at that retreat." Peter, James, and John had the ultimate mountaintop experience. They were on the mountain, now called the *Mountain of Transfiguration*. Some believe the Mountain of Transfiguration is Mount Tabor, and others believe it is Mount Herman. Our tour guide told us he believed the transfiguration of Jesus took place on Mt. Herman. This is also my belief.

Peter had just declared that Jesus was the Christ, the Son of the living God. We know the disciples were gathered in Caesarea Philippi when this dramatic statement about Christ's identity was made. Many believe the Church was born at Pentecost, but I believe the Church was birthed at Caesarea Philippi. In another Gospel after Peter made this statement, Jesus said to Peter, "On this rock I will build My church" (Matt. 16:18). The rock is this very declaration Peter made. In our church, no one can join the church until they have made this very declaration.

When we were in Israel, we stood near the very spot where Peter boldly identified who Jesus is. We were in Banais, a beautiful wooded area with falls and springs that originate from the melting snow of Mt. Herman. These waters from Mt. Herman form the headwaters of the Jordan. We could see majestic snowcapped Mt. Herman in the distance, as we stood in the very place Peter made this marvelous declaration.

Jesus probably journeyed with His disciples to the top of Mt. Herman where Peter, James, and John beheld the glorified Christ. Jesus looked exactly like He did when He revealed Himself in all of His glory to John, the Revelator. Moses and Elijah joined Jesus. After this mountaintop experience, Peter wanted to build three tabernacles in honor of Jesus, Moses, and Elijah. This is a natural response after a mountaintop experience. We want to set up camp on the mountain and never return to the valley. We cannot do this, however, because people are waiting in the valley to hear all about our mountaintop experiences. We do not have to keep silent about our experience, as the disciples were instructed to do. We can shout it from the rooftops. Have you shared your mountaintop experience with someone today?

> *Lord, thank You for all the mountain top experiences I have had in my life. Help me to share them with others.*

Daily Deposit: One day we will experience the ultimate mountaintop experience when we climb the mountain leading to the Throne of God. He sits on the mountain, on the sides of the north. We don't have to wait till then, however, to know His presence and to boldly enter His Throne Room. We can do it today! What are you waiting for?

April 2

The Day and the Night Are Yours
Psalms 74:1–23

"From the rising of the sun to the going down of the same, the Lord's name is to be praised." This is a chorus we sing in our church and it is based on one of David's psalms. In Psalm 74:16 David wrote, "The day is Yours, the night also is Yours."

What would our days and nights be like if we said, "Today is Yours, Lord. Tonight is Yours, Lord"? When we commit our way to the Lord, He is able to bring His will to pass in our lives. When we commit our days to the Lord, He is able to go ahead of us and prepare the way for each day. One of the things I like to pray every morning is: "Lord, I commit this day to You. You alter it according to Your plan. I also commit every work to You so You can establish my thoughts."

When I pray this prayer, I give the Lord the right to change my own plans and to interrupt my plans at any time in the day. He becomes Lord of my day. The day belongs to Him anyway, but if I insist on doing my own thing and going my own way, the Lord is not able to do what He longs to do in my life that day.

I also give my nights to Him when I pray this simple prayer, "Thank You for giving Your beloved sleep, and speak to me in the night." God has given me many dreams in the night that have delivered His wisdom and revelation knowledge to me about certain circumstances in my life.

This week try giving your days and nights to the Lord. Whatever we give to the Lord, He is able to bless and multiply. Remember the feeding of the five thousand. The days I release to the Lord become meaningful and fruitful. When I forget to release my days and nights to Him, my days sometimes become stressful and my nights restless.

Lord, I give my day and night to You. Help me to remember to do this daily.

Daily Deposit: There are works the Lord has for you today that will have an eternal impact. Commit the day and night to Him.

April 3

What Causes Us to Rejoice?
Luke 10:13–37

This passage gives us four reasons we can daily rejoice and give thanks to God.

1. *Rejoice because we have power over satan.* The seventy had just returned from ministering to the multitudes. They were rejoicing because demons were subject to them in His name. Jesus responded to them and said they should rejoice because their names were written in heaven.
2. *Rejoice because our names are written in the Lamb's Book of Life.* If you have received the Lord as your Savior and made Him Lord of your life, you can rejoice because your name is written in the Lamb's Book of Life. We can know for sure that we will see Jesus face-to-face when this Book is opened and He reads our name and says, "Enter into the joy of My Kingdom in Heaven."
3. *Rejoice because God has revealed the hidden things to us.* As we read God's Word, He is able to give us wisdom and revelation knowledge. He can reveal His plans for us personally and also for the whole earth. When our eyes are enlightened, we can see better how to minister to others on this earth. We can also better discern which direction we need to take.
4. *Rejoice because Jesus Christ, the Son of God, has revealed the Father to us.* There are many who believe in the God of the Universe, but the only way we can know God as our Heavenly Father is through Jesus Christ, His Son. Jesus is the fullness of the Godhead, bodily. Jesus came to empower us with the Holy Spirit. When He went to be with the Father, He sent the Holy Spirit to lead and guide us into all truth, to comfort us, to bring things Jesus said to our remembrance to gift us, and to take the things of Jesus Christ and reveal them to us. Jesus shows us by the Holy Spirit who the Father is in character and action, as we read the Gospel accounts of Jesus on earth. With all of these reasons to rejoice, we should be able to joyfully declare every day of our lives: "This is the day the Lord has made I will rejoice and be glad in it."

Lord, help me always to remember these four reasons to rejoice.

Daily Deposit: The joy of the Lord is our strength, and we will be strengthened to get through every day when we rejoice in Him. His joy is eternal.

April 4

Obedience and Curses
Deuteronomy 26:1–27:26

This passage gives us another reason to rejoice. God wants us to rejoice in every good thing He has given to us and our households. (See Deuteronomy 26:11.) He instructed the Children of Israel to lay aside a tithe of their increase to Him.

Our relationship to God is a win-win situation if we obey His commandments and walk in His ways. We cannot "out give" God. He has an abundant storehouse in heaven. When we give to Him from a heart of love, He opens the windows of heaven and sends showers of blessings upon us. The blessings we receive are not all material blessings. We can also receive the spiritual blessings of joy, peace, and righteousness when we sow into the kingdom of God here on earth. God does not need our money. He owns the cattle on a thousand hills. The instructions to tithe were for the benefit of the children of Israel. It is always more blessed to give than to receive, and God wanted His children to be blessed. Curses would be the consequences of not obeying God's commandments.

When the children of Israel reached Mt. Ebal, God instructed them to set up an altar and to present their offerings to Him. Moses then divided the tribes into two teams. One team included the tribes of Simeon, Levi, Judah, Issachar, Joseph, and Benjamin. This team was to climb on top of Mt. Gerizim and shout out the blessings of God to the people. The other team included Reuben, Gad, Asher, Zebulun, Dan, and Naphtali. This team climbed Mt. Ebal and declared the curses Israel would experience if they did not obey God's commandments.

Twelve curses and fourteen blessings were declared on that day. The good news is that Jesus on the cross became a curse for us so we can now be delivered from every curse. We can break generational curses now because of the blood of Jesus. The children of Israel had many commands to obey. Jesus narrowed the commands we have to obey down to only two—to love the Lord God with all of our hearts and to love our neighbor as ourselves. (See Matthew 22:37–40.) We only have the power to keep these two commandments as we daily allow Jesus to be Lord of every area of our lives. Whenever we refuse to give Jesus any area of our lives for Him to control, we miss the blessings He desires to give us in that area. Is there anything you are holding onto today that you need to release to the Lordship of Jesus Christ?

Lord, show me the areas of my life I need to surrender to You.

Daily Deposit: As we give God our first fruits, we are laying up treasures in heaven.

April 5

Read: Deuteronomy 28:1–68; Luke 11:14–36; Psalm 77:1–20; Proverbs 12:18

Overtaking Blessings
Deuteronomy 28:1–68

The goal of every runner in a competition is to win the race. Believers in Christ are also in a race. Our goal is to finish well this race on earth.

We do not want our adversary, the devil, to overtake us. We know through the scriptures that we will win the race in the end. However, people often get temporarily knocked off the racetrack that God has ordained for them. Some people get pushed off the track through various circumstances in their lives. They go through trials, and, instead of getting better, they get bitter. Others fall into sin for a season, and they run the risk of not finishing the race as well as the Lord intended. Still, others are offended by fellow believers or wounded by them; so they withdraw for a season from fellowship.

The scene at Mt. Ebal and Mt. Gerizim was completed. All the curses and blessings had been declared. The rules of the race were clearly defined by God. The major condition for winning the race of life was to diligently obey the voice of the Lord and observe to do His commandments. If the rules were followed faithfully, the runners in this life would be assured of complete victory. Blessings, not the enemy, would overtake all those who heeded God's Word.

There is a great difference between reading God's Word and heeding God's Word. James compares the person who does not apply God's Word to his life in humble obedience to a man who looks at himself in the mirror and then walks away. God has already given us the blood of Jesus to cover our sin, and He has also given us the Word of God to correct any sins. The Word is both a mirror to show us our own sin and a rod of correction to help us stay on the racetrack God has set before us.

The blessings that will overtake us as we keep on God's track are: fruitfulness, prosperity, victory over our enemies, establishment as a holy people, good weather, and promotion. This should challenge us all to stay on the track by heeding God's Word. Are you still on the right track?

Lord, I don't want to waste time by getting off the track of life that You have set before me. Help me to heed Your Word.

Daily Deposit: Heeding God's Word today will reap rewards for eternity.

April 6

Nothing Hidden
Luke 11:37–12:7

Jesus confronted the Pharisees, scribes, and lawyers with their hypocrisy. He said the Pharisees were only interested in looking good on the outside. He called them a bunch of hypocrites. He upbraided the Pharisees because they were only interested in their own position in the synagogues. He compared the Pharisees and scribes to graves that are not seen and are walked over. In other words, the Pharisees and scribes were living dead men who had no true spiritual life within them.

Then He turned to the lawyers and said they were no better than the Pharisees and scribes because, instead of releasing people from their burdens, they put more burdens upon them. He said the blood of the prophets shed from the foundation of the world were on their hands. He accused the lawyers of taking away the key to knowledge from others, while they slammed the door of true knowledge in their own faces.

The leaven of the Pharisees was hypocrisy. When they were in the synagogue, they looked so spiritual, but in the dark, they were disobeying God's commands. Jesus said these chilling words to them: "For there is nothing covered that will not be revealed, nor hidden that will not be known. Therefore whatever you have spoken in the dark will be heard in the light, and what you have spoken in the ear in inner rooms will be proclaimed on the housetops" (12:2–3). When I hear these words of Jesus, I am challenged to keep my life clean and my words pure.

One of the prayers I pray is, "Lord, bring everything that is hidden to light." I prayed this prayer almost daily when two of our boys were in the world. They had gotten off the track God had set before them. One son was on drugs and everything he ever did in the dark was brought to light. One morning we got a call from the police station telling us that our son was caught smoking marijuana in the woods. We had to go down to the police station to talk this over with the other parents of the boys who were caught. Thank God, the police were merciful and did not put this incident on their records. Our son then knew he could not get away with anything. Today that son is a missionary to Hungary. He fell for a season, but he got back on the right track.

Is there anything in your life now that you would be embarrassed for God to find out about? God already knows everything about you. He hears all your words and He sees every action. He wants you to repent of everything that is pulling you off the track that He has set before you. Today is a great opportunity to come clean with God and to receive the cleansing He has for you as you repent and confess your sins to Him.

Lord, shine a light on any hypocrisy in my own life.

Daily Deposit: Every sin we confess and repent of here on earth will be removed from the record in heaven.

April 7

Passing the Torch
Deuteronomy 31:1–32:29

We ran one half block down to the main street near our house. The crowds were already gathered as they lined the streets to see a special event. The event was the passing of the Olympic Torch. Atlanta hosted the Summer Olympic Games in 1996. Runners chosen for their leadership in their respective communities were to run several miles with the Olympic Torch. We watched the exchange from one runner to another. The crowds cheered as the torch was passed and, in a matter of minutes, the new runner took off, with torch in hand, to run his designated miles.

The children of Israel had been under the leadership of Moses for more than forty years. It was time now to pass the torch of leadership to his successor, Joshua. Moses was 120 years old, and he made it clear to the children of Israel that he would not be able to cross over the Jordan with them. It was not his age that hindered his ability to cross over the Jordan. He was commanded by God not to cross over because he had disobeyed God at the Waters of Strife. The land that Moses dreamed about was within sight. God did allow Moses to view the land from a mountain. His feet, however, would never tread on this Promised Land. So often we miss seeing the promises of God fulfilled in our lives. Why? Because we disobey Him. The promises of God can only be fulfilled if we will trust God with all of our hearts and obey His Word. Moses summoned Joshua before the assembly and told him to be strong and courageous.

Whenever we enter a new situation there is an element of fear. Our hearts pound as we go for our first day in college. When we experience our first day on our new job we are anxious about what our new boss will think of us. The children of Israel were faced with a new situation. They had been totally dependent upon Moses for over forty years. Now Joshua was in command. They had to trust Joshua to lead them into the Promised Land. More than that, they had to trust God to give them victory over the giants in the land.

The only way to overcome fear is to trust the Lord. David experienced many fearful times, but he said, "Whenever I am afraid, I will trust in [the Lord]" (Ps. 56:3). We should join in making the same confession when fear tries to overwhelm us.

Today you may be facing a new situation, and fear may be knocking at the door of your heart. You can close the door in the face of fear when you say, "I will trust the Lord and not be afraid."

Lord, I put my trust in You. Let me not be afraid.

Daily Deposit: Fear can neutralize our effectiveness, as we go forward to possess the land for Jesus' kingdom. Resist fear by trusting the Lord and you will win souls for eternity.

April 8

The Song of Moses
Deuteronomy 32:30–52

The Song of Moses is a collage displaying both the faithfulness of God and the unfaithfulness of His chosen people. The Song is a somber song reminding us all of God's character. God is a merciful and loving God, but at the same time He is a just God Who is both jealous and unrelenting in His call for a rebellious people to repent. He is always ready to forgive, but He metes out His justice with His mercy to enforce His boundaries upon a restless, wandering nation.

Moses emphasized the strength of God when he called Him their Rock. We sing a song in our church called, "There is No Rock Like Our God." Moses portrayed God as protector, leader, and provider of the children of Israel. Moses compared God's protection of Israel to an eagle hovering over her young and then spreading her wings to carry them. God guided Israel and provided the best of the fruit of the land for them. *The Song of Moses* ended by reviewing Israel's disobedience. The children of Israel became fat and satisfied and soon forgot God. They provoked Him to jealousy when they sought after other gods. God had to judge the children of Israel.

Like the children of Israel, one of my sons went his own way and sought the pleasure of drugs, more than he did God. During his rebellion, the Lord gave me a word of warning for the church. I was awakened about 4 a.m. to the sound of an alarm. It was not an audible sound, but I could hear it with my spiritual ears. The alarm sounded just like the alarm at a dam nearby that was used to warn people to get off the river because the floodgates were going to be opened. I heard these words spoken to my spirit, "I am about to open the floodgates. There will be a flood of good and of evil. Tell my saints to hide themselves in the Rock, Jesus, so they will not be swept away in the flood of evil."

I told my son this word I felt the Lord had given me. He said, "Mom, I don't think I'm hiding in the Rock and I'm afraid." I comforted him with the words of Isaiah that the Lord had given me earlier as a promise for my children. Isaiah prophesied that God would pour water on all those who are thirsty and floods on the dry ground. He will pour His Spirit on all your descendants and His blessing on your offspring, and they will spring up among the grass like willows by the watercourses. (See Isaiah 44:3–5.) Earlier that year, I had cursed a willow tree because its roots kept clogging our pipes. Two weeks later the tree was struck by lightning and died. Even after we had someone grind the trunk of the tree, two months later I noticed a small willow at the bed of our creek. There was enough life left in that tree to spring up again. I told my son that even though he felt dry, there was enough life in him to spring up like a willow, and he did.

Lord, help me daily to hide myself in You.

Daily Deposit: Hide yourself in the Rock, Jesus, today.

The Blessings of the Father
Deuteronomy 33:1–29

This passage records the blessings that Moses declared over all the tribes of Israel. Moses had been like a father to the children of Israel, and he had attempted to reveal God to them as their loving Heavenly Father. The children of Israel failed to grasp this concept of God. They knew God's works, but they did not know His ways. They constantly doubted that God was for them and not against them. They doubted God's goodness, His provision, and His protection. These deep-seated doubts about God's true character caused them to be paralyzed with fear in the wilderness for forty years.

Recently, there has been a move in the body of Christ to teach fathers how they can bless their children. A multitude of seminars are taught in various churches about the responsibilities of fathers to speak blessings over their children. After one of these seminars, I was determined to set up a time when my husband could declare his blessings over our three sons. We decided to go down to a Christian retreat in Florida. This would provide the perfect atmosphere for Tom to bless his three sons. They all decided to go deep-sea fishing together. I decided to stay behind at the retreat center so Tom could use this time to bless our boys. As I prayed for them in my room, I pictured Tom and the boys in a boat similar to the one in Jesus' day. I envisioned Tom sitting in a boat gently rocking in calm seas as he prayed a blessing over each of them.

They were gone for several hours. When they returned, I noticed Tom looked a little pale. They began to tell me all about their blessing experience. The boat had fifty other people on it and the seas were rough. Tom got seasick, so the blessing time they experienced was not like the one I had envisioned. Tom managed to have a special blessing time with the boys when we returned home.

It is sad to say that in our society many fathers spend more time cursing their children than blessing them with God's blessings. When blessings are declared over us, we have a desire to walk in those blessings. The father's blessings help set the sails of the ships of our lives to sail in the direction God desires. If you have never declared blessings over your children, it is not too late. You can also declare blessings over your grandchildren.

Lord, give me the words I need to pray a blessing over my children and grandchildren.

Daily Deposit: Blessing children today can shape their destiny for eternity.

April 10

A Mother's Heart
Luke 13:23–14:6

Yesterday we talked about the father's blessing. Throughout the struggles in the wilderness, Moses tried to reveal the Father's heart to the children of Israel. They feared God, but not in the way we should fear Him. They were afraid of God. The children of Israel failed to see the glorious character of God. God is love. God is good. God is faithful and forgiving, merciful and just.

As I think of God's character, my mind goes back to my mother who, throughout her life, displayed the love of God. Her heart was tender towards her three daughters, and she wanted us all to live pure lives. She often would say to us, "Girls, don't do anything you would not want Jesus to see." She also told us never to take what others said personally. She exhorted us to think about the person who wrongs us as a person who needs lots of love. She taught us to reach out in love to our neighbors and friends. She wanted to protect us from harm's way and prayed for us continually.

God has both a mother and a father heart. Jesus expressed the mother heart of God when he cried out over Jerusalem: "O Jerusalem, Jerusalem, the one who kills the prophets and stones those who are sent to her! How often I wanted to gather your children together, as a hen gathers her brood under her wings, but you were not willing!" (13:34). When we were in Jerusalem we had the opportunity to stand in what is believed to be the very spot where Jesus cried over Jerusalem. The panorama of the city below was breathtaking. There was a small chapel shaped in the form of a teardrop where people could gather and pray over Jerusalem. I imagine Jesus is still weeping over Jerusalem. Only three percent of all Israel even believes in the God of Abraham, Isaac, and Jacob.

The Bible is clear about what those in Israel will face in the days ahead, as we draw near to the Second Coming of our Lord. We should all be moved to tears as we intercede for the peace of Jerusalem. Join me as I pray for God's beloved people in Israel.

Lord, You wept over Jerusalem and Your heart's desire was to gather them all to Yourself and keep them from harm's way. Set your angels round about Jerusalem and Israel, and defend Your people. Peace be on Israel.

Daily Deposit: Today we can weep with Jesus over Jerusalem, just as He did. God will bottle those tears and will one day send them down as a latter-day rain of blessing upon Israel.

April 11

Standing in the Heap
Joshua 3:1—4:14

On our many tours to Israel, we had the joy of seeing many of our friends baptized in the River Jordan. We usually made our trips in May. At that time, the River Jordan looks more like a creek than it does a river. At harvest time, however, after the rains, the Jordan often overflows its banks. It was during harvest time, when the banks of the Jordan were about to overflow, that Joshua and the priests crossed over it. God wanted to exalt Himself in the sight of all Israel, just as He exalted Himself when Moses and the children of Israel crossed the Red Sea. God wanted to show the children of Israel that He was just as much with Joshua as He was with Moses.

Instructions were given to appoint men from each tribe to cross over the Jordan as the priests carried the ark of the covenant. The moment the soles of their feet hit the waters of the Jordan, the waters parted and became a heap on each side of them.

God wants to exalt Himself today in the midst of the troubled waters you may be going through. You may feel like those waters are going to drown you, but God promises not to allow those waters to overwhelm you as you walk through your troubles. (See Isaiah 43:2.) The troubled waters will be parted and stand as a heap on either side of you if you will only hold on to your faith! God loves to exalt Himself in the midst of trouble. He will part the waters and you will be able to walk across on dry ground. You will be able to stand with faith in a heap of troubles, whenever you keep your focus on Jesus as He goes before you to make a way where there seems to be no way. God is just as much with you as He was with Moses and Joshua.

Lord, help me to hold on in faith when troubled waters come my way.

Daily Deposit: Every trial we experience on earth is a test of our faith. Whenever we pass these tests, we add to our heavenly rewards in heaven. Every fiery trial we have experienced on earth will turn into jewels in heaven, if we hold on to our faith during those trials.

Repentance and Rejoicing
Luke 15:1–31

The angels rejoice when one sinner comes to repentance. I always have a mental picture when I read this passage. I see Jesus as Captain of the Heavenly Hosts. He blows the heavenly shofar to gather all the angels. The saints hear the shofar and bells also begin to ring loudly to rally everyone in heaven. God announces the exciting news that one soul has repented. A song of praise begins, and the saints and angels dance with joy.

Jesus gave several parables about how God seeks to save those who are lost, and how He and all His angels rejoice when one repents and joins the kingdom. The parable we are most familiar with, of course, is the parable of the prodigal son. We experienced two prodigal sons in our lives. Those days were not easy. My husband and I prayed every day for our sons to return to the Lord. We longed for the day when we would see the fruits of our prayers. It was painful to see the glazed eyes of the son on drugs. The other son, during his college years, only attended church on Mother's Day and Christmas.

Like the father in the parable of the prodigal son, we never gave up hope. In the parable, the father went into the fields every day and looked expectantly for his son to return from his wanderings. The day of his son's return finally came and the rejoicing of that father paled in comparison to the rejoicing in heaven. The father threw a party and so did those in heaven. There was one, however, who did not rejoice. The elder brother was jealous of his brother because his father gave a party for his brother. The father's words to the elder brother are what we all need to hear. He said, "Son, you are always with me, and all that I have is yours" (v. 31). After we have repented and come to know God as our Heavenly Father through Jesus Christ, we can rejoice everyday. Why? Because we are joint heirs with Christ! All that the Father in Heaven has becomes ours, because we have received Jesus as our Lord and Savior.

Our prayer daily should be for all of our loved ones to come to know Jesus Christ in a personal way so they, too, can rejoice over their great inheritance. When our family members and friends come to repentance we can join the party in heaven and rejoice. Repentance brings rejoicing to us personally when we give our hearts to the Lord. It also brings rejoicing when we see others repent and come to know Jesus, as well.

Lord, I pray that soon there will be many parties in heaven when those
I have been praying for come to know You.

Daily Deposit: Your prayers today for the salvation of your loved ones, friends, and others will pave the way for great rejoicing in heaven.

April 13

What Are True Riches?
Luke 16:1–18

The parable of the wise steward is one that has always troubled me. Why would Jesus tell us to "make friends for yourselves by unrighteous mammon, that when you fail, they may receive you into an everlasting home" (v. 9)? The unjust steward was complimented by his master because he cleverly forgave the debts of those who owed money to his master so that they would befriend him after he was fired as a steward. The master intended to fire the steward because he was accused by others of wasting his master's goods.

Jesus was saying that we need to be wise stewards who are familiar with the world's ways of doing things. We have to recognize that we are in the world, not of the world. Because we are in the world, we must operate daily in the world system. The world system is entirely opposite from the kingdom's system. In the world system people push their ways to gain finances and power. In the kingdom's system, we humble ourselves and trust the Lord to promote us and to provide what we need. We seek to please God and not man. At the same time, we must not be ignorant of the world's system. We cannot be friends of the world, but we can learn to be skillful in financial matters. Our worldly earnings, however, are not our true treasures.

Jesus said, "Therefore if you have not been faithful in the unrighteous mammon, who will commit to your trust the true riches?" (v. 11). I believe God looks for men and women who are skilled in the operation of finances on earth because He knows such people will handle His true treasures well.

What are our true treasures? Our true treasures are not on this earth, but they are in heaven. This devotional book has emphasized how we can daily lay up for ourselves treasures in heaven by witnessing to people, praying for others and generations to come, studying God's Word and sharing it with others, and speaking words about the Lord on earth. You may want to review some of the "Daily Deposits" in this book to ignite that desire in your heart to be a good steward of heavenly treasures.

My husband and I are about to finish teaching a two-year study on handling our finances on earth. This study has opened our eyes to the reason we must understand how to be financially wise. How we use our money on earth reveals where our hearts are. A quick peek into your own checkbook ledger will reveal where your heart is. We must remember that monies invested in kingdom work will last eternally.

Lord, help me to be wise with the monies you give to me.

Daily Deposit: Review your checkbook ledger today and pray about sowing more into God's kingdom in the future.

April 14

Inquiring of the Lord
Joshua 9:3–10:43

A turning point came in my life when I was living in Savannah, Georgia. My children were young. I was so involved in doing good works that the day came when my husband, my mother, my Lord and a friend confronted me with my business.

One evening I had not prepared dinner because I had spent all day at the hospital with a friend who was dying of cancer. I was exhausted. When my husband came home, he asked, "Where's dinner?" I told him where I had spent my day. He said, "Linda, don't you think you're doing too much and forgetting about your own family?"

When my mother came for a visit, she was exhausted after a day of accompanying me to a visit to the hospital, to a counseling session with someone in a mental institution, and to a teaching I had to give at my church. At the end of the day, mother said, "Linda, I think you should consider taking care of your own family before you get so involved with all this outreach."

One morning shortly after that, the Lord spoke to my heart and said, "Linda, you need to take care of your natural fruit before you take care of other fruit." The final blow came when my friend and I were going to visit someone in a mental institution. I was sharing with my friend how I hated making these visits because they seemed so unfruitful. My friend asked me, "Linda, did the Lord ask you to do this?" I responded, "No, my pastor dumped this duty on me, and, frankly, I resent it." My friend said gently, "Linda, you need to inquire of the Lord before you get so involved with doing things in His Kingdom."

Maybe you're doing a lot of things that God never asked you to do. Take it from me; it is better to please God than man. Our passage today details how Joshua and the men of Israel failed to ask counsel of the Lord before they made a covenant of peace with the men from Gibeon. The men from Gibeon pretended to come from a far country when actually they were the next enemy that Joshua would have to conquer to claim the Promised Land. The true identity of the men from Gibeon was discovered after three days, but by then it was too late. The children of Israel could not conquer Gibeon, and Gibeon continually remained as a thorn in Israel's side.

This story should challenge us all to be sure to seek counsel from the Lord before we go about doing what seems to us as a good thing. God does not want us to do good things if these things are not His will. He wants us to be led of His Spirit to do the things He desires. When we inquire of Him and then obey Him, we can be assured that all of our good works will be fruitful.

Lord, always remind me to inquire of You.

Daily Deposit: Only those works done through Christ will last eternally.

April 15

Trust and Blessings
Psalms 84:1–12

Whenever we put our trust in the Lord we will be blessed. This psalm ends with these words, "Blessed is the man who trusts in You!" The full content of this psalm describes the man who trusts in the Lord. The man who trusts in the Lord:

- Loves to be in His presence (v. 2).
- Cries out for fellowship with the living God (v. 2).
- Praises the Lord (v. 4).
- Goes from strength to strength (v. 7).
- Serves willingly and humbly in the house of God (v. 10).
- Never doubts the goodness of God (v. 11).

When we trust in the Lord we become totally dependent upon Him. We enter a resting position in His loving arms. We wait expectantly and patiently for Him to reveal His strength and goodness on our behalf even when we are in the midst of a great trial.

Trusting in the Lord is a choice we have to make daily. When we trust in the Lord, we do not have to make scenarios about our possible future. We know the Lord will bring good out of every situation because we have turned every situation over to Him. One of the greatest blessings of trusting the Lord is the absence of fear. We are able to quietly and confidently expect God to see us through the fire, the flood, and whatever may try to hurt or overwhelm us. Whenever we trust our circumstances into the hands of the Lord He is able to take action on our behalf. If we refuse to give our difficult circumstances to Him, and try to work things out ourselves without any assistance from the Lord, our efforts to get relief will be futile.

I was faced with the choice to trust in the Lord, rather than the arm of flesh. When I hit a young boy with my car his parents sued me for damages. The lawyer from our insurance company called me and said, "Mrs. Sommer, I think you better hire another lawyer in addition to our lawyer because this could get messy." I told him I already had another lawyer. My lawyer was Jesus Christ and, as I talked with my "Lawyer," He told me not to be bitter against the young boy's parents because their lawyers had talked them into suing me. I released all into the hands of my faithful "Lawyer" and joy welled up within me. After a whole year passed, I was notified that all had been settled out of court. The trust I had during that year gave me the blessing of peace and the absence of fear.

Lord, help me always to trust in You.

Daily Deposit: Trust in the Lord today, and your tomorrows will be in His hands.

April 16

Never Lose Heart
Luke 18:1–17

There are several things we should do when we pray. They are as follows:

- Have faith.
- Pray according to God's will (what He says in His Word).
- Pray without ceasing and with thanksgiving.
- Never lose heart when we pray.
- Wait upon the Lord.
- Forgive (make sure there is no unforgiveness in your heart).
- Humble yourself before God.

In my fifty and more years I have seen many answered prayers. I wish I had kept a prayer journal so I could have a record of all of these answers. The above list is certainly not complete by any means, but I know if I am faithful to do the seven things listed, I can have confidence that God will hear me and answer my prayers. He may not always answer the way I want Him to, but He will always do what He knows is best.

People often ask me if they should keep asking God repeatedly for something. Some feel we show a lack of faith if we keep asking. In response to this question, I always lead such people to this passage. Jesus gave a parable that reveals how He feels about repeatedly asking for something in prayer. He made this statement, "Men always ought to pray and not lose heart" (v. 1). The parable He gave tells about a widow who constantly came to the judge to ask for justice from her adversary. The judge did not even fear God, but because of her constant insistence for justice from the judge, the judge avenged her. Then Jesus explained that God speedily avenges those who cry out to Him in prayer day and night. He closed this parable with this chilling question, "When the Son of Man comes, will He really find faith on the earth?" (v. 8).

The second parable Jesus gave in this passage reveals how we should pray. We learned earlier that God is concerned with our attitude, not just with our works. Jesus told the parable of the Pharisee and the tax collector. (See Luke 18:10–14.) The Pharisee had a haughty attitude when He prayed. Sometimes I see this in the body of Christ. People feel like God owes them something, and they pray presumptuous prayers. The tax collector could not even lift his head and he beat his breast as he cried out for God's mercy. God heard and answered the tax collector's prayer. When we have a humble heart that persists in prayer we will see our prayers answered.

Lord, help me to humbly pray with faith and never give up.

Daily Deposit: The prayers we pray in faith with a humble and right attitude will avail much. Such prayers can affect lives for eternity.

April 17

Boldness in Action and Asking
Joshua 15:1–63

Faith always pleases God. God also is pleased when we come boldly into His throne room with confidence that He will both hear and answer our prayers. We learned yesterday that the attitude of our heart is what God sees when we pray. He hears our hearts before He hears our words. The passage today speaks of boldness in action and asking.

Caleb was eighty years old. He had asked to take the giants on the mountain. He was bold and courageous in his old age. God honored his boldness and Caleb was able to take this mountain. Caleb drove out the three sons of Anak (all giants). Caleb did not stop there. He went on to possess more land. He said, "He who attacks Kirjath Sepher and takes it, to him I will give Achsah my daughter as wife" (v. 16). Othniel took it and Caleb kept his promise, and Othniel and Achsah were married. Achsah went to her husband and persuaded him to even ask for a field. Then she went to her father and asked for the upper and lower springs as a blessing to her. Caleb granted her request.

This story inspires me to think big when I act upon God's Word, and when I pray to the Father in Jesus' name. Jesus is my Husband and, because He died on the cross for me and shed His blood for me, I now have the right to come boldly into the Father's throne room and make my requests known to Him. The Father is always pleased when I ask big in Jesus' name!

So often, we limit our prayers. I have had people say to me, "You are praying for the impossible!" I think God loves for us to pray for the impossible because He is the God of the impossible. All things are possible through Him.

Today pray BIG! Don't settle for less than God's best. Today take bold actions! God is always pleased with boldness. If we pray according to God's Word, we can pray boldly.

Lord, I want to pray BIG!

Daily Deposit: I believe we will find out in heaven what we could have had on earth, if we had just prayed with more boldness!

April 18

Read: Joshua 16:1–18:28; Luke 19:1–27; Psalm 87:1–7; Proverbs 13:11

Possessing the Land
Joshua 16:1–18:28

The possession of the Promised Land continued under the leadership of Joshua. Some of the tribes, however, put off receiving their inheritance. Joshua asked these tribes, "How long will you neglect to go and possess the land which the LORD God of your fathers has given you?" (Josh. 18:3). They were told to survey the land first, so Joshua could cast lots for the possession of the land they claimed.

We are in a war with Iraq as I write this devotional. Tanks are advancing quickly through the desert terrain of Iraq. Their goal is to possess the capital city, Baghdad. As I watch this war on TV, I think about the spiritual war we are in daily. The Bible tells us there is a land filled with three enemies. If we fail or neglect to possess this land, we will have trouble moving ahead in our walk with Christ. That land is the land of our souls—the land of the mind, the will, and emotions.

We have three lustful areas in our souls that will conquer us, if we do not possess the land of our souls. The three enemies are our three lusts—the lust of the flesh (seeking to satisfy our five senses in an addictive way), the lust of the eyes (vain imaginations, fantasies, and covetousness in our minds), the lust of the pride of life (trusting in our own ability and our own resources more than we trust in God and His provision). (See 1 John 2:16.) If we neglect to possess the land of our souls and resist these three enemies, we will experience a defeated Christian walk.

The key to overcoming these enemies in our souls is to walk in the Spirit. If we walk in the Spirit, we will not fulfill these three lusts. If we neglect to walk in the Spirit, we will not be able to claim our full inheritance as joint-heirs with Christ. The way to overcome the lust of the eyes (mental idolatry) is to cast down vain imaginations and every high thought that exalts itself against the knowledge of God. We are to take those thoughts captive to the obedience of Jesus Christ. All of the strongholds in our souls are in our minds. Our minds are the devil's battlefield. The way we can win the victory over our fleshly lusts is to send Jesus to do battle for us when we are tempted to overindulge our five senses. Our five senses are given to us to enjoy God's creation, but addictive habits, such as overeating, drugs, or alcohol, will develop if we begin to overindulge our five senses. Our only hope to overcome the pride of life is simply to humble ourselves by casting every care upon Jesus. The bottom line is that a person who walks in the Spirit will have his/her mind renewed by the Word of God, will display the fruits of self-control and patience, and will live a humble life of dependency upon God for everything.

Lord, I trust You to battle for me as I possess the land of my soul.

Daily Deposit: Victory over the lusts of our souls now will bring heavenly rewards.

April 19

Read: Joshua 19:1–20:9; Luke 19:28–48; Psalm 88:1–18; Proverbs 13:12–14

The Stones Will Cry Out
Luke 19:28–48

We could hear the birds chirping loudly as they celebrated the beginning of spring in Israel. It was early May and all the roses were in bloom throughout Israel. As we descended the tour bus, our tour guide told us to gather in groups of four and walk down through the Mount of Olives. He said, "As you walk, think about Jesus' triumphal journey from the top of this mountain to Jerusalem." As we journeyed down the mountain, my mind flashed back to the scene described in our passage today. I could hear the disciples loudly crying out, "Blessed is the King who comes in the name of the LORD! Peace in heaven and glory in the highest!" (v. 38). Some of the Pharisees told Jesus to get control over His disciples and tell them to keep silent. Jesus responded, "I tell you that if these should keep silent, the stones would immediately cry out" (v. 40).

My eyes glanced downward as my feet walked on the very path Jesus traveled on this triumphal day. He was riding a colt and the crowds threw their clothes on the road as Jesus continued His journey to Jerusalem. Jesus prophesied that the day would come when Jerusalem would be surrounded by her enemies and destroyed. Those enemies would not leave even one stone upon another when they destroyed the temple and the Holy City. Jesus' prophecy was fulfilled in 70 A.D.

> I continued my walk down the Mount of Olives, but this time I recalled another day Jesus walked this path. It was early dawn, on the first day of the week, when Jesus traveled this same path. There were no crowds and only the birds were celebrating His victory walk. Our Lord descended the mountain to tell His disciples about His resurrection. The disciples would continue to cry out once again, "Blessed is the King who comes in the name of the Lord!" That victory chant would be heard throughout the world as the disciples carried the gospel to every nation.

We join their victory chant every time we share the Gospel with someone. The stones are still crying out this victory chant. Audio and videotapes are made from crushed stone, and people throughout the world are hearing the victory cry. The day will come soon when Jesus will split the Mount of Olives and all will say, "Blessed is He who comes in the name of the Lord."

Lord, help me to be faithful to spread the Gospel!

Daily Deposit: A Book of Remembrance is kept in heaven. Every time we talk about the Lord to others, God adds to our personal Book of Remembrance. How big will your book be?

April 20

Control Issues
Luke 20:1–26

Throughout the Bible we see control issues repeatedly revealed. For example, some of the children of Israel did not like Moses and Aaron to have control over them, so the sons of Korah banded together to take control. Coups in nations happen because of control issues. Wars are fought over control issues. Church splits happen because of control issues. Pride is the root of all control issues. We think we can do a better job than those in authority over us so we want to seize control.

In our passage today, we see the Pharisees asking Jesus "who gave Him the authority to do what He was doing?" Jesus answered their question by asking another question. This is the classical Jewish way of discussion. Jesus asked them if the baptism of John was from heaven or from men? They remained silent because they knew if they said it was from men, they might be stoned. For many believed John to be a prophet. If they said, "From heaven" they knew then Jesus would ask them why they did not believe in John's baptism. Because they could not answer this question, Jesus responded, "Neither will I tell you by what authority I do these things" (v. 8).

Later in the passage, the chief priests and scribes tried to trap Jesus. They asked him if it was lawful, or not, for them to pay taxes to Caesar. They were hoping Jesus would tell them not to pay taxes to Caesar; because if He did, they would have reason to incite the Romans against Jesus. Jesus, once again escaped their trap and asked for a denarius. Then He answered their question with this question, "Whose image and inscription does it have?" They responded, "Ceasar's." Jesus told them to "render therefore to Caesar the things that are Caesar's, and to God the things that are God's" (v. 25).

Jesus answered the control issue, once and for all, with His skillful responses to their questions. Jesus was saying: God in Heaven is in control of all things. He said this in such a way, however, that they could argue with Him no more. When we understand the fact that God is sovereign and He is the ultimate authority over all things, then we no longer have control issues. Pride is uprooted and we all can humble ourselves before God by casting all of our cares upon Him. God is the One who places men in authority, not political parties or church committees. These leaders are obligated to obey God's mandate. If they do not, God will deal with them according to His justice.

Lord, whenever I want to control things, forgive me and help me to
cast every care upon You.

Daily Deposit: When we humble ourselves and recognize God's sovereignty we have nothing to worry about. All of our striving ceases. We can be at peace because we know everything is under control—God's control!

April 21

The God of the Living
Luke 20:27–47

We have experienced a multitude of evangelistic training courses over our forty and more years as believers. Most of these evangelism courses emphasize the gift of eternal life. They usually say something like this: "If you want to receive the gift of eternal life, then you can do this by receiving Jesus as your Lord and Savior." We forget that everyone will have eternal life. The just and the unjust will be raised to stand before God. We will all live eternally. The question we need to ask people when we share the gospel is, "*Where* do you want to spend eternity?" God truly is the God of the living, not the dead.

Jesus revealed the truth that God is the God of the living in this passage. The Sadducees did not believe in the bodily resurrection. They asked Jesus to tell them who would be the husband of a woman who had been widowed seven times. He told them that there would be no giving of marriage in heaven. He reminded them of how both Moses and David knew God was the God of the living, not the dead. Moses called God the God of Abraham, the God of Isaac, and the God of Jacob. David wrote in the Book of Psalms: "The LORD said to my LORD, 'Sit at My right hand, till I make Your enemies Your footstool'" (Ps. 110:1). David was speaking of God the Father and God the Son in this passage. Jesus proved to them by this psalm that He was of the lineage of David, but He truly was the Son of God, not the Son of David.

When we receive as truth that God is the God of the living, we are forced to examine our brief life here on earth. What we believe and how we live our lives here on earth will determine both where we will spend eternity and the rewards we will receive in eternity. This is a sobering thought that challenges me to submit myself daily to God and to resist the devil.

Lord, I pray that all my loved ones will spend eternity with You.

Daily Deposit: Today may be the day you can share the living God with someone who could believe and receive the privilege of living eternally in God's presence.

April 22

Me and My House
Joshua 24:1–33

"But as for me and my house, we will serve the Lord" (v. 15). When we visit my husband's sister in Alaska, we see this sentence written, framed and hanging in several rooms in their home. Years ago when our brother-in-law was saved, he made the same declaration Joshua did in our passage today.

The Lord spoke through Joshua and reminded all the Children of Israel of His faithfulness to them even in the wilderness. He rehearsed His faithfulness to them, from the time of Abraham to the present time. God reminded them of all the victories He had given them over all the "ites" in the Land. God had given them a land for which they did not labor. They could now enjoy cities they did not build and vineyards and olive groves they did not plant.

Joshua exhorted them to fear the Lord and to serve Him in sincerity and truth. He warned them not to get involved with other gods, as they had done in the past. It was time now to choose who would be their God forever. Joshua had already made his decision. He said, "But as for me and my house, we will serve the Lord" (v. 15). The people responded and said, "Far be it from us that we should forsake the Lord to serve other gods" (v. 16). Joshua warned them again not to have any other gods before the Lord. He told them if they served the foreign gods in the land, God would chasten them. Once again, they said, "No, but we will serve the Lord!" (v. 21).

Joshua said they had witnessed against themselves. They said again, "The Lord our God we will serve, and His voice we will obey!" (v. 24). Joshua wrote on a stone and recorded the promise of the Children of God to be faithful to the Lord.

We can make many declarations and promises to God. We can even write them in stone. However, if we do not carry out our promises and daily demonstrate with our lives what we have promised with our mouths, we are no better than the scribes and Pharisees who were hypocrites. They said one thing and did another. God is not interested in what we say. He is interested in what we do. We make a declaration in our church weekly. The declaration is that our church will be trained in the fear of the Lord. Our lives will show whether or not we are just mouthing this promise to God or if we truly mean it.

Lord, thank You for Your faithfulness. Help me to always be faithful to You.

Daily Deposit: The day will come when we will have a new name written on a white stone. I pray my new name will be "Faithfulness."

April 23

A Prayer of Moses
Psalms 90:1–91:16

The children of Israel were in the process of claiming the Promised Land. Moses, Aaron, and Joshua were dead. Time would tell whether or not they lived up to all the promises they made to Joshua. Unfortunately, we know the rest of the story. The children of Israel were unfaithful and served other gods. God allowed many enemies to come up against Israel to chasten them. God raised up judges to deliver them whenever the children of Israel repented. Joshua told them that God would "not forgive [their] transgressions nor [their] sins" (Josh. 24:19). Joshua was telling the children of Israel that God would not ignore their unfaithfulness. He would deal with it, and we see throughout scripture this pattern – unfaithfulness by the children of Israel, God's chastisement for their unfaithfulness, their repentance, and their deliverance.

Whenever God allows our enemies to come against us, He is trying to bring us to repentance. He is giving us a wake-up call. I cannot help but think of the tragedy of September 11, 2001. This was a wake-up call heard throughout the world. God was not punishing individuals for their disobedience to Him, nor did He cause this tragedy. However, He did not intervene to spare us this tragedy. He desires that none perish, but that all come to repentance. God is interested in our eternal souls.

Moses revealed our Heavenly Father's heart in this prayer he wrote centuries before 9/11. He said, "You turn man to destruction, and say, 'Return, O children of men'....You have set our iniquities before You, Our secret sins in the light of Your countenance. For all of our days have passed away in Your wrath; we finish our years like a sigh. The days of our lives are seventy years; and if by reason of strength they are eighty years, yet their boast is only labor and sorrow; for it is soon cut off, and we fly away. Who knows the power of Your anger? For as the fear of You, so is Your wrath. So teach us to number our days, that we may gain a heart of wisdom" (vv. 3, 8–12).

Throughout Israel's history, God gave numerous wake-up calls. When Israel responded and repented, they were delivered. Have there been personal wake-up calls in your own life? We all need to know how brief our life is here on earth. We desperately need to count each day as precious and live daily in the fear of the Lord because we have no assurance that there will be a tomorrow.

Lord, help me to live each day of my life as thought were my last day on earth.

Daily Deposit: As we daily commit ourselves to do the will of God, our tomorrows will be filled with fruitfulness. Our goal is simply to win souls. This is God's goal. Proverbs 11:30 reads, "He that wins souls is wise." Whomever we win with the help of the Holy Spirit to the Lord will be spared God's wrath. We do not want anyone to perish.

April 24

The Servant Spirit
Luke 22:14–34

One of the goals of every Christian should be to cultivate a servant spirit. Jesus was a servant of servants. In this passage, He shared with the disciples how different God's Kingdom is from the world's system. In the world's system, rulers rule, but in God's Kingdom, rulers serve. Jesus said, "The kings of the Gentiles exercise lordship over them, and those who exercise authority over them are called 'benefactors.' But not so among you; on the contrary, he who is greatest among you, let him be as the younger, and he who governs as he who serves" (vv. 25–26).

I had the opportunity to explain servanthood to our younger son, when he was asking me many questions about our eternal future. I told him that we were in training on earth and one day we would rule over angels and nations. He exclaimed "Momma, I don't want to rule over nations!" I assured him that if he was chosen to rule over nations, he would be a great servant. I shared, "Those who rule over the most people will get to serve the most people." Ray responded excitedly, "Momma, I can do that! I love to serve!"

A fast way to develop a servant spirit is to be the only woman in a home of four men. This was my plight in life and I was forced to cultivate a servant spirit. However, on many occasions I found myself serving these men out of duty, rather than love. I often even murmured and complained as I picked up their dirty clothes or cooked three meals a day for them. I was serving, but I did not have a grateful attitude. When we exhibit the servant spirit it will be our joy to serve others.

When Jesus washed the feet of the disciples, He gave them an example of servant-hood. He demonstrated the joy of serving others. After He finished washing their feet, He said, "For I have given you an example, that you should do as I have done to you. Most assuredly, I say to you, a servant is not greater than his master; nor is he who is sent greater than he who sent him. If you know these things, blessed are you if you do them" (John 13:16).

We will be blessed (happy) if we enter our role as servants with a grateful attitude. Once I repented of my ungrateful attitude as I served my family and others, I was filled with joy.

Lord, thank You for being a Servant to us as well as a Friend.

Daily Deposit: When you begin your day, ask the Holy Spirit to show you ways in which you can do special acts of service for your family members or friends. The Holy Spirit knows exactly what will bless them on this day.

The Cup of Wrath
Luke 22:35–54

A topic few want to discuss is the wrath of God. We don't like to think of having God's wrath poured out upon us. Jesus had the same problem we have. He wished He could have avoided God's wrath. On the cross, the wrath of God towards the sins of the whole world was poured out upon Jesus. Jesus agonized in the garden and prayed, "Father, if it is Your will, take this cup away from Me; nevertheless not My will, but Yours, be done" (v. 42).

We had the opportunity to visit the Church of All Nations in Israel, at the foot of the Mount of Olives, which was next to the Garden of Gethsemane. The altar of this church has a great white stone, which is believed to be the very one Jesus leaned upon as He prayed for God to remove this cup away from Him. A wrought iron fence resembling the crown of thorns protects this rock. The people on our tour bowed their heads and prayed as they remembered Christ's anguish in the Garden and His sacrifice for them. We could hear weeping.

Jesus knew exactly what price He would pay when He was crucified. He knew the pressure of the sins of the world laid upon Him that would cause His heart to physically break. He knew He would be the substitute to take upon Himself, not only the sins of the whole world, but also the wrath of God. Yet, for the joy set before Him, He pressed on to Jerusalem where He would be arrested, tried, and crucified.

Those who make Jesus Christ the Lord of their lives and who accept His finished work on the cross will be spared God's wrath. The Bible tells us that believers are not appointed to wrath. This challenges me to intercede more for lost souls and to boldly witness to the lost. The heavens rejoice every time one soul comes to repentance.

Lord, help me to lead many souls to You.

Daily Deposit: Jesus paid the ultimate price for our sins. Are you willing to pay the small price of inconvenience to reach out to someone with the Gospel today? We can spare many from the day of wrath if we will be faithful to share the gospel with others.

April 26

Is the Lord With Us?
Judges 6:1–40

We all have times in our lives when we question whether or not the Lord is with us. When the tragedy of 9/11 happened, many asked, "Where was God when the twin towers in New York were destroyed?" Gideon asked this same question. The Children of Israel had gone after other gods and done evil in God's sight, so He had delivered Israel into the hands of Midian for a period of seven years. The Midianites were cruel enemies of Israel. They hid themselves in strongholds in the mountains and waited until Israel had sown their fields. Then they swept down from the mountains and destroyed all of their fields. Israel was greatly impoverished because of the Midianites. When the Children of Israel cried out to the Lord, He sent a prophet who reminded them of their disobedience. He said through this prophet, "'I *am* the LORD your God; do not fear the gods of the Amorites, in whose land you dwell.' But you have not obeyed My voice" (v. 10). After sending a prophet, God sent an angel to Gideon. Gideon was a simple farmer and was hiding from the Midianites in the winepress near where he worked threshing wheat.

> And the Angel of the Lord appeared to him, and said to him, "The Lord is with you, you mighty man of valor!" Gideon said to Him, "O my lord, if the LORD is with us, why then has all this happened to us? And where are all His miracles which our fathers told us about, saying, 'Did not the Lord bring us up from Egypt?' But now the Lord has forsaken us and delivered us into the hands of the Midianites."
>
> —JUDGES 6:12–13

Then the Angel of the Lord revealed God's plan to Gideon. God had chosen Gideon to deliver his people from the Midianites. Gideon couldn't believe his ears, so he asked for a sign as proof that God was truly choosing him. The Angel consumed with fire the sacrifice Gideon prepared, and Gideon knew he had been with the Angel of the Lord. Gideon was instructed to destroy the idols to Baal that his father had erected. Gideon obeyed God and later defeated the Midianites.

Whenever we feel like God has forsaken us, God may use us to prove His strength, power, and presence to others. Like Gideon, the response of many who lost loved ones on 9/11 was first to ask God where He was on that fateful day. There were many Gideons who God used to show Himself strong on behalf of them. There were many Gideons on that day who delivered the trapped and suffering. The testimonies I heard from many who experienced loss inspired me to never question God's presence.

Lord, thank You for Your promise never to leave us nor forsake us.

Daily Deposit: When we experience fiery trials, we are the Gideons chosen to show God's strength, comfort, mercy, and power to all those who witness these trials.

Who Crucified Jesus?
Luke 23:11–43

Our son is now diligently working in Hungary to pull down the walls of anti-Semitism. Eastern Europe and Russia are countries steeped in anti-Semitism. There seems now to be a rise of anti-Semitism even in the United States.

The hatred of the Jews is nothing new. This hatred is inspired by the devil himself who would like to destroy every Jew on earth. Satan has made futile attempts to do this. First, there was the attempt to kill every Jewish baby boy when the Jews were in bondage in Israel. Then, once again, Satan inspired Herod to give instructions to kill every Jewish baby boy in Israel after Jesus was born. Herod feared he would lose his power when he heard of the birth of this child in Bethlehem. There were the crusaders who killed Jews in the name of Christ. Those who did the killing were demonized. They were not true Christians. They claimed the label *Christian*, but their hearts were far from God. Later, the tyrants, Hitler and Stalin, killed multitudes of Jewish people. Throughout history, people who do not truly serve the God of Abraham, Isaac, and Jacob have hated the Jews.

The Jews have wrongly been accused of killing Jesus Christ. For centuries since Jesus was crucified, the label *Christ Killer* has been placed upon Jewish people. When we read today's passage, one might make the assumption that it was the Jewish religious leaders who killed Jesus. Granted, those Jewish leaders whose hearts were far from God, yelled, "Crucify Him, crucify Him!" on that fateful day two thousand years ago. The Roman soldiers also played their part when they nailed Jesus to the cross and pierced His side with a spear, but they did not kill Jesus. Then who killed Jesus?

No one killed Jesus. Jesus willingly surrendered Himself to the will of God the Father and laid His life down for the sins of the world. Our sins were laid upon Jesus on the cross. The weight of these sins pressed heavily upon Jesus' heart and his heart broke under that weight. Truly, He has born our transgressions and taken away our sins. Who killed Christ? We all did. The good news is that He forgave the whole world and was raised again on the third day. Are you guilty of Christ's death? The answer is "yes." The good news is that He has forgiven you for every sin He bore on the cross for you. Have you received His forgiveness? Do you believe He has washed all your guilt away when He shed His blood just for you? What a Savior! We killed Him, but He now gives us the right to live eternally in His presence if we accept Him as our Savior. He provided the perfect sin sacrifice that satisfied all God's requirements for atonement.

Lord, thank You for Your sacrifice.

Daily Deposit: The cross gives me the right today to live in victory.

April 28

Who Rules?
Judges 8:17–9:21

The judges were raised up to deliver the Children of Israel. Gideon did such a great job in his victory over the Midianites that everyone wanted him to rule over them. Whenever someone is valiant and courageous we naturally think he or she would make a great ruler over us. However, in reality, there is only one true ruler, and Gideon knew this. The people said to Gideon, "Rule over us, both you and your son, and your grandson also; for you have delivered us from the hand of Midian." Gideon responded, "I will not rule over you, nor shall my son rule over you; the LORD shall rule over you" (vv. 22–23).

The day would come when Israel would no longer be satisfied with the judges God appointed to deliver them. They would ask Samuel, one of God's appointed judges, to give them a king. They wanted to be just like the other nations that had kings. God wanted to be their one and only king. Israel was not satisfied. They wanted a king they could see with their physical eyes. God granted their request, and Samuel anointed Saul the first king over Israel. Later God would reveal Himself to Israel in the form of the King of the Jews, Jesus Christ. At that time they would be able to see the One and Only King in the flesh. This did not satisfy them either, because they wanted a king who would deliver them from the Roman oppression. The oppression Jesus delivered them from on the cross made the deliverance from Roman oppression pale in its significance.

Gideon knew that the ultimate ruler was the Lord. He is the one who promotes and demotes. He is the one who rules over all. If more of us recognized whose rule we are under, we would not hesitate to submit ourselves to Him. God is the King of the whole Universe. He has all power, knows all things, and can even subdue nations on our behalf.

The only reason people do not bow their knee to God, the Ultimate Ruler, the King of Kings and Lord of Lords, is because they want to be in control of their own lives. They want to trust in themselves and their own resources, rather than trust in God and His provision. People who are subject to the lust of the pride of life will never submit themselves to the Lordship of Jesus Christ. One day, however, every knee will bow and every tongue will confess that Jesus Christ is Lord.

> *Lord, I pray for those who are in pride now and refuse to receive Jesus Christ as their Lord and Savior. May they all humble themselves before the mighty hand of God now, before it is too late.*

Daily Deposit: We can invite people today who have resisted God in the past to humble themselves and receive Jesus. If they accept our invitation, we will see them in heaven.

April 29

Slow of Heart
Luke 24:13–53

M any times when we share the Gospel with others, we use this scripture: the Word is near you, in your mouth and in your heart (that is, the Word of faith which we preach). The Bible says, "If you confess with your mouth the Lord Jesus and believe in your heart that God has raised Him from the dead, you will be saved. For with the heart one believes unto righteousness, and with the mouth confession is made unto salvation" (Rom. 10:8–10). This scripture reveals that saving faith has to come from our hearts.

Cleopas and a friend were on the road to Emmaus. Jesus, that very day, had been raised from the dead. He joined the two as they walked and asked them what they were talking about. They were astonished that Jesus did not know the events of the day. They did not recognize Jesus and they probably thought He was a stranger to Jerusalem. The two shared the events of the day and how certain women who followed Jesus said angels appeared to them at the tomb and said Jesus was alive. Some of His followers ran to the tomb and found it to be just like the women told them.

Jesus said to the two, "O foolish ones, and slow of heart to believe in all that the prophets have spoken!" (v. 25). Then Jesus reviewed all the prophets and the Scriptures that foretold that Christ must suffer and die before He entered His glory. They invited Jesus to come in and sup with them. Jesus broke the bread and blessed it, and in that moment they recognized Him. Then He vanished from their sight. They said to one another, "Did not our heart burn within us while He talked with us on the road, and while He opened the Scriptures to us?" (v. 32).

The major sin we have to continually resist in our Christian journey is that of unbelief. We receive Jesus as our Lord and Savior. We believe in our hearts that He was raised from the dead, and we confess this fact with our mouths. Some wrongly believe that the battle with unbelief is settled on that great day when we were saved. Truly, the battle with unbelief begins on the day of our salvation. Before we received Jesus we lived in unbelief and did not even recognize it. Now we are new creatures in Christ Jesus. Our spirits have been awakened to newness of life and we now know when we doubt God's promises and question His presence. Now we have to daily fight the battle of faith.

Jesus chose not to intervene when Peter denied Him, but He told Peter He would pray that Peter's faith would not fail. Faith is our lifeline to God, and without it we will sink quickly. The devil knows this, Jesus knows this, and now we know it. Whenever we have a battle with doubt and unbelief, we need to cry, "I believe. Jesus, help my unbelief!"

Lord, thank You for Your faithfulness to give me faith when I need it.

Daily Deposit: Faith operates in the *now*, but it pays great dividends in eternity.

April 30

The Fight Over Land
Judges 11:1–12:15

The land of Israel had been promised to the children of Israel. The borders of this land extended in to what we know today as Iraq, Iran, Syria, and Jordan. The tribes of Israel faced war after war to possess the land that was promised them. We cannot help but ask the question, "So what is new?" The battle for Israel still rages and will not be settled until the Lord comes again. In the meantime, we now are in a conflict with Iraq. Will we also go into Iran? Only God knows. He has His timetable. Our part is to do what He gives us to do concerning Israel. Right now we seem to be in the role of protector, but the day will come when we also will turn our backs on Israel. The Bible says that every nation one day will be gathered against Jerusalem. (See Zechariah 14:2.)

In our passage today, the people of Ammon were ready to fight against Israel. Jephthah was asked to be the commander of Israel. He sent a message to the King of Ammon, saying, "What do you have against me, that you have come to fight against me in my land?" (Judges 11:12). The king of Ammon replied, "Because Israel took away my land when they came up out of Egypt, from the Arnon as far as the Jabbok, and to the Jordan. Now therefore, restore those lands peaceably" (v. 13). Does this sound familiar to you? The Palestinians believe Israel belongs to them. They want, what they consider, their land returned to them. They especially want Jerusalem.

The reply Jephthah gave to the king of Ammon also sounds familiar. Jephthah said to him, "Israel did not take away the land of Moab, nor the land of the people of Ammon; for when Israel came up from Egypt, they walked through the wilderness as far as the Red Sea and came to Kadesh" (Judges 11:15–16). The children of Israel bypassed Moab and Edom, because they were not allowed to enter. Israel was forced to fight when Sihon, the king of the Amorites, came against Israel. Israel won this battle and took all the territory of the Amorites from Arnon to Jabbok and from the wilderness of Jordan. The Lord God dispossessed the Amorites from before His people Israel.

The rest of the story is told in this passage. The king of Ammon did not listen and he came against Israel and was defeated. Will this be the rest of the story in our present-day situation with the Arab nations surrounding Israel? We can rest assured that God knows the rest of the story. If we read our Bible, we also know the rest of the story. One day, King Jesus will rule and reign from the city of Jerusalem. We will have to wait until that day to have lasting peace in the Holy City. Until that time, we are commissioned by the Lord to pray for the peace of Jerusalem. Join me, as I pray today for Jerusalem.

Lord, Israel is Your home country and Jerusalem is Your hometown.
I pray for the peace of Jerusalem to be established. This will happen
when You come again.

Daily Deposit: The prayers I pray today for Israel will avail much.

May 1

What Will Be Your Children's Work?
Judges 13:1–14:20

We have been blessed to have eight grandchildren in a period of six years. As we look at the shining faces of these little ones, I wonder what they will be when they grow up. Wouldn't it be wonderful if an angel visited each of us and told us what our children or grandchildren are called to do while they are here on earth? An angel did visit Menoah and his wife. He told them they would have a son and Menoah asked the angel, "What will be the boy's rule of life, and his work?"

An angel did not visit me, but I was told during a prayer time exactly what my boys were called to be while they lived on earth. When I asked the Lord a question like Menoah asked the angel, I heard this reply with my spiritual ears:

- Your oldest son will be a bridge between races.
- Your middle son will be a bridge between nations.
- Your youngest son will be a bridge between families.

We have seen all three of our sons fulfill their callings in life. Our oldest son has reached out to many races. He seems to have a special love for people of different ethnic backgrounds. Our middle son has served as an English teacher in China for almost three years. He plans to return to China with his wife and four children in God's timing. Our youngest son is in Budapest now, teaching on Jewish roots. His call is to join the family of God (Jew and Gentile) together as he seeks to pull down the walls of anti-Semitism.

You do not have to wait for an angel to come and tell you what your children are called to do in their lives. The Lord will show you, if you will just ask and wait for the answer. I have not yet asked the Lord about the future of my grandchildren. You might join me and pray for your children and grandchildren.

> Lord, there are works from the foundation of the earth You have
> ordained and prepared for my children and grandchildren to complete
> while they are on this earth. I ask you to reveal through Your Word
> and by Your Holy Spirit their callings and destinies.

Daily Deposit: Many children today lack a sense of destiny. As you share with your children and grandchildren what you hear from God about their callings, they will gain a sense of destiny that will help keep their lives focused on the Lord in this life and into eternity.

The Birth of Sin
Judges 15–16:31

Menoah and his wife gave birth to Samson who was called to be a deliverer of Israel. He accomplished that calling, even though he was seduced and gave in to his own lusts. When I review the life of Samson, I think of the verse, "He who calls you is faithful, who also will do it" (1 Thess. 5:24).

God was faithful to fulfill His call in Samson's life, even though Samson sinned. This calling had been birthed in God's heart long before Samson was born. Samson birthed sin in his own life through giving in to his own lusts. When we look at Samson's life, we see just how satan's influence can be compared to the stages in the birth of a child:

Natural Birth	The Birth of Sin
Conception—sperm meets egg	**Conception**—enticing agent meets lust
Gestation—nine months of growth	**Gestation**—lustful thoughts grow in the mind
Labor—battle of child to be born	**Labor**—battle between lust and the Spirit
Delivery—child is born; life comes	**Delivery**—sin is born; death comes

Seducing Spirits are the agents sent by satan to tempt us. Samson was seduced by lustful thoughts about women. Delilah was able to discover his weakness because he gave in to his own lusts. Seducing spirits cannot read our minds, but they can discover our weak areas if we speak about them or give in to them through our actions.

We are led astray by our own lusts when we give in to the suggestions of seducing spirits. If we dwell on lustful thoughts, we are on our way to birthing sin. However, our own will can still win over temptation. We can take those thoughts captive to the obedience of Jesus Christ. If we pull down the strongholds and the vain imaginations in our minds, we will be able to abort the birth of sin in our lives. Once we have given in to our lusts, by receiving the suggestions to sin by seducing spirits, and we have refused to reject lustful thoughts, our only hope of overcoming is to cry out to Jesus for help and to repent. Samson repented just before he destroyed the Philistines when he pulled down the pillars of their temple. It is never too late to repent.

Lord, help me not to give in to my lusts.

Daily Deposit: Closing the door to our own lusts today will reap eternal rewards.

May 3

The Birth of the Spirit
John 3:1–21

We learned yesterday about how sin is birthed in our lives. Today's passage explains how the Spirit of God is born in our lives.

Nicodemus, a Pharisee who was a ruler of the Jews, came secretly to Jesus in the night. He had heard Jesus preaching about the Kingdom of God in the synagogue. Nicodemus knew Jesus was of God because of the many signs and wonders he had demonstrated. Jesus got right to the point when he talked with Nicodemus. He told Nicodemus, "Most assuredly, I say to you, unless one is born of water and the Spirit, he cannot enter the kingdom of God" (v. 5). Nicodemus did not understand because he was thinking only of natural physical birth. Jesus explained that man must be born of the Spirit, not just of water (the natural physical sperm).

Jesus continued his conversation with Nicodemus and said, "For God so loved the world that He gave His only begotten Son, that whoever believes in Him should not perish but have everlasting life. For God did not send His Son into the world to condemn the world, but that the world through Him might be saved" (John 3:16–17).

When a baby is born physically, he leaves the darkness of the womb and enters the bright light of the delivery room. The same thing happens to us when we are born again. We leave the darkness of sin and enter the light of the Kingdom of God. We are translated from darkness into the light. In physical birth, if a baby is caught in the birth canal for too long, he will be born dead. The spiritual birth canal in our own lives can be compared to our wills. If we keep refusing to come to the light, when we are told about Jesus over and over again, we run the risk of dying in the darkness of our own sin. "Light has come into the world, and men loved darkness rather than light, because their deeds were evil" (v. 19).

> *Lord, I pray for all those I know and love who have chosen to remain in darkness. May Your light shine upon them and open the eyes of their understanding to the Truth. May they embrace You—the light of the world—as their Lord and Savior.*

Daily Deposit: Someone today may be stuck in the spiritual birth canal. The words of truth you speak to them could bring them into God's light.

May 4

Receiving
John 3:22–4:4

When my boys were infants, I wrapped them in receiving blankets. The hospital nurses taught me how to wrap my new little bundles from heaven. The blanket had to be tight around the baby, so that he would feel as warm and secure as he did when he was in my womb. The baby's head had to be covered to keep heat from escaping his body. Whenever I changed my baby, I wrapped him quickly again in the receiving blanket so he would not be chilled.

When we are born again, God wraps us in His love. His Holy Spirit, the Comforter, provides security and comfort to us immediately. We cannot, however, remain babies forever. The day comes when the Holy Spirit does more than comfort us. He empowers us to walk in the Spirit. As sons and daughters of God, we begin to be led by the Spirit. As we walk in the Spirit, we begin to receive all Jesus has for us.

When we are born again we become new creatures. Old things are passed away and all things become new. We now have resurrection life, the very life of Jesus within us. But, at the same time, we still live in a body that is subject to sin. We still have a soul that has three lustful areas (the pride of life, the lust of the eyes, and the lust of the flesh). This is why Paul told us to reckon ourselves dead to sin and alive to Jesus Christ.

When we receive the greatest gift from heaven, the Lord Jesus Christ, the battle between our soul and spirit begins. Until we were born again, there was no battle. We were beings controlled by our own soul. Paul defined the battle we all have, when he said he often did the things he did not want to do and failed to do the good he wanted to do. Then he shared that there was a war going on inside of him. Sin still dwelled in his mortal body. (See Romans 7:13–25.) His only hope and our only hope is to daily lift our flesh (the soul and body), that wants to sin, to Jesus Christ. Jesus is the Bishop, or Captain, of our soul and only He can enable us to win this daily battle. Only Jesus can deliver us from the body of sin and death. Thanks be to God who always causes us to triumph through Jesus Christ. (See 2 Corinthians 2:14.) The moment the chilling effects of sin are felt in our lives, we need to confess our sin and allow the Holy Spirit to wrap us, once again, in the warmth of Jesus Christ, who not only forgives us, but who also cleanses us from all unrighteousness.

Thank You, Lord, for receiving me just the way I am and for delivering me from sin and death.

Daily Deposit: Lift your mind, emotions, will, and the members of your body up to Jesus today and He will enable you to be more like Him. He will use you to touch and transform lives.

Clinging to Christ
Judges 21:1–Ruth 1:22

We have been talking about spiritual development after we have been born again. The battle between the flesh (body and soul) and the spirit begins at our new birth. We will only have success in this battle if we cling to Jesus Christ. Christ now lives in us by the Holy Spirit.

The Holy Spirit is the Great Teacher of God's Word and He also teaches us how to pray. Without the daily feeding of God's Word and the daily spiritual exercise of prayer, we will never become spiritually mature. To win the victory over our flesh, we must become totally dependent upon the Holy Spirit. When we daily submit ourselves to the control of the Holy Spirit, we will do what pleases God instead of what pleases us. God wants us to have pleasure in this life. This is why He created us with five senses. However, whenever we seek to please ourselves more than we seek to please God, we have opened the door for satan who continually seeks to draw us away from God.

Many things please God, but there are three things that please Him the most. These three things are faith, obedience, and witnessing. Without faith it is impossible to please God. Without obedience it is impossible to walk in the spirit and not fulfill the lusts of our flesh. Jesus told His disciples not to fear; because it was His Father's good pleasure to give them His Kingdom. The Kingdom of God is not meat or drink. It is righteousness, peace, and joy in the Holy Spirit. Whenever we witness to others about the righteousness, peace, and power of the Holy Spirit they can obtain when they receive Jesus Christ as their Lord and Savior, we have done something that not only pleases God, but also can change a person's life eternally.

The two daughters-in-law in our passage today can represent our flesh and our spirit. Naomi was ready to return to Bethlehem (House of Bread). Naomi told both widowed daughters-in-law not to go with her, since she could not supply them with more sons to marry. Orpah returned to Moab. Ruth decided to cling to Naomi. Because Ruth made this decision, God provided a kinsman redeemer (Boaz) to be her husband. Whenever we choose to cling to the Holy Spirit, instead of fulfilling the lusts of our own flesh, we have a kinsman redeemer (Jesus Christ) who will provide all we need to win the victory over temptation. Boaz and Ruth had a child, Obed, who was the father of Jesse, who was the father of King David. When we are born again, the fruitfulness of our lives depends upon our dependency upon our new husband (Jesus Christ).

Thank You Lord, for being my Husband. Help me always to cling to You.

Daily Deposit: My dependency upon Christ today will enable me to do works that will last for eternity.

May 6

The Miracle Mode
John 4:43–54

We learned earlier this month that faith is one of the things that pleases God and, without faith, it is impossible to please God. The kind of faith, however, that pleases God the most is *believing faith*. Believing faith is not based on what we see. Believing faith is based upon what we have heard. "Faith comes by hearing, and hearing by the word of God" (Rom. 10:17). Our passage today reveals the heart of many people today. People refuse to believe, unless they can see proof or evidence. "Seeing is believing" is the motto of such people. As Jesus began to do miracles on earth, many people got into the miracle mode. They wanted to see a miracle or a sign before they committed themselves to believing in Jesus.

The miracle ministry of Jesus began in Cana at the wedding when Jesus turned the water into wine. The people in Cana remembered this miracle, and when Jesus returned to Cana, they were in the miracle mode. They wanted to see Jesus do another miracle. A nobleman came to Jesus and implored Him to heal His son who was dying. Jesus said to Him, "Unless you people see signs and wonders, you will by no means believe" (v. 48).

People were seeking the hands of Jesus, not His heart. They sought Jesus for what He could do, not for who He was. Jesus tested the nobleman. He told him to return home because his son was alive. At that point, this nobleman had a choice to believe what Jesus said was true or to reject the statement Jesus made about his son. The nobleman believed what Jesus said was true, and he went home. He never doubted that the words he heard Jesus speak could heal his son. As the father was going his way, a man came to him from his home and told him that his son lived. The nobleman asked when his son got better and the man told him the hour his son made a turn for the better. It was the very hour Jesus spoke healing to his son.

We do not have to wait to see evidence that the Word of God is true. All we have to do is believe God's Word, receive God's Word, and obey God's Word to see daily miracles in our lives. Whatever God has promised us, we can believe it now, receive it, and thank Him for the miracle! The miracle may not happen as we think it should. The miracle God always has in His heart to perform is the miracle of salvation. Salvation means *wholeness in body, soul, and spirit*. The faith that pleases God is the faith that believes His Word before any evidence is manifested on earth.

Lord, may my faith always please You.

Daily Deposit: Every time we believe and receive God's Word as true, even though we do not see any evidence, we have added to our account in heaven. Our assets in heaven are based upon the faith we have manifested on earth.

May 7

Rejection
John 5:1–23

Our guide rushed us through the Sheep Gate past St. Anne's Church to see the remains of the Pool of Bethesda. We looked down from a height of about ten feet and saw the five porches spoken of in this passage. I closed my eyes and tried to picture the scene described in our reading today.

The pool was whirling as relatives and friends rushed to help their infirmed loved ones dip in the waters before the waters were calm again. They believed that an angel stirred the waters and one could only be healed if he entered the whirling waters. One lame man sat alone, while others rushed past him. Jesus, however, did not rush past him. When Jesus saw this man, He stopped and asked, "Do you want to be made well?" The lame man told Jesus that he had no one to put him in the water. Jesus then said, "Rise, take up your bed and walk." The man immediately took up his bed and walked.

The man had been infirmed for thirty-eight years. There are many like this man who have had an emotional infirmity called rejection. For years they have waited for someone to pay attention to their loneliness. For years they have felt sorry for themselves because they felt no one cared. While others were enjoying the whirling waters of the river of life, they stood on the shore. The years of rejection robbed them of every intimate relationship and they felt no one loved them.

Rejection overwhelms people and can even cause a root of bitterness to join with the root of rejection in their hearts. Rejected people often envy those who seem to have a full life with meaningful relationships. People who have been rejected have received this lie, "Nobody cares."

The emotional infirmity of rejection has paralyzed many people and they alone cannot receive the waters of healing. They must have someone to put them in the water. Only Jesus can heal rejected people, and only He has the living waters that can heal their broken hearts. We are the ones God has chosen to help rejected people get into the living waters where they will find their healing. We are the ones who lift their heads to see Jesus who has always been standing in front of them to heal them. The fear of rejection that has paralyzed them for years will leave when we reach out in love to those who have broken hearts and lives. Have you been helping rejected people receive Jesus? Only He has the waters of life that can heal their broken hearts.

Lord, aid me in helping rejected people to see Jesus.

Daily Deposit: Today, look for opportunities to reach out in love to rejected people. Heaven will be filled with rejected people who were loved on earth by people like you and me.

May 8

Resurrection
John 5:24–47

Less than two months ago, we all celebrated what many Christians call Easter Sunday. When I found out that Easter was a pagan holiday that celebrated the fertility god, I decided to no longer call this high point in the Christian calendar Easter Sunday. I now either call it Resurrection Sunday or the Feast of Firstfruits. Jesus was raised from the dead on the day the Hebrews celebrated the Feast of Firstfruits. This feast was always celebrated just two days after the first Sabbath of the Passover Season, which was always the first day of the Feast of Unleavened Bread. Passover began on the fourteenth day of Nisan, and this was a day when no one was to work. Two days later on the sixteenth day of Nisan, the Feast of Firstfruits was celebrated. The Hebrews observed the Feast of Firstfruits by bringing an omer (five pints) of the barley from their first harvest as a wave offering before the Lord. This omer was the proof of a good future harvest.

The fact that Jesus was raised on the day of the Feast of Firstfruits symbolizes that Jesus was the firstfruit of all who will be resurrected. He was the first person who died, was resurrected, and lived on earth in a glorified body. When Jesus observed the Passover with His disciples, He blessed the bread and broke it and said, "Take, eat; this is My body" (Mark 14:22). Jesus is the bread of life broken for us. He had to be broken before He could be raised to newness of life. The resurrection of Jesus is the guarantee and the beginning of the final harvest when all mankind will be raised from the dead. Jesus spoke about this final harvest when He said (vv. 28–29):

> For the hour is coming in which all who are in the graves will hear His voice and come forth-those who have done good, to the resurrection of life, and those who have done evil, to the resurrection of condemnation.

We all will experience a resurrection day. Some will be raised to life and some will be raised to condemnation. People often say the only sure things in this life are death and taxes. We could add to this statement and say the only sure thing after death is the resurrection. If our lives are hid in Christ Jesus, we will look forward to this resurrection with joy. If we reject Jesus Christ while we live on this earth, the resurrection from the dead will not be something we will anticipate with joy.

Lord, help me to be faithful to share with others the good news of the resurrection to newness of life in Jesus Christ.

Daily Deposit: Today share the good news about the resurrection with someone you know.

May 9

Read: 1 Samuel 5:1–7:17 John 6:1–21; Psalm 106:13–31; Proverbs 14:32–33

The Seas of Life
John 6:1–21

Our tour boat stopped in the middle of the Sea of Galilee. It was time for our devotional and prayer time. My husband read this passage from John; then we sang a song about Jesus walking on the water. When we bowed our heads for prayer, there was a moment of silence. All we could hear was the gentle waves of the sea brushing against the boat. It was hard for us to envision the stormy sea the disciples experienced when they saw Jesus walking on the water. Our tour guide told us that forceful winds from the Golan Heights can suddenly cause the sea to be dangerous and tempestuous.

The disciples left the shore of Tiberius to go to Capernaum. It was dark. Jesus remained behind to pray. They were about four miles out from shore when a horrific storm came up suddenly. The disciples feared the boat would capsize when they saw Jesus walking on the sea near the boat. He said to them, "It is I; do not be afraid" (v. 20). Then he entered their boat, and the seas were calm once more.

This story is an example of the repetitive pattern we all experience in life. Just when the circumstances in our lives seem to be calm because our priorities are in order, and we are making progress, suddenly a stormy trial comes that troubles the calm sea of our lives. We feel like we are going to capsize and everything will be lost. We are paralyzed with fear for our future. Some of the circumstances that can beat violently against us are: the job we held for twenty years suddenly folds, a loved one dies, or our good health we enjoyed for over fifty years begins to fail.

When the stormy trials of this life seem to overwhelm us, we need to look up. Jesus is walking through the storm to reach us. He wants to enter our lives so that He can calm the raging seas around us. We can hear His voice over the waves of the sea. He says, "Fear not." Our focus is no longer on our circumstances, but we now can see Jesus.

His very presence brings hope and peace to our anguished souls. Jesus is with us. We can make it to shore.

What would have happened to the disciples if Jesus had not entered their boat? What will happen to us if we refuse to allow Jesus to enter our lives? We will surely sink and be overwhelmed by the waves of adversity. If you are experiencing a stormy trial, cry out to Jesus. He longs to help, but we have not, because we ask not. So often we think we can handle everything on our own.

Lord, thank You for helping me through the rough seas of this life.

Daily Deposit: The trials of my faith here on earth will be turned to jewels in heaven.

May 10

Give Us a King!
1 Samuel 8:1–9:27

Samuel was old. His sons did not walk in the ways of the Lord. The people wanted to be like other nations that had kings. They cried out to Samuel, "Give us a King!" Samuel was grieved because he knew they already had a King. God was their King. God, however, told Samuel to heed the voice of the people because they had already made their choice. For years, they chose other gods over the God of Abraham, Isaac, and Jacob. God told Samuel the people had rejected His leadership and rule over them. God said the people had not rejected Samuel, but they had rejected Him, the one true God.

God told Samuel to warn the people about what they would experience when they had an earthly king. The description given was exactly what happened when King Solomon reigned over them. Samuel warned that an earthly king would possess the best vineyards for himself. He would hire the best cooks and keep the best perfumes for himself. He would take their best men and women as his servants. He would draft their young men into his army. Even after this warning, the people still cried out for a king.

Who is your king? If you have rightly chosen, Jesus is the King of Kings over your life. As your King, Jesus will not take your best men and women as his servants. Jesus said that He came to serve. He did not come to be master. He told His disciples that they were no longer his servants. They were His friends. As your King, He will not take the best of your possessions. Instead, He will give all He possesses to you as your inheritance. Jesus is the Captain of the Heavenly Hosts and He does have a mighty army of saints. But all of His army are volunteers. They willingly serve in the Lord's army.

Have you made Jesus King of your own life? If you have, you can enjoy His Kingdom of peace, righteousness, and joy every day you live on earth.

Thank You Lord for being my King. It is a joy to dwell in Your Kingdom.

Daily Deposit: The Kingdom we enjoy on earth is nothing compared to what we will enjoy in heaven. When we make Jesus our Lord and King, we can look forward to living in a Kingdom that will never end.

Read: 1 Samuel 10:1–11:15; John 6:47–71; Psalm 107:1–43; Proverbs 15:1–3

A Meal Fit for a King
John 6:47–71

I can remember my father sitting in his easy chair in front of the TV while he waited for my mother to serve him his dinner on a TV tray. I always thought he was like a king waiting while all of his servants busied themselves to serve a meal that was fit for a king. Sometimes mother was late with dad's dinner. When she was late, he always exclaimed, "Frances, a piece of shoe leather would taste delicious by now." In our passage today, we read about a meal that King Jesus has prepared for us. We learned earlier that King Jesus came to serve us, not to be master over us. The meal He has prepared for us is fit for a king.

The meal King Jesus has prepared for us is Himself. Jesus said that He is the living bread that came down from heaven. When we eat this bread, we will never die. Jesus told them (vv. 53–55):

> Most assuredly, I say to you, unless you eat the flesh of the Son of Man and drink His blood, you have no life in you. Whoever eats My flesh and drinks My blood has eternal life, and I will raise him up at the last day. For My flesh is food indeed, and My blood is drink indeed.

Many left, following Jesus, after He made this statement that sounded cannibalistic to them. When one of my sons was about six years old, he asked me, "Mom, will we eat in heaven?" I responded, "In heaven we won't need food because we will feed on Jesus."

My son exclaimed, "I hope some of Jesus is left by the time we get to heaven!"

Jesus laid His life down to prepare us a meal fit for a king. Because of the death, burial, and resurrection of Jesus, we can now enjoy spiritual food that will last eternally. Jesus not only prepares us the meal as our Servant King, but He also is our daily spiritual food and drink. Whenever we are in His presence we can drink from His fountain of living water and feed on the manna of His Word. He offers us the new wine of His Spirit every day. Have you feasted on Jesus today? He promises to give you living water that will quench your spiritual thirst forever. His presence will sustain you throughout this day.

Lord, thank You for being the living bread. Thank You for preparing a meal fit for a king for me every day. Help me never to pass by Your table without taking time to eat.

Daily Deposit: When we take time to sit at the Lord's table, we will eat the spiritual food that will last eternally. Don't miss your meal today!

May 12

Read: 1 Samuel 12:1–13:23; John 7:1–30; Psalm 108:1–13; Proverbs 15:4

The Suffering Christ
John 7:1–30

Jesus was willing to suffer for our sakes. He was able to go to Jerusalem and face the cross, for the joy that was set before Him. He looked forward to seeing our joy as we sit at His Table and fellowship with Him. Jesus suffered much even before the cross. He faced five types of persecution: death threats from the religious Jews, misunderstanding from His own family, hatred from the world, false accusations, and unbelief.

As Jesus suffered, we also will suffer. One of the persecutions I have experienced is misunderstanding by my own family. I can remember that my mother-in-law, for a long time, did not understand my zeal for the Lord. The day came, however, when she understood and Jesus imparted to us both His baptism of love. One of the most memorable events in my life happened when I met a Christian lady who was eighty-eight years old. I had heard about her work in my community. She was one of the pastors of an African Methodist Episcopal Church in town. She led a little rhythm band for underprivileged children. When we met, we had no words, only tears. As we hugged one another, she said, "You know, as I know, the sufferings of Christ."

I believe one of the greatest things Jesus suffered was the unbelief of His own family members. His brothers urged Jesus to go to Jerusalem to show His stuff to the people. They said, "Show Yourself to the world" (v. 4). The very brothers Jesus grew up with misunderstood Him and were still looking for more proof. They did not believe He was the Christ until after His resurrection.

It was time for the Feast of Tabernacles in Jerusalem. This was one of the three pilgrim feasts that every Jewish male was required to attend. The Feast of Tabernacles is called *The Feast*. It is a joyful time of celebration when families gather together in their *sukkots* (little shelters attached to their homes) to share their meals for seven days. The families joyfully remember and share all of God's goodness to them as they eat delicious food under the stars that twinkle through the opening of their thatched roofs.

Jesus went to Jerusalem in secret because He knew it was not His time yet to be arrested. When I read these scriptures, I envisioned Jesus hiding in the shadows as He watched His family laughing joyfully at their table in their sukkot. The suffering of that moment was what many rejected people feel. They always seem to be on the outside looking in at people who are having a good time. Do you feel that way sometimes? Jesus has already identified with your pain.

Lord, thank You for suffering for my sake.

Daily Deposit: Today, reach out in love to someone who has been on the outside looking in. Your acceptance of the rejected will be recorded in heaven.

May 13

The Living Water
John 7:31–53

Yesterday, we saw Jesus hiding in the shadows observing the celebration of the Feast of Tabernacles. He decided to come out of the shadows to go into the Temple to teach. Everyone was amazed at His doctrine. It was tradition on the last day of the Feast of Tabernacles to have a water libation ceremony. The priests paraded through the streets of Jerusalem to the Pool of Siloam, where they drew water to take back to the Temple. After filling their pitchers, they marched back to the courtyard of the Temple. There they poured the water on the altar. It was a ceremony to celebrate the abundant rains that would water their fields during the fall harvest.

While the priests were pouring the water on the altar, a loud voice came from the corner of the courtyard. A hush came over the crowd. It was Jesus. He stood and cried, "If anyone thirsts, let him come to Me and drink. He who believes in Me, as the Scripture has said, out of his heart will flow rivers of living water" (vv.37-38). Jesus was speaking about the Holy Spirit, who would fill all those who believe in Him.

Jesus can give us the water that will always quench our thirsty souls. He can pour out the river of His Holy Spirit on those who will receive this living water. Some, however, will refuse to drink of this living water. Their souls will remain parched. They will miss the power energized by the River of Life.

Today you can go to the well and drink from this living water. Each day of our lives we need to be refreshed by this water. Most nutrition experts recommend that we drink between six and eight glasses of water each day. Could it be that we need to drink from this spiritual living water between six and eight times a day? David praised the Lord seven times a day. It might be a good idea to establish this pattern of praise in our daily lives. Every time we praise the Lord, we are drawing water from the wells of salvation with joy. When we establish such a pattern of praise, our souls will never become parched.

Lord, thank You for the living water of Your Spirit.

Daily Deposit: This would be a great day to begin your spiritual health regimen. Try praising Jesus eight times during this day. Your praises will be recorded in the Book of Remembrance in heaven. (See Malachi 3:16.)

May 14

Celebrate Forgiveness
John 8:1–20

We rushed out of our rooms when we heard booming noises below us. We were in the Seven Arches Hotel on the Mount of Olives. The hotel overlooks the city of Jerusalem. We saw flashing lights and, with hearts pounding, we gathered under the seven arches. To our relief, we saw a huge display of fire works. Israel was celebrating the birth of their nation.

It has been our privilege to be in Israel on at least six of its birthdays. Whenever May 14 arrives, I remember those happy occasions in Jerusalem and I look forward to the day when Messiah will be revealed to Israel! That great day is recorded in Zechariah 14. Zechariah records that in that day His feet will stand on the Mount of Olives which faces Jerusalem on the east and that the mountain will split in two. On that day, Israel will know the forgiveness Jesus Christ purchased for them on the cross. They will look at His pierced hands and they will go as families into their homes to weep. A fountain of cleansing will be opened for them and all of Israel will be saved on that day.

Our passage today records the forgiving power of Jesus Christ, even before He experienced the cross. A woman was caught in adultery. The religious leaders and the people were ready to stone her. The scribes and the Pharisees reminded Jesus of the law of Moses, stating that anyone who committed adultery was to be stoned to death.

"Stone her! Stone her!" The crowds continued to shout when Jesus quietly knelt and began to write something in the sand. Jesus was probably writing the various sins the scribes and Pharisees had committed. Then he raised His head, looked into their angry eyes and said, "He who is without sin among you, let him throw a stone at her first" (v. 7). One by one, the crowds dispersed. The woman was left alone with Jesus. Jesus asked her, "'Woman, where are those accusers of yours? Has no one condemned you?'" She said, 'No one, Lord.' And Jesus said to her, 'Neither do I condemn you; go and sin no more'" (vv. 10-11).

Jesus did not come into the world to condemn the world, but that the world through Him might be saved. What great news! I wish everyone would believe this. I look forward to the day when all of Israel will believe this. Do you believe Jesus forgives all of your sins – past, present, and future? If you do, rejoice with me today as I celebrate both the birth of Israel and the forgiveness of Jesus Christ.

Lord, thank You for Your total forgiveness!

Daily Deposit: Is there someone today who needs to hear about Jesus' forgiveness? Ask God to lead you to that one who needs to know this wonderful news. This news can make an eternal difference in someone's life.

May 15

The Power of the Past
1 Samuel 17:1–18:4

The past has the power to defeat us or to give us great victories. People who dwell on their negative past and refuse to forgive those who have wronged and hurt them will live defeated lives. People who forgive and remember the victories in their past will always be able to conquer their foes in the present. David was a man who remembered his victories. That memory of past victories gave him the courage to face both the present and the future.

The story related in our passage today is well known to even people who never read the Bible. The story of David and Goliath causes us all to remember the times in our past when we have faced giants. The giants may have been illness, unemployment, or the loss of a loved one. The story of David and Goliath gives us the key to victory over every negative circumstance in our lives. The key is to remember the victories of the past.

David had no doubt that he could slay Goliath; because, with God's strength he had killed both a bear and a lion. The uncircumcised Philistine who now defied the armies of Israel was a piece of cake for David. David was able to slay Goliath with five smooth stones hurled from his slingshot.

Someone told me that they kept five smooth stones in a glass jar in their home. Tied to each stone was a small piece of paper with a note recounting five past victories in this person's life. This person shared how he would pull the stones from the jar and read about his past victories whenever he faced another giant in his life. Five is the number for grace. Grace has the word *race* in it. Have you ever thought about that? When we receive God's grace, we are enabled to run God's **RACE** well. We will win every race in this life when we call upon God's grace to face the giants in our lives! Also remember: God's grace enabled us to win the victories in the past.

Lord, thank You for past victories.

Daily Deposit: Make a list today of your past victories. You will be amazed at how many times God has shown Himself strong on your behalf. While you write your list, another list will be written in your *Book of Remembrance* in heaven. I believe we all have a chapter in our Books of Remembrance called, "*The Victories of the Lord.*"

May 16

Jealousy
1 Samuel 18:5–19:24

After David killed Goliath, David became like a brother to Saul's son, Jonathan. David was invited to live in Saul's palace, but soon Saul became jealous of David. David kept winning victories over Israel's enemies. When David returned from one of these victories, the daughters of Israel shouted, "Saul has slain his thousands, and David his ten thousand," (v. 7). This saying rang in Saul's ears, and so, he sought to kill David.

Saul's jealousy grew to such a point that he became mentally tormented. God sent an evil spirit to torment Saul. The Bible tells us where there is envy and strife there is confusion and every evil work. Saul's jealousy opened the door for him to receive tormenting spirits that brought confusion and anguish to his soul. Only the songs David played on his harp were able to calm Saul's troubled soul.

Jealousy has great power to destroy lives. The first murder on earth was caused by jealousy. Cain slew Abel because God accepted Abel's offering and rejected his.

Jealousy leads to anger, and anger leads to murder. The only way this vicious cycle can be broken is for the jealous person to confess his sin and receive God's forgiveness. Saul never repented; as a result, he spent his life trying to kill David.

Recently, I saw a demonstration of jealousy in my own living room. Two little girls were playing nicely together, until a neighbor of mine walked in the room. The neighbor enjoyed playing with the girls and tried desperately to pay equal attention to each girl. This became impossible, since the little five-year-old girl kept clinging to her. Suddenly, I noticed the ten-year-old sister in the corner of the room. Her countenance was dark and she was curled in a fetal position. The mother of the girls arrived and said that the older girl was so jealous of her little sister. Whenever we are jealous, our countenance becomes dark and our days also become dark. There is no pleasure in jealousy! The jealousy we express today can affect generations to come.

Lord, help me to never be jealous.

Daily Deposit: Be on guard daily against jealousy. Rejoice when someone receives honor. Make it your goal to esteem everyone higher than yourself. When you do this, you will never be jealous.

May 17

Work, for the Night Is Coming
John 9:1–41

My older sister lives in Seattle, Washington. During the summer months, Seattle experiences daylight until 10 p.m. She said she is always relieved when this season is over because everyone in her neighborhood works in their yards until 10 p.m. She and her husband are not interested in devoting their evenings to yard work.

As I advance in my golden years, I have the desire to make every day count for the Lord. We are co-laborers with Jesus and the harvest is ripe. Jesus said, "I must work the works of Him who sent Me while it is day; the night is coming when no one can work. As long as I am in the world, I am the light of the world" (vv. 4-5). The day would come when the earth would be in darkness for three hours in the afternoon. The light of the world would be suffering on the cross for our sake. As the light of Jesus was flickering, darkness settled like a shroud over the earth. The moment Jesus released His Spirit into the hands of the Father, light shined into the place called Abraham's bosom. Jesus received the keys to death and hell. Peter records this scene when he wrote:

> For Christ also suffered once for sins, the just for the unjust, that He might bring us to God, being put to death in the flesh but made alive by the Spirit, by whom also He went and preached to the spirits in prison, who formerly were disobedient, when once the Divine longsuffering waited in the days of Noah, while the ark was being prepared, in which a few, that is, eight souls, were saved through water.
> —1 PETER 3:18–20

Jesus, the light of the world, even while His body was in the grave, was still sharing His light with the world. On the dawn of the third day, Jesus was raised from the dead. For forty days He walked the earth in His glorified body. Many believed in Him as He walked the shores of Galilee once again. After forty days, Jesus ascended into heaven, but His light was still on earth. We—who now take His light to those who are in prison—are the light of the world. Is your light shining? The day will come when we can no longer labor with Christ on earth to set people free. Until that day, keep shining your light for Jesus.

Lord, help me to keep Your light burning brightly in me.

Daily Deposit: As the days draw closer to Jesus' return, the world grows darker, but the path of the just grows brighter and brighter. The way to keep your light burning bright for Jesus is to daily receive fresh oil (the anointing of the Holy Spirit).

May 18

The Door
John 10:1–21

Every time we go to Israel we visit the *Biblical Gardens*. We always look forward to this part of the tour because we are able to see exactly how different aspects of life in Israel were when Jesus walked on the earth. I recall, on one occasion, our guide took us to a square of pasture land fenced by large rocks. As we stood in front of this area, our guide explained all about shepherding in the days of Jesus. He said, "This is where the sheep sleep at night." We noticed an opening in the stone fence. Then he said, "This is the door to the sheepfold." Then he explained how the shepherd puts his body in this opening at night after all the sheep have entered the fold. The shepherd sleeps with his head buried between his knees and guards the sheep from robbers, wolves, and wild beasts. The shepherd actually becomes the door. This visual picture I embraced that day has helped me understand this passage in John.

> Then Jesus said to them again, "Most assuredly, I say to you, I am the door of the sheep. All who ever came before Me are thieves and robbers, but the sheep did not hear them. I am the door. If anyone enters by Me, he will be saved, and will go in and out and find pasture."
>
> —JOHN 10:7–9

Jesus continued to share His function as our Good Shepherd. Jesus said He would protect His sheep from the thieves and robbers who would seek to steal and kill them. He said He not only will protect the sheep, but He will give them abundant life. A sheep is totally dependent upon his shepherd to lead him both to water and to good pasture land. Jesus leads us to the still waters where our souls are calmed by His presence. Jesus leads us to His Word where we find sustenance for the day.

Jesus said that His sheep always follow Him because they know His voice. We had the opportunity when we were in Israel to stay at a kibbutz that overlooked the Shepherd's Fields in Bethlehem. We were amazed as we watched a shepherd call for his sheep. The moment he called, a group of sheep immediately flocked around his feet. When another shepherd called out, those sheep around the first shepherd stood motionless. We saw other sheep gathering around the second shepherd who called for his sheep. Jesus' sheep know His voice and they just will not follow anyone else.

I just read a letter from a woman who was falsely accused and is in prison for life without parole. She wrote, "God doesn't need prison doors to open or the keys because Jesus is the door." She is one of the Good Shepherd's sheep. Are you?

Lord, thank You for being my Good Shepherd.

Daily Deposit: Pray for those who do not yet know the Good Shepherd's voice.

May 19

Read: 1 Samuel 24:1–25:44; John 10:22–42; Psalm 116:1–19; Proverbs 15:20–23

The Feast of Dedication
John 10:22–42

During our May devotionals we have discussed a couple of feasts—the Feast of Tabernacles and the Feast of Firstfruits. In our passage today, we see another feast mentioned. This feast is called the Feast of Dedication. The passage begins, "Now it was the Feast of Dedication in Jerusalem, and it was winter. And Jesus walked in the temple, in Solomon's porch" (vv.22–23). I always wondered when the celebration of Hanukkah began. When I researched this passage I learned that the Hebrew word for Hanukkah means *dedication.*

Hanukkah is usually celebrated near Christmastime, in the month of December. Jesus went to the temple at the time of this feast. To understand the significance of Jesus' visit to the temple during the Feast of Dedication, it will be helpful for us to learn more about The Feast of Dedication.

This holiday celebrates the re-dedication of the temple in 165 B.C. It is always celebrated seventy five days after Yom Kippur. The Hanukkah story preserves the epic struggle and the heroic exploits of one of the greatest Jewish victories of all time–their independence from Greco-Syrian oppression in 165 B.C. Hanukkah is an eight-day feast. It begins on the twenty-fifth day of Kislev, the ninth Hebrew month (corresponding roughly to December). Hanukkah is often called the Festival of Lights.

Jesus, the light of the world, walked into the temple at the beginning of the Festival of Lights and identified Himself as the God/man. He said, "I and the Father are one" (v. 30). The Jews were furious and accused Jesus of blasphemy. Jesus exhorted the Jews to believe in Him, simply because He did the works of His heavenly Father. The works He did proved that He was the Son of God and was both divine and human.

> The Jews did not believe Jesus' words, and they doubted His divinity. This problem still exists today. Many believe Jesus was a historical prophet, but they do not believe He was God in flesh form. That day, Jesus was experiencing more than an intellectual battle with the Jews. Jesus was face-to-face with the spirit of antichrist. We have to remember that we do not fight against flesh and blood, but against principalities and powers, rulers of darkness, and wickedness in high places. (See Ephesians 6:12.) That wicked spirit had the power to blind the eyes of the Jews in Jesus day. Many are blinded today by that same spirit. But we now have the power to bind the spirit of antichrist and to loose people to the power of the Holy Spirit. It is the Holy Spirit, alone, who can open the eyes of people's understanding. Jesus, the light of the world, has given us the authority in His name to open the eyes of those who are spiritually blind. Have you used your authority today?

Lord, thank You for giving me Your authority.

Daily Deposit: When we use the authority we have in Jesus name to open the eyes of those who are spiritually blind, we will see the fruit of our warfare in heaven.

May 20

Springtime
John 11:1–53

S pringtime in Atlanta enters like an elegant bride adorned in fine white lace. Bright purple, pink, and red azaleas form her bouquet. The birds provide music for the bridal procession, as Spring dances down the isles of Atlanta's streets that are lined with pure white dogwood trees, intermingled with flowering peach trees and redbuds. The stunning bride named *Spring* is ready to meet her Bridegroom and Creator.

One of my favorite spots to visit when the azaleas are in full bloom is a local cemetery. In the midst of this cemetery is a replica of the tomb where Jesus was raised from the dead. Two statues of women with vessels in their hands stand near the open tomb. They represent Mary and Martha, who visited Jesus on the day of His resurrection. Above the tomb is a sign that reads, "He is not here! He is risen!" Bright multi-colored azalea bushes form a natural amphitheater. Just to the left of the two statues is a pulpit with an open Bible, both made of stone. Engraved on the open Bible is John 11:25–26:

> I am the resurrection and the life. He who believes in Me, though he may die, he shall live. And whoever lives and believes in Me shall never die.

Jesus spoke these words to Martha just before He raised Lazarus from the dead. Jesus asked Martha if she believed what He said. Martha replied, "Yes, Lord, I believe that You are the Christ, the Son of God, who is to come into the world" (v. 27). This faith statement has been declared by millions over the centuries. The day will soon come when the millions who declared by faith their belief in Jesus will be resurrected. Just as Lazarus heard the words, "Come forth," these millions will hear the same voice and the same words. On that day, the Bride of Christ will receive the bridal gown of a glorified body. The Bridegroom will embrace His bride and they will experience eternal springtime together.

Lord, thank You for the beautiful springtime. The beauty of spring will not compare, however, to the beauty we will see when we experience the resurrection.

Daily Deposit: We do not have to wait for the resurrection to experience eternal springtime in our hearts. Jesus is the Resurrection and the Life and we can experience His presence every day. Enjoy the beauty of His Holiness today.

May 21

The Perpetual Poor
John 11:54–12:19

We just returned from Jamaica where we ministered to over ten churches. Most of the people who attended would be considered poor, by American standards. On our trips to India and Mexico we saw people who lived in shelters of cardboard. The poverty we have seen all over the world is not limited to foreign countries. We have the same kind of poverty in America. We will always have the poor with us, no matter how many social programs are administered to relieve the poverty situation. Many of the people we have seen, who would be considered poverty stricken, are millionaires in the spirit. They have joy unspeakable through Jesus Christ who gives them strength to live each day in dire conditions.

Today our passage reveals how Jesus sees people. It was six days before the Passover when Jesus returned to visit the home of Mary, Martha, and Lazarus. Mary took a pound of expensive oil and anointed Jesus' feet. She wiped his feet with her tears and the house was filled with the sweet fragrance of this costly oil. Judas was offended and asked, "Why was this fragrant oil not sold for three hundred denarii and given to the poor?" Jesus answered, "Let her alone; she has kept this for the day of My burial. For the poor you have with you always, but Me you do not have always" (vv. 5, 7). Judas did not care about the poor. He wanted the oil to be sold and put in the money box so he could steal from it.

Jesus was not at all cavalier in His attitude towards the poor. He cared for the poor then, and He cares for them now. He knew, however, that soon He would return to the Father. Mary was preparing Him for His burial.

On the cross, Jesus broke the poverty curse. He became poor, so that we might be made rich through Him. Does this mean that we should not have poor people existing after the cross? We will always have the poor with us, even as Jesus said. It is our responsibility to reach out to the poor to alleviate their suffering. Jesus wants to alleviate the suffering of both the physically poor and the spiritually poor. Anyone who does not know Jesus Christ in a personal way is spiritually poor. Will you reach out to the spiritually poor when you encounter them?

Lord, thank You for caring for both our physical and spiritual conditions.

Daily Deposit: You have a care package you can deliver to the poor today. The care package is this Word of God that exhorts us to cast all of our cares upon Jesus because He cares for us. (See 1 Peter 5:7.)

The Grain That Dies
John 12:20–50

Jesus continued to try to prepare His disciples for His death. He told them Mary was preparing Him for burial. He told Philip and Andrew that "the hour has come that the Son of Man should be glorified" (v. 23). The word *glorified* meant nothing to Philip and Andrew. They both probably asked themselves, "What on earth is Jesus talking about?"

Jesus knew the battle Andrew and Philip were having as they tried to understand His words. Jesus, once again, attempted to clarify what would happen to Him and why it had to happen, when He said, "Most assuredly, I say to you, unless a grain of wheat falls into the ground and dies, it remains alone; but if it dies, it produces much grain" (v. 24). Jesus was telling Andrew and Philip that His body was just a shell. His body would die and be buried, but He would be raised again. When He was raised, many others would believe in Him and His life would be lived through many people after His death and resurrection.

When I entered my golden years, I realized that my shell is growing old. It will soon die and be buried. My prayer is always that through my death, many will come to know Jesus Christ as their Lord and Savior. When this old mortal body dies, my real life will continue and will last forever. When we know Jesus in a personal way, we have His life within us, and His life is eternal. When I accepted Jesus Christ, He began to live within me. The life that I live in the flesh today, I am able to live because of the faith I have in Jesus Christ. The mystery of our faith is "Christ in us the hope of glory." The day will come when my body will be glorified, even as the body of Jesus was glorified. The older I get, the more I long for this glorified body that will never tire, will never wrinkle, and will never have pain.

Several years ago, I spoke with my mother's neighbor. She was an amazing woman who still lived in her own apartment by herself at the age of 105 years old. I asked her to share with me the secret to her old age. She replied, "Knowing the Lord and eating All Bran." I asked her how she was feeling. She laughed and said, "I am just tired of myself." She had lived in her shell for 105 years and she was tired of her shell. She was weary of living in her mortal body. She loved her life in Jesus, but she was ready to lose the shell of her body so she could put on a body that was incorruptible. She was ready to be glorified.

Lord, thank You for dying so I can live forever in newness of life.

Daily Deposit: We do not have to wait for our glorified bodies to glorify Jesus. We can glorify Him today in everything we do and say.

May 23

Shall the Sword Devour Forever?
2 Samuel 2:12–3:39

Jesus warned that in the last days there would be wars and rumors of wars, but this was only the beginning of sorrows. As I write this, we just finished another war. It was our second war with Iraq. In my lifetime I have seen five wars. There has been a war almost every decade of my life. Will there ever be a day when we will have lasting peace?

"Will the sword devour forever?" was the question Abner asked Joab when Joab was pursuing his life. Joab had had enough war. In response to Abner's question, Joab blew a trumpet. All his army stood still and did not pursue Israel anymore, nor did they fight anymore.

The day will come when there will be no more war. The swords will be beaten into plowshares and people will study war no more. This will not happen, however, until the millennial reign of Jesus Christ on earth. A lion will lie down with a lamb and children will even be able to play with snakes and not be harmed.

The day will come when Jerusalem will earn its name as the *City of Peace*. There will be the sounds of joy in Zion, instead of the loud sirens of ambulances in the streets of Jerusalem. Many in Jerusalem today, however, do not know about the great day of peace coming to Jerusalem. They think they will experience peace in their lifetime. There will be no lasting peace until Jesus comes again.

We do not have to wait until wars cease in order to enjoy the peace that passes our understanding. Jesus has already established peace in our hearts, and this peace will last forever.

Lord, thank You for the peace You have given me as my inheritance today.

Daily Deposit: People are looking for peace today. You know where they can find it. Why don't you tell them? Those who receive their inheritance of peace today will be able to daily add to their treasures in heaven.

May 24

The Zeal of the Lord
2 Samuel 4:1–6:23

Sometimes, in our zeal for the Lord, we make mistakes. We need to always fear the Lord—to stand in awe and walk in obedience to the Lord. However, we always need to recognize our dependence upon the Lord. The moment we fail to inquire of the Lord and begin to move in our own strength when trying to accomplish something for Him, we are subject to failing miserably. Such was the case when David attempted to return the ark to Jerusalem.

David was a man after God's own heart, but he also was a man subject to sin. The Bible describes the various ways in which David failed. Today's passage is a warning to us all. For the most part, David was able to remain humble in his spirit, even though he was a great king. He knew that his position as king was ordained by the Lord. He knew that God had established him as king, to fulfill His purposes for Israel. David had great success over his enemies because he remained humble. God gives grace to the humble; it was God's grace that enabled David to be triumphant.

The day came when David failed to obey the instructions for transporting the ark. David knew the scriptures well, but in his exuberance to return the ark to Jerusalem, he did not follow the instructions given in the law about the transport of the ark. The priests were the only ones allowed to carry the ark. The priests were instructed to bear the ark upon their shoulders whenever the ark was transported. David knew this, but he put the ark of the Lord on an oxcart. The ark became unstable when the road got bumpy and Uzzah reached to steady the ark. The anger of the Lord was aroused against Uzzah and God struck him dead.

David was both angry and fearful after this happened. David decided not to continue the transport of the ark to Jerusalem. He placed the ark in the home of Obed-Edom, the Gittite, for a period of three months. David then got the courage to take the ark from Obed-Edom's home and transport it to Jerusalem. This time David transported the ark according to the instructions God had given in the law.

We learn from this story of the dangers of going ahead of the Lord when we are excited about accomplishing His work. Jesus goes before us to do the works of the Father through us. We must join Him in these works with a humble and grateful heart. It is the grace of God that labors through us, and it is His grace that enables us to wait upon the Lord, instead of moving in haste.

Lord, help me to wait upon You always.

Daily Deposit: Offer yourself today to the Lord and allow Him to work through you, both to will and to do of His good pleasure.

May 25

Why Israel?
2 Samuel 7:1–8:18

Today, the eyes of every nation are focused on Israel, a nation the size of the state of New Jersey. The last great battle will be fought on the soil of this small nation. Jesus was born in this nation and He will rule and reign in this nation. God has promised that His presence will dwell continually in this nation. David asked:

> And who is like Your people, like Israel, the one nation on the earth whom God went to redeem for Himself as a people, to make for Himself a name-and to do for Yourself great and awesome deeds for Your land-before Your people whom You redeemed for Yourself from Egypt, the nations, and their gods?
>
> —2 SAMUEL 7:23

One cannot help but ask the question, "Why Israel?" There are many nations greater and more powerful than Israel, but Israel is called "the apple of God's eyes." God answered this question when he shared that He did not choose Israel because they were many in number. He chose Israel because He loved a man named Abraham who managed his household well. God knew Abraham could be a great father of nations. He saw a faithful Syrian man who had faith. God knew He could count on Abraham. God covenanted with Abraham to make his offspring as great as the number of the sands on the seashores and the stars in heaven.

God chose Abraham because he knew Abraham had a willing heart. God chose David because David was a man after God's own heart. God chose Abraham to bless a nation because He loved a man. God loves us and chooses us because He loves Jesus. God loves us with the very same love that He has for Jesus. We are His chosen generation. We are His chosen priests ordained to declare His love to the nations. When we ask, "Why Israel?" we must also ask "Why me, Lord?" He has chosen me, simply because He loves me. This makes me want to celebrate His love.

Lord, Your love is better than life.

Daily Deposit: There are those you will meet or talk with today who need to know God's love. Choose today to share His love with someone.

May 26

Dining With the King
2 Samuel 9:1–11:27

If you are near my age, you probably remember the many butler movies made in the forties. The lady of the house sits like a queen at the table, while the cook in the kitchen puts the finishing touches on a delicious meal. Then the lady rings the crystal bell in front of her and a butler appears. One arm has a towel neatly folded over it and the other arm reaches out to serve the meal fit for a king. This picture is certainly one that is seldom seen in America today. In fact, few families even sit down for a meal together anymore.

One of my secret desires was to experience a dinner like the one in the movies. I told my desire to my children just before Christmas one year and they arranged a Christmas surprise for me. Just a few days before Christmas, they told me we were having a surprise for dinner. They asked me to dress in my best clothes and come to dinner when I was called. One of my sons pulled my chair and seated me at the table. Next, the French student who was visiting came into the dining room. She was dressed like a French maid. My husband, dressed in a dress shirt and tie, entered. I noticed he had a towel draped over his arm. There was a crystal bell in front of my place setting. My husband announced that dinner was served. My dream was fulfilled.

As I think back on that lovely evening, I experienced both unbelief and delight. Mephibosheth, the son of Jonathan, I'm sure, experienced these same feelings when he was invited to eat at King David's table. His invitation was not just for one evening. He was invited to sit at the king's table the rest of his life. Mephibosheth's life before this invitation was laced with many trials. His nurse had dropped him in her desperation to save him, as she fled for safety when the enemy was approaching the king's palace. Mephibosheth became lame, as a result of this incident. After Saul and Jonathan were killed in battle, Mephibosheth was all but forgotten.

King David remembered his oath to Jonathan and asked if there was anyone left in the house of Saul he could show kindness to. When he was told Mephibosheth was still alive, he sent for him. When Mephibosheth saw David he fell on his face and said, "Here is your servant." He also exclaimed, "What is your servant that you should look upon such a dead dog as I?" (See 2 Samuel 9:6,8.) David returned all of Saul's riches to Mephibosheth and Mephibosheth ate at the king's table from that day forward.

Have you ever felt like a dead dog? Have you ever felt like a servant who gets no reward? King Jesus wants to invite you to the table He has prepared for you today. He wants to share all of His riches with you. Don't refuse His gracious invitation.

Lord, thank You for Your invitation.

Daily Deposit: Invite someone to the King's Table today.

May 27

Covering Sins
2 Samuel 12:1–31

Have you ever tried to cover your sins? I have certainly had this experience more than once in my lifetime. One time I told a bold-faced lie to my husband. I spent a whole week of sleepless nights. I was so afraid my husband would discover that I had lied to him. The day came when he discovered I lied to him. That week of torment I spent was one that I never want to repeat.

Fear always brings torment. My fears were unfounded because, when my cover-up was uncovered, my husband forgave me. However, he was hurt because I did not believe he would be so forgiving. I was afraid he would be angry. My fears and my cover-up were the fruit of a lack of trust.

God grieves when we try to cover our own sins. He has provided a covering for our sins. That covering cost Him the death of His only Son. When Jesus died on the cross, His blood was sufficient to cover our sins. Whenever we confess our sins, Jesus is faithful—not only to forgive our sins, but also to cleanse us from all unrighteousness. We no longer have to fear God's wrath. Jesus drank from the cup of wrath when He died for us on the cross.

King David tried to cover his sins. He deliberately had the husband of Bathsheba killed in battle so he could marry her. God saw his sin and sent Nathan, the prophet, to speak to David. Nathan told David a story about a poor man who had only one lamb. He had nourished this little lamb for years. A rich man, who had many lambs, came and took the poor man's lamb. He killed the lamb and dressed it and invited strangers to come and dine with him.

When David heard the story, his anger flared and he said the rich man should die for this dastardly deed. Then Nathan told David he was the man. Nathan rehearsed David's sins of adultery and murder. David's sins were uncovered. His sins, however, had never been covered in the sight of the Lord. David learned how fruitless it is to hide our sins from God. He wrote, "If I regard iniquity in my heart, the Lord will not hear" (Ps. 66:18). David paid a great price for his sin. Nathan told him the sword would never depart from David. If David had confessed his sins before God instead of trying to cover them up, David would have received both God's forgiveness and restoration. It is futile for us to try to cover our sins.

Lord, help me to always be truthful with You. I always want to confess my sins to You.

Daily Deposit: We can have a clean record in heaven if we will confess our sins and receive the cleansing of the blood of Jesus.

May 28

Iniquities
2 Samuel 13:1–39

God has forgiven us of our past, present, and future sins. So far as the east is from the west, so far has He removed our transgressions. The prophet Isaiah spoke of what Jesus would do for all of mankind through His death on the cross. Most of us are familiar with the wonderful Messianic passage, found in Isaiah 53, that states Jesus was wounded for our transgressions, bruised for our iniquities, chastened for our peace, and by His stripes we are healed. The atonement Jesus purchased for us on the cross, when He shed His blood, was *total atonement*. Our transgressions, iniquities, sins, and illnesses were all paid for on the cross.

I have always wondered what *iniquities* are. When I heard a message about iniquities, I finally understood how iniquities and transgressions differ. *Iniquities* are sins of the heart and *transgressions* are sins against others. Iniquities are the desires in our hearts to disobey God. God told Moses that the iniquities of the fathers would be passed on to the third and fourth generations. This means that the "want to," or the inclination, to sin in certain areas may be passed down from generation to generation. A biblical example of this is the tendency to lie, which was passed from Abraham to Isaac, and, later on, to Jacob.

Today, our passage also illustrates how the iniquities of the fathers are visited upon our descendents. David committed adultery with Bathsheba and his sin led him to murder Bathsheba's husband. When he committed these sins, David opened the door for his descendents to be weak in the area of sexual temptation and murder. Amon, David's son, committed incest with his half-sister, Tamar, who was Absalom's sister. When Absalom found out about the incident, he made plans to kill Amon and later did.

These stories should cause us all to think twice before we give in to temptation. When we sin today, our sins could affect generations to come. The good news is that the tendency to obey God can be passed on to future generations. The great news is that because of Jesus' death on the cross, we can break the curse of generational iniquity upon our children, their children, and their children's children. We can release ourselves from this pattern, when we confess the sins of our forefathers, forgive them, and apply the blood of Jesus to our bloodlines. We can pray a prayer like this:

> *Father, in the name of Jesus, I confess the sins of my forefathers back to four generations. I forgive them, and I break all ancestral ties by placing the blood of Jesus over my bloodlines.*

Daily Deposit: Share the good news with someone today—that they can be freed of all generational curses.

May 29

The Church of the Chicken
John 18:1–24

One of the most authentic places we visit when we tour Israel is nicknamed "The Church of the Chicken." The Catholics have built a lovely chapel over what was the palace of Caiaphas. Peter denied Christ three times in the courtyard of this palace. Jesus told Peter earlier that he would deny Him three times, before he heard the rooster crow. This is why this ancient place is called "The Church of the Chicken."

Every time we visit this spot, I am overwhelmed by the presence of the Lord. We usually visit the lovely chapel and then our tour guide leads us down to the place Jesus was held before he was sentenced to death. The place is called *the pit*. In the cellar of Caiaphas' home was a dark stone pit where prisoners were held. While the Pharisees, priests, and Sadducees argued over the fate of Jesus, Jesus was all alone in this pit.

As I looked into the darkness of this pit, I remembered Jeremiah and how he was lowered into a pit and left to die. Jesus has experienced every trial any man could ever experience. On the cross, Jesus, who knew no sin, became sin for us. Every sin ever committed on earth was laid upon Jesus. I cannot even begin to imagine the emotional torment and physical pain our sins caused Jesus to experience.

In tomorrow's reading in John, we see how Peter denied Christ because he feared for his life. It took Peter's denial of Christ three times to reveal to Peter that he was a weak man. Peter, the man who had declared he would follow Jesus, even if it meant prison or death for him, had denied Jesus even with an oath. Jesus warned Peter that satan wanted to sift him like wheat. Jesus promised to pray for Peter, that Peter's faith would not fail. Then Jesus told Peter to strengthen his brethren after he was converted. The conversion of Peter happened in the courtyard of Caiaphas. Peter's dependence upon his own strength was crushed. The "I" in Peter was dealt with and the "I" became "Thy." Peter was converted from self-confidence and pride to humble confidence in Jesus and in Him alone. Peter became totally dependent upon the grace of God.

God is able to use the very weapons that the enemy forms against us, for our good. Peter momentarily gave in to the temptation to deny Christ, but God used that dreadful scene in the courtyard of Caiaphas's palace to change Peter forever. Peter could now strengthen his brethren because he finally knew that his only strength came from the Lord.

Lord, thank You for always turning what satan means for evil into something good.

Daily Deposit: Reach out to someone today who may feel he has failed. Tell that person how God can work all things for good.

May 30

King Jesus
John 18:25–19:22

On one of our tours to Israel we had a female tour guide. Even though she was Jewish, she loved a certain song we sang, and she sang right along with us every time we sang this song. The song was "Hail, Jesus. You're My King." Every time this Jewish tour guide sang this song, she was declaring the truth. Truly, Jesus is our King. He is not only our personal King, but He is also King of the Universe. He is King of kings and Lord of lords.

After the Jewish religious leaders could not agree on Jesus' fate, they decided to take Him to Pilate. Pilate asked Jesus directly if He was a king. Jesus responded:

> You say rightly that I am a king. For this cause I was born, and for this cause I have come into the world, that I should bear witness to the truth. Everyone who is of the truth hears My voice.

Then Pilate asked him another question, "What is truth?" Jesus never answered Pilate, but He could have said, "I am the Way, the Truth, and the Life." Jesus knew, however, that Pilate would not receive the truth. Because Pilate was a man pleaser, he allowed Jesus to be crucified. Before Jesus left the Praetorium, some Roman soldiers mocked and scourged Him. They dressed Him in a purple robe and crowned him with a crown of thorns. Then they exclaimed, "Hail, King of the Jews!" Just as our tour guide did not know she was declaring truth when she sang "Hail Jesus. You're my King," these Roman soldiers had no idea they were declaring the truth about Jesus.

We can declare the truth about Jesus; however, this is not enough to save us. We need both to declare the truth that Jesus was crucified, was dead, buried, and raised from the dead, and we must also believe this truth in our hearts. Are there people you know who speak the truth about Jesus, but who have never believed this truth in their hearts? Pray for these people to believe in their hearts the truths that they speak.

Lord, thank You for being the Way, the Truth, and the Life.

Daily Deposit: Ask God today to help you reach out to someone who has never believed in his or her heart that Jesus Christ is Lord. Your witness to them could change a life for eternity.

May 31

Read: 2 Samuel 17:1–29; John 19:23–42; Psalm 119:132–155; Proverbs 16:12–13

Three Marys
John 19:23–42

Only four people did not abandon Jesus when He was crucified. Today, we read in our passage that Mary, Jesus' mother; Mary, his mother's sister; Mary Magdalene, and John were the only ones who remained faithful to Jesus. Jesus told John to take care of His mother. John would become like a son to Mary. After Jesus said this, He said, "I thirst!"

The thirst Jesus had that day was more than physical thirst. As He looked down from the cross at the four who were faithful, I know He longed to see the other disciples. Where were they? They had abandoned Him just like Jesus said they would. Jesus was thirsting for the fellowship He so enjoyed with His disciples. He was thirsting for their laughter, their support, their stories, their presence.

Did you know Jesus thirsts to have fellowship with you? Every day Jesus longs for you to spend time with Him. He wants to hear about your burdens, so He can take care of all of your cares. He wants to hear about your joys, so He can rejoice with you. He wants to hear about your sorrows, so He can weep with you. Will you fill His thirst today and spend time with Him? He loves you and desires for you to draw near to Him.

The three Marys chose the one thing needful. Jesus earlier praised another Mary for choosing the one thing needful. The one thing needful that Mary, the sister of Lazarus, chose was to sit at the feet of Jesus. Have you sat at His feet today? The three Marys stood at the foot of the cross on that day and I know they sat at the feet of Jesus for the rest of their lives.

Lord, help me never miss a day of fellowship with You.

Daily Deposit: When we sit at the feet of Jesus, we will receive His Words that will last eternally.

June 1

What Are You Worth?
2 Samuel 18:1–19:10

My father lived in a house full of girls: my mother, my twin sisters, my older sister and me. Dad was outnumbered five to one. Dad seldom got to say a word, but when he did speak, he had something to say. One of the questions he loved to ask us was, "Girls, what do you think you are worth to me?"

We always replied, "We don't know." Then he asked another question, "How much do you think all the tea in China is worth?" Again we replied, "We don't know." He smiled and exclaimed, "You girls are worth more to me than all the tea in China."

Today, in our passage, we learn that King David was told by his army that he was worth more than ten thousand of them. David always had a great strategy to overcome his enemies. This time, the enemy David faced was not one of his choosing. Absalom, his beloved son, had turned against him. Now David had to come against Absalom. David divided his army into three camps and he planned to go with them against Absalom. However, the people told David not to go with them. They said, "You shall not go out! For if we flee away, they will not care about us; nor if half of us die, will they care about us. But you are worth ten thousand of us now. For you are now more help to us in the city" (2 Sam. 18:3). David remained by the gate of the city, but he gave special instructions to his army generals to deal kindly with his son Absalom.

Shortly after the battle began, Absalom was slain. While riding his mule, Absalom got his hair caught in the branches of a tree. One of David's men saw Absalom's plight and reported it to Joab. Joab asked the man why he did not kill Absalom. The man replied, "Though I were to receive a thousand shekels of silver in my hand, I would not raise my hand against the king's son. For in our hearing the king commanded you and Abishai and Ittai, saying 'Beware lest anyone touch the young man Absalom'" (2 Sam. 18:12). Joab was enraged and he quickly went to the tree where Absalom was hanging. He took three spears and thrust them into the heart of the king's son.

David's life was precious to his men, and Absalom's life was precious to his father, King David. David's life was worth more than ten thousand men, and Absalom's life was worth more than one thousand shekels. How much are you worth? Do you know how precious you are to the Lord? A psalm reads, "Precious in the sight of the Lord is the death of His saints" (Ps. 116:15). The word *precious* in Hebrew means costly. When your life ends, it will cost God a living witness of His glory on earth. You are worth the price of the blood of God's only Son.

Lord, thank You for paying such a great price for my soul.

Daily Deposit: Today affirm someone and tell them how much they are worth.

June 2

Returning Home
2 Samuel 19:11–20:13

David had to leave his home because Absalom, his son, had gathered his own followers to depose David from the throne. As David left his beloved city, the scene was not a pretty one. David's head was covered, he was barefoot, and he feared for his life. Sheimi saw David and mocked him as David fled.

David was still grieving the death of his son, but at the urging of his commanders, he returned to his home to resume his throne. Sheimi, the one who had mocked David as he fled from Absalom, now begged David for mercy. David had mercy on Sheimi and did not kill him, even though his commanders wanted David to rid himself of this mocker. Jonathan's son, Mephibosheth, met David. Mephibosheth had not shaved or taken care of his feet the whole time David was away. David asked Mephibosheth why he did not flee with him. Mephibosheth replied that his servant, Ziba, deceived him. Ziba told him he would saddle a donkey for Mephibosheth, but he did not return to get Mephibosheth. Deception and mocking were the farewell David experienced as he fled his city.

What awaited him upon his return was no better. The men of Judah helped David cross the Jordan. They were greeted by Sheba, the son of Bichri, a Benjamite. Saul was a Benjamite, and the hatred Saul had for David was still brewing in those men who were followers of Saul. Bichri shouted, "We have no share in David, Nor do we have inheritance in the son of Jesse; Every man to his tents, O Israel!" (20:1). Only the tribe of Judah remained loyal to David.

The bloodshed continued throughout King David's reign. Nathan, the prophet, had prophesied after David's sin with Bathsheba that the sword would never depart from David. David's son was dead. Jonathan, his beloved friend was dead. Mephibosheth, Jonathan's son, was like a dead man. David's return home was not triumphant. His last days would be spent grieving for his son Absalom, and there was famine in the land.

David only had the Lord to cling to. The Lord was his strong tower and his rock throughout his life, but more than ever David knew the comfort only the Lord could give.

Whenever we return to our former homes, we discover that things are not as we remembered them. The home we lived in might even be gone, and many of our friends may have died. The comforts of home are temporary, but our home in the Father's heart will remain forever. David knew this, and this knowledge kept him through many trials.

Lord, thank You for the security of living in Your heart and home forever.

Daily Deposit: There's no place like home, especially when we know our true home is with our Heavenly Father forever. Share that hope with someone today.

The Promise and the Power
Acts 1:1–26

The last words a person speaks on earth are usually worth noting. Many, on their deathbeds, have related their love to their family, or have given instructions to take care of various family members. Jesus' last words on earth were words of instruction. He instructed his disciples not to depart from Jerusalem, but to wait there for the power of the Holy Spirit to come upon them. He said, "It is not for you to know times or seasons which the Father has put in His own authority. But you shall receive power when the Holy Spirit has come upon you, and you shall be witnesses to Me in Jerusalem, and in all Judea and Samaria, and the end of the earth."

The disciples had already received the Holy Spirit. Earlier, after Jesus was resurrected, He breathed into the disciples the Holy Spirit. Jesus imparted the Holy Spirit to those who believed and followed Him. On that occasion He said to them, "'Peace to you! As the father has sent Me, I also send you.' And when He had said this, He breathed on them, and said to them, 'Receive the Holy Spirit. If you forgive the sins of any, they are forgiven them; if you retain the sins of any, they are retained'" (John 20:21-23). Now it was time for the Holy Spirit not only to be within them, but also to come upon them.

Jesus was filled and directed by the Holy Spirit the whole time He was on earth. However, His empowerment by the Holy Spirit for ministry did not occur until the Holy Spirit descended on Him like a dove when He was baptized in water by John the Baptist. (See John 1:32.) If Jesus needed this empowerment before He began His earthly ministry, how much more do we need that same power to come upon us!

There is still a debate in the body of Christ about the baptism in the Holy Spirit. The scriptures, however, tell us exactly the reason for the baptism in the Holy Spirit and the need for this baptism. The Holy Spirit first came upon Jesus and then, later, His disciples were empowered for their ministry. They did not just receive tongues. They received the full sevenfold anointing of the Holy Spirit: the spirit of wisdom and understanding, the spirit of might and counsel, the spirit of knowledge and the fear of the Lord, and the Spirit of the Lord.

I have stopped debating. I decided to receive all Jesus had to give me. I asked Jesus to baptize me in the Holy Spirit, and He did. The major difference I saw in my life after the Holy Spirit came upon me was in my hunger for the scriptures and my boldness in witnessing. Have you asked Jesus to baptize you in the Holy Spirit?

Lord, thank You for the Promise of the Father.

Daily Deposit: This is a great day for you to be empowered by the Holy Spirit.

June 4

Power to Witness
Acts 2:1–47

It was one of those cloudless blue skies in May, around A.D. 30. Throngs of Jewish worshipers crowded the Temple courts. It seemed like people from every nation had made their pilgrimage to Jerusalem to celebrate Shavuot, the Feast of Weeks. Fifty days were counted from the Feast of First Fruits, the day Jesus was raised from the dead. He had been with the disciples and others for forty days. Just before He ascended into heaven, He gave them instructions to wait in Jerusalem until they received the Promise of the Father. One hundred and twenty of His followers waited with one heart in one place.

Suddenly the sound of a rushing mighty wind interrupted the worship of the thousands in the courts of the temple. Some of the worshippers ran to see where this wind was coming from. As they reached the outer court and viewed the city below, they saw flashes of light over a home not far from the temple. They rubbed their eyes in unbelief and tried to focus again on this mysterious phenomenon. They had just read Ezekiel and Habakkuk, as part of their feast celebration. They questioned among themselves, "Could it be that those prophesies we read about the return of God's Shekinah glory, after 600 years is being fulfilled right before our eyes?"

Then Peter and the other disciples walked out of the house. They seemed to be weaving back and forth like drunk men, but it was only nine o'clock in the morning. As they began to speak, everyone understood their speech because they were speaking in the languages of all the nations gathered in Jerusalem on that day. The crowds were amazed, because they knew most of those who came from this home were simple, unlearned Galileans who had never been schooled in languages. The crowds hushed as Peter began to speak, "Men of Judea and all who dwell in Jerusalem, let this be known to you, and heed my words. For these are not drunk, as you suppose, since it is only the third hour of the day. But this is what was spoken by the prophet Joel" (vv. 14–16). Then Peter opened the Hebrew scriptures and read Joel's prophecy about how God promised to pour out His Spirit on all flesh. Peter continued to expound the scriptures to them. He read from the Book of Psalms and told them that God had made Jesus, whom they crucified, both Lord and Christ.

Fire from heaven had fallen. What appeared to be divided tongues of fire had ignited the 120 followers of Jesus with the Holy Spirit anointing—the spirit of wisdom and understanding, might and counsel, and knowledge and the fear of the Lord. Unlearned Galileans were transformed into bold witnesses on that day of Pentecost. Peter assured the crowds that this power they had received was also promised to them and their children. This power to witness is also for you. Have you received this power?

Lord, thank You for making this same power available to me.

Daily Deposit: Be empowered by the Holy Spirit to witness boldly today.

June 5

Counting the Numbers
2 Samuel 23:24–24:25

We love to visit a messianic congregation on Fridays. The rabbi of this congregation has been a friend of ours for years. Because of our schedule, we are only able to attend about once every three months. When we have the opportunity to talk with this rabbi, he always asks the same question, "How many is your church running these days?" I am always tempted to say jokingly, "We are running a lot off these days!" The rabbi is concerned with numbers, as many pastors are. They feel numbers represent the strength of their church; they feel that they are not successful if the numbers in their congregation drop off. However, this is not true. God is concerned with souls, not numbers.

Our son's father-in-law pastors a church in Alabama. This church has never grown past about one hundred members. Yet, this pastor and this church have supported missions all over the world. The congregants are bold witnesses for the Lord and many have come to know Jesus through their witness. This church is interested in increasing the number of souls in the Kingdom of God, not their church. In fact, if my son's father-in-law hears a congregant murmuring and complaining, he tells them they might like to try another church in the town. He says, "There are plenty of good churches in this town, and you just might find a better fit at another church."

David was concerned about numbers. He gave in to the temptation to number Israel and Judah to discern the strength of his army. He must have forgotten about Gideon and how God commanded Gideon to reduce his forces against the Midianites, because God wanted to be their strength, not numbers. Even Joab, David's right arm general, warned David not to number the troops. David did not heed his warning and Joab followed David's orders, reporting back the number of soldiers in each tribe. David recognized his sin and confessed it to God. God forgave David. Still, there are always consequences of sin.

God gave David a choice of seven years of famine, continual flight from his enemies, or three days of plagues as a retribution for his sin. David chose the plague. He had rather fall into the hands of a merciful God than in the hands of his enemies.

David interceded for the people. The prophet Gad gave the word of the Lord to David and instructed him to erect an altar on the threshing floor of Araunah, the Jebusite, and to do sacrifice there. God promised to stop the plague after David followed these instructions. David wanted to buy the threshing floor, but Araunah wanted to give it to David. David insisted on buying it. David said, "No, but I will surely buy it from you for a price; nor will I offer burnt offerings to the LORD my God with that which costs me nothing" (2 Samuel 24:24). The plague ceased. David learned a hard lesson.

Lord, give me a heart for souls.

Daily Deposit: Today, see people as souls, not numbers.

The Rod of Correction
1 Kings 1:1–53

We are instructed in God's Word to never rebuke an elder, but to entreat him as a father. (See 1 Timothy 5:1.) However, there is a place for rebuke in the church, as well as in families. It has been said that as the family goes, so goes the church, and so goes the nation. Today, we are reaping what we sowed in the fifties and sixties when parents became lax in the discipline of their children. We have many rebellious adults who are lawless. It is wrong for a child to rebuke his parents. However, it is just as wrong for a father not to rebuke his son.

David did not rebuke Adonijah during his childhood. Now Adonijah, the brother of Absalom, had a spirit like Absalom. Adonijah wanted to be king. Nathan, the prophet, told Bathsheba of Adonijah's plans and asked her to warn King David. King David had promised Bathsheba that her son, Solomon, would be king after him. David heeded the warning of Bathsheba and Nathan, the prophet, and Zadok, the priest, anointed Solomon as king. When Adonijah found out that David had made Solomon the king, he ran to take hold of the horns of the altar and all of his followers fled in fear. Solomon had mercy upon Adonijah and did not kill him.

What would have happened if David had rebuked Adonijah and disciplined him when he was a child? David never questioned Adonijah about why he was disobedient. David just let things slide. He was too busy fighting wars to discipline his own children. The rebellious spirit of pride in Absalom and Adonijah could have been broken if David had been diligent in the discipline of his children. We see other examples of lack of discipline in the life of Samuel and his guardian father, Eli the priest. Both Samuel and Eli had rebellious sons. (See 1 Samuel 3:13; 8:2–3.) Pride is the root of rebellion. If the rod is not applied to pride, that root will always flourish and bear fruit.

Proverbs 13:24 says that a man hates his child if he refuses to discipline him. The rod my husband and I used when our children were young was the wooden spoon. When my children were older, I continually discovered wooden spoons my children had hidden from us when they were young. The rod of correction our Heavenly Father uses is His Word. His Word is able to instruct us, correct us, and reprove us. (See 2 Timothy 3:16.) We have a choice in life. We can submit ourselves to the rod of correction (God's Word) or face being chastened in other ways. God chastens those He loves because He considers us as His sons and daughters. God never hesitates to discipline us because He is an honorable Father. Submitting to God's rod of correction (His Word) is the way I want to be disciplined by God. If I refuse this rod of correction, God will use other means to correct me.

Lord, help me to daily submit myself to Your Word and obey it.

Daily Deposit: Today I choose to submit to God's rod of correction.

June 7

God's Discipline
Acts 5:1–42

Yesterday, we talked about God's discipline. God chastens those He loves. Today's passage illustrates what happens when we do not obey God's Word. Ananias, with Sapphira his wife, sold a possession and kept back part of the proceeds, instead of giving it all to the church. God saw what they did and He told Peter about it. We have to remember that God sees all and knows all and He will do everything in His power to help us not to sin.

However, if we decide in our hearts to blatantly disobey His Word, God will chasten us. Peter gave Ananias a chance to repent, when he told Ananais he had lied to God. At that moment, Ananias could have confessed and repented. But fear came upon him and he dropped dead. Three hours later, when his wife came in, Peter gave Sapphira a chance to redeem herself. He asked her whether she sold the land for a certain price. Sapphira told the same lie Ananias told Peter. Peter asked why she and her husband both agreed together to test the Spirit of the Lord. Sapphira then dropped dead. What happened to Ananias and Sapphira brought the whole church into an awesome fear of the Lord.

This story has always bothered me and I am sure has troubled others. The question is asked, "How could a loving God cause the death of two of His saints?" The answer to this question is simple. God did not cause the death of these two saints. Their own sin caused the death of Ananias and Sapphira. Sin always brings death. This is why God longs for us to heed His chastening and His rod of correction, before it is too late. God knew the hearts of Ananias and Sapphira. They tested the Holy Spirit, and as we know, Jesus said to satan, "You shall not tempt the LORD your God" (Luke 4:12). When we tempt the Lord, the consequences are usually fatal.

The result of this incidence brought fruitfulness to the church. Believers were increasingly added to the Lord and multitudes of men and women became followers of Christ. Peter and the other apostles were asked not to teach anymore in the name of Jesus. They responded, "We ought to obey God rather than men." They feared God more than they feared man. This true story of Ananias and Saphhira ought to put the fear of the Lord in our hearts. We cannot play games with God, because He can discern our hearts.

Lord, try my heart and know my ways and keep me in Your ways always.

Daily Deposit: God's ways are given to us to keep us out of trouble. When we refuse to go His way, our disobedience can lead to sins that can affect generations to come. Choose to go God's way today.

June 8

Read: 1 Kings 3:3–4:34; Acts 6:1–15; Psalm 126:1–6; Proverbs 16:26–27

The Face of an Angel
Acts 6:1–15

What do angels look like? I have never seen one, but I know people who have. Their description fits what the Bible teaches about angels. Those I know who have seen angels tell me that angels look like strong men. They are usually around seven feet tall. When the Lord appeared to Abraham, three men were standing by Him. The Lord and these three men (angels) ate dinner with Abraham. (See Genesis 18.)

In our passage today, the council that questioned Stephen saw Stephen's face as the face of an angel. Stephen was full of faith and power. He did great wonders and signs among the people. He was also a wonderful servant. The apostles had just laid hands on seven men of good reputation, full of the Holy Spirit and wisdom, to take care of the distribution of food to the widows. Stephen was among these seven men. As we look at the character of Stephen, we begin to get a picture of what the face of an angel would look like. The face of an angel must reflect great power and wisdom. At the same time, the face of an angel must reveal humility and servant-hood. We learn in the Bible that angels are ministering spirits sent to minister to the saints. (See Hebrews 1:14.) The face of an angel shines with God's glory.

When our son was serving as a teacher of English in China, several of his students asked him, "What makes your face shine?" He was able to tell them that the light of God's glory brightened His face. We know the Shekinah glory of God shone so brightly on the face of Moses that he had to cover His face when he came down from Mt. Sinai. Moses had spent forty days and nights in the Lord's presence. That time spent with God on the mountain changed the countenance of Moses. The time Stephen spent in the presence of God changed Stephen's countenance. Gazing at God's glory as we spend time in the presence of the Lord causes our faces to shine like the face of an angel.

I was privileged to see the face of Jesus in a vision, as I was waking up from a Sunday nap. His face appeared to me in a ball of light. The joy, love, and peace on His face was beyond expression. His eyes were like laser beams penetrating the very core of my being. His smile was contagious, and the peace on His face enveloped me.

I asked the Lord then if I could have a video of His face to show the whole world. I knew anyone who looked into the face of Jesus would instantly repent because of the compelling love expressed in His face. I heard the following with my spiritual ears: "I have not chosen to reveal myself to all of mankind in this way. I have chosen to reveal my face in the faces of every believer on earth." As we spend time with Jesus, He is able to brighten our countenance with His glory, and like Stephen, we can have the face of an angel.

Lord, brighten my countenance today.

Daily Deposit: Time spent with Jesus today is time well spent.

June 9

History—His Story
Acts 7:1–29

This chapter of Acts is worth outlining. Stephen was empowered by the Holy Spirit, as he reviewed all the Hebrew Scriptures with the council who sought to kill him. Stephen was refreshing the memory of all those who heard. We, too, can have our memories refreshed as we read Chapter 7 of Acts. He began with Abraham and reviewed the history of the Hebrew people, up to the crucifixion. History became His (Jesus') story.

My husband had the opportunity to share this same history with a Chinese professor of economics. We had the joy of hosting one of my son's Chinese students for five years, while she finished her education in the United States. We prayed often for her father, who was not a believer. The day came when we were able to have her father as a guest in our home for six months. We were able to arrange an invitation to him from Georgia Tech to come and study in the states for six months. He only spoke Mandarin; so when he arrived at Georgia Tech, they said they could not help him in his research. He decided just to do research from our home.

After two months with us, he had completed his work. We suggested that he use the next four months to try to learn some English. We gave him a Bible that paralleled a Mandarin and English translation of the Bible. He took our suggestion. After only two weeks into the Word of God, he asked us an unusual question. Through his daughter who interpreted, he asked, "Why was Jesus so mean to the Jews? I thought Jesus was a Jew." We had suggested that he begin his study of the Bible with the Gospel of John. We knew, after this question, that we needed to sit down and explain some things to our guest. So we set a time for the next Saturday.

Tom began to expound the scriptures to him, beginning with Abraham, and ending with the cross. This took three hours, since his daughter had to interpret everything to him. We suggested that we meet again and discuss more of the Bible. Suddenly, he said something to his daughter in Mandarin; she looked surprised. Then, she shared, "My dad wants to receive Jesus Christ now as his Lord and Savior. He told me that he could see that Christianity was the only religion based on love. All other religions are based on fear. That day, the journey through the scriptures from Abraham to the cross availed much. We will see in our next devotional that Stephen's review of the Hebrew Scriptures, unfortunately, did not have the same result.

Lord, help me never to forget Your History lessons.

Daily Deposit: Today is a good day to review His-story. We need to be ready to share, as Stephen did, with those who have not understood or even read the scriptures. When we store God's Word in the computer of our minds, the printout we share with others can change lives for eternity.

June 10

Read: 1 Kings 7:1–51; Acts 7:30–50; Psalm 128:1–6; Proverbs 16:31–33

Outline of His Story
Acts 7:30–50

As we look together at what Stephen shared with the council, we see an unfolding of God's eternal plan. My husband, Tom, shared with our Chinese guest exactly as Stephen shared. I was thankful Tom did not begin the story with the beginning of time. Stephen was used to speaking to Jewish leaders and I am sure this is why he began his review of His-story with Father Abraham. He outlined the following:

The Appearance of God's Glory to Abraham: God told Abraham to "get out of your country, From your family And from your father's house, To a land that I will show you" (Gen. 12:1). Abraham obeyed and left the land of the Chaldeans and dwelt in Haran. Then he continued his journey into the Promised Land. God told Abraham that his people would dwell in bondage for 400 years in Egypt. God would judge Egypt and deliver His people from bondage. God gave Abraham the Covenant of circumcision and Abraham begot Isaac. Isaac begot Jacob, and Jacob begot the twelve patriarchs.

The Appearance of God's Glory to Joseph: Jacob was the father of all twelve patriarchs. He favored his youngest son, Joseph. Joseph's brothers became jealous. They sold Joseph into slavery. Joseph served in Egypt as a slave and he found favor in the sight of Pharaoh, who made Joseph governor of all Egypt. There was famine in Israel, so Jacob (Israel) sent some of his sons to Egypt where there was food. Joseph eventually made himself known to his brothers and invited his father and all of his brothers to dwell in the land of Goshen. Seventy five people came with Israel to Egypt.

The Appearance of God's Glory to Moses: When Joseph died, a cruel Pharaoh ruled in Egypt and enslaved the Children of Israel for 400 years. Moses was born and was delivered from Pharaoh's plan to kill all the newly born sons of Israel. Moses killed an Egyptian when he was forty years old, and fled to the wilderness, where God appeared to Moses in a burning bush. God instructed Moses to deliver His people from bondage. God sent plagues upon Egypt and Moses delivered his people from cruel bondage. The Children of Israel were disobedient and dwelled in the wilderness forty years before they entered the Promised Land. Moses erected a tabernacle of witness.

The Appearance of God's Glory to Joshua, David, and Solomon: The Commander of the Hosts of the Lord (Jesus Christ) appeared to Joshua and encouraged him to possess the Promised Land (Joshua). Joshua fought many enemies and claimed The Promised Land. The Children of Israel lived in this land under the many judges and kings, including King David who wanted to build a house for God. Solomon built the house for God.

Lord, help me to remember Your story.

Daily Deposit: His-Story can make a difference in the eternal history of others.

June 11

Read: 1 Kings 8:1–66; Acts 7:51–8:13; Psalm 129:1–8; Proverbs 17:1

Hear in Heaven
1 Kings 8:1–66

The lady swept tiny pieces of paper, gathered them with her hands, and threw them into the waste bin. I thought to myself, "What if my prayer was one of those now in the waste bin?" We were by the Wall in Jerusalem, where thousands come to offer their prayers to God daily. The Wall looks like a collage, mingled with green, gray, and white colors. Green sprays of hyssop grow out of the gray wall and tiny white pieces of paper are tucked in the spaces between the stones of the wall. Written on those pieces of paper are prayer requests made by Jerusalem pilgrims from every nation. Whenever we go to Israel, people give us more written prayer requests to tuck in the Wall. I often wondered what happened to the requests that fell from the wall. On this day, I discovered their fate. Does God still hear the prayers that are swept away?

The Western Wall in Jerusalem is one of the holiest sights in all of Israel. We try to visit the Wall as often as possible while we are in Jerusalem. I believe God hears every prayer prayed at the Wall, simply because He honors the prayers Solomon prayed at the dedication of the Temple thousands of years ago. Solomon prayed for God to hear from heaven all the supplications and prayers prayed towards the temple. He asked God to hear from heaven the following prayers: prayers to justify the righteous, prayers of confession of sin, prayers to break drought conditions, prayers to end every kind of plague and sickness, all the prayers of foreigners who visit this holy sight, and prayers for victory in wartime and deliverance from captivity. God heard Solomon's prayer. I believe He hears every prayer prayed at the Western Wall. God sees even those tiny prayer requests that fall from the wall and are swept away. God hears our hearts before He hears our words.

We don't have to go to the Western Wall in Jerusalem to have our prayers answered. God is listening today to your requests and supplications. He hears your heart whenever you cry out to Him in prayer.

Lord, thank You for hearing my heart as I pray to You.

Daily Deposit: God loves for us to make our requests and supplications to Him. We can thank Him even before the answers to our prayers come, because God is a faithful God. The prayers you pray from your heart today can make a difference in the hearts of others, for eternity.

June 12

The Gift of God Is Free
Acts 8:14–40

Whatever God chooses to give us is absolutely free. Salvation is a free gift from God. However, it cost His Son, Jesus Christ, His life to purchase this free gift for us. The gift of the Holy Spirit is free, as well. God longs to give us the gift of the Holy Spirit.

To receive a gift from God, we simply need to know it exists, and then we must ask for it. Peter and John went to Samaria and discovered that the believers there had not yet received the gift of the Holy Spirit. The Holy Spirit had not fallen upon them as it had those in the room where the 120 were gathered at Pentecost. Peter and John laid hands on the believers in Samaria and they received the gift of the Holy Spirit.

Simon, who had practiced sorcery in Samaria, had been converted and baptized. When he saw what happened to the believers, when they received the gift of the Holy Spirit, he offered money to Peter and John because he wanted the same ability to impart the gift of the Holy Spirit.

I believe Simon saw and heard these believers speak in tongues. Peter said to him, "Your money perish with you, because you thought that the gift of God could be purchased with money!" (v. 20). It was evident Simon's heart was not right with God. Peter told Simon that he needed to repent because he was poisoned by bitterness and bound by iniquity. Simon asked for Peter and John to pray for him.

Anyone who has been saved can ask for the gift of the Holy Spirit. The gift of the Holy Spirit is the same special anointing that came upon the disciples gathered in the house at Pentecost. I am so glad I asked Jesus to baptize me with the Holy Spirit when I was twenty-six years old. The first manifestation I received after asking for the Holy Spirit to come upon me was a hunger for God's Word and a boldness to witness. Two years later I received my prayer language. I was so thankful I could pray in tongues, as well as in English.

Eight years after I received my prayer language, I hit a little boy with my car. I was in such distress I could not pray in English. I was so grateful I could pray in tongues, even when my mind was in anguish.

Lord, thank You for the gift of the Holy Spirit.

Daily Deposit: If you ask, seek, and knock today, you will receive. What you receive from God today will empower you to touch other lives for eternity.

June 13

Read: I Kings II:1–12:19; Acts 9:1–25; Psalm 131:1–3; Proverbs 17:4–5

A Damascus Road Experience
Acts 9:1–25

Many times, I have prayed for people to have a "Damascus Road Experience." The experience Paul had on the road to Damascus was dramatic and he was changed from a persecutor of believers to a converter of unbelievers to have faith in Jesus Christ. As he traveled to Damascus, a light suddenly shone around him from heaven. Then he fell to the ground and heard a voice say, "Saul, Saul, why are you persecuting Me?" (v. 4). Saul asked who was speaking to him, and he heard the Lord say, "I am Jesus, whom you are persecuting. It is hard for you to kick against the goads." Saul was astonished and trembled as he asked, "Lord, what do You want me to do?" (v. 5). Then the Lord said, "Arise and go into the city, and you will be told what you must do" (v. 6).

Ananias was told by the Lord to visit Saul. Saul was blinded by the bright light. He was alone praying in his room, when he had a vision of a man Ananias who came to him and laid hands on him. In the vision, the Lord restored Paul's sight. Ananias was told by the Lord to go lay hands on Saul, and Ananias obeyed. The Lord assured Ananias that Paul was a chosen vessel to bear His name before Gentiles, kings, and the children of Israel. Ananias obeyed and layed hands on Saul, and he was filled with the Holy Spirit, receiving his sight. Paul let no grass grow under his feet. He immediately preached Christ in the synagogues and told everyone that Jesus truly was the Son of God.

To have a "Damascus Road Experience" a person needs to have the scales knocked off his eyes. The light of God needs to burn so brightly that a person is translated from the darkness of this world, with its sin, into the light of the Kingdom of God. I prayed for years for my brother-in-law to have a "Damascus Road Experience." He was not a believer, and his wife was ready to divorce him. One Friday night, I prayed with his wife and another friend. My brother-in-law had not darkened the door of a church in the eight years of their marriage. As we prayed in the spirit for my brother-in-law, I had a vision. I saw a light coming from heaven down upon him, but there was a block of wood that blocked this light from shining fully on him. When we broke generational curses over him and prayed more in the Spirit, I saw that block of wood move, and then the light from heaven was shining fully upon him. The Sunday after we agreed in prayer, my brother-in-law came to our door and told his wife they had to quickly return to their home, so they could go to church together. He son exclaimed, "Daddy are you sick?" My brother-in-law was saved the next Thursday and was baptized with the Holy Spirit two weeks later. He had a "Damascus Road Experience!"

Lord, thank You for "Damascus Road Experiences."

Daily Deposit: Your prayers for people to have a *Damascus Road Experience* will reap great rewards in this life and the next.

June 14

Read: 1 Kings 12:20–13:34; Acts 9:26–43; Psalm 132:1–18; Proverbs 17:6

Multiplication
Acts 9:26–43

David got in trouble because he was interested in numbers and he counted his army to determine his strength. Our strength comes from the Lord, not the numbers of our army. Whether we like it or not, when we became believers, we were drafted into the Lord's army. I have no idea how many are in that army to date, but we know the strength of that army is in the Lord, not in the numbers. Even though we understand that God does not concern Himself with numbers, most pastors would like to see their churches grow. We all would like to see the Kingdom of God grow.

We make a declaration in our church every Sunday, over our church. We declare in agreement that our church is strong, empowered by the Holy Spirit, that we are growing in numbers, and that everyone is being trained to live in the fear of the Lord! In this declaration, we see the secret to growth in the church, as well as in the Kingdom of God.

We read in our passage today (v. 31):

> Then the churches throughout all Judea, Galilee, and Samaria had peace and were edified. And walking in the fear of the Lord and in the comfort of the Holy Spirit, they were multiplied.

Peter was empowered by the Holy Spirit after he was baptized with the Holy Spirit at Pentecost. Saul also had received this power when Ananias laid hands on him. Paul spoke boldly in the name of the Lord Jesus and disputed against the Hellenists. Peter went to Lydda and healed Aeneas, a man who had been bedridden for eight years. Then he traveled to Joppa where he raised Dorcas from the dead. The apostles continued to do the very same miracles that Jesus had done while He walked on earth. The empowerment of the Holy Spirit gave them great boldness to witness and to pray for people to be healed and raised from the dead.

The church grew in numbers because the believers walked in the fear of the Lord. The fear of the Lord is expressed when our awesome respect and honor of God leads us to obey Him with our hearts, as well as our actions. The church was edified (built up) and was at peace because the believers walked in the fear of the Lord. Strength is not in numbers; however, the Kingdom of God is always multiplied when believers are empowered by the Holy Spirit and walk in the fear of the Lord.

Lord, empower me today with Your Holy Spirit. Help me to walk in the fear of the Lord.

Daily Deposit: Our rewards in heaven will be based upon our motivation to obey God. The works we do that are motivated by duty or pleasing man will be burned, but the works we do, because we love the Lord, will remain.

We Are Kings
1 Kings 14:1–15:24

As we read about the various kings of Judah and Israel, we see there were very few good kings. In fact, we could count the good kings all on one hand. In our passage today, we see several kings mentioned: The kings mentioned are Jeroboam, Rehoboam, Abijam, Asa, Jehoshaphat, Nadab, and Baasha. Only two of these kings were good kings. I can remember my dad teaching a study on 1 and 2 Kings. He often spoke of "Good King Asa." King Asa and his son, Jehoshaphat, were the only two good kings in the list above.

Why should we even spend time studying the various kings? As we discover both the character and the deeds of the different kings, we can learn exactly what makes a good king. Believe it or not, we are all kings! God has made us kings and priests. (See Revelation 1:6.) As kings, we represent God's kingdom here on earth. Asa and Jehoshaphat were good kings because they pulled down the idols in their land. Asa was king over Judah for forty-one years, and "Asa did what was right in the eyes of the LORD, as did his father David" (1 Kings 15:11). Asa banished the perversion out of the land and removed all the idols. He even removed his own grandmother from being queen mother because she had made an obscene image of an idol.

If we want to be a good king in God's kingdom here on earth, we also have to destroy the idols in our lives. Idol shattering is not easy. First, we have to identify the idols in our lives, and then we have to repent from our idolatry. Recently, I heard this definition of an idol: An idol is anything we think about more than we think about God. When I heard this, I had to begin to examine my thought life. When I did, I discovered many idols.

One of my major idols is clothes. I think about clothes a lot. In fact, when I am worshiping God in church, I often think about what I am going to wear the next day. A quick way to identify the idols in our lives is to pay attention to what distracts us in the middle of worship. Some women plan their menus in the middle of worship. Some men think about their schedule the next day.

The next time you are worshiping God in church, pay attention to what distracts you. It is mind-boggling to discover what stupid idols we have. When you identify the idol, you then have to smash it by taking your thoughts captive to the obedience of Jesus Christ. You may have to do this many times before your mind is free from idolatrous thinking. God is faithful, however, to help us as we take seriously the challenge to smash the idols in our lives. Today would be a good day to start smashing the idols in our lives.

Lord, thank You for helping me identify the idols in my life.

Daily Deposit: Taking our thoughts captive today to Jesus will reap eternal rewards.

We Are Included
Acts 10:24–48

A gentle breeze cooled us as we sat in the sunlight in the amphitheatre in Caesarea. My husband read this passage from Acts. He shared how important this site was to us as Gentiles, because it was here the first Gentiles received the Gospel. Most of us are familiar with the story of Cornelius, a centurion. Cornelius was fasting and praying when an angel of God appeared to him in a vision. The message the angels delivered to Cornelius reveals how God sees everything we do, and He hears every prayer we pray. The angel said, "Your prayers and your alms have come up for a memorial before God" (v. 4). Then he instructed Cornelius to send for Peter who was staying at the home of Simon the Tanner. We had the opportunity to visit the very home where Peter had his vision of the unclean things. I could just picture Peter receiving this vision on the roof, when his thoughts were interrupted by a knock on the door. It was the men Cornelius sent to invite Peter to his home.

God prepared Peter's heart to go to the home of Cornelius. Before this time, Peter was extremely exclusive in sharing the Gospel. He only went to the Jews and he only fellowshipped with Jews. God had to show Peter that no man was to be considered common or unclean. Peter finally understood the truth that God shows no partiality—that every nation who fears Him and works righteousness is accepted by Him. Truly Jesus is Lord of all. Peter began to share the Gospel. As he preached, the Holy Spirit fell upon all those gathered in Cornelius' home. The gift of the Holy Spirit was poured out upon the Gentiles and they began to speak in other tongues.

Most cults are exclusive. You usually have to do certain things or be from a certain backgrounds to belong to a cult. Many religions are exclusive also. We were all too familiar with the cast system in the Hindu religion when we were in India. The good news is that the Gospel is for all nations. The only condition for being a Christian is to believe in and receive Jesus as Savior. Paul wrote in Romans about how we can be admitted into the Kingdom of God through salvation. He said all we have to do is confess with our mouths and believe in our hearts that Jesus Christ is Lord and that He was raised from the dead to be saved and to enter into the Kingdom of God (Rom. 10:9:10, paraphrased). Faith and confession are the only two keys necessary to unlock the Kingdom of God that includes righteousness, peace and joy, and all the riches in glory through Christ Jesus. The invitation is open to all. Why do so many people refuse so great a salvation?

Lord, I pray for everyone I know who still refuse You.

Daily Deposit: Today you can share this inclusive invitation with someone. Your personal invitation to know Jesus personally can change a life for eternity.

June 17

Read: 1 Kings 18:1–46; Acts 11:1–30; Psalm 135:1–21; Proverbs 17:12–13

Exhortation
Acts 11:1–30

There are many gifts in the body of Christ. One of these gifts is the gift of exhortation. I have heard few teachings on this gift. (See Romans 12:8.) However, it is one of the most important gifts in the body of Christ. We are told in the book of Hebrews to exhort one another daily. (See Hebrews 3:13.) Few in the body of Christ take the time to call someone on the phone or to write a note of thanks when we see someone giving of themselves in service to the Lord. We are to exhort one another to love and good deeds. Many in the body of Christ have not found their place in the body. These are people who need to be exhorted to discover their gifts and to use them to strengthen the body of Christ.

I am convinced that the counseling sessions in churches would be greatly reduced if the people in the body of Christ would daily use the gift of exhortation. Most people who need counseling have a root of rejection that keeps them from giving and receiving love. If rejected people were exhorted to use the gifts God has given them in service to the body of Christ; I believe they would be fulfilled, and the thoughts of self would be changed to thoughts of service. Many counseling sessions in churches are devoted to individuals who are having trouble in their marriages. Marriages could be saved if the husband and wife made a practice of exhorting one another daily.

Today's passage gives an example of the gift of exhortation and how it works in the body of Christ. Barnabas was known for encouraging believers. We see a little of his character and his lifestyle revealed in our reading today. Barnabas was sent to Antioch. When he arrived, he saw how the grace of God was operating there, and he was glad. Then he exhorted the believers in Antioch to cleave to the Lord with purpose of heart.

Barnabas was described as a good man, who was full of the Holy Spirit and faith.

As we look at this passage, we see the qualities of an exhorter. An exhorter is filled with faith and the Holy Spirit. He is known for his goodness and always allows the grace of God to operate through him.

The Holy Spirit is an exhorter par excellence. When we are filled with the Holy Spirit, exhortations will naturally flow out of our mouths. When we are filled with the Holy Spirit, we will have faith, no matter what trials we may face. We will not only be able to rejoice in the midst of trials, but we will also be able to encourage others when they go through trials. We can conclude that to be an excellent exhorter, we must stay filled with the Holy Spirit.

Lord, help me to stay filled with the Holy Spirit. I want to be an excellent exhorter.

Daily Deposit: Exhort someone today who needs encouragement.

June 18

Read: 1 Kings 19:1–21; Acts 12:1–23; Psalm 136:1–26; Proverbs 17:14–15

Activation of Angels
Acts 12:1–23

The book of Acts describes the many acts of the believers in Jesus Christ after He ascended. These followers of Jesus were able to do the same works—and even greater works—that Jesus did on earth. One of the reasons they were able to do so many great works is that they were not alone. These men and women of God were filled with the Holy Spirit and they were assisted by myriads of angels. Wouldn't you like to be assisted by myriads of angels?

Psalm 103 reveals the secret to activating angels. Angels hearken to the voice of God's Word. (See Psalm 103:20.) Hebrews tells us that angels are spirits sent to minister to the saints. (See Hebrews 1:14.) One of our main assignments on earth is to give God's Word voice.

When we declare God's Word in prayer, things begin to happen in the spirit realm. We cannot see what is happening, but we know angels are helping us. How do we know this? When Daniel fasted for Israel, it took three weeks before he had his answer. After three weeks, the angel Gabriel appeared to him and told him that God heard his prayer the very first day he began to pray, but there was warfare in heaven that delayed the answer. Michael came and helped Gabriel fight against the Prince of Persia—another angel who did not want Daniel's prayer to be answered. (See Daniel 10.)

In our passage today, a group of believers were assembled in the home of Mary and were praying for Peter. Their prayers activated the angels and an angel came and got Peter out of prison. Peter was chained between two guards when the angel of the Lord appeared to him and set him free. Everything happened so fast that Peter thought he was having a vision. When Peter knocked on the door where these believers were praying, they thought they were having a vision.

These believers were probably praying for God to judge Herod, since he was the one who arrested Peter. Angels were also activated as a result of their prayers and, later, Herod was struck dead by the angel of the Lord. I am challenged by these stories to speak God's Word more often as I pray.

Lord, thank You for ministering angels who can assist me.

Daily Deposit: Every time we give God's Word voice here on earth, those words are added to our Book of Remembrance in heaven. (See Malachi 3:16.)

June 19

Read: I Kings 20:1–21:29; Acts 12:24–13:15; Psalm 137:1–9; Proverbs 17:16

God of the Hills and Valleys
I Kings 20:21–29

When I go to retreats, I usually have a mountaintop experience and I want to remain on the mountain. I dread going back to the routine of life when the business of every day crowds out my times in the presence of the Lord. I forget that the Lord is present with me always, whether I feel His presence or not. He is present with me, even when I miss my quiet times in the morning. God is present with me when I go through hard trials. God is truly the God of both our hills and the valleys.

Nature reveals that the valleys are much more fruitful than the mountains. We had the opportunity to drive through the Napa Valley in California. We were amazed at the lush vineyards in the valley. As our bus left to travel up the mountains, we noticed that the vegetation dwindled. There is a spiritual lesson we can learn from this natural phenomenon. During the valleys in our lives, we have the greatest opportunity to bear fruit. The fruit of the Spirit is love, joy, peace, long-suffering, kindness, goodness, faithfulness, gentleness, and self-control. (See Galatians 5:22–23.) If we trust in the Lord and draw strength from His Word during our trials, the fruit of the Spirit is developed in our lives. Others will notice the peace we have in the midst of tragic circumstances. They will observe the sustaining joy that overflows from us in the midst of sorrow.

I had a high school friend who lost two husbands in private plane crashes. When we had a high school reunion, so many of her fellow students asked her why she had such strength during these tragedies. Their questions opened the door for her to share her faith and to tell them it was the Lord who strengthened her.

In our passage today, the Lord delivered Israel from Syria because Syria thought Israel's God was only the God of the mountains. They decided to war with Israel in the plains, and Israel won the battle. We forget that the battle is the Lord's and the victory is ours.

Jesus will win every battle for us if we will trust Him to be the Lord of both the mountains and the valleys in our lives. We don't have to dread the valleys. It is in the valleys that the Lord shows Himself strong on our behalf. It is in the valley experiences of our lives that the fruit of the Spirit is cultivated and developed in us. A life without valleys is a life without victories. This is the victory that overcomes the world, even our faith. As we release our faith in the valley seasons of life, we will see great fruit birthed and developed in our character. We also will see a harvest of souls—people who will come to the Lord because of our witness during the valley seasons of life.

Lord, thank You for being Lord of the mountains and the valleys in my life.

Daily Deposit: When we trust the Lord in the valleys on this earth, we will receive great rewards in heaven. Our trials of faith will be more precious than gold.

June 20

Justified by Faith
Acts 13:16–41

The glad tidings Paul was preaching was that we are justified by faith, not by works. Paul said that all who believe in Jesus are justified by Him, not by the law of Moses. (See Acts 13:39.) The word *justified* can mean "just as if I never sinned." When we believe and receive what Jesus did on the cross for us, and we confess that Jesus was raised from the dead, and confess Him as Lord of our lives, we are saved and we are justified. (See Romans 10:8–10.) The blood Jesus shed on the cross purchased both our salvation and our justification. It is not what we do in this life that justifies us. It is what Jesus has done for us, over 2,000 years ago when He died on the cross, that justifies us.

As I write this devotional, we are ministering in many churches in Jamaica. We just discovered that many in these churches have no assurance of salvation. They believe that if they sin they can lose their salvation. If it were true that committing sin can cause us to lose our salvation, then we would all be doomed. We all sin and fall short of the glory of God.

When we believe we are justified by faith, not by works, we will be able to have the full assurance of our salvation. When Jesus died on the cross for our sins, He forgave us of all of our sins (past, present, and future). Nothing can separate us from the love of Jesus Christ. Jesus paid the full debt for our sins on the cross. Our sins can separate us from our fellowship with God, but our sins will never separate us from our relationship with Jesus Christ.

John 3:16 says, "For God so loved the world that He gave His only begotten Son, that whoever believes in Him should not perish but have everlasting life." This is the scriptural basis we have for total justification. God did not send His Son to condemn the world, but to save the world.

We learn in our next reading that the Gentiles in Antioch who heard this good news about justification begged Paul to preach these same words on the next Sabbath. We should not have to be begged to preach this great news about our justification through Jesus' death on the cross. We should be shouting it from the housetops. Have you shared this good news with someone this week?

Lord, thank You for Your salvation that is so full and free!

Daily Deposit: When you share the good news about justification with someone, that person's life could be changed for all eternity.

The Light of the Gospel
Acts 13:42–14:7

Jewish people were the first to take the light of the Gospel to the nations. They were chosen by God to be a light to the Gentiles. The message of justification Paul preached was well received by the Gentiles. The next Sabbath, when Paul preached, the whole city gathered to hear the Word of God. Many of those gathered were Gentiles.

Some of the unbelieving Jewish people became jealous because the Gentiles were being stirred to receive Jesus Christ. Some of the Jews even contradicted and blasphemed the words spoken by Paul. Paul told them how God offered the gospel first to the Jews. Paul explained that since many Jewish people rejected the message, it was time for him to reach out to the Gentiles with the good news of justification.

When Paul left Antioch to go on to Iconium, many of the Jews followed him. Their mission was to disrupt Paul's gatherings. God was faithful, however, and signs and wonders were manifested to convince the people that Paul's words were true. Even with these signs and wonders, unbelieving Jews and Gentiles came against Paul and plotted to stone him.

Persecution by unbelievers continued throughout Paul's journeys. One time he was stoned and left for dead. The disciples and Paul, however, were never daunted by this persecution. They continued to preach the gospel from city to city, "and the disciples were filled with joy and with the Holy Spirit" (v. 52).

There will always be those who oppose the Gospel. Darkness hates the light. Jesus said, "Blessed are those who are persecuted for righteousness' sake, For theirs is the kingdom of heaven" (Matt. 5:10). The blessing we receive when we are persecuted for sharing the Gospel is overwhelming joy. When persecution comes, we realize that we are making an impact against the forces of darkness, and this brings great joy to our hearts.

The greatest persecution we experienced, as we traveled through the world to share the Gospel, was in Russia. We had an outreach to bring the Gospel to Russian Jews through free musical festivals. At these festivals, religious Jews gathered and picketed and tried to get people not to go into the concert hall. We felt like we were reliving this Acts account. These religious Jews were unsuccessful and thousands of Jewish people came to know Jesus as their Messiah. There was an outbreak of joy at these concerts. Those who shared the Gospel and those who received the Gospel were filled with joy and the Holy Spirit. The light of the Gospel will always produce great joy even in the midst of persecution.

Lord, thank You for Your joy that strengthens Your disciples today.

Daily Deposit: Reach out to someone with the good news today!

June 22

A Sure Promise
Acts 14:8–28

We love to quote all the Scripture promises, but there are some promises we seldom quote. Such a promise is found in our reading today. The quote is, "We must through many tribulations enter the kingdom of God" (Acts 14:22). These were the encouraging words of exhortation Paul gave to the disciples when he returned to Lystra, Iconium, and Antioch. Many in these cities had believed the Gospel and were now disciples who were sharing this good news with others. Paul's goal, as he revisited these cities, was to strengthen the souls of these new disciples. Why would this message strengthen souls?

If someone came to your church today preaching the message that through much tribulation you would enter the kingdom of God, what would be your reaction? I'm afraid many of us would not receive this message. We don't like to think about tribulation. We want our faith in Christ to protect us from tribulation. However, the truth is that if we are true believers, we will experience much tribulation. The world will hate us because of our message, and we will be persecuted for righteousness sake. Jesus told us that we would have tribulation, simply because we live in a fallen world. He also exhorted us to be of good cheer because He had overcome the world. (See John 16:33.) James, the brother of Jesus, told us to count it all joy when various trials come upon us. (See James 1:2.)

The sure promise is that we will all experience tribulation. Another sure promise, however, is that we can experience joy in the midst of tribulation. How can this be?

One day when I was squeezing lemons to make lemon pie, I had an understanding of this promise. I first cut the lemons in half. Then I pressed the cut lemon against the raised pillar of the glass juicer. After the juice came from the lemon, I strained the juice so there would be no pulp or seed in the juice that I was adding to the pie. What that lemon went through, to produce a delicious lemon pie that brought joy to everyone who tasted it, can be compared to what we go through during tribulation times. First, we begin to have our flesh cut away, as our minds are renewed by the Word of God. Next, tests and trials begin to press the essence of the fruit of the Spirit (love) from our lives. Finally, these trials and tests, during tribulation times, all blend together to form a life that displays Christ.

Joy is one of the manifestations of the fruit of the Spirit (love). "The Kingdom of God is not eating and drinking, but righteousness and peace and joy in the Holy Spirit" (Rom. 14:17). The joy of the Lord is our strength, and His joy is able to come forth from our lives when we are pressed and pruned. To enter into the kingdom of God, where we can experience the true essence of the joy of the Lord, we must experience tribulation.

Lord, help me to be conformed to Your image, as I experience tribulation.

Daily Deposit: Eternal rewards await those who pass through tribulation.

June 23

Salvation Plus
Acts 15:1–31

There was a dispute among the Jews about circumcision. Some of the Jews felt the Gentile believers should be circumcised. Peter stood up and declared that it was not necessary for the Gentiles to be circumcised, because they were saved by grace, not the works of the law. After much discussion, it was decided that the Gentiles should not be burdened by having to follow Jewish laws of circumcision. In Ephesians, there are some powerful lessons learned:

- Faith + Grace = Salvation. This is the equation for salvation given in Ephesians 2:8–9:

  For by grace you have been saved through faith, and that not of yourselves; it is the gift of God, not of works, lest anyone should boast.

- The equation for salvation is not: Faith + Grace + Works = Salvation

We should all rejoice that God has required nothing of us to be saved, except faith. And even faith is a gift of God. All we have to do is receive the gift of salvation by faith. Salvation is a free gift to all who will believe and receive it. We cannot even brag about our faith. The only thing we have a right to brag about is the Lord Who has given His life to purchase our salvation. A good definition of grace is this acronym:

God's
Riches
At
Christ's
Expense

How can we refuse the great gift of salvation? It is free, but it cost Jesus everything. The major block to receiving any gift is pride. No man can come to know Jesus Christ unless the Father draws him. The effective prayer of a righteous man avails much, and your effective prayers for the salvation of your loved ones and friends will avail much.

Lord, help me to effectively pray for the salvation of others.

Daily Deposit: Use your weapons of warfare today to pull down the strongholds that block people from receiving the gift of salvation.

June 24

Come to My House
Acts 15:32–16:15

One of the greatest joys I have experienced over the years has been hosting many guests in our home. We even built a little apartment next to our home to house people as they came through our city. We had a Chinese girl come to spend one night with us, and she stayed with us for five years. We had a Russian young man come, as an exchange student, to live with us for one year, and he was with us for seven years. When I share these stories with others, they often laughingly ask us if they could come spend the night in our home. At one time we had people from Israel sleeping upstairs and people from Colombia sleeping downstairs in our home. We have housed people from Israel, China, Russia, England, France, Italy, Germany, Australia, Japan, Ukraine, Hungary, Africa, South America, and Israel.

Several scriptures exhort us to be hospitable. Peter exhorts us to be hospitable to one another without grumbling. (See 1 Peter 4:9.) The writer of Hebrews tells us that if we entertain strangers, we might be actually entertaining angels. (See Hebrews 13:2.) I don't believe any of those we hosted over the years were angels, but many of them were true saints!

We see in our reading today that Lydia had the gift of hospitality. She was at the river, probably washing her clothes, when she overheard Paul and Silas praying. She asked them to baptize her, and then she invited them to come to her home. Because Lydia was willing to open her home to Paul and Silas, the first church in Macedonia was established in her home.

When we bought our home, we prayed this prayer as we anointed the doors of our new home: "Lord, may everyone who enters our home be saved and anointed and filled by Your Holy Spirit"

When I shared this prayer with some of my friends, they made a special effort to have their unsaved relatives and friends come to our home. One of my neighbors sent her unsaved husband to borrow some bread.

The gift of hospitality will continue in heaven. I heard that the size of our mansions will be determined by the number of people we have led to the Lord. We will be hosting these people from time to time in eternity. How big will your mansion be?

Lord, help me always to be given to hospitality.

Daily Deposit: Demonstrate brotherly love today by inviting someone for coffee or for a meal.

What Is in Your Heart?
2 Kings 8:1–9:15

Elisha began to weep when he spoke to Hazael. Hazael had come to Elisha to ask him if King Ben-Hadad would die from his present illness. When Elisha told Hazael that the king would not die, Hazael was not happy about what seemed to be good news. Elisha began to weep, as God revealed to him what was in Hazael's heart. Elisha prophesied that Hazeal would set young men on fire and even rip babies out of pregnant women. Hazael was alarmed that such wickedness would ever come from him, but Hazael had a wicked heart. Elisha told Hazael he would be king of Syria. Hazael took matters into his own hands and smothered King Ben-Hadad when he was in his own bed.

We cannot hide the wickedness in our hearts from God. We are capable of committing every sin known to man, because we all have fleshly lusts. The Bible tells us that our hearts are despitefully wicked. Who can know our hearts? We do not even know our own hearts. Only God knows our hearts. This is why we have to ask God daily to search our hearts and to reveal to us any wickedness in us. We can pray as David prayed, "Create in me a clean heart, O God, And renew a steadfast spirit within me" (Ps. 51:10).

The good news is that when we receive Jesus Christ as our Lord and Savior, we also receive a new heart. The law of God is written upon our hearts, and the love of God can now be shed abroad in our hearts. When we accept Jesus as our Savior and Lord, we receive a heart transplant. We become new creatures with new hearts. We are still capable of sin, but we now have the ability to not give in to temptation when satan tempts us in the area of our three lusts (the lust of the flesh, the lust of the eyes, and the pride of life). Our carnal nature is still capable of sinning, but as we daily reckon that carnal nature dead, and consider ourselves by faith to be alive to Jesus Christ, we will begin to experience the joy of walking in the Spirit.

If we stay filled with the Holy Spirit we will not fulfill the lusts of our flesh. The new heart we have will keep pumping Christ's life through us, as we daily submit our bodies to the Lord as a living sacrifice. We are the body of Christ and He has given us a heart that is capable of the same love that He has.

Lord, help me to stay filled with the Spirit so that the love of God can always be shed abroad in my heart.

Daily Deposit: Allow the love of Jesus Christ to fill your new heart and overflow to others today.

June 26

What's On Your Mind?
Acts 17:1—34

Yesterday we talked about what is in our hearts. Often what is in our hearts is revealed by what is on our minds. Whatever captures our thoughts is a result of the condition of our hearts. The accusations whirled at Christians is that they are too narrow-minded. Those in the world often tell us we need to be more open-minded. Today's reading discusses both the closed mind and the open mind.

The Jews in Thessalonica were closed to what Paul taught. They were envious, because Paul was gaining many followers as he taught in their city. These Jews attacked Jason who was hosting Paul and Silas, and Paul and Silas had to flee for their lives to Berea. In Berea the Jews were more open-minded about Paul's message. Paul described the Bereans as fire-minded people who received the word with all readiness and searched the scriptures daily to find out whether these things were so.

The Bereans did what we all need to do. We need to check out everything with the scriptures. Only the Word of God has the power to discern the thoughts and intents of our hearts and to also reveal who is speaking to our hearts. There are three broadcasters who speak daily to our hearts. Satan speaks to our hearts and tries to capture our thought life through his strategy of seduction. Our own flesh speaks to our hearts and says, "I feel, I think, and I want." This is the voice we usually hear. The Holy Spirit speaks to our hearts through the scriptures and through His still, quiet voice. When we know the scriptures well, we will be able to immediately recognize which voice is speaking to us.

Open-mindedness is only good if we check what our spiritual receptors are receiving. Paul found the Athenians were extremely open-minded because they were always looking for something new. This mindset describes the mindset of today. New Age has its roots in this kind of open-mindedness.

There are five receptors that transfer messages to our minds. These five receptors are our five senses–touch, taste, sight, hearing, and smell. These receptors are the gates of our mind. We can choose daily to open these gates to receive worldly or godly thoughts. What we choose to taste, touch, see, hear, and smell will determine our thought life. What is on your mind today?

Lord, help me to keep my mind stayed upon You today.

Daily Deposit: Hide some of God's Word in your heart today by memorizing and meditating on the scriptures. Your renewed mind will go with you to heaven.

June 27

Repairing the Damages
2 Kings 10:32—12:21

God is interested in the physical condition of the buildings on our church properties, but He is more interested in the living stones that make up the building of the body of Christ here on earth. When I was a little girl, we used to play a little game with our hands. We folded our two hands together and interlocked our fingers. We lifted our two index fingers to form a church steeple, and used our thumbs as doors. Then we said this little jingle, "Here is the church, here is the steeple, open the doors (we opened our thumbs out), and see the people." Then we moved our fingertips inside our interlocked hands to represent a multitude of people. The true church of God is people.

You have probably heard the expression, "The church is a hospital for sinners, not a haven for saints." Many of the living stones in the body of Christ need repair. Their hearts have been hurt through rejection and offense. We can have a lovely church building, but if the people in the church are not daily being restored and repaired, we have a church in disrepair.

Our passage today tells about how the temple was in disrepair, both physically and spiritually. Athaliah, the mother of Ahazriah had killed all the king's sons, with the exception of Joash. The daughter of King Joram hid Joash from Athaliah. Athaliah had control over the land until Joash became king when he was seven years old. At that time Athaliah was killed. During Athaliah's reign, the temple was used for Baal worship, and it was in need of both physical and spiritual restoration.

When Joash became king, Johoida the priest made a covenant to dedicate the people and the king to the Lord. The altars to Baal were torn down and the land was purged from idol worship, with the exception of the high places. A box for offerings to repair the temple was placed in the temple, and the work of physical restoration of the temple began.

What is the condition of your church? Are there hurting, rejected people to whom you need to reach out? Only Jesus can heal the broken heart, but all of us can be His physician assistants as we pray with and for hurting people. The first priority of every church should be to minister to the Lord and then to the people. When Jesus is allowed to heal the brokenhearted, set the captives free, give beauty for ashes, and the garment of praise to those who are heavyhearted, the church will be beautified both physically and spiritually.

Lord, help me to reach out to those who are heavy in heart.

Daily Deposit: Is there someone you need to encourage today? One word of encouragement may change a life for eternity.

June 28

The High Places
2 Kings 13:1–14:29

As we study the various kings of Judah and Israel, we often see this phrase, "However the high places were not taken away, and the people still sacrificed and burned incense on the high places" (2 Kings 14:4). Because the high places were not taken away, both Israel and Judah were often defeated by their enemies. The high places were groves of trees on the mountaintops where people gathered in secret to worship idols.

Some cults today meet on high places to practice their satanic rituals. I have prayed for the destruction of many high places in several cities. One of the places I went to pray had places for burnt sacrifices. Our prayer team used our weapons in the spirit to pull that high place down.

Most of us would never think of burning incense to idols in high places like some cults do; however, we do daily give our allegiance to various idols in our lives. The high places in our lives consist of thoughts that exalt themselves above the knowledge of Jesus Christ. Anything that captures our thought life other than Jesus is an idol.

The way to identify the idols in our lives is to pay attention to our thought life. What consumes most of our thoughts daily? Is it our family, our jobs, our friends, or even our church? All of these things are worthy of our thoughts, but if they possess our thought life, we are guilty of idolatry. You have heard the expression, "An idle mind is the devil's playground." This is a true statement, but just as true is the statement that a mind filled with the cares of this world is also the devil's playground.

When we are worried and fearful about worldly things, we are in idolatry. We have not released our cares to the Lord. Instead, we try to work out our problems without His help. When we do this, we are in pride and the idol we are worshiping is ourselves.

Prideful thoughts are the high places in our minds that most of us need to pull down. Pride always exalts itself against God. If the high place of pride is not pulled down in our minds, we will live a continual life of defeat. We will have both God and the devil as our enemies. God resists the proud, but He gives grace to the humble. The source of strife is pride, and strife opens the door to every evil work of Satan.

Have you dealt with the high places in your life? Think now about what consumes your daily thoughts. Then pull down these thoughts by using the weapons of the Word of God and prayer. When the high places are pulled down, God will cause you to ride upon the high places in the Spirit with Him.

Lord, help me to pull down the high places in my mind.

Daily Deposit: Take your thoughts captive today to the obedience of Jesus Christ.

June 29

Reasons to Praise the Lord
Psalms 147:1–20

One of the ways to take our thoughts captive to the obedience of Jesus Christ is to live a life of continual praise. King David praised the Lord seven times a day. He wrote many songs of praise. David wrote in the psalm in today's reading, "Praise, the LORD! For it is good to sing praises to our God; For it is pleasant, and praise is beautiful" (Ps. 147:1–2). In this psalm David gives a multitude of reasons to praise the Lord. Here are just a few:

1. The Lord gathers the outcasts of Israel (v. 2).
2. The Lord heals the brokenhearted and binds their wounds (v. 3).
3. The Lord calls the stars by name and counts them all (v. 4).
4. The Lord's power is great and His understanding is infinite (v.5).
5. The Lord lifts up the humble and casts down the wicked (v. 6).
6. The Lord prepares rain for the earth and makes the grass to grow (v. 8).
7. The Lord gives food to the beast (v. 9).
8. The Lord blesses the children within you (v. 13).
9. The Lord makes peace in your borders and fills you with the finest of wheat (v. 14).
10. The Lord causes His Word to run swiftly (v. 15).
11. The Lord gives snow and scatters the frost (v. 16).
12. He causes the wind to blow and the waters to flow (v. 28).

These are just twelve reasons to praise the Lord. The next time you are having a battle in your thought life, think of these reasons to praise the Lord. Begin to declare them out loud. When the devil comes against you with vexing thoughts, you can vex him and put him to confusion when you begin to praise the Lord. Have you praised Him today?

Lord, help me to live a continual life of praise like King David did.

Daily Deposit: When we praise the Lord on earth, we are able to add to His glory in heaven. God is dressed in garments of glory and He dwells in the midst of our praises. As we praise God on earth, God's glory intensifies.

June 30

Idol Worship
2 Kings 17–18:12

We talked earlier about the high places where both Israel and Judah set up shrines and pillars and burned incense to other gods. God allowed Assyria to successfully invade Israel. God was so angry with Israel that He removed them from His sight and delivered them into the hands of plunderers (17:20). The king of Assyria brought the people of Babylon—Cuthah, Ava, Hamath, Sepharvaim—and placed them in the cities of Samaria, instead of the children of Israel. These people brought their own gods with them, and Israel began to worship these gods. When I looked up the names of some of the gods, I was shocked to find out some of these gods were exactly the gods or idols our nation worships today.

The men of Babylon made *Succoth Benoth*. Succoth Benoth was the name of the tents that were set up to house prostitutes. These tents would be similar to our brothels or houses of prostitution. Israel worshipped this god of Babylon. The men of Cuth made a god called *Nergal*. Nergal was similar to the Egyptian sun god. They worshipped the sun and bowed down to it. The men of Hamath made *Ashima* (a sex goddess). The Avites made *Nibhaz* and *Tartak*. Nibhaz was the god of pleasure, and Tartak was the worship of a past hero (hero worship). The Sepharvites burned their children in fire to *Adrammelech*. Adrammelech was the son of Sennacherib (a war hero).

Our nation today is inundated by pornography, prostitution, and pleasure seeking. One only has to attend a national sports event or a rock concert to see the hero worship connected with sports heroes and rock singers. "Fun in the sun" is the theme of many Americans, especially in the summertime.

The statement about Israel was that they feared the Lord, yet served their own gods, according to the rituals of the nations from among whom they were carried away (17:33). There was a real spiritual mixture in Israel. That same mixture exists in America today. Even new age philosophy is beginning to invade mainline denominations. I pray that God will not remove us from His sight as He did Israel.

Lord, deliver our nation from idolatry.

Daily Deposit: The result of idolatry is always destruction. As believers, we have the responsibility to warn people about the consequences of idolatry and challenge them to fear the Lord with all their hearts. Are there people whom you love today who need to be warned? Your warning could save their lives for eternity.

July 1

The Martyr Spirit
Acts 21:1–17

Recently, I heard the testimony of a missionary to Mexico. He said he would count it a privilege to be martyred for Jesus Christ. He told us how he went alone into a dangerous area in the mountains of Mexico. There had been many robberies and murders in this area, but he felt he needed to preach the Gospel there. Bandits attacked him and pulled him off his horse. He was beaten badly and left for dead. His horse fled during the attack, but there was enough strength left in the man to whistle for his horse. As this man lifted his badly beaten body over the saddle of his horse, some Gospel tracts fell out of his saddlebag. The horse returned the man to his home. A young teenager watched the robbery from a hillside, but he was afraid he would be killed if he tried to help. After the man left, this teenager walked down the hill to have a closer look at the scene of the crime. There was a piece of paper on the ground. He picked up the paper and read it.

Several years later this man returned to preach at a church in those same mountains. A young man came to talk with him after the service. The young man told how he had seen the robbery from a nearby hill. He said after he read the tract, the Lord saved him and he was now preaching the Gospel.

Even though great fruit came forth from this robbery, I do not think it is God's will for us to put ourselves in harm's way with the thought we might be martyred. I may be wrong, but I believe a living witness is better than a dead one. In our passage today, Agabus, a trusted prophet, told Paul he would be bound by the Jews and given over to the Gentiles if he went to Jerusalem. The disciples wept and begged Paul not to go to Jerusalem. He was not persuaded, and said, "The will of the Lord be done."

Paul had many opportunities to be martyred, but the Lord spared him until his work was finished on earth. Paul wanted God's will first, not his own will. He trusted his life into God's hands and always sought to be in the center of God's will. We know that Paul was eventually martyred, along with many of the other disciples. Paul's focus was doing the will of the Lord, even if it meant martyrdom. When our first priority is to do the will of our Heavenly Father, I believe we can confidently put the length of our days in His hands. I often pray this prayer:

> Lord, put me in the right place at the right time, and keep me in the center of Your will. I place my days into Your hands. Allow me to live out the days that are promised me in my book of life.

Daily Deposit: Yesterday is history, tomorrow is a mystery, but today is a gift. Let God have His way with your day today, and you will accomplish His will today.

July 2

Jewish Roots
Acts 21:18–36

J ust in the last ten years there has been a movement by Messianic Jewish believers to inform Christians about their Jewish roots. Some Gentile Christians have forgotten that the early church was mostly Jewish. They also do not realize that the Bible is written by Jewish people, with the exception of the books of Acts and Luke. Gentile believers owe a great debt to the Jewish people. Jesus Christ is a Jew. God graciously has included Gentiles in His plan of salvation, but Jesus' first call was to declare the Gospel of the Kingdom of God to Jewish people. Our youngest son is presently in Budapest, Hungary, where he is teaching the local churches all about their Jewish roots. He hopes to pull down some of the strongholds of anti-Semitism in Hungary. God hates anti-Semitism.

Our passage today reveals a problem between Jewish and Gentile believers. Through Paul's ministry, many Gentiles had become believers in Jesus Christ. Paul shared with James, the head of the church in Jerusalem, all about his ministry to the Gentiles. When the church in Jerusalem heard Paul's experiences with the Gentiles, they all glorified the Lord and gave thanks.

James shared with Paul that many Jews were saying that Paul wanted them to forsake the law of Moses. This is the exact argument given by Jewish people who resist the Gospel today. They believe that if they accept Jesus as their Messiah, they will have to forsake their Jewish roots. The truth is that Jewish believers in Jesus do not forsake their Jewish roots. In fact, their roots even grow deeper into their magnificent Jewish heritage.

The Church in Jerusalem decided not to require Gentiles to fulfill the Jewish laws of purification, with only these exceptions: they were to "keep themselves from things offered to idols, from blood, from things strangled, and from sexual immorality" (v. 25). When Paul brought the Gentiles into the temple, many of the religious Jews were infuriated and sought to kill him, but a Roman centurion intervened and saved Paul's life.

The goal of our Heavenly Father is to gather all unto Himself (both Jews and Gentiles). We are at liberty to keep our unique customs, but we are to be one in the Spirit. The law of Moses is still to be observed, but the good news is that Jesus has fulfilled the whole law. As believers, we now have the law written upon our hearts. The promise to Jewish people is that one day the law also will be written upon their hearts. (See Jeremiah 31:33.)

Lord, thank You for including me in Your great plan of salvation.

Daily Deposit: Take every opportunity to express your love and gratefulness to Jewish friends and neighbors.

The Ministry of the Moment
Acts 21:37–22:16

Many Christians look forward to the day when their ministries will be fruitful. They spend their lives in preparation for their ministries, but they forget the "Ministry of the Moment." One of the tricks of satan is to keep us looking forward to the future or dreading the future, so that we cannot walk by faith in the present moment. He also tries to keep us bound by the hurts of our past, so we cannot be used by the Lord in the present.

If we look carefully at the life of Paul and the life of Jesus we see the secret of their successful ministries. They believed in the "Ministry of the Moment." They both understood the truth that faith can only operate in the present moment.

Jesus ministered to whoever was in front of Him at the moment. We see in our passage today how Paul took every opportunity to share the Gospel. After his arrest, as he was climbing the stairs of the Roman barracks, he asked permission to speak to the people. He was given permission and Paul boldly shared his testimony in Hebrew to the people.

Paul never missed a moment to share the Gospel. We know he continued to use his moments to share the Gospel both to the Romans when he was in prison and to encourage the churches through the letters he wrote when he was in prison. I learned the "Ministry of the Moment" when I almost died from the loss of blood after a miscarriage. When my life was draining out of me and my spirit was leaving my body, I knew I might not have another moment. When I awoke from the anesthesia, administered to me before the doctors operated to stop the bleeding, I was so grateful that I had more moments to express my love to Jesus and to others.

In my first devotional this month I shared this saying: "Yesterday is history, tomorrow is a mystery, but today is a gift." I would change that saying to read, "Yesterday is history, tomorrow is a mystery, but this moment is a gift." We have no guarantee that we will have another moment.

Lord, help me to minister to whoever I encounter in the moments of this day.

Daily Deposit: What you share with others in your telephone conversations and face-to-face encounters with others today could change a life for all eternity.

Our Citizenship
Acts 22:17–23:10

We unfolded our camp chairs and got in position to see the largest display of fireworks in the Southeast. It was the 4th of July, and we had to wait almost two hours. One of my favorite hobbies is people watching. We sat and enjoyed this hobby together, as we observed people from ever nation pass by us. A lovely African family hurriedly passed by. The father was giving instructions to his children in some African dialect. A Chinese family smiled at us when we said, "Nehou" (the Chinese greeting of hello). We picked up familiar words in Spanish, when a Spanish couple was rushing to find their position to watch the show. It seemed like every nationality was present in Atlanta to celebrate Independence Day.

Since gaining our independence from England in 1776, our nation has opened its arms to people from every nation. Many of these people have become U.S. Citizens. Our Russian son who lived with us for seven years is going to receive his citizenship this year.

Our passage today tells how Paul avoided scourging by the Romans, because he proved he was a Roman citizen. When the Romans discovered his heritage, they took him to be heard by the Jewish council. Paul, once again, used this opportunity to share the Gospel. He discerned that some of the Jews were Pharisees and others were Sadducees. Paul knew how to skillfully share the gospel with people from every nation, culture, and religion.

Paul declared that he was a Pharisee who believed in the resurrection. The Sadducees did not believe in the resurrection. Soon, dissensions began to erupt between these two religious sects. Once again, a Roman centurion intervened and took Paul into the barracks for his protection.

Paul's true citizenship was in heaven. He wrote that we are ambassadors for Christ here on earth. (See 2 Corinthians 5:20).

As ambassadors, we represent our King, Jesus, and our country, Heaven, wherever God sends us. We have the message to carry to all nations that will bring them peace, joy, and love, and most of all salvation.

Lord, help me to skillfully share the Gospel with people from every nation.

Daily Deposit: Ask Jesus today to sharpen your presentation of the Gospel. Be ready to share effectively with people of different religions and cultures.

Faithful to the Call
Acts 23:11–35

My middle son's favorite scripture is "Faithful is He that calls you, who also will do it" (1 Thess. 5:24). My life verse is, "For it is God who works in you both to will and to do for His good pleasure" (Phil. 2:13). We all have the call to fulfill God's will and to do things that please Him. Each of us also has a unique calling. God sees to it that we are equipped to fulfill that call.

Paul was trained from his youth to fulfill His calling. His calling was to be a witness to every nation. He went to the Jews first. When his message was rejected by them, he took the Gospel message to the Gentiles. Because Paul was both a citizen of Rome and a student of the Hebrew Scriptures, he was effective in his witness to both Jews and Gentiles.

Paul was always willing to give His personal testimony to anyone who would listen. His personal testimony included how Jesus pursued and persuaded him on the road to Damascus. Paul was faithful to his calling, and Jesus went ahead of him to open doors for him to witness. Sometimes we do not know what doors God will open for us to witness.

Jesus opened prison doors in Macedonia for Paul and Silas to witness to a prison guard and his family. Now Jesus was closing the prison door in Rome for Paul to be a witness there. Jesus, Himself, appeared to Paul while he was in the Roman barracks. Jesus told Paul that, just as Paul testified of Him in Jerusalem, he would be given the opportunity to testify of Him in Rome.

I am corresponding now with a lady in a women's state prison in California who is in prison for life without a chance of parole. She wrote me that in prison she found Jesus, and, although she is enclosed by prison walls, she is free and liberated in the Spirit. God is using her to be a witness to others who are bound.

Jesus holds the keys of David. He can open the doors that no man can open and close the doors that no man can shut. The doors he may open for you to be a witness may not be of your own choosing. You can rest assured, however, that Jesus will go before you to prepare the hearts of the hearers wherever He opens a door of witness for you.

Lord, I trust You to open the doors for me to be Your witness.

Daily Deposit: Wherever you find yourself today is a good place to witness.

July 6

Does God Hear Every Prayer?
Psalm 4:1–8

"Hear me when I call, O God of my righteousness! You have relieved me in my distress; Have mercy on me, and hear my prayer" (Ps. 4:1). David cried out to God to hear his prayer. People have asked me this question, "How can I be sure God hears my prayers?"

In these last days, we have to have confidence that God both hears and answers our prayers. In 1 John 5:13–15, we are told to have confidence that God both hears our prayers and that He also will grant our petitions. John exhorts us to continue to believe in the name of the Son of God. Then he writes that we can have confidence that God hears us if we ask according to His will. The only way we can know we are asking according to God's will is to ask according to God's Word. God reveals His will in His Word.

John tells us that we can know God hears our prayers, but there are conditions we must fulfill in order to have such confidence. These conditions are outlined both in this passage in 1 John 5 and Psalm 4. In order to know for sure that God will hear our prayers, we need to:

1. Continue to believe in Jesus, and pray with faith (1 John 5:13).
2. Ask according to God's will (1 John 5:14).
3. Confess our sins (Ps. 4:4).
4. Continue in God's Word (Ps. 4:4).
5. Put our trust in the Lord (Ps. 4:5).

Have you ever felt like your prayers were just hitting the ceiling instead of ascending to heaven? At those times, we need to ask the Lord to reveal to us any sins we need to confess. David in another psalm cried out to God to search him and know his heart and reveal any wicked way within him. (See Psalm 139:24.) When we confess our sins, God is faithful and just to forgive us of our sins and to cleanse us from all unrighteousness.

In Psalm 4:5, David exhorts us to offer the sacrifices of righteousness. I believe we need to offer our sins to God, and when we do He is able to create within us a clean heart and renew a right spirit within us. Another psalm of David tells us that if we regard iniquity in our hearts, God will not hear our prayers. (See Psalm 66:18.) We regard iniquity in our hearts when we do not confess our own sins before the Lord. The psalm concludes with this statement, "You have put gladness in my heart…I will both lie down in peace, and sleep" (Ps. 4:7, 8). Whenever we put our full confidence in the Lord and know that He will answer our prayers according to His will, we can have that same gladness and peace David experienced. Do you have this confidence?

Lord, help me to pray with confidence.

Daily Deposit: Before you pray today, ask God to search your heart.

July 7

Fulfillment
Acts 25:1–27

We play a great part in the fulfillment of prophecy in our lives. You have probably heard the term, "self-fulfilling prophecies." When we blurt out the things we fear and dread the most, those fears often come to pass. We learn in Job that the things he feared the most came upon him. We do have to watch what we say with our mouths, simply because there is an unseen audience that hears what we confess with our mouths. Demonic spirits cannot read our minds, but they do hear what we say. On the positive side, however, God's angels also can hear our confessions. In Psalm 103, we learn that angels hearken to the voice of God's Word.

I have learned over the years never to confess what I fear. Instead I confess just the opposite, by declaring what God's Word says. For example, there was a time in my life when I feared the little boy that I hit with my car would die. God gave me a word before this fiery trial. He told me I would soon be tested with fire, but like Shadrach, Meshach, and Abednego, I would come out of that fire with not even the smell of smoke. I held on to this word during this fearful time in my life and cried out to God to give me faith to believe. I said out loud, "Lord, you promised to deliver me out of this fire."

When God gives us a word, we need to hold on to it in faith and we also need to declare it and act upon it. Jesus gave Paul a word of prophecy when Paul was in the Roman barracks in Jerusalem. Jesus said, "Be of good cheer, Paul; for as you have testified for Me in Jerusalem, so you must also bear witness at Rome" (Acts 23:11). Paul remembered those words of Jesus. He held on to those words in faith and he acted upon those words. Faith always speaks, and faith always acts. Paul was transferred from those barracks to Caesarea where Festus asked him if he wanted to return to Jerusalem to be judged by the Jews. Paul responded, "I appeal to Caesar." Paul knew his destination was Rome because Jesus told him he would bear witness in Rome. Paul cooperated with the word Jesus gave him, and he knew the way to Rome was to appeal to Caesar.

The sure word of prophecy given to us will be fulfilled, but we also must act upon the word that has been given us. We must, however, know for sure that the prophecy we have received was from Jesus, not mere man. The spirit of prophecy is Jesus. When we know we have heard from the Lord without any doubt, then we must begin to act on that word by faith. Abraham heard the Lord tell him to leave his home and go to the land He had promised him. Abraham obeyed what he heard and he acted upon it. Is there a word of prophecy you know the Lord gave you many years ago? Have you acted upon it?

Lord, help me to act upon the words You have given me.

Daily Deposit: Begin to act today on the words Jesus has spoken to your heart.

July 8

The Purpose of a Testimony
Acts 26:1–32

During my many years as a Christian I have heard numerous testimonies. I have noticed that some people testify more about themselves than they do about Jesus. I cringe when I hear the dirty laundry list of sins committed before a person came to know Jesus. Some of the details of these sins add nothing to the person's testimony. Perhaps we sometimes feel if we tell how bad we were before Christ, this will give people hope. However, hope needs to be built upon God's Word, not what we experienced before Christ. Our hope is built on nothing less than Jesus Christ and His righteousness.

Paul knew how to testify about Jesus. In fact, in our passage today Paul skillfully communicated the very words Jesus spoke to Him. A careful study of these words reveals *Paul's call, Paul's purpose, and Paul's message.* Paul spoke boldly to King Agrippa as he relayed exactly what Jesus told him on the Damascus Road (vv. 14-18).

Paul's call was to open the eyes of the Gentiles to turn from darkness to the light of Jesus and to deliver them from the power of satan. *Paul's purpose* was to be a witness of the things he had seen and heard, and what Jesus had revealed to him. *Paul's message* was to speak of the great inheritance freely given to all those who will believe in Jesus Christ (v. 18).

Paul's powerful testimony about Jesus' appearance and His words to him on the Damascus Road almost persuaded King Agrippa to become a believer. We do not know if King Agrippa later received Christ. We do know, however, that Paul was able to plant some good seeds in King Agrippa's heart.

Whenever we give our testimony, we need to be careful to speak the words of Jesus, not just our own words. The words of Jesus are the seeds that can be planted in the hearts of our audience. If those who hear our testimony do not respond immediately, we can trust that we, at least, have sown seeds that could be watered later by another laborer.

Our testimonies should always include God's Word. No one will ever be born of the Spirit of God if the seeds of God's Word are not planted. It is the Word of God and the Spirit of God that give new birth. The faith for our audience to believe in Jesus Christ is imparted as we deliver God's Word. Faith comes by hearing and hearing by the Word of God.

Lord, help me to skillfully deliver Your Word when I give my testimony.

Daily Deposit: Today might be a good day to review your own testimony. Make sure some of God's Word is included in your testimony. Use scripture to back up your experiences.

July 9

Lighten the Load
Acts 27:1–20

Tempestuous seas awaited Paul as he sailed to Italy in the Roman ship. The only hope of sparing both the ship and the souls aboard was to lighten the ship. After they lightened the ship, many days passed when neither sun nor stars were seen. Paul fasted during these days.

We all go through tempestuous seas of trials, testing, and temptations. During those times, we often feel like we are going to be overwhelmed and drown in the sea of troubles we are experiencing. Darkness envelopes us and we lose sight of the Light of the World: The Bright and Morning Star, our Lord Jesus. However, the truth is that Jesus has not forsaken us. In fact, He is in the boat with us! He can speak to our souls, "Peace be still." His message to us during these troubled times is simple: "Lighten the load!" We lighten the load when we cast all of our cares upon Him. He cares for us.

As we begin to release our burdens to Him, we slowly receive the assurance that we will make it to shore safely. Our lives may appear to be shipwrecked, but our souls will be saved as we cast all of our cares upon Jesus. Jesus invites us to come to Him, take His yoke upon us, and learn of Him meekness and lowliness of heart. Then He promises us that He will give rest to our souls because His yoke is easy and His burden is light (Matt. 11:30). The moment we cast our cares upon Jesus and release our burdens to Him, He is able to throw light on our circumstances. He is able to give us His wisdom. He is able to dress us in the garment of praise that lifts the spirit of heaviness off of us. He both enlightens our spiritual eyes and lightens the burdens that are on our shoulders.

The souls who watch us as we go through various trials can also be enlightened. When they observe the peace and joy we have in the midst of hard times, they begin to desire what we have. They may even ask us why we are experiencing hope, peace, and joy in our dark hour.

Lord, help me to always cast my cares upon You.

Daily Deposit: Is there something you are burdened about today? Cast that care upon the Lord. Then begin to praise Him for taking care of all of your concerns. He can perfect those things that are a concern to us, but only if we release those concerns to Him.

July 10

The Dangers of the Dark Side
1 Chronicles 9:1–10:14

Many great literary classics have compared evil to dark and good to light. We see this comparison in the Bible also. Jesus exhorted, "Therefore take heed that the light which is in you is not darkness" (Luke 11:35). Whenever we see a "therefore" in the Bible we need to find out what it is there for. Jesus said just before this exhortation that the lamp of the body was the eye. If we are careful to put good things before our eyes, our whole body will be full of light. We are warned not to seek enlightenment about our future from the occult. Deuteronomy 18 tells us all about the dark side. It warns us not to consult mediums, witches, sorcerers, or soothsayers.

Saul paid a great price when he decided not to inquire of the Lord, but instead he sought answers about his future from the witch of Endor. This witch was like a modern day fortune-teller, and she was under the influence of a familiar spirit. Our passage today tells us that "Saul died for his unfaithfulness which he had committed against the Lord, because he did not keep the word of the Lord, and also because he consulted a medium for guidance" (1 Chron. 10:13).

This account should warn us all to stay away from any occult involvement. When we participate in any occult activities, such as séances or going to fortune-tellers, we have entered the dark side (the realm of satan). If we enter the dark side through one of these activities, satan, the prince of darkness, then has the legal right to darken the eyes of our understanding.

I heard a real story that relates how easily darkness can come into our lives. Corrie ten Boom, a famous Dutch evangelist, told an experience she had when she shared the Gospel with a lady. Corrie shared the gospel effectively with this lady, but every time the lady tried to pray the prayer to accept Jesus as her Lord and Savior, she could not speak those words out loud. After several tries, Corrie went aside to pray. She asked the Lord what was blocking this lady from confessing with her mouth that Jesus Christ was Lord. The Lord told Corrie to ask the lady if she had ever been to a fortune-teller. When Corrie asked the lady this question, she responded, "Yes, I went to a fortune-teller when I was a teenager, but it was just in fun." Corrie asked the lady to confess seeking a fortune-teller as a sin and to ask the Lord to forgive her. She confessed her sin, and immediately she was able to pray the prayer to accept Jesus. Have you ever entered the dark side even for fun? I know I had to confess the sinful acts of playing with Ouija boards, tarot cards, and eight balls when I was young.

Lord, show me what I need to confess as sin today.

Daily Deposit: God can shine a light on any darkness in your life as you ask Him today to reveal what you need to confess to Him.

191

July 11

Mighty in the Spirit
1 Chronicles 11:1–12:18

We recently completed a five-month Bible school called "Mighty in the Spirit." The man who founded this school had a fervent spirit for the Lord. He died suddenly at the age of fifty-two, but his wife took over his ministry. One of the teachings this man loved to give was based on our passage today. He loved to talk about David's mighty men.

He told us David was able to win the victory over his enemies, because he was careful to surround himself with mighty men. He shared one of the secrets of becoming mighty in the spirit—to hang around people who are mighty in the spirit. The anointing of God has a way of rubbing off on us when we rub shoulders with anointed people.

We learn in this passage about several of David's mighty men. Jashobeam the son of a Hachmonite lifted up his spear and killed three hundred men at one time. Three of David's mighty men risked their lives when they went into the enemy camp to draw water from the well in Bethlehem to give to David. Benaiah, the son of Jehoiada, was a valiant man who did mighty deeds. On a snowy day, he lowered himself into a pit to face a lion and kill it. When our teacher told about Benaiah, he said Benaiah was a man who couldn't wait to be challenged with trouble. If trouble wasn't anywhere around him, then he sought to find it and defeat it. He said Benaiah was fearless.

What are the character qualities we need to look for in order to identify mighty men in the spirit? All we have to do is look at Jesus. He is divine, but also, He is a human. Jesus always honored His heavenly Father by doing what He saw His heavenly Father do, and by speaking what He heard His heavenly Father say. Jesus was willing even to lay His life down to honor His Father's will. David's mighty men also honored David and they were willing to risk their lives to please David and to grant David's desires.

Those who are mighty in the spirit today are those who overcome satan by the blood of the lamb and by the word of their testimony. They love not their lives, to the death. If we love our own lives more than we love Jesus, we will never become mighty in the spirit.

Lord, help me to become mighty in the Spirit.

Daily Deposit: You may have the opportunity to lay your own life down today when you willingly take time out of your busy schedule to pray with or to counsel someone.

July 12

The Army of the Lord
1 Chronicles 12:19–14:17

As I write this, my nephew is taking a test to rejoin the army infantry. His mother and I have mixed feelings about his possible reinstatement into the army. We live in a day where there are many wars. Anyone who enlists in the army today might have to actively fight in one of these wars.

Like it or not, as believers, we are all enlisted in God's army. Most of us have to face front line spiritual battles daily. We are fighting an unseen enemy, but at the same time our ranks are bolstered by an unseen army of angels. That unseen army of God enabled David to win many victories over his enemies.

Our passage today reveals how God's unseen army came to David's rescue when he faced war with the Philistines. When David inquired of the Lord whether or not he should go against the Philistines, God gave him specific instructions. God told David to attack the Philistines, only after he heard the sound of movement in the tops of the mulberry trees. God told David He would go before him to fight the Philistines.

David waited for the sound of the rustling of the tops of the mulberry trees. David could not see what was happening, but he could hear the sound of the breeze in the treetops. I believe a mighty army of angels was going before David, marching on the tops of the mulberry trees. God had sent His mighty unseen army ahead of David. David only had a mop-up job to accomplish.

It gives me great comfort to know that the Lord Sabaoth, the Lord of Hosts, goes before us with His mighty army in every battle we face! Are you facing a battle today? Take heart! The battle is the Lord's! And He is going before you to give you the victory!

Lord, thank You for fighting my battles for me.

Daily Deposit: Comfort someone today with these words, "If God is for you, who can be against you?" (See Romans 8:31.)

July 13

The Second Chance
1 Chronicles 15:1–16:36

We serve a God of the Second Chance. The only time in our lives God will not give us a second chance is after our death. After death we will not have a second chance to receive Jesus Christ as our Lord and Savior. We have to do this while we are still on earth. Reincarnation is nonexistent. The scriptures tell us that it is appointed to man once to die and then the judgment. (See Hebrews 7.) We see the long-suffering character of God when He gives us a second chance. One of these times is in our reading today.

David had blown it. In his excitement and determination to return the ark to Jerusalem, he failed to follow God's instructions. He put the ark on an oxcart, and when Uzza tried to steady the ark, God struck Uzza dead. David was so grieved by this because he knew he failed to carry out God's instructions to allow only the Levites to carry the ark on poles. No one was ever to touch the ark because if they did, they would instantly die.

This whole incident so frightened and discouraged David that he allowed the ark to be kept in the home of Obed-Edom, where it remained for three months. Obed-Edom's house was blessed as long as the ark resided in his home. The time came when David got over his fear, anger, and discouragement and he tried again to return the ark of God to Jerusalem. This time he carefully followed all of God's instructions for the transport of the ark, and only the Levites were allowed to carry the ark. David prepared a place for the ark and pitched a tent over it.

The instructions were given for all the priests to sanctify themselves before they transported the ark. This time, they transported the ark with joy and God helped the Levites who bore the ark of the Lord. David danced before the Lord with all of his might. There was great celebration when the ark arrived in Jerusalem and David supplied all of Israel with a feast. On that day David delivered a song, "O give thanks to the Lord! Call upon His name; make known His deeds among the peoples! Sing to Him, sing psalms to Him; talk of all His wondrous works. Let the hearts of those rejoice who seek the Lord. (See Psalm 105:1–3.) David's anger and discouragement was transformed to joy.

Sometimes we blow it by not following through with God's instructions, but He is the God of the second chance. When we get over our fears, anger, and discouragement and gain enough confidence to try again, God is waiting to help and strengthen us. He wants us to finish the race of life well, and He will always pick us up when we are willing to move in faith from the position of failure to the promise of success. Jesus is the glory and lifter of our heads.

Lord, thank You for the second chances You give me.

Daily Deposit: Today move in faith and receive with joy God's second chance.

July 14

Do All That Is in Your Heart
1 Chronicles 16:37–18:17

Throughout our lifetimes we have so many righteous and good desires. The Bible tells us that the Lord will grant the desires of the righteous. (See Proverbs 10:14.) I often tell people that when God plants His desires in our hearts, He grants what He plants.

We see in our passage today that David had a desire to build a house for God. When he communicated this desire to Nathan the prophet, Nathan responded by saying, "Do all that is in your heart, for God is with you" (1 Chron. 17:2). That evening Nathan was awakened in the night with a word from God. God said, "Go and tell My servant David, 'Thus says the LORD: "You shall not build Me a house to dwell in. For I have not dwelt in a house since the time that I brought up Israel, even to this day, but have gone from tent to tent, and from one tabernacle to another"'" (1 Chron. 17:4–5). God continued speaking to Nathan and said that none of the judges ever had the thought to build him a house, but the day would come when He would no longer move from place to place. He would see to it that His house would be built in Jerusalem. David's son would be appointed to build God's house in Jerusalem and God would establish His Kingdom and the throne of David forever.

David had a good desire, but God did not plant it in David's heart. David felt guilty because he had such a beautiful home and God did not have His own home. The desire David had was good, but God had another plan. David could have been very disappointed when Nathan told him he was not the one chosen to build God's house. Instead, David got alone with God and began to praise Him. He said, "O LORD, for Your servant's sake, and according to Your own heart, You have done all this greatness, in making known all these great things" (1 Chron. 17:19).

When David knew God's plan, he began to prepare, plan, and pray. David could have said, "Well, God this is your plan so You do it." We forget that even though God's plan differs from ours, we still need to help establish His plan on earth. This is why we pray, "Thy Kingdom come, thy will be done on earth as it is in heaven." David found it in his heart to pray before God for the fulfillment of His plan on earth.

Have you had a good plan that you thought surely was God's plan? Have you seen that plan go up in smoke just as the burnt offering went daily up in smoke? I know I have experienced this often in my life. When this happens, I pray and ask God how I can cooperate with His plan. I ask Him to reveal His plan to me. He always shows me how I can cooperate with His plan.

Lord, I ask You to reveal Your heart's desires and plans for me.

Daily Deposit: Release your own plans to God today and ask Him to establish His plan in your life.

July 15

God's Faithfulness
Romans 2:24–3:8

Jesus once asked, "When the Son of Man comes, will He really find faith on the earth?" (Luke 18:8). This question has always pierced my heart. It indicates that there will be a great falling away from the faith before Jesus returns. The Bible speaks of a time when men's hearts will fail them because of fear, and men's hearts will wax cold. There is no question that the hearts of people sometimes can be fickle. The faith they once held often fails during crisis times. The seed of the Word of God that causes faith to spring up in the heart becomes parched during drought times or hard times. It never produces fruit. Those hearts, however, which are rooted and grounded in the love of Jesus Christ, will always be fruitful.

Many will fall away in the end days because trials will become more intense. There will be those who even deny their faith because of persecution. The only way we can hold onto our faith is to have our focus continually upon Jesus Christ, the author and the finisher of our faith. We have to put our faith in God's faithfulness.

Our passage today asks the question, "For what if some did not believe? Will their unbelief make the faithfulness of God without effect?". Paul answers that question when he says, "Certainly not! Indeed, let God be true but every man a liar" (Rom. 3:3–4).

There are two things God cannot do. God cannot lie, and God cannot be unfaithful. This should comfort every doubting heart. Many doubted God's goodness and His faithfulness when the twin towers in New York fell, but God's faithfulness will stand even when everything else in the world is falling and failing. Whenever we are assailed by doubt, we need to turn our focus on Jesus Christ and take our eyes off the world and what is happening in our present day.

Some people believe God has abandoned us. God may give us up to our own lusts if we continually sin, but He will never abandon us.

Jesus promised, "I will never leave you nor forsake you" (Heb. 13:5). We need to know for sure and settle it in our hearts that Jesus was not lying when He said those words. Don't allow the chief of liars, satan, to rob you of your faith in God. When those doubts come, and they certainly will, say out loud, "God is good and God is faithful." We overcome the wicked one with the Sword of the Spirit (the Word of God).

Lord, help me to focus on You, the Author and Finisher of my faith.

Daily Deposit: Today use the Sword of the Spirit (God's Word) to stab the devil. Find verses in God's Word that you can declare out loud when Satan comes against you.

July 16

Building God's Temple
1 Chronicles 22:1–23:32

David said, "Solomon my son is young and inexperienced, and the house to be built for the LORD must be exceedingly magnificent, famous and glorious throughout all countries. I will now make preparation for it" (1 Chron. 22:5). David was speaking of building a physical house for God. He gathered all the physical materials to build the first Temple, and then his son Solomon performed the actual building of it.

We are all building a house for God. Every day, we are gathering the materials to build this house. This house is not made of stone. Rather, it is made of living stones who believe in Jesus Christ. Like David, we may not be able to actually do the building of this house, but we can daily make preparations and gather the materials for this magnificent house for God. The materials we use need to be excellent and our preparations need to be thorough.

What are the materials we use to build or to prepare God's dwelling place? God said in His word that the day would come when He would dwell among us and we would no longer need a temple made with hands to contain Him. That day has come! Those who believe in Jesus are His dwelling place! We are the temple of the living God. The materials we use in building this temple must be excellent and magnificent. They must be glorious because they contain God's glory. The materials cannot be wood, hay, or stubble. They must be gold and precious jewels.

The gold we gather for God's dwelling place is the trials we go through daily. We all will face trials, but these trials will only stand the test of fire when they are made of gold.

Every gloomy trial we face can be turned to gold when we turn to the Lord Jesus Christ for help in the trial. Jesus is the Master Builder who is able to build more of His character in us through the various trials we experience. The precious jewels that make up a glorious house for God are people. We are His precious jewels and, every time we share our faith with people, we are gathering jewels for God's house. Are you gathering these magnificent materials for God's house today?

Lord, I want to daily help to build Your dwelling place.

Daily Deposit: There are precious jewels in your own neighborhood that need to be gathered together. Have you shared your faith with your own neighbors? You can start today.

July 17

The Established Heart
Psalm 13:1–6

Our devotionals for the last two days spoke of God's faithfulness and how we can build a house for Him. We talked about the last days and how men's hearts will grow cold and how many will fall away from the faith. Yesterday, we discussed the magnificent materials necessary to build a dwelling place for God. When our hearts are established, we will be able to remain faithful to God and also continue building His house and His kingdom throughout our lifetime. Today's passage gives us the secret to establishing our hearts. It was written by King David who once said, "[I] will not be afraid of evil tidings; [my] heart is steadfast, trusting in the LORD" (Ps. 112:7). David knew how to keep his heart from failing and being conquered by doubt.

We hear his struggle with doubt as he says, "How long, O LORD? Will You forget me forever?" (v. 1). We all have times like this in our lives when we feel like God has forgotten us? During several crisis times in my life, I have screamed, "Where are you, God?" I am sure many in the United States on 9/11 were screaming this very question.

When horrific times come into our lives, doubt is waiting at the door to rob us of faith. What can we do at these times to overcome the doubt that assails our minds and our emotions? David employed the following five things when he had periods of doubt:

1. He asked God to enlighten his eyes (v. 3).
2. He trusted in God's mercy (v. 5).
3. He rejoiced in God's salvation so freely given to him (v. 5).
4. He sang to the Lord (v. 6).
5. He remembered how bountifully God had dealt with him in the past (v. 6).

Five is the number for *grace*. We all need grace when we go through periods of doubt in our lives. The next time doubt drapes its darkness over your mind and heart, ask God to enlighten your eyes to see things as God sees them. When you experience a trial, trust in God's mercy. Truly His mercy always outweighs His judgment. Whenever you feel like God is far away, begin to rejoice in His salvation. You have been given the gift of eternal life with God forever. This life is only temporal and is so short. When you feel like you cannot face another day, begin to sing to the Lord. The garment of praise will envelop you and the veil of darkness will be stripped away.

When you start to wonder if God still loves you, despite what you have done in the past, remember how bountifully He has dealt with you in the past. If you do these five things, your heart will be established.

Lord, forgive me for my doubts. Help me to establish my heart in faith.

Daily Deposit: Write down some of the times God has helped you.

Standing Without Wavering
Romans 4:14–5:2

Yesterday we learned how King David was able to establish his heart when he had periods of doubt. Today's passage gives us more insight into how faith always wins the battle over doubt. We face this battle continually.

When I hit a little boy on his bicycle and he was critically injured, I experienced the raging battle between doubt and faith. One day I had faith that this little eight-year-old boy would be healed. The next day I was paralyzed with fear because I thought he would die. The only thing that helped me win this battle was God's promise to me. Six months before the accident, God had given me a promise. I was having communion in my church when I heard God's still, quiet voice speak this to me.

> You are going to go through a fiery trial, but just as Shadrach, Meshach, and Abednego came out of the fire without even the smell of smoke on their clothes, you also will come out of this fire without the smell of smoke.

This promise was based on the story in *Daniel* when King Nebuchadnezzar threw Daniel's companions into the fire because they did not worship him. The King expected them to be burned instantly, but as King Nebuchadnezzar's counselors watched the fire they saw another man who looked like the Son of God walking with them through the fire. The fire had no power over Daniel's companions. Their garments were not affected by the fire. Their hair was not even singed. (See Daniel 3:13–27.) I held onto this promise during the fiery trial I went through, and Jesus was with me throughout the trial. The boy was healed. Even though his parents bore false witness against me and sued me, my insurance did not go up.

God also gave Abraham a great promise. He told Abraham that he would have a son who would be the father of many nations. Abraham refused to be weak in faith and he did not look at the weakness of his own body or the deadness of Sarah's womb. He had to wait many years before this promise was fulfilled, but he did not waver because of the promise God had given him. He was fully convinced that what God had promised him, He was able to perform. Abraham's stand in faith was accounted to him for righteousness. To stand in faith without wavering and to win the battle between faith and doubt, we must hold onto the promises God has given us. God's promises are like a strong pillar that we can wrap our arms around so that the winds of adversity will not blow us down. Has God given you some promises to embrace? Embrace them and stand in faith!

Lord, help me to embrace Your promises and stand in faith believing.

Daily Deposit: Today, hold on with faith to those promises God has given you!

July 19

Searching and Seeking
1 Chronicles 28:1–29:30

Most people played the game hide-and-seek when they were children. I can remember my favorite hiding place. I always crawled under the bed, while my sister counted to ten. She shouted, "Coming, ready or not!" My heart pounded rapidly as I saw her feet standing right next to the bed. I tried to not even breathe and I hoped my pounding heart would not help her discover my hiding place! Suddenly the feet I saw from my secret hiding place were exchanged for the bright, joyful face of my sister as she bent down, pulled the bed covers up and shouted, "I found you! I found you!"

Shame, fear, and guilt became a part of our nature when Adam and Eve gave into satan's temptation in the garden. When Adam and Eve sinned, they tried to hide from God. They discovered their nakedness and they were ashamed of their bodies. Before they sinned, their bodies were cloaked in the glory of God. There was no guilt, shame, or fear. Adam and Eve's hearts were pounding as they hid themselves where they thought God could not find them. Then God cried out, "Adam, where are you?" Adam's response was, "I heard Your voice in the garden, and I was afraid because I was naked, and I hid myself" (Gen. 3:10).

Many of us, from time to time, have tried to hide from God. My way of hiding from God is simply to stop my quiet times with Him. I do not want to be in His presence because I am afraid He will tell me something I don't want to hear. Something in my life has separated me from desiring to fellowship with God—and that something is sin. When those times happen in my life, all I have to do is confess my sins. Instantly God not only forgives my sin, but He also cleanses me from all unrighteousness. Sin causes the garment of glory in our lives to be replaced with the garment of shame.

Our passage today tells us that we cannot hide from God. David said these words to Solomon his son:

> As for you, my son Solomon, know the God of your father, and serve Him with a loyal heart and with a willing mind; for the LORD searches all hearts and understands all the intent of the thoughts. If you seek Him, He will be found by you; but if you forsake Him, He will cast you off forever.
>
> —1 CHRONICLES 28:9

When we receive Jesus as our Lord and Savior, God will never leave us or forsake us, because Jesus has purchased us the right through His death on the cross to live in God's presence without shame, guilt, fear, or condemnation. Instead of hiding from God, we can freely seek Him and enter His throne room through the blood of Jesus. There, we can confess our sins before God and be liberated from shame, guilt, and fear.

Lord, forgive me for the times I have tried to hide from You.

Daily Deposit: Ask the Holy Spirit to reveal any sins you need to confess.

July 20

Standing in His Righteousness
Psalm 16:1–11

When we stand on the promises of God and stand giving our praises and thanksgiving to God daily, we are preparing ourselves to face whatever adversities come our way. When adversity comes, and it most definitely will, we continue in the mode of faith in His promises and continual thanksgiving and praise. As we take our stand against adversity by employing these weapons against the enemy, we also need to be sure that we are standing in the righteousness of Jesus Christ, not our own righteousness. In Ephesians 6, we are given the armor we must put on as we take our stand against the enemy. This armor includes the helmet of salvation and the breastplate of righteousness. These are defensive parts of the full armor of God that enable us to be protected against the fiery darts of the enemy. We also employ our offensive weapons against the enemy every time we lift the shield of faith and we embrace the sword of the Spirit, and every time we declare God's Word out loud.

We must make sure we have on this armor when we do battle with the enemy. The breastplate of righteousness is placed upon us whenever we understand and declare that we are standing in the righteousness of Jesus Christ, not our own righteousness. We cannot withstand the enemy in trials, if we are not cloaked in the righteousness of Jesus Christ.

David knew the secret of standing in the righteousness of God whenever he faced his enemies. Even though Jesus Christ had not come in the flesh when he wrote this psalm, David did know Jesus in the spirit. David said, "My goodness is nothing apart from You" (Ps. 16:2).

We must credit any goodness within us to God. Our righteousness is of the Lord Jesus Christ! Whenever we make this statement out loud, the enemy runs in terror. We see this promise given clearly in Isaiah 54:17:

> "No weapon formed against you shall prosper, and every tongue which rises against you in judgment you shall condemn. This is the heritage of the servants of the LORD, and their righteousness is from Me," says the LORD.

To win the battle between faith and doubt and all battles with our enemies (the lusts of our own souls and satan and his demons), we stand in the righteousness of Jesus Christ against them. No weapon that is formed against us will prosper if we have the breastplate of righteousness firmly in place before we do battle.

Lord, help me to remember to stand in Your righteousness when I fight my enemies.

Daily Deposit: Today I place the breastplate upon me by confessing that Jesus Christ is my righteousness.

July 21

Your Offspring
Romans 7:1–14

One of the main purposes of marriage is to be fruitful and multiply. When a man and woman marry, they usually desire offspring. When we marry Christ, we should also desire spiritual offspring. Paul said we are married to "Him who was raised from the dead, that we should bear fruit to God" (v. 4).

Whether we like it or not, the offspring we produce through marriage will usually resemble us physically. When I look at my grandchildren, I see a collage of the facial features of both their mothers and dads. Often I even see personality traits that remind me of their mothers and dads.

The goal of our marriage to Christ is to produce spiritual offspring who develop the same character traits as Jesus. What an awesome responsibility we have to share our faith with others and also to disciple them so they become more like Jesus. When we have natural children, we have the challenge of training and teaching them until they are adults. We often forget that we have this same responsibility to those whom we lead to Jesus Christ! Jesus did not command us to go into all the world and save the world. When He commissioned all those who believed on Him before His ascension, He said:

> All authority has been given to Me in heaven and on earth. Go therefore and make disciples of all the nations, baptizing them in the name of the Father and of the Son and of the Holy Spirit, teaching them to observe all things that I have commanded you; and lo, I am with you always, even to the end of the age.
> —Matthew 28:18–20

As spiritual mothers and fathers, we are expected to teach and train our spiritual children. Often this is impossible because of time and distance. However, we do have the responsibility to make sure that every person we lead to Jesus Christ has spiritual parents who can disciple them.

There is a recurring dream I have that troubles me. I often dream about abandoning my own babies. In the dream, I suddenly realize the babies are missing and I go back to get them. I usually find the babies both underfed and without proper clothing. Perhaps the Lord is telling me in those dreams that I have left spiritual babies alone without someone to care for them. I know I am guilty of that. My challenge from this day forward is to make sure the new converts I lead to Jesus Christ have both a spiritual mother and a spiritual dad to nurture them. Paul never married, so he had no children, but he had many spiritual offspring whom he nurtured, trained, and taught. Have you abandoned any of your spiritual offspring?

Lord, forgive me for neglecting my spiritual children.

Daily Deposit: Today, you might want to write a note or call one of your spiritual children to tell them you love them and want to be available to help them.

July 22

The Promise Keeper
2 Chronicles 6:14–8:10

You may be familiar with a movement called *Promise Keepers*. The purpose of this organization is to strengthen marriages by teaching men how to be better husbands. We talked yesterday about being married to Christ and bearing spiritual offspring. None of us would want to be married to someone who is a promise breaker. We need to thank God daily that He has provided a wonderful Husband (Jesus Christ) for us, Who always keeps His promises. Today's passage speaks about God's faithfulness to keep His promises. It was time to dedicate the Temple. At the dedication Solomon declared:

> Lord God of Israel, there is no God in heaven or on earth like You, who keep Your covenant and mercy with Your servants who walk before you with all their hearts.
> —2 CHRONICLES 6:14

It should give us great comfort to know that God will never break His covenant with us. He always keeps His promises to us.

A similar passage is given to us in the New Testament. Paul spoke of God's promise-keeping ability to the Corinthians when he wrote:

> For all the promises of God in Him are Yes, and in Him Amen, to the glory of God through us.
> —2 CORINTHIANS 1:20

We do not have to fear that Jesus will ever be an unfaithful husband. He has promised never to leave us or forsake us. When we experience the faithfulness of our spiritual husband, we are challenged to remain faithful to Him.

Lord, thank You for Your faithfulness. Forgive me for the times I have been unfaithful to You.

Daily Deposit: Talk with someone today about God's faithfulness to you. When you speak of God's faithfulness, your words are recorded in the Book of Remembrance in heaven. (See Malachi 3:16.)

July 23

Flesh and Spirit
Romans 8:9—23

Every day we live we face the continual battle between doing our own thing, when we submit to our fleshly lusts, or doing God's thing when we submit to His will. The only way we can win this battle is to submit ourselves, moment by moment, to be led by the Holy Spirit.

We recently talked about nurturing and training our spiritual children until they mature. We learn in our passage today that those who are led by the Spirit become not just children of God, but they become sons of God (v. 14). We never want to stay spiritual babies. We want to develop to spiritual maturity.

I remember talking with my oldest son and challenging him to be led by the Holy Spirit daily. He asked me what that looked like. I couldn't answer his question right away, but, after careful thought, I discovered in the Word what being led by the Holy Spirit looks like. Since Paul and other apostles often spoke of the importance of growing up spiritually, I searched out some of their letters and found out what a person must do daily to cooperate with the Holy Spirit as He seeks to mature us spiritually. A person who is led by the Holy Spirit daily:

- Submits to God and resists the devil (James 4:7, 1 Pet. 5:6–9).
- Humbles himself by casting every care upon Jesus (1 Pet. 5:6–7).
- Seeks God's wisdom by consulting His Word (James 1:5).
- Receives and hides God's Word in his heart (James 1:21).
- Commits his body as a living sacrifice to God (Rom. 12:1).
- Commits the members of his body to be used as God's instruments of righteousness (Rom. 6:13).
- Sings psalms, spiritual songs, and hymns, and makes melody in his heart (Eph. 5:19).
- Allows patience to have its perfect work in him (James 1:2–4).
- Orders his conversation aright (James 1:26–27, 3).
- Both hears and does God's Word (James 1:22–25).

Of course, there are many other scriptures that reveal what being led by the Holy Spirit looks like. However, this list should be sufficient to challenge us all daily to be more diligent to cooperate with the Holy Spirit as He seeks to lead, teach, and mature us.

Lord, I want to keep maturing spiritually. Help me to be more diligent as I daily seek to be led by Your Spirit.

Daily Deposit: Review this list, and ask the Holy Spirit to help you do what is necessary to be led by Him every moment of this day.

The Gentle Warrior
Psalm 18:35–50

D avid extolled the Lord in this psalm. He gave God thanks for delivering him from Saul. The picture David painted of God as our strong deliverer was not only vivid, but also full of contrasts. David spoke of God's shield of salvation. Salvation truly is a shield to cover those who believe and trust in the Lord. We are covered by the shield of faith whenever we declare what the blood of Jesus has done for us. Whenever I encounter a spiritual battle, I like to declare out loud that the blood of Jesus enables me to be:

- Sanctified (set apart for His service)
- Justified (just as I had never sinned)
- Forgiven
- Healed
- Redeemed
- Saved
- Delivered

We overcome satan by the blood of Jesus and the Word of our testimony. (See Revelation 12:11.) When we testify out loud about what the blood does for us, satan has to flee. This is the way we can lift the shield of faith, so that every fiery dart of the enemy is quenched.

Jesus is our strong deliverer. David said in this psalm that God's right hand held him up and His gentleness made David great. David had not seen Jesus in person, but he had seen Jesus in the Spirit as his strong deliverer, just as Joshua saw Jesus as his mighty warrior and deliverer. David also saw the meekness and gentleness of Jesus in the Spirit.

When we think of Jesus as our deliverer, like David, we can picture Him as our gentle warrior. Jesus is both mighty and meek. Jesus is the only one who can teach us meekness and lowliness of heart.

David could easily identify himself with Jesus. He was a gentle warrior, because he was a shepherd, even as Jesus is our Good Shepherd. God avenged David of all of his enemies, just as David defeated both the lion and the bear when they tried to attack his flock.

At the same time, David gently ministered to his sheep as he led them to the still waters and to good pastureland. As we meditate on this psalm, we see that meekness is great strength under control. The strength of the Lord is imparted to us to overcome our enemies. He is the rock of our salvation who valiantly does battle for us when we trust in Him. Even during the battles of life, however, we need to take time to drink from the still waters and allow Jesus to teach us. Daily, we must answer His invitation to spend time with Him for Him to teach us meekness and lowliness of heart.

Lord, before I resist the devil, I need to sit at Your feet and learn meekness.

Daily Deposit: Before your day gets busy, take time to sit at Jesus' feet.

Grieving and Glory
Romans 9:1–24

I recently attended a grief seminar that opened my eyes to the grieving process. The seminar leader shared with us that it often takes three years or more to get over a divorce and many years to get over the loss of a spouse by death. There is nothing wrong with grief. It is a natural process that enables us to weep with those who weep. Many who lose loved ones fail to go through the necessary steps of grieving. When this happens, often the one who has experienced loss will have emotional pain that is not transferred to Jesus. Jesus was a man of sorrows who was acquainted with grief. Isaiah prophetically spoke of how Jesus bore our griefs and carried our sorrows. (See Isaiah 53:3–4.)

Jesus bore our griefs and sorrows on the cross so that we now have the power to go through the grieving process with emotional stability and strength. Why? Because Jesus goes through grief with us.

Another kind of grief that we must transfer over to Jesus is the grief over those who are lost. In our passage today, Paul speaks about the grief he experienced because so many of his own Jewish people (friends, family, coworkers, and countrymen) were lost. He said (vv. 2–5):

> I have great sorrow and continual grief in my heart. For I would wish that I myself were accursed from Christ for my brethren, my countrymen according to the flesh, who are Israelites, to whom pertain the adoption, the glory, the covenants, the giving of the law, the service of God, and the promises; of whom are the fathers and from whom, according to the flesh, Christ came, who is over all, the eternally blessed God. Amen.
>
> —ROMANS 9:2–5

As I read these words of Paul, I want to cry. I'm sure he was weeping when he wrote these words. Paul was so burdened for his lost Jewish countrymen and brethren that he was willing to be accursed if it would mean their salvation. He said he grieved continually. This type of grief is to God's glory. The kind of burden that Paul had for the Jews was a gift from God. It enabled Paul to be an effective intercessor for his own people.

Continually, Paul interceded for the lost Jews. He laid his life down and stood in the gap for all the lost Jews. When we have a burden for souls, God has granted us the privilege of experiencing a great part of His own heart. Jesus wept over Jerusalem because He was unable to collect His Jewish brothers and sisters unto him like a mother collects her young chicks. Do you have such a burden for souls? If you don't, ask God to give it to you. You will never be the same, and you will become both an effective intercessor and a laborer in this End Time harvest.

Lord, give me a burden for souls.

Daily Deposit: The prayers for the lost today will reap an eternal harvest.

July 26

The Favor of the Lord
2 Chronicles 17:1–18:34

I often pray for the favor of the Lord. When I send material to publishers or when I have to go before those in authority, I pray for the favor of the Lord. Favor is something most of us want to be manifested in our daily lives. We might just desire favor in the market place so that we can be good stewards and save money to sow into the kingdom. We may long for favor with our fellow employees so there will be harmony in our work situations. The favor of the Lord, however, is to be most desired. We can learn a lot about the favor of the Lord as we read this historical account in Chronicles of King Jehoshaphat, who had the favor of the Lord:

> Now the LORD was with Jehoshaphat, because he walked in the former ways of his father David; he did not seek the Baals, but he sought the God of his father, and walked in His commandments and not according to the acts of Israel.
> —2 CHRONICLES. 17:3–4

God established Jehoshaphat's kingdom and gave him great favor because he was a man after God's own heart, even as David was. If we want to have the favor of the Lord, we must be people who are after God's own heart. How can we be such a people who continually experience the favor and blessings of the Lord? The verses quoted above give the answer to this question. We will have the favor of the Lord when we:

- Are after God's own heart.
- Give up our idols.
- Seek God with all of our hearts.
- Obey His commandments.
- Refuse to act like disobedient, rebellious people.

We must understand that the favor of the Lord does not guarantee that we will have no suffering in our lives. In fact, the very favor of the Lord will often cause suffering in our lives. We will suffer for the sake of Jesus Christ, just as Paul suffered. We will suffer, simply because we are walking in a righteous manner. We will suffer persecution, ridicule, and even abandonment by friends and family because we make the decision to serve the Lord with all of our hearts. I know a man whose wife left him simply because he committed his life to Jesus Christ. She did not understand why he had changed and she did not like the new man-in-Jesus he had become. Suffering for righteousness sake, however, is a small price to pay when we can continually experience the favor of the Lord!

Thank You Lord for Your favor.

Daily Deposit: Trust and obey the Lord today and you will have His favor!

July 27

The Battle Is the Lord's
2 Chronicles 19:1–20:37

One of my favorite expressions is: "The battle belongs to the Lord, and the victory is ours!" We need to remember this whenever we go through trials or spiritual warfare. We can learn so much from this account recorded in Chronicles.

Jehoshaphat was a great king, as we learned yesterday, because he had the favor of the Lord. We learned how to obtain the favor of the Lord. Today we can learn what to do when we are faced with, what seems to be, an overwhelming battle.

Jehoshaphat was facing a great enemy. The people of Moab, along with the people of Ammon, came to battle against Jehoshaphat. Jehoshaphat was afraid, so he set himself to seek the Lord and proclaimed a fast (2 Chron. 20:3). We can certainly identify with Jehoshaphat, when he was fearful. Whenever we face trials or the enemy comes against us in force, it is natural for us all to be fearful. The frontal attack of satan is always fear. When we are anesthetized by fear, we are paralyzed and helpless to do anything to defend ourselves. It is then when satan can perform his filthy operations on us and carry out his diabolical plans.

Jehoshaphat did not give in to fear. Instead, he "set himself to seek the LORD and proclaimed a fast throughout all Judah. So Judah gathered together to ask help from the Lord" (2 Chron. 20:3–4). Then, Jehoshaphat went into the sanctuary and reminded God in heaven of His past victories. He declared that he and his people would remain faithful to God, no matter what calamity faced them (2 Chron. 20:5–13). All of Judah stood before the Lord and the Spirit of the Lord came upon Jahaziel, one of the priests. Jahaziel offered these comforting words:

> Listen, all you of Judah and you inhabitants of Jerusalem, and you, King Jehoshaphat. Thus says the LORD to you: "'Do not be afraid or dismayed because of this great multitude, for the battle is not yours, but God's."
> —2 CHRONICLES 20:15

> You will not need to fight in this battle. Position yourselves, stand still and see the salvation of the LORD, who is with you, O Judah and Jerusalem!
> —2 CHRONICLES 20:17

Encouraged by these words, Jehoshaphat appointed singers to sing and praise the Lord as they went out before the army. When we are faced with what seems to be an impossible battle with the enemy's opposing force, we can:

- Set our hearts to seek the Lord.
- Ask for others to fast with us about the battle.
- Pray with others about the battle.
- Sing and praise the Lord.

Lord, thank You for winning so many battles for me.

Daily Deposit: Set your heart, today, to seek the Lord in these ways.

July 28

Read: 2 Chronicles 21:1–23:21; Romans 11:13–36; Psalm 22:1–18; Proverbs 20:7

Unbelief Blinds
Romans 11:13–36

Today is my husband's birthday. He is in the second half of his sixties and I praise the Lord everyday for what He has done in my husband's life. For so long, my husband doubted many things in the Bible. He did not understand the victory that is ours through Jesus Christ. He was raised in a mainline denomination that did not emphasize salvation through new birth, and he did not have a lot of grounding in the Word of God. He was blinded about many things because he had unbelief. Unbelief is what keeps us from a personal relationship with God the Father through Jesus Christ.

Many on earth believe there is a God. However, they do not believe that we can enter into the great privilege of personally knowing the God who created the whole universe, when we come to know Jesus Christ as our Lord and Savior!

We learned earlier how much Paul longed to reach his Jewish brethren and how he was so grieved because many of them still remained in unbelief. God had partially blinded them because of their unbelief. The day will come, however, when all Israel will be saved. Paul did not see that day, and we might not see that day.

The day spoken of here is when Jesus returns and sets His feet on the Mount of Olives. The mountain will split in two, and Israel will recognize Jesus as their own Messiah.(See Zechariah 12.) A fountain of cleansing will be opened for them and their sins will be taken away. (See Zechariah 13.)

If Jewish people are now partially blinded, until the fullness of the Gentiles has come in, should we share our faith with Jews today? If God was able to partially blind their eyes, He also has the power to unveil their eyes and enlighten the eyes of their understanding!

We have a great responsibility to share with everyone our faith. The Bible tells us to go to the Jews first. We are deeply indebted to the Jewish people because, without them, we would not have a Savior, the Word of God, or the twelve apostles. Jesus was commissioned by God the Father to go first to the Jewish people with the message of His kingdom. We have the same commission. We must pray that God will remove the veil from the eyes of the Jewish people to whom we go with this great message of salvation!

Lord, I pray for all of my Jewish friends. Please unveil their eyes.

Daily Deposit: When you pray for the peace of Jerusalem today, also pray for all of Israel to be saved. Ask God to open doors to share the Gospel with Jewish people.

July 29

What Is God's Will?
Romans 12:1–21

Over the years, many have asked me to pray for God's will to be done in their lives. It's easy for me to agree with someone for this request because we do have confidence that we are praying according to God's will. God wants us to know what His will is so we can pray with confidence that God hears our request to know His will and He answers that request. (See 1 John 5:14–15.)

God not only will grant our request to know His will for our lives, but He has already shown us clearly what His will for us is in His Word. Our passage today reveals the will of the Lord for every person. It is God's will that we:

1. Present our bodies as a living sacrifice (v. 1).
2. Be transformed by the renewing of our minds (v. 2).
3. Be humble (don't think of ourselves too highly) (v. 3).
4. Use the gifts God has given us (v. 5–9).
5. Love without hypocrisy (v. 9).
6. Abhor evil (v. 9).
7. Cling to that which is good (v. 9).
8. Be kindly and affectionate towards one another (v.10).
9. Remain fervent in the spirit (v. 11).
10. Rejoice in hope (v. 12).
11. Be patient in tribulation (v. 12).
12. Continue steadfast in prayer (v. 12).
13. Distribute to the needs of the poor (v.14).
14. Be given to hospitality (v. 13).
15. Bless those who persecute you (vs. 14).
16. Rejoice with those who rejoice and weep with those who weep (v. 15).
17. Do not be high-minded, but make friends with the humble (v. 16).
18. Do not repay evil with evil (v. 17).
19. Do not avenge ourselves (v. 19).
20. Overcome evil with good (v. 21).

After reviewing this list, we no longer will have to ask the question, "What is God's will for me?" Instead we should pray:

Lord, help me to be faithful to do these twenty things while I'm here on earth.

Daily Deposit: Review this list and ask the Holy Spirit to help you remember this list. Challenge yourself to not only remember this list, but also to daily do this list.

July 30

Finishing the Race
2 Chronicles 26:1–28:27

You have probably heard the quote, "It does not matter if you win the race; it is how you run the race that counts." The Christian walk is often compared to a race. Paul said, "I have finished my course, I have run the race and now it is time to receive my crown."

God is interested in both how well we run the race of the Christian life and how we finish the race. Moses, in Psalm 92, asked God to teach us to number our days so that we might apply our hearts to wisdom. Each day is a gift from God, and He watches to see how we will use that gift. Yesterday is history; tomorrow is a mystery, but today is a gift.

Our passage today reveals the sad account of Uzziah's life. He began to rule when he was sixteen years old and ruled in Jerusalem for fifty-two years. He began the race of life well. He prospered and defeated all of his enemies. When things seemed to be going so well, Uzziah gave in to the pride of life. He quit trusting in God and began trusting in himself. He took it upon himself to go into the sanctuary to burn incense to the Lord. Only the priests were allowed to burn incense. In response to Uzziah's disobedience and pride, God struck him with leprosy. He remained a leper the rest of his life.

There is nothing more to say. Whenever we take things into our own hands and think we can disobey God without facing destructive consequences, we have deceived ourselves. Uzziah had many days of serving the Lord, but his one act of pride cost him his health for the rest of his life.

Uzziah was sixty-eight years old when this happened. This should sober every senior who might read this devotion. We will only finish the race well when we daily humble ourselves before God. The moment we become prideful and take things into our own hands is the moment that might cost us everything.

Lord, help me to both run the race of life well and also finish it well.

Daily Deposit: Today humble yourself before God by casting every care upon Him, because He cares for you. He does care that you both run His race well and finish His race well.

July 31

Carry Out the Rubbish
2 Chronicles 29:1–36

My dad did not do a lot around the house to help my mother because his work was so demanding. One thing, however, he never failed to do was to carry out the garbage. Even though I had four men in my home (my husband and three sons), I often had to carry out the garbage. They always seemed too busy with studies and jobs to do this. I was often tempted not to carry out the garbage for a whole week. If I had done this I am sure someone would have made the comment, "Why haven't you carried out the garbage?" Then I would have replied, "Why haven't you carried out the garbage?"

It is so important that we learn to carry out our own garbage daily. I don't mean physical garbage. I mean spiritual garbage. In the account today, Hezekiah gave orders for the temple and the priests to sanctify themselves. The first step to sanctify themselves was to carry out the rubbish from the holy place because their forefathers had sinned (v.6). Their forefathers had desecrated the holy place and this is why God had allowed their enemies to conquer them. If we do not daily carry out our spiritual garbage, the enemy will often defeat us.

What is our spiritual garbage? Our spiritual garbage consists of the containers filled with what we see, what we hear, and what we speak. What we see, what we hear, and what we speak will determine both how much spiritual garbage we have and the quality of that spiritual garbage. If we do not guard our eye gates from beholding evil, our ear gates from hearing the wrong kind of teaching and music, and our mouth gate from speaking things contrary to the Word of God, we will have smelly garbage in our brains that will cause us to live stinking lives.

We can only live sanctified lives if we are careful about what we put in the temple of the living God (our bodies). "Garbage in, garbage out" is a well-known saying, especially in the computer world. What we feed our lusts with will determine the quality of the garbage we contain in our temples. When we feed our lust of the flesh by overindulging in what God created for us to enjoy, we will soon lose the sweet savor of the Lord's presence in our lives. When we fill our eyes with wicked things like pornography and sensual movies, our eyes will soon be shut to the enlightenment God wants to give us through His Word. When we stuff our ears with loud music that does not glorify God or hear teachings that are contrary to the Word of God, we will have a dirty wax buildup in our spiritual ears that will block us from hearing the voice of the Lord. Have you taken your garbage out today?

Lord, help me to be diligent to take my spiritual garbage out daily.

Daily Deposit: Be honest when you pray today, and confess all the garbage you have allowed to remain in your temple.

August 1

Patience
Romans 15:1–22

All the ladies around the table were eighty-years-old and older. I was teaching them the book of James. I shared with them that trials are allowed by God to help us develop patience. I explained that the word *patience*, in this letter James wrote, does not mean never being frustrated or irritated. The word *patience*, in Greek, means "bearing up under a heavy burden or simply being able to suffer long without complaining."

"Long-suffering" is a fruit of the Spirit, and it is only developed in us when we go through suffering. James exhorts us to allow patience to "have its perfect work" in us when we go through trials (James 1:4). Patience begins to work perfectly in our lives when we learn to release every care to Jesus. When we are able to wait upon the Lord, with the expectant faith that He will give us the strength to go through the trial and also bring something good out of the trial, we are allowing patience to have its perfect work in us. Everyone experiences trials in this life, but only those who love the Lord and seek His Word in the midst of trials will be able to cultivate the fruit of patience in their lives.

In his letter to the Romans, Paul called God the God of patience (v. 5). Patience, or long-suffering, is not a human trait. Only God has perfect patience, but He is able to perfect His fruit of patience within us when we seek His wisdom, His Word, and His help in the midst of a trial. None of us will ever have perfect patience. The word *perfect*, here, means "mature." Patience will grow and mature in us as we refuse to murmur and complain, maintaining instead an attitude of gratitude throughout our trials.

How can we cooperate with the Holy Spirit as He forms the fruit of patience within us? Paul wrote (v. 4):

> For whatever things were written before were written for our learning, that we through the patience and comfort of the Scriptures might have hope.

We will develop patience when we read God's Word. When I look at the lives of some of the patriarchs and apostles, I am amazed at how they survived so many trials.

The life of Paul alone should inspire us all to have the hope that we can survive all the trials we face. The life of Jesus should comfort us and give us hope that He has already won the victory for us over the various trials we face. He has gone before us and made a way of escape out of every temptation and trial. Are you allowing patience to have its perfect work in you?

Lord, help me to cooperate with Your Holy Spirit as He begins to establish patience in me.

Daily Deposit: Show me, in your Word today, someone who has experienced a trial like I am now experiencing. Thank You for Your comfort and Your gift of faith.

The Fellowship of the Saints
Romans 15:23–16:7

"When I get my million, I want to buy a large houseboat that I can use for fellowship times with my Christian friends. We'll have plenty of good food and, best of all, we'll enjoy sharing God's food (His Word) together." These were the words of a friend of ours who just loves to fellowship with the saints. He longs to have a big gathering place where he can invite Christians to be refreshed and renewed.

What our friend was describing is definitely on God's heart! God loves to see His children having fun and fellowshiping together. The early feasts in the Hebrew scriptures were such times when family and friends gathered to worship and praise their God. Jesus loved breaking bread with His followers. The early church sprang from fellowship times in homes where the saints broke bread together.

Paul had been many places and had seen a multitude of faces, but what he loved almost as much as he loved preaching, was fellowshiping with and ministering to the followers of Christ. In his letter to the Romans, Paul said he could not come to them right away because he had to minister to the saints in Jerusalem first (v. 25).

He asked the Roman believers to pray that his service for Jerusalem might be acceptable to the saints so he could come to them with joy. He looked forward to being refreshed together with them (vv. 31–32).

It has been our joy to also go many places and see many faces. We have traveled on mission trips to almost every continent on earth. Our happiest memories of those trips are the times when we sat at the table and broke bread with the saints in those countries. In India, we sat on the mud floor of little huts and our food was served on large banana leaves. In China, we joined in the celebration of the Spring Festival (celebration of the new year) by eating *zhaozi* (a New Year's dish). In Mexico, we enjoyed goat stew at the open campgrounds. In Peru, we ate chicken and rice at all of our gatherings. In Jerusalem, we shared falafels and prayed for the peace of Jerusalem. We loved to minister to the laborers in those countries and hoped that the Lord's ministry through us refreshed and renewed them.

I'm looking forward to continued fellowship with all of these saints when we meet in heaven. Maybe the mansion of our friend will be a houseboat on the River of Life in heaven.

Lord, help me to be hospitable and fellowship often with Your saints.

Daily Deposit: Fellowship with a Christian friend today. If you cannot have them come to your home, call them on the phone. Whatever you share together about the Lord will be recorded in your Book of Remembrance in heaven.

August 3

Read: 2 Chronicles 33:14–34:33; Romans 16:8–27; Psalm 26:1–12; Proverbs 20:19

The Holy Kiss
Romans 16:8–27

When we were in India, we were instructed by the pastors there not to be publicly affectionate with our spouses. We were told that this would offend the Indians.

When we were in South America, we were told it was customary to greet one another with a kiss and a hug. We just returned from Hungary where everyone greets each other with a kiss on each cheek and a hug.

The manner of greeting varies from country to country. When we were in England, a firm hand shake was the usual greeting. Christians, however, are instructed by Paul in this letter to greet one another with a holy kiss.

We have a Puerto Rican lady in our church who is disappointed if we do not greet one another with a holy kiss. When someone does not respond to her affectionate kiss, she often exclaims, "Haven't you heard that the Bible tells us to greet one another with a holy kiss!"

It is a great custom to greet one another with a kiss and also to say good night to one another with a kiss. I can remember one of the happiest memories of my childhood was when my father kissed each of the three girls in our family with a kiss on the cheek and said "Girls, good night and have sweet dreams." The one thing I didn't like about those kisses, however, was that Dad often drank a big glass of buttermilk just before he kissed us. I can remember bracing myself and thinking, "Oh no! Here comes the juicy kiss from Dad."

I believe when we see Jesus face to face, He will greet us with a holy kiss. However, I don't have to wait until I see Him face-to-face to feel the warmth of His love.

Every morning when I have my early prayer time, I can almost feel His gentle kiss on my cheek. Jesus can't wait to greet you with the holy kiss of His presence as you take time to be with Him. Have you given Him time morning by morning to greet you with the kiss of His presence?

Lord, forgive me for the times I leave the house without spending time
in Your presence. Help me not to miss any more of Your kisses.

Daily Deposit: If you are not the kissing type, there are many ways you can show your affection to your Christian friends. You can give a friend a kiss by writing a note or giving him/her a telephone call. Think of other ways to give people a holy kiss with acts of kindness and love.

The Law That Frees
2 Chronicles 35:1–36:23

God gave Moses the law on Mt. Sinai. The law was given to define *sin*. Moses appointed seventy elders to help him judge the people according to the law. As long as Israel obeyed God's laws, they did well. God allowed Israel's enemies to come against them and defeat them, when Israel rebelled against His laws. Later, God raised up judges who would relay God's Word to the people, so they could return to God after their seasons of rebellion. After the period of the judges, kings were anointed and appointed to lead the children of Israel. The kings who read God's Word and instructed the people in the laws and statutes of God always prospered. Josiah was one those kings.

After the book of the law was found and read to King Josiah, he first tore his clothes and wept. Then he prepared and held the largest Passover ever recorded. Josiah told the Levites to no longer carry the law from place to place on their shoulders. They were given orders to place the ark inside Solomon's temple and allow it to rest there.

The law was never meant to cause bondage, nor to be a burden in our lives. The law was given by God to instruct us in His ways, so that we could live our lives free of bondage. It was not long before the children of Israel found it impossible to keep all the laws. They soon recognized their dependency upon God's mercy and love.

God humbled Himself and became the only human being to obey the law perfectly. Jesus Christ did not come to destroy the law. He came to fulfill the law for us.

Recently I finished a study of Leviticus and I often paused in my study to praise God, because I no longer had to keep all those laws. That would be a real burden.

The law of God finally found its resting place in the temple. Through Jesus Christ, the law of God can find its resting place in our temples (our bodies). The law of God is no longer written on tablets of stone. The law is now written on the hearts of everyone who believes in Jesus.

Today, we do not have to strive to obey the law. Jesus sent the Holy Spirit to enable and empower us to keep the two laws we are commanded to keep. The whole law is fulfilled when we love God with all of our hearts and souls, and when we love our neighbor even as we love ourselves. We now have the law of liberty in our hearts. Jesus can now obey the law through our temples of flesh. We can enter a resting place when we look to Jesus to fulfill God's Word through us.

> Lord, thank You for fulfilling the whole law for me. Thank You for
> nailing the curse of the law on the cross when You became a curse for
> my sake.

Daily Deposit: Take time today to review the Ten Commandments. (See Exodus 20.) Memorize them and then read Jesus' words in Matthew 22:36–40.

A House Fit for God
Ezra 1:1–2:70

Cyrus, the king of Persia, was stirred in his spirit to proclaim throughout the kingdom to return to Jerusalem to build a house for God. Nebuchadnezzar had desecrated Solomon's temple and had taken much of the gold, silver, and holy articles out of the temple. The Spirit of God commissioned Cyrus to restore the temple and Ezra was one of the Jewish leaders sent to oversee this restoration.

God no longer dwells in a temple made with hands. God dwells within those who believe in His Son, Jesus Christ. Does your temple need restoration? Has the Spirit of God moved on you to cooperate with Him as He does some repair work on your heart?

What blueprint does God want us to follow as we allow the Holy Spirit to restore our temples (body, soul, and spirit)? In Proverbs 24:3–4, we are given the answer to this question:

> Through wisdom a house is built, and by understanding it is established; by knowledge the rooms are filled with all precious and pleasant riches.

I remember reading a tract about allowing Jesus into the rooms of our hearts. The tract was called "My heart, Christ's home." It described how Jesus walked into each room of our hearts. The tract began with a picture of Jesus knocking on the door of our hearts. The door was opened and Jesus began to clean the rooms that were filthy in our hearts. The closets were cluttered with suggestive reading material. The kitchen had rotting, spoiled food. We failed to feed ourselves with the fresh manna available through His Word daily. The fireplace in the den of our hearts was warm and welcoming, but we didn't have time to sit down with Jesus and enjoy the warmth with Him. Our hearts were busied with the mundane routines of life and our thoughts were far from Him.

I was convicted when I read this tract because I knew my heart needed cleansing, restoration, and refreshing. To rebuild our temples and to restore our hearts, we need to first pull down the strongholds of pride and erect the walls of understanding and humility.

To have a holy dwelling place for Jesus Christ, we must learn to fear the Lord (have holy, reverent, and obedient hearts). We need to wallpaper our hearts with God's Word by hiding His Word in our hearts. We need to tune the radios of our hearts to hear God's voice and obey His voice. We need to shut off the TV of our hearts, filled with wrong images, and to open the eyes of our understanding to behold the goodness of the Lord. Daily, we need to get rid of the rotten garbage (unconfessed sins) in our hearts and spray the fresh air of His presence in every room of our hearts. Are you ready to do some heart building and cleaning today?

Lord, create within me a clean heart and a right spirit.

Daily Deposit: Start building a house fit for God today, by spending more time in God's Word and less time in front of the television.

August 6

Goodness and Mercy
Ezra 3:1–4:24

Most of us are familiar with Psalm 23. David declared in this psalm that the Lord's mercy and goodness would follow him all the days of his life. This should be the testimony for every Christian.

When we look back at even the difficult trials we have experienced, we can see how something good resulted from these trials. God allows every trial in our life for our good and for His glory.

The Israelite's captivity was over for a season. It was time to rebuild the temple. Before they even restored the temple, they began to establish again the feasts and the sacrifices God had commanded them to observe once again. They also gave all the money needed for rebuilding the temple. The Levites began to oversee the work of the house of God, and all the people responded as one to undertake the mammoth task of rebuilding the house of God.

The time came to lay the foundation for the new temple. What a joyous celebration. When the foundation was laid, the priests stood in their beautiful apparel and blew the trumpets. The cymbals of the sons of Asaph clashed in rhythm with the shouts of the people. What were the people shouting? They were shouting and giving thanks to the Lord by saying, "For He is good, for His mercy endures forever toward Israel" (Ezra 3:11).

The Children of Israel had come through a great trial. They had experienced the cruel bondage of Babylon. Many I'm sure asked the questions, "Where are You God? Why have You forsaken us?" God had not forsaken Israel. He brought them out of Babylon and now they could rebuild His temple. As they shouted and praised the Lord, many of the older priests began to weep because they remembered when the foundation was laid for Solomon's temple. They longed to have that temple again, but the new temple would not compare to the glory of Solomon's temple.

When we experience destruction and bondage in our lives, we can hold on to the hope that restoration will eventually come if we keep seeking the Lord. We will not have to weep when this restoration process begins because God will make all things new. We travel from glory to glory even when we pass through the wilderness of trials. God is good all the time! His mercies are new every morning!

Lord, forgive me for the times I have not seen Your goodness in some of the trials I have experienced.

Daily Deposit: Take time today to write down how God has shown His mercy and goodness to you through some of the trials of your life. What you write down will be recorded in the Book of Remembrance in heaven.

August 7

Read: Ezra 5:1–6:22; 1 Corinthians 3:5–23 Psalm 29:1–11; Proverbs 20:26–27

The Voice of the Lord
Psalm 29:1–11

When I speak or teach I often share what I have heard the Lord speak to my heart. I have never heard an audible voice, but often, the Holy Spirit impresses me with scriptures and words for my instruction, correction, and reproof. The Holy Spirit also gives me words from God's Word to share with others. Someone once said, "If you have to hear an audible voice from God, your spiritual ears are stopped up."

We all have had seasons where we have had a hard time hearing from the Lord. I have come to believe that when I have those times, I need to examine my own heart and ask these questions: "Am I daily reading God's Word? Am I seeking to be taught of the Holy Spirit as I read God's Word? Am I careful to guard my physical and spiritual ears, instead of filling them with voices and music that clutter my ears? Am I asking God questions and taking time to wait for an answer?"

Psalm 29 describes God's voice. David wrote: "The voice of the Lord is over the waters; the God of glory thunders" (v. 3). "The voice of the Lord is powerful; the voice of the Lord is full of majesty" (v. 4). "The voice of the Lord splinters the cedars of Lebanon and makes them skip like a calf" (v. 6). "The voice of the Lord divides the flames of fire" (v. 7). "The voice of the Lord shakes the Wilderness and makes the deer give birth" (vv. 8–9).

If any of us heard the audible voice of the Lord with all of its strength, majesty, and power, we would probably die of a heart attack. When the Children of Israel heard the voice of God from Mt. Sinai, they trembled and asked Moses to relay God's word to them from that day forward. We don't have Moses to relay God's voice to us today, but we do have the Holy Spirit who gently filters God's voice to us so that we can hear God's voice and respond in love, not fear.

God speaks to us in a still, quiet voice. The Holy Spirit gives us gentle impressions and instructions, as we read God's Word. We talked earlier about tuning our spiritual ears to hear God's voice by getting rid of the worldly buildup of other voices and music that stop up our spiritual ears. The day will come when we will hear God's voice with all of its majesty and power. That day will occur when Jesus gives a loud victory shout and calls forth those in the graves to join Him in their glorified bodies. We can look forward to that great Resurrection Day. We don't have to wait until that day, however, to hear God's voice. Are you listening carefully for God to speak to you today?

Lord, forgive me for the times I have not taken the time to listen for Your voice. Holy Spirit, tune my ears to hear God's voice today.

Daily Deposit: Take time today to ask God questions and wait for an answer. Your life may be changed forever.

August 8

Preparing Our Hearts
Ezra 7:1–8:20

We talked, yesterday, about hearing the voice of the Lord. We hear His voice with our hearts. The exhortation in the early scriptures many times was, "Hearken to the voice of the Lord." The word *hearken* means "listen; listening." Jesus said, "He who has an ear to hear, let him hear" (Rev. 2:29). If we are going to be able to hear the voice of the Lord, we need to prepare our hearts to hear.

There have been many times in my life when I had seasons of reading God's Word without receiving God's Word into my heart. Also, there have been many times when I have read God's Word and did not have a clue about the meaning of what I just read.

Moses prayed in Psalm 90 for us to number our days that we may apply our hearts to wisdom. (See Psalm 90:12.) Solomon spoke of how David taught him to let his heart retain God's words so he could keep His commands and live. David exhorted Solomon to obtain wisdom and understanding and never to forget or forsake God's Word. (See Proverbs 4:4–6.) Solomon exhorted his own sons to lend their ears to understand God's Word. (See Proverbs 5:1.)

To hear God's voice through His Word, we must prepare our hearts to hear by guarding our physical ear gates and by sharpening our spiritual ears. We read in our passage today:

> For Ezra had prepared his heart to seek the Law of the LORD, and to do it, and to teach statutes and ordinances in Israel.
>
> —EZRA 7:10

Ezra prepared his heart to seek God's Word. His motivation was to obey what he heard and to teach what he learned to the people God had given him to lead.

How can we daily prepare our hearts to hear God's voice? Jesus gave the answer to this in the Parable of the Sower, presented in Luke 8. This parable is about hearing God's voice with our hearts. Jesus described four conditions of the heart:

1. Callous heart—Our hearts cannot hear because they are hard (vv.5, 12).
2. Careless heart—Our hearts cannot hear because they are not rooted and grounded in love (vv.6, 13).
3. Cluttered heart—Our hearts cannot hear because they are filled with the cares, riches, and pleasures of this world (vv. 7, 14).
4. Contrite heart—Our hearts hear because we are obedient, meek, and humble (vv. 8, 15).

Lord, create in me a clean heart so I can hear Your voice.

Daily Deposit: Prepare your heart today to seek His Word and hear His voice.

August 9

Read: Ezra 8:21–9:15; I Corinthians 5:1–13; Psalm 31:1–8; Proverbs 21:1–2

Ministers for the House of God
Ezra 8:21–9:15

"I'm a son of Levi!" the elderly man in the wheelchair proudly exclaimed when I introduced myself to him, inviting him to the Bible study I was teaching in his retirement home. Dr. Levin later, on several occasions, visited my study. I wanted to share with Dr. Levin that I was also a daughter of Levi, but I did not think he would understand.

Our passage today speaks about one of the problems Ezra faced as he tried to rebuild God's house in Jerusalem. After reviewing all the households present, Ezra realized that there were none present from the household of Levi. He gave the command to Iddo and his brethren to bring to him the ministers for the house of God. By God's grace, Iddo found a man of understanding of the sons of Levi. Eventually, over 200 sons of Levi were found and gathered together to minister for the House of God.

No church today should face the problem Ezra had. Why? Because we are all priests called to minister, both to the Lord and to His people. Have you recognized your priestly role? Daily, you have the opportunity to minister to the Lord and His people. The Lord is always present to receive our adoration, as we minister to Him with our songs of praise and worship. His people are always present with us, also, to receive our love, prayers, praises, exhortations, and encouragement.

I can remember a period of two years when I was without a car. My husband had a company car, but we decided not to purchase one for my use. During this season, I daily prayed, "Lord, if you want me to minister to someone today, bring them to my door or have them call me."

I had just prayed that prayer one morning, when the doorbell rang. It was a neighbor I had just met the night before at our neighborhood garden club. She asked if she could come in and talk with me about something. I welcomed her and listened to her request. She said, "Last night when I met you, I knew you were a Christian. I desperately need a prayer partner in the days ahead, as I am going through a divorce. Would you be willing to be my prayer partner?" I responded strongly, "Yes, I would love to be your prayer partner!" She exclaimed, "Now don't say yes right away. This is serious, and I think you need to pray about it before you give me an answer." I then shared with her how I had already prayed that morning for the Lord to send me someone I could minister to.

Lord, help me to always be ready to minister to You and to Your people.

Daily Deposit: Minister to the Lord by spending time worshiping and praising Him. Ask Him in prayer today to lead you to minister to one of His beloved.

August 10

Godly Sorrow
Ezra 10:1–44

The Word of God tells us that there are only two things that can produce repentance in our lives. In 2 Corinthians 7:10, it states: "For godly sorrow produces repentance leading to salvation, not to be regretted; but the sorrow of the world produces death."

In Romans 2:4, it says: "Or do you despise the riches of His goodness, forbearance, and longsuffering, not knowing that the *goodness of God* leads you to repentance" (emphasis added).

Repentance is a gift from God. No one without the Holy Spirit's help even has a desire to repent. Our hearts are despitefully wicked. The Holy Spirit often will bring godly sorrow upon us. Suddenly, we realize how our lives have grieved God. We don't like ourselves and we want to change. When we reach this point in our lives, we cry out to God. He hears us; we repent of our sins. We are saved from our sins when we accept Jesus Christ as our Lord and Savior. Godly sorrow produces repentance unto salvation. We are translated from the kingdom of darkness to the kingdom of light.

Both the goodness of God and godly sorrow can produce repentance in us after we are saved. We see the long-suffering of God over and over again in our lives. We see His hand of mercy and experience the strength of His grace. We are convicted of our ungratefulness and our lack of commitment when we meditate on the goodness of God. We repent of our lack of discipline and commitment, and we receive God's grace to help us in our weak areas. We repent of our pride and willfulness. We are transformed by the renewing of our minds and recognize that our total dependency upon God to work in and through us.

Godly sorrow often overwhelms us as we read God's Word and we see how we have grieved the Holy Spirit by sinning in specific ways. This kind of godly sorrow was experienced after Ezra spent hours reading the law to the people. As soon as they heard the law, they realized how they had sinned by marrying foreign women. They began to mourn because of their transgression of the law. It was as if God, Himself, was joining them as they wept over their own sin. When we look into God's Word, God's light reveals our sin and we cannot help but repent and cry out for God's mercy.

Have you ever had godly sorrow produce repentance in your life? I guarantee that if you spend time in God's Word, you will be touched by God's sorrow over your sin, and you will receive the gift of repentance.

Lord, thank you for Your Word that shines a light on my sin. Nothing will change in my life if I refuse to recognize my own sin.

Daily Deposit: Look into the mirror of God's Word today and ask God to reveal to you the things in your life that grieve Him.

August 11

Read: Nehemiah 1:1–3:14; 1 Corinthians 7:1–19; Psalm 31:19–24; Proverbs 21:4

Keeping On Keeping On!
1 Corinthians 7:1–19

Over thirty years ago, my sister-in-law came for a visit. She had been married for seven years, and her husband was not saved. She shared with me that she was ready to divorce her husband. I led her to this chapter in Corinthians. I explained to her that since she was a believer, she was not to depart from her husband if he was willing to stay with her. Paul made this statement, "And a woman who has a husband who does not believe, if he is willing to live with her, let her not divorce him" (v.13).

In obedience to what Paul shared about marriage, my sister-in-law decided she could not leave her husband. A few years later, her husband was gloriously saved. He was a deer hunter and spent many weekends hunting deer. On one of those hunting weekends, my sister-in-law came up to visit us in Atlanta.

One of her friends spent the night on a Friday night and we decided to intercede for my-sister-in-law's husband. As we sat around the breakfast room table, we began to pray. I had just learned the spiritual principle of breaking ancestral ties by confessing the sins of the forefathers back to four generations. (See Exodus 20:5.) I shared with them that we had tried everything in prayer for her husband, but we had not broken these generational ties. We were so desperate that we fumbled through the prayer from a little tract I had about breaking the ancestral ties. As we prayed, I saw with my spiritual eyes a block of wood over her husband's head. That piece of wood was blocking a heavenly light that was shining down on his head. We continued in prayer and then I saw that block of wood move. The light from heaven was shining on her husband. I exclaimed excitedly, "Wow! I don't know what happened, but I think we have had a spiritual breakthrough for your husband!"

The Sunday after we prayed those prayers, her husband showed up early in the morning to pick up my-sister-in law. We were shocked when he said, "I came early, because we have to reach home in time to go to church. With his mouth wide open in disbelief, their son asked, "Dad, are you sick?" They went to church that morning, and their church was in revival. The preacher was loud and forceful, and my sister-in-law thought, "Boy, my husband will never come back to church!" The revival continued all week and, on Thursday night, her husband suddenly said, "Let's go to church!" The message was about deer hunting. It turns out that the preacher was a big deer hunter. That night, my sister-in-law's husband was gloriously saved.

We found out later what happened on the night we prayed together. That night her husband shot a deer and he couldn't find where the deer fell. He made a deal with God and prayed, "God, if you will help me find that deer, I promise I will go to church on Sunday." He looked just a few feet ahead and there was the deer.

Lord, help me to keep on keeping on in faith when I face trials.

Daily Deposit: Pray with faith today for your lost loved ones.

August 12

Abiding in Your Call
1 Corinthians 7:20–40

S o many singles are anxious about finding their life partner. Marriage occurs when one male and one female join themselves in a covenant with God and they become one flesh under God. When we speak our vows to one another on that great wedding day, God sees us as one flesh. However, the process of becoming one spiritually, physically, mentally, and emotionally usually spans the lifetime of a marriage. The blending of two personalities into unity is even more difficult than skin grafting. Skin grafting is an extremely painful process. I have a relative who was burned over 80 percent of her body. It took years for her to recover after receiving what seemed like endless skin grafts. Even after the skin grafts, there were noticeable scars.

When a man and woman marry, the grafting process begins. Two wills, two minds, two emotional conditions, two bodies, two past experiences, and two spirits slowly become unified as one. The only thing that will make this grafting process less painful is the engrafted Word of God. If both marriage partners have engrafted the Word of God in their hearts, they will be more likely to submit to one another in love and to esteem their marriage partner higher than they esteem themselves.

Both partners bring into the marriage the scars from their past. They both may have suffered rejection and wounds in past relationships. Only Jesus Christ can heal the broken heart. If both partners are willing to receive the skillful touch of the Surgeon's knife (the Word of God), they will be spared a lot of pain and misery in their marriage.

Paul recommended that people not marry, simply because he was convinced that the Lord would return soon. He felt it was not wise to enter marriage, because he knew it took time for husband and wife to become wedded and unified in the various areas of their lives. He knew that when people are married, they have to be concerned about commitment to one another, as well as their commitment to the Lord. Paul desired for the followers of Jesus to be undivided in their focus upon Jesus.

Paul was not against marriage. In fact, he wrote to the Ephesians that marriage is an example of Christ and the church. If no one ever married, we would not have this beautiful illustration of Christ and the church (His bride).

Many may feel as Paul did when he wrote this letter. They may feel that the Lord will return very soon. I would advise singles to seek the Lord about their calling in these days. If they are called to be married, they should marry. If they are called to be single, they should remain single. We all should remain in our callings as the days approach the return of the Lord.

Lord, speak to the singles I know and show them what their calling is.

Daily Deposit: Call a single person today and encourage him or her to ask the Lord about their calling.

Preventing Stumbling
1 Corinthians 8:1–13

Not long ago, I traveled with a woman in a wheelchair. She was able to walk with a walker for only short distances, because her legs were so weak. I prayed continually that I would be able to see ahead of her when she walked, so I could remove anything that might cause her to stumble and fall. When we love someone, we do not want to do anything that would physically harm or emotionally hurt them.

Paul exhorts us, in this passage, not to do anything that would cause our weaker brother in Christ to stumble. He warned the Corinthian Christians not to offend their brothers and sisters by partaking of food given to idols, when they were in the presence of those who believed such a practice was sin.

When we share the Gospel in different countries, there are many cultural customs we need to be aware of. When we were in India, we were told not to show any open affection towards one another, even though we were married. We were told this would offend the Indian people. When we were in Mexico, the women on our mission team were told to always wear skirts because many Mexicans felt it was a sin for a woman to wear slacks. When we were in Russia, the women on our team were asked not to wear makeup. When we visited the Western Wall in Israel, the women were told to cover their heads, since this was the Jewish custom. Paul was familiar with the customs of the various countries he visited. He wrote:

> And to the Jews I became as a Jew, that I might win Jews; to those who are under the law, as under the law, that I might win those who are under the law…to the weak I became as weak, that I might win the weak. I have become all things to all men, that I might by all means save some.
>
> —1 Corinthians 9:20–22

When our appearance, actions, and words are not in line with the customs in a country, the Gospel message we deliver may not be received because we have created a stumbling block before the people of that land. Also, if we know our Christian brothers are offended by certain things we do, we should avoid doing those things when we are in their presence. We have a responsibility as Christians not to cause our brothers and sisters in Christ to stumble.

Lord, help me to be sensitive to the beliefs of my brothers and sisters in Christ. Help me to never cause them to stumble by something I do or say.

Daily Deposit: At the end of our days, our words and deeds will be judged for reward. Having this eternal perspective should encourage us all to be discreet and discerning about our actions and words.

August 14

The Priceless Gospel
1 Corinthians 9:1—19

To charge people money to hear the Gospel of Christ is, I believe, an abomination to God.

A recent practice of well-known preachers and evangelists is to refuse to speak anywhere, unless a certain fee is guaranteed or unless a certain number of people will be present to hear their message. Such a practice is not scriptural.

Paul was not dependent upon people to supply his needs as he preached in different locations. He was dependent upon God to meet his needs. Offerings were often gathered before Paul even reached the city where he planned to deliver a message. These offerings were meant to help Paul with his journeys and housing expenses. They were not used by Paul to gain riches for himself.

Preachers and evangelists must provide for their families. However, they should depend upon God to meet their needs. God can cause men to give to them generously. They can pray for God to lay upon the hearts of the people what they should give as a love offering. Most pastors in America are salaried. What would happened if these pastors told their board of elders that they would just receive a love offering from the people instead of being on salary? So far, I have never seen a pastor do this, but it would open the door for them to pray more and be more dependent upon God.

Paul wrote, "If we have sown spiritual things for you, is it a great thing if we reap your material things?" (1 Cor. 9:11). However, Paul did not use this right, because he did not want to hinder the Gospel. He was free to travel wherever the Lord led him to go, and he trusted the Lord to provide the means by which he should live and travel. Paul always preached the Gospel without charge, so he never was guilty of abusing his authority in the Gospel. Paul's needs were always met because he trusted the One who supplies all. Who do you trust to be your provider?

Lord, forgive me for the times I have been anxious about my financial condition. Help me to cast this care upon You.

Daily Deposit: Pray for God to give you wisdom as you sow monies into various ministries.

August 15

Things in Common
1 Corinthians 9:20–10:14

No matter what your doctrine or denomination may be, there is one thing you have in common with every Christian. That one thing is the experience of temptation. Satan has no particular denomination or doctrine in mind when he targets Christians for temptation. When we go through trials and temptations, satan is targeting us for destruction, and God is testing our faith. Sometimes, however, when I go through trials I think, "No one has ever been faced with what I am facing now." However, Paul wrote:

> No temptation has overtaken you except such as is common to man; but God is faithful, who will not allow you to be tempted beyond what you are able, but with the temptation will also make the way of escape, that you may be able to bear it.
> —1 Corinthians 10:13

Temptation is common to man. Even non-Christians go through trials and temptations. However, Christians have Jesus as their way of escape when they go through various temptations. Everything we face in this life has already been faced by Jesus. He has gone before us in every trial. The unbeliever has to wade through trials and temptations in their own strength. I feel sorry for them.

Trouble, tribulation, trials, and temptations are the four "T's" that will be our constant companions through life. If we are seeking to walk in the ways of the Lord, we can rest assured that God will not allow us to be tested or tempted beyond what He knows we are able to bear. I recently heard the testimony of a man who lost both his wife and his child to AIDS. His wife hemorrhaged during childbirth and had to receive a transfusion. The blood she received transmitted the AIDS virus to her. Later she became pregnant with another child, and that child was born with AIDS. When I heard this man's testimony, I was amazed at his faith. He was not bitter, and God used his experience to inspire him to write a book that has helped thousands through their trials.

Our faith does not grow through trials unless we seek the help of Jesus (our way of escape) and His Word in the midst of the trial. When we read the history of the children of Israel, we see how they often failed the "faith test." They were examples to warn us all of our vulnerability to defeat when we do not walk in God's ways. We have much more going for us, however, than they did.

We now have Jesus (the author and finisher of our faith) who can supply us with all the faith we need to go through every trial and temptation, if we will only turn to Him in complete trust.

Lord, thank You for being my way of escape.

Daily Deposit: Today, write down the many times Jesus has been your way of escape in the midst of trials. Your words will be added to your Book of Remembrance in heaven.

August 16

Good Days and Long Life
Psalm 34:11–22

We are friends with a couple who always present a constant challenge to us. We celebrate our anniversaries and birthdays with them because we are the same age and have both been married for forty-four years. Our two friends go to the gym every day, eat all the right foods, and are disgustingly in great shape. Even when we were on a cruise together to celebrate our fortieth anniversary, they hit the weight room every day and only ordered the low calories meals. My husband and I do not have the discipline or the diligence to keep up with their healthy habits. Sometimes we laugh and ask, "Do they plan to live forever?"

No matter how disciplined we are with our health habits, we all have to face the fact that one out of every one people die. We all have our appointment with death. This psalm, however, reveals a way that will guarantee us both long and good days, and it has nothing to do with our physical condition. It has everything to do with our spiritual condition. David wrote (vv. 12–14):

> Who is the man who desires life, and loves many days, that he may see good? Keep your tongue from evil, and your lips from speaking deceit. Depart from evil and do good; seek peace and pursue it.

If we want to see long days, we must be careful about what we say and what we do. David's son, Solomon, agreed with his father when he wrote:

> Death and life are in the power of the tongue, And those who love it will eat its fruit.
>
> —PROVERBS 18:21

> Whoever guards his mouth and tongue keeps his soul from troubles.
>
> —PROVERBS 21:23

If we want to see long days, we must be careful about what we say and what we do. Keeping our speech pure will affect our souls and also add years to our lives. If we pursue peace, we will also see good and long days. I knew a woman who lived to be 105 years old. I noticed she never murmured or complained, and she always encouraged others. When I asked her what her secret to long life was she exclaimed, "I love the Lord and I love people. Oh, I also eat All Bran!" To sum it all up a formula for long life is:

Speak good things + do good things + seek peace + All Bran = Long life.

Lord, help me to speak Your words and do Your work.

Daily Deposit: Try to speak only those things that edify today.

August 17

Our Covering
1 Corinthians 11:3–16

When we read some of Paul's letters, we might conclude that he is a male chauvinist. Today's reading certainly would lead one to believe that Paul was not a big fan of women. However, when we look deeper into the culture of Paul's day, we are able to have a better understanding of his views.

In Paul's day, prostitutes shaved their heads. Paul felt that men should not have their heads covered during worship, since they are the image and glory of God, and women should have their heads covered when they prayed or prophesied. If we read a little further, Paul states that all things are from God. Paul ended his dissertation on head coverings with these statements (vv. 15–16):

> But if a woman has long hair, it is a glory to her; for her hair is given to her for a covering. But if anyone seems to be contentious, we have no such custom, nor do the churches of God.

Paul was simply speaking about the customs. He was not issuing commandments. Paul, of all people, would never want us to be bound by custom or tradition. Paul neither condemns the custom nor commends the custom.

In our own church, we used to have several women who wore head coverings as a symbol that they were under the authority of their husbands. Many Catholics and Jewish women carry on the tradition of having their head covered when they attend church or synagogue.

As women, we do display the glory of our husbands. I was on a search team for a pastor once, and our team made sure we approved of the wife of the pastor before we offered him a job. When we look at a man's wife, we usually can discern what kind of man is married to her. David, however, wrote that we all were created for the praise and glory of God.

Whatever our religious tradition is, both men and women are called to demonstrate God's glory in their actions and words. When we do honor the Lord in our words and deeds, we will all be covered by His glory. A prayer I like to pray daily is:

Lord, be glorified in my life today.

Daily Deposit: We make deposits in our heavenly bank accounts whenever we glorify God in our words and deeds on earth.

August 18

Communion
1 Corinthians 11:17–34

The order of a communion service varies from church to church and from culture to culture. When we were in a church in Paris, France, we were invited to come to the altar to drink wine from a common cup and to tear a piece of bread from a common loaf. When I was a Southern Baptist, we celebrated communion once a quarter. This was also the tradition of the Presbyterian Church I joined after I married. Both churches passed a tray with grape juice and a tray of tiny little wafers to represent the body of Christ. The church I now attend observes communion every Sunday. In those moments of quiet reflection, the Lord often speaks to my heart.

Verses 24 and 25 in our passage today are usually quoted before communion services in most churches. We had the opportunity, when we were in Israel, to visit the Bible Institute where they had a replica of the upper room. We ate a meal there and took communion. I closed my eyes and imagined Jesus standing before the disciples and saying (v. 24):

Take, eat; this is My body which is broken for you; do this in remembrance of Me.

When I heard those words in that special setting, my spiritual ears heard these personal words spoken to my heart:

I love you with the same love my Father loved me. I gave my body willingly on the cross for you. If you had been the only person on earth, I still would have died for you. This is how much I love you.

With my eyes still closed, I used my divine imagination to picture Jesus lifting the cup and saying (v. 25):

This cup is the new covenant in My blood. This do, as often as you drink it, in remembrance of me.

Again I heard the still, quiet voice of the Holy Spirit say, "Through the blood of *Jesus* you have been sanctified, justified, forgiven, redeemed, restored, and healed."

Lord, help me to remember those words spoken to me in Israel.

Daily Deposit: You can celebrate communion in your own home today. Communion can mean co-union and communication with Christ Jesus.

August 19

Jesus Is Lord
1 Corinthians 12:1–26

It was the usual Episcopal service at the church in Seattle where my aunt attended. However, instead of ending the service with his weekly Sunday morning benediction, the priest did something that changed my aunt's life forever. With his microphone in hand, the priest left the pulpit, stepped off the platform, and walked among the congregation. Then he gave these instructions, "As I walk among you today, I will stop in front of each one of you and say, 'Jesus Christ is Lord.' I ask each person present to make that same good confession as I hold the mike in front of you."

As the priest traveled down each row of pews, my aunt became more and more self-conscience and nervous. My aunt's heart was pounding as the priest stood only two people away from her. Then her turn came. With a dry throated, shaky voice, my aunt confessed, "Jesus Christ is Lord." Suddenly she felt a peace flood her soul and she no longer was trembling. It was the first time she had made that public confession. As the words of faith came out of her mouth, she was born again. Until that day she was a religious observer. After that day, she became a part of the family of God. Her religiosity was transformed into a relationship with the living God.

Paul wrote (v. 3):

> Therefore I make known to you that no one speaking by the Spirit of God calls Jesus accursed, and no one can say that Jesus is Lord except by the Holy Spirit.

Paul also wrote:

> But what does it say? "The word is near you, in your mouth and in your heart" (that is, the word of faith which we preach): that if you confess with your mouth the Lord Jesus and believe in your heart that God has raised Him from the dead, you will be saved. For with the heart one believes unto righteousness, and with the mouth confession is made unto salvation.
>
> —Romans 10:8–10

Jesus Christ is my Lord and Savior to the glory of God.

Daily Deposit: Make that good confession often today. Each time you speak these words, your words will be recorded in your Book of Remembrance in heaven.

The Esther Victory
Esther 8:1–10:3

E very Purim, the Esther story is celebrated by Jewish people throughout the world.
Dramatic portrayals of the story of Esther are presented in temples and homes. We had the opportunity to visit a Jewish home during Purim. The children and adults wore costumes. Haman was played by a burley, bearded man with a fake handlebar mustache. He truly looked the villain. Every time he came on stage, adults and children alike twirled and shook various noisemakers and shouted, "Boo, boo!" Whenever Esther or Mordecai appeared on stage, there was a great victory shout.

The story of Esther is certainly a victory story. What seemed to be certain destruction for all the Jews in the over one hundred provinces from India to Ethiopia that King Ahasuerus ruled was averted through united prayer and fasting and two obedient servants of the Lord, Esther and Mordecai.

This story always inspires me to be bolder in my faith. With fear and trembling, Esther was willing to risk her life to go before King Ahasuerus, without being invited. Mordecai boldly refused to bow down to Haman, the king's right hand administrator, when he passed through the streets of Shushan.

Our passage today begins with these words, "On that day King Ahasuerus gave Queen Esther the house of Haman, the enemy of the Jews" (Esth. 8:1). The king took off his signet ring (the very ring he had previously given to Haman) and gave it to Mordecai. Esther appointed Mordecai over the house of Haman. Esther pleaded with the king to counteract the decree to kill all the Jews Haman had coerced the king to sign. However, the king could not reverse the letters devised by Haman to annihilate the Jews, because it was the law. The king asked Queen Esther to write another decree concerning the Jews and to seal it with the king's signet ring. The new decree permitted the Jews who were in every city to defend themselves and to destroy, kill, and annihilate all the forces of any people that would try to assault them.

Even though the book of Esther never mentions God, the story is a dramatic portrayal of what God did for us when He gave His only begotten son, Jesus Christ, to be crucified for our sins. Through the crucifixion and resurrection of Jesus Christ, satan's house was delivered to the church (the bride of Christ). We were given the right to make declarations that decree the destruction of satan. We were given the Holy Spirit (the seal of King Jesus that gives us all authority over satan). Jesus Christ was crucified on the cross; satan's kingdom was given to us, and now we have the authority and the power of the Holy Spirit to make satan's accusations and plans of destruction against us null and void. We can all shout the victory shout!

Lord, help me never forget that I have been given all power over satan.

Daily Deposit: Use your authority today to resist the devil.

August 21

Read: Job 1:1–3:26; 1 Corinthians 14:1–17; Psalm 37:12–28; Proverbs 21:25–26

Edification
1 Corinthians 14:1–17

Have you ever thought about why you need to attend a corporate gathering of believers on a weekly basis? Often we get into the routine of attending a church or a fellowship, just because the Word of God exhorts us not to forsake the assembling of ourselves together. Of course, the major purpose we attend church is to worship the Lord in a corporate setting. However, we also gather together unto the Lord Jesus Christ so we can be built up or edified. Edification is essential for the Bride of Christ, especially in these last days. If we leave our church service without being edified, something is wrong. We need to be edified by the message, the music, and the ministry.

The subject of *edification* was discussed in this passage. Paul was exhorting the church at Corinth to be careful to use their gifts to edify the church. Many in the church were able to pray and sing in tongues, and Paul thanked God that he spoke in tongues more than them all. However, he challenged them to prophesy because prophecy edifies the church. He believed, also, that tongues should only be used in a public gathering if the tongues were interpreted so that all present could understand the message. He wrote (vv. 10–11):

> There are, it may be, so many kinds of languages in the world, and none of them is without significance. Therefore, if I do not know the meaning of the language, I shall be a foreigner to him who speaks, and he who speaks will be a foreigner to me.

We experienced what it is like to be a foreigner who does not understand the language. When we visited our son in Budapest, we attended a service that was delivered in Hungarian. Thank God there was an interpreter! If there had not been an interpreter, we would have left the church without being edified. When we attended Christ Church in Jerusalem, several prophecies were given. Two prophecies were given in Hebrew and I did not understand what was being said. I prayed, "O Lord, if there is another prophecy, please let an English speaking person deliver it." The next prophecy was given by an English speaking saint who delivered words that not only edified me, but also changed my life. The words were, "You will be tried by fire, but you will be like shining crystal after it is fired, and you will stand on the crystal sea with all the saints and rejoice." I was familiar with the passages about the saints being refined like silver and gold through trials, but what did this word about crystal mean? Later I looked up the process for making crystal. I discovered that the temperature of the fire used to make crystal is much higher than that used to refine gold. I then understood that no matter how hard, heavy, and hot the trials get in these last days, God's promise is to beautify His church and to present them faultless and flawless. That word edified me. How about you?

Lord, thank You for all of Your gifts. May I always use them to edify.

Daily Deposit: Use your gifts today to edify your friends and family.

233

August 22

Targeted and Tested
Job 4:1–7:21

In over thirty years of reading the Bible through in a year, I still do not look forward to reading the book of Job. Chapter after chapter in Job reveals who tests us and who targets us in this life. However, Job and his friends did not fully understand the concept of testing and targeting.

Throughout our lives, we are tested by God. He allows circumstances and relationships to test us. What is God testing? Every trial we face is a test of our faith. God tests us to see if we will trust Him in our trials or trust in ourselves. Like Job, we sometimes may sigh and ask God, "Why have You set me as your target?" (Job 7:20). Job did not realize that God had allowed satan to target him because God had faith that Job would be victorious over satan.

God knows exactly which tests to give us in the school of life. If we turn to Him in complete trust, He will never give us a test that we cannot pass. If we fail to pass a test because we trust in ourselves more than we trust in God, we can be confident that God will give us a make up test. Have you had any of those make up tests lately?

Do you remember when Peter denied Christ three times? Peter trusted in himself more than he trusted in God, and this is why the test was given. It was not a pop quiz either. Jesus told Peter ahead of time that satan would sift him as wheat, but He would pray that Peter's faith would not fail. (See Luke 22:31–32.) Peter really blew his first test, but later Jesus gave him the opportunity to pass when he asked Peter three times if he loved Him. Peter passed his make up test, and his faith, though it wavered during his first test, ultimately did not fail. (See John 21:15–17.)

Peter's temptation to deny Christ was allowed by God to bring Peter to a place of total dependency upon God. Jesus even told Peter, "When you have returned to me, strengthen your brethren" (Luke 22:32). From his test, Peter gained a testimony that would be used often to strengthen those who seem momentarily weak in their faith.

We understand from the book of Job and from the temptation of Peter that God allows satan to target us for failure; while at the same time, God is testing us for success. God knew that both Peter and Job would pass their final faith exam.

Job did not understand this sequence of testing and targeting. He felt like God was punishing him, but he could not figure out why he was being punished, because he felt like he had done everything that God required. At the end of the book of Job, Job finally sees how utterly dependent he is upon God. Job was on the edge of becoming bitter, instead of better, through his various trials. But when he prayed for his friends, all was restored to him. When we do not become bitter in trials, God can make our walk with Him better than it even was before the trial.

Lord, help me to never become bitter when I go through trials.

Daily Deposit: Today, call someone and strengthen them by sharing a testimony you gained through a testing time in your life.

August 23

By the Grace of God
1 Corinthians 15:1–28

Yesterday, we talked about how Job was tested by God and targeted by satan. Throughout our lives, we, too, are tested and targeted, but we have much more going for us than Job had. We are living on the other side of the cross.

Jesus was tested and targeted, but through His death and resurrection, we now have all the power we need to resist the devil when we are tempted. Job longed for a *daysman* (someone to stand in the gap and do battle for him) when he was tempted. God has blessed us with this *daysman*. (See Job 9:33.) His name is *Jesus*. If we will call upon Jesus when we are tempted, we will always win the victory! Why? Because the battle is the Lord's and the victory is ours (2 Chron. 20:15). Through Christ Jesus, we now can enter God's throne room and find grace (God's supernatural ability) in our time of testing and targeting.

Paul took no credit for his ability to be victorious during his testing and targeting times. He said that it was grace that labored through Him. The list of Paul's tests probably exceeds most of ours. When I review Paul's trials listed in 2 Corinthians 11:27, I stand in awe of how he was able to get through them.

Jesus said to Paul, "My grace is sufficient for you, for My strength is made perfect in weakness" (2 Cor. 12:9). Paul wrote, "By the grace of God I am what I am, and His grace toward me was not in vain" (1 Cor. 15:10). When we depend totally upon God's ability and not our own to get through the testing and targeting in our lives, we will also experience what Paul did. We will know that God's grace is sufficient.

If you are going through a testing and targeting time right now, admit your weakness to God. Call on His grace, and allow His grace to operate through you. If you will do this, you will come through this difficult time in your life victoriously.

Lord, thank You for Your grace.

Daily Deposit: One of the gifts we will be able to present Jesus when we see Him face-to-face is that of our trials. I believe we will have a review of every trial, and we will see those trials turn to gold and jewels in heaven. The prophet Malachi wrote:

> Then those who feared the LORD spoke to one another, and the LORD listened and heard them: so a book of remembrance was written before Him for those who fear the LORD and who meditate on His name. "They shall be Mine," says the LORD of hosts, "on the day that I make them My jewels."
>
> —MALACHI 3:16–17

Read: Job 12:1–15:35; 1 Corinthians 15:29–58; Psalm 39:1–13 Proverbs 21:30–31

The Miracle Mirror
1 Corinthians 15:29–58

When we understand two basic facts about our life here on earth, we will be challenged to number our days so that we can apply our hearts to wisdom.

The first fact is that we are mortal. The flesh of our bodies will perish. Every day I look at myself in the mirror and I say, "Lord, I need a miracle!" My face is beginning to show the signs of aging, and every part of my body has dropped or is drooping. The pull of gravity is taking its toll on me. No matter what I do, I cannot beat "Father Time." This flesh will one day turn to dust.

The second fact about our lives on earth is definitely more encouraging. If we are believers in Christ Jesus, we can look forward to the resurrection and transformation of our mortal bodies. Mortality will clothe itself in the garments of immortality, and we will have new bodies that will never die or see corruption again.

The only way I can daily be reminded of this truth is to look into another mirror. I call this mirror the *Miracle Mirror*. This *Miracle Mirror* is the Word of God. When I look into this mirror daily, hope and faith are stirred in my heart and I receive a facelift. Jesus is the glory and lifter of my head. When I focus upon Him, my countenance is beautiful.

Paul wrote:

> The body is sown in corruption, it is raised in incorruption. It is sown in dishonor, it is raised in glory. It is sown in weakness, it is raised in power. It is sown a natural body, it is raised a spiritual body. There is a natural body, and there is a spiritual body.
>
> —1 CORINTHIANS. 15:42–44

Wow! What a miracle! Those words give me a facelift. How about you?

Lord, help me to daily look into the Miracle Mirror of Your Word.

Daily Deposit: When you put on your cosmetics today, focus on Jesus and your face will be brightened with His glory.

August 25

Read: Job 16:1–19:29; 1 Corinthians 16:1–24; Psalm 40:1–10; Proverbs 22:1

Miserable Comforters
Job 16:1–19:29

R ecently I attended a Grief Seminar. The goal of this seminar was to help all those attending to know how to better comfort the grieving. The leader exhorted us not to say these things:

- I know you will miss _____, but you will see them in heaven.
- These things happen in life.
- We don't need to ask why; we just need to ask God what we can do now.
- Jesus said, "In the world you will have tribulation," so what else can we expect?
- Well, you can always have another child or marry again.
- Maybe through this, God is trying to get your attention.

Even though some of these statements are based on scriptures, a grieving person does not need to be banged over the head with a Bible. He needs to have loving arms placed around him, and in most cases, it is best to say nothing. If you have to say something, just say, "I am praying for you daily."

Job was surrounded by miserable comforters who seemed to have all the right answers. Some of the things they shared with Job were absolutely true, but their timing was off. Job questioned them, "Shall words of wind have an end?" (16:3). Often when we try to speak words of comfort, they simply become "words of wind." Such words never comfort. In fact, they can add to the discomfort of those who are grieving.

The only words that we should speak to the grieving are words that are anointed and blown upon by the wind of the Spirit. We need to ask the Holy Spirit to give us the words to comfort the brokenhearted and the grieving. If we receive nothing, it would be better to say nothing.

I have no recall of the words spoken to me when my mother died, but I do remember the presence of many loving people. Their presence gave me more strength than any words they could have spoken to me.

Job said this (vv.16:4–5):

> If your soul were in my soul's place. I could heap up words against you, and shake my head at you; but I would strengthen you with my mouth, and the comfort of my lips would relieve your grief.

We need to put ourselves in the place of the grieving and ask the Holy Spirit to give us the words to say. If we receive nothing to say, then we just need to strengthen the grieving with our presence.

Lord, help me to become a skilled comforter.

Daily Deposit: The Holy Spirit-led words we speak on earth are recorded in heaven.

August 26

Crisis and Comfort
2 Corinthians 1:1–11

We have been talking this month about trials. We mentioned the four "T's" (troubles, trials, temptations, and tribulations). When we experience these four "T's," we need to be aware of what is happening in the spirit realm.

When crisis times invade our lives, we often ask, "Is this something I need to resist or is this something allowed by God to test my faith?" The answer to this question can be found in today's passage. This passage reveals the following:

Troubles and Tribulations—We experience these "T's" because we live in a fallen world (a world that is on a corruption course). Jesus said:

> In the world you will have tribulation; but be of good cheer, I have overcome the world.
>
> —JOHN 16:33

Trials and Temptations—God allows trials to test our faith. At the same time, however, Satan tempts us to be discouraged, angry, or bitter when we go through trials. This is why James tells us to rejoice in the midst of trials because God is testing our faith and developing the fruit of joy and patience in us. We are comforted when we see there is always a purpose for the various "T's" that invade our lives. Paul was always sure that no matter what Satan meant for evil in his life, God would work all things together for his good. (See Romans 8:28.)

Paul gives several reasons we suffer in this life in today's passage:

- We suffer because we are righteous, and satan hates us (v. 5).
- We suffer because through our suffering we are able to console and comfort those who experience similar troubles (v. 4).
- We suffer to strengthen the body of Christ. When we suffer, others are called to pray and do warfare on our behalf. Both those praying and those receiving prayer are strengthened (v. 11).

We can rest assured that when we suffer in this life, our suffering is never in vain, if we depend upon God and His Word in the midst of the suffering.

Lord, help me always to remember that You allow suffering to accomplish Your purposes.

Daily Deposit: One day we will understand more fully the reasons for our suffering. That day may not come until we are in heaven.

August 27

Yes and Amen!
2 Corinthians 1:12–2:8

One of the most common words in every language is *yes*. We have learned to say "yes" in almost every language. Germans say "Da," and Spanish speaking countries say, "Si." In India, people simply shake their heads from left to right to convey a "yes."

Another common word in every language is *amen*. In fact, this word is the same in every country. *Amen* means "so be it" in Hebrew.

Paul wrote:

> For all the promises of God in Him are Yes, and in Him Amen, to the glory of God through us.
>
> —2 Corinthians 1:20

No matter what language we speak, we can all understand what the *Yes* and *Amen* mean in this verse. When Jesus died on the cross to forgive us of our sins, there was a resounding "Yes!" in heaven. *Yes* could also be heard from the portals of hell. Satan and his legions of demons were convinced that they had won, when Jesus died. On Resurrection Day, the angels and saints in heaven were shouting, "Yes and Amen!" Shrill and shocked cries were heard from satan's territory, and their "Yes" was changed to "Oh no!!" There was no "Amen!" heard in hell. Satan's supposed triumph was turned to defeat. Death and hell were swallowed up in victory.

When we face the four "T's" in this life, we need to remember that God stamped *Yes* and *Amen* on the stone that was rolled away on Resurrection Morning. All of God's promises were sealed on that great resurrection morning.

Lord, help me never to forget that glorious Resurrection Morning!

Daily Deposit: Whenever you remember that resurrection morning, your thoughts about Jesus will be recorded in your book of Life in heaven.

August 28

Where Is Wisdom and Understanding?
Job 28:1–30:31

My heart goes out to Job, because he lived in a day when his *daysman* (his interces-sor, Jesus Christ) was not yet born on earth, and the Word of God, as we know it today, was not yet written. Job is the oldest book of the Bible. No wonder Job cried out (v. 12):

> But where shall wisdom be found? And where is the place of understanding?

We know exactly where wisdom and understanding can be found. Wisdom can be found in the living Word (Jesus Christ, who is all wisdom) and in the written Word (the Bible). Understanding is freely given to those who ask the Holy Spirit to teach them as they open their Bibles daily. Solomon said that wisdom and understanding were found in God's Word when he wrote:

> My son, if you receive my words, And treasure my commands within you, So that you incline your ear to wisdom, And apply your heart to understanding; Yes, if you cry out for discernment, And lift up your voice for understanding, If you seek her as silver And search for her as for hidden treasures; Then you will understand the fear of the LORD, and find the knowledge of God. For the LORD gives wisdom; From His mouth come knowledge and understanding.
>
> —PROVERBS 2:1–6

What a blessing it is to live in this age! Job's miseries were multiplied because he did not have complete access into God's throne room. We now have that access, through the blood of Jesus. Whenever we are submerged in the four "T's" (tribulations, troubles, trials, and temptations), we can instantly and boldly enter God's throne room and find help in our time of need. God then graces us with His wisdom and His understanding.

Father, thank You for the sacrifice of Your Son Jesus. Now I can enter Your throne room and find grace to help me when I am in need.

Daily Deposit: God hears all your cries for help when you are in need. God answers those cries by giving you all the wisdom and understanding you need. Ask Him for wisdom and understanding today, and your day will be a heavenly day.

August 29

Read: Job 31:1–33:33; 2 Corinthians 3:1–18; Psalm 43:1–5; Proverbs 22:8–9

Reviewing Our Righteousness
Job 31:1–33:33

Poor Job scratched his head and probably asked God, "Where did I go wrong? What did I do to deserve this treatment?" When we experience the four "T's" in this life, we may ask these same questions. Somehow, we believe, as Job did, that God is punishing us for something we did or said. We may even try to justify ourselves in the sight of God as Job did. In this passage Job reviews his own righteousness. The list is extensive. Here are just a few examples from his review:

1. I have made a covenant with my eyes not to lustfully look upon a woman (Job 31:1).
2. I have always told the truth, and I am a man of integrity (Job 31:6).
3. I have walked in Your ways, and my hands are spotless (Job 31:7).
4. I have never coveted another man's wife (Job 31:9).
5. I have treated my servants well (Job 31:13).
6. I have always given and been kind to the poor (Job 31:16-21).
7. I have never made money my god (Job 31:24–25).
8. I have never gotten involved with astrology (Job 31:26–28).
9. I have never rejoiced over the destruction of my enemies (Job 31:29).
10. I have never sinned with my mouth (Job 31:30).
11. I have always been hospitable to strangers (Job 31:32).
12. I have always confessed my sins to You and to others (Job 31:33–34).

Wow! What a list! Could you live up to even half of Job's righteous life? Job was not being punished. Job was being tested, simply because he was a righteous man. God gave satan permission to test Job. Through the testing, Job realized that all of his own righteousness was as filthy rags in the sight of our great God who framed the universe by His Word.

Job cried out (vv. 31:35–36):

> That my Prosecutor had written a book! Surely I would carry it on my shoulder,
> and bind it on me like a crown.

This was Job's major failing. He saw God as his Prosecutor, not his advocate. Have you ever felt like God was punishing you for your sins? Jesus Christ bore our punishment once and for all on the cross. Rejoice! God is for you, not against you!

Lord, thank You for being my advocate.

Daily Deposit: Today, list just a few of the things God did for you through the death and resurrection of Jesus Christ, His only Son. Your heart will rejoice and your words will be recorded in heaven.

Hearing Test
Job 34:1–36:33

As my husband and I age, we have noticed that we have to speak louder and more distinctly to one another. Sometimes I find myself almost shouting. Our passage today reveals a great secret that will enable us all to gain knowledge, understanding, and wisdom from the Word of God. Many people daily read their Bibles, but they do not experience the change of heart that God can cause as they read their Bibles. People often read the Bible with their minds and not their hearts. Knowledge of the Word of God will simply puff us up, but applying that knowledge to our hearts will change our lives.

Even though Job had miserable comforters, some of them gave marvelous truths that will help us all. In today's passage Elihu said (vv. 34:2–3):

> Hear my words, you wise men; give ear to me, you who have knowledge. For the ear
> tests words as the palate tastes food.

We have to do more than just read God's Word. We need to hear it. Paul wrote, "So then faith comes by hearing, and hearing by the word of God" (Rom. 10:17).

Paul must have read Elihu's words. Wisdom is applied knowledge, and it will not come unless we hear God's Word with our hearts, not just our heads.

Elihu was addressing Job's other miserable comforters, but his message is one we all need to hear. God tells us daily to listen to Him and learn to fear Him (reverence and obey Him). Obedience to God's Word will never happen until we hear God's Word with our hearts. I'm sure you have had the experience of giving commands to your children, and your commands fall on deaf ears. We need to pray daily that our spiritual ears will be open to hear God's Word. We also need to pray daily that God will grace us with an obedient heart to do what His Word tells us to do.

The Children of Israel remained in the wilderness for forty years because they did not hear God's Word. And therefore, they never obeyed God's Word. God promised them if they would hear His Word and obey His Word, they would live a life of blessing. A cursed life would be what they would receive if they failed to hearken (listen with an obedient heart) to the voice of God.

Have you lived a life of blessing? If your answer is "no," perhaps you are not chewing on God's Word enough. You have not tasted and seen that the Lord is good.

Lord, forgive me for the times I have just read Your Word with my
mind and not my heart.

Daily Deposit: Today, when you eat your meals, take time also to chew on God's Word. Listen to God's Word with your heart. Three meals of God's Word a day can change your spiritual diet forever.

August 31

Read: Job 37:1–39:30; 2 Corinthians 4:13–5:11; Psalm 44:8–26; Proverbs 22:13

The Breath of God
Job 37:1–39:30

No matter how hard we try, we cannot define the Trinity with our finite minds. In the past I have come up with my own explanation for the Trinity. I know God must smile at my feeble attempt, but here goes:

- God, the Father, is the speaker or voice.
- God, the Son, is the Word of God made flesh.
- God, the Holy Spirit, is the breath of God.

Whenever we think of the Holy Spirit, we often think of wind and breath. Elihu continued his list of God's wonders in our passage today. Many of these wonders include descriptions of God's wind and breath:

- From the chambers of the south comes the whirlwind.
- Cold comes from the scattering winds of the north.
- By the breath of God ice is given and the broad waters are frozen.
- He quiets the earth with the south wind.
- He clears the skies with His wind so the brightness of the sun shines.

After Elihu's speech, which was quite eloquent, God answered Job out of the whirlwind and Job was awestruck. God still speaks through a whirlwind. His voice is only truly heard when He breathes the Holy Spirit on His Word. The Holy Spirit is the *Great Teacher* who is able to give God's Word the power to blow away all the cobwebs from our minds, so that the light of His glorious Son will shine brightly on our hearts to warm and change our hearts.

Have you asked the Holy Spirit to breathe on God's Word today as you read it?

I guarantee that if you will ask, He will answer, and the Word will become life to you, not just black and red marks on a white page.

Holy Spirit, blow on God's Word as I read from it today.

Daily Deposit: Begin today by asking *The Great Teacher* to take the things of Jesus Christ and show them to you. I promise you will experience a bright, sunny day in the Spirit, and the clouds of your present circumstances will be blown away.

September 1

Why Do the Righteous Suffer?
Job 40:1–42:17

What a relief! We are almost through the book of Job. In my first book, *Around the Word in 365 Days*, I avoided most of the Job passages in the *One Year Bible*. Job is not an easy book to read or to interpret, but I truly have enjoyed my journey through Job this year. I hope you have also. Books have been written to try to answer the question, "Why do the righteous suffer?" The satisfactory answer to this question can be found in the book of Job and no other book. When we look at the book of Job through other pages of the scriptures, we can conclude the following:

The righteous suffer because:

1. Many are the afflictions of the righteous, but the Lord delivers them out of them all. (See Psalm 34:19.) We have adversity because God allows the righteous to be tested even as He allowed Job to be tested. He promises, however, to deliver the righteous out of every affliction.
2. We live in a world that is on a destructive course of corruption. This course of corruption began when Adam and Eve sinned. Jesus warned us that, "In the world you will have tribulation; but be of good cheer, I have overcome the world" (John 16:33).
3. God allows the righteous to experience trials so that we will learn to submit to Him and resist the devil. (See James 4:7.) Just as Job experienced, we often do not recognize our total dependency upon God until we go through hard times. We often do not use our spiritual weapons against the enemy until we encounter hard times. The psalmist David went through many trials, and he said, "He teaches my hands to make war" (Ps. 18:34).
4. God allows the righteous to suffer so that they might understand and have more compassion upon the suffering. Paul wrote (2 Cor. 1:3–4):

> Blessed be the God and Father of our Lord Jesus Christ, the Father of mercies and God of all comfort, who comforts us in all our tribulation, that we may be able to comfort those who are in any trouble, with the comfort with which we ourselves are comforted by God.

Lord, help me to trust You and Your Word in my times of suffering.

Daily Deposit: Thank God today for seeing you through all of your trials.

September 2

Now Is the Day of Salvation
2 Corinthians 6:1–13

There are probably many people whom you are praying and asking the Lord to save. I know my list grows daily. Today's scripture gives me great encouragement as I pray for the salvation of others. It says:

> In an acceptable time I have heard you, And in the day of salvation I have helped you.
>
> —2 Corinthians 6:2

The moment we pray for the salvation of another, we can be assured that God hears our prayers. Not only does He hear our prayers for the salvation of others, but He also answers such prayers. We can base that fact upon the following scripture:

> Now this is the confidence that we have in Him, that if we ask anything according to His will, He hears us. And if we know that He hears us, whatever we ask, we know that we have the petitions that we have asked of Him.
>
> —1 John 5:14–15

The Bible tells us that God is "not willing that any should perish but that all should come to repentance" (2 Pet. 3:9). When we pray for the salvation of another person, we know that we are praying according to God's will so we should have the confidence that God both hears our prayers and that He answers our prayers for the salvation of others.

I used this Scripture to convince a lady that God wanted to save her son who was on drugs. She doubted if God would save him because of his strong rebellion. When I gave her this passage, she repented of her unbelief and then prayed, believing for her son's salvation. The day we agreed in faith believing for her son's salvation, God heard us, and her son's salvation was manifested on earth a year later.

Does this encourage you to pray for all those on your *Salvation List* with faith?

Lord, forgive me for ever doubting that You want to save my loved ones. Help me to pray with faith for each one of them today.

Daily Deposit: Today offer the list of names on your *Salvation List* to God with full confidence that He will hear your prayer and that He will answer those prayers. You can have confidence that you will meet them all in heaven.

September 3

Read: Ecclesiastes 4:1–6:12; 2 Corinthians 6:14–7:7; Psalm 47:1–9; Proverbs 22:16

Unequally Yoked
2 Corinthians 6:14–7:7

There is a Christian computer dating service called "Equally Yoked." I know people who have actually found their mates by using this service. Paul warned believers not to be unequally yoked with unbelievers. This warning can encompass much more than marriage. We should be careful not to be unequally yoked with partners in business, as well. We warned a young man recently not to get into a partnership with a man who was not a believer. He heeded our warning, and his life was spared much misery. Later the shady business practices of this possible partner came to light, and our friend gave thanks to God for sparing him disaster.

The concept of yoking is one that was understood better in Paul's time than in ours, unless you are a farmer. In his day, the necks of two oxen were placed in two joined, wooden collars. These collars kept the two oxen from going separate ways when a farmer was plowing his field. If a farmer had a stubborn ox who wanted to go his own way instead of following the farmer's way, the ox that was attached to the rebellious ox would be pulled off the path and hindered from making the progress needed to get the work done.

Paul knew that if we associated with unbelievers on a regular basis, our spiritual progress would be hindered. The fields that were white and ready for harvest would not be efficiently plowed. Paul asked these questions (vv. 14–16):

> What fellowship has righteousness with lawlessness? And what communion has light with darkness? And what accord has Christ with Belial [a worldly idol]? Or what part has a believer with an unbeliever? And what agreement has the temple of God with idols? For you are the temple of the living God.

The words *fellowship, communion, accord, part,* and *agreement* all connote some type of union, either in thought or action. Of course, we are in the world and we are called to be lights shining in the world. But at the same time, we are not to allow the darkness of worldly friends to invade and hinder our spiritual lives.

We saw the result in our own family of how ungodly friends can pull us away from being effective laborers in this End Time harvest. Two of our sons surrounded themselves with ungodly friends when they were in high school and college. These friends did bring darkness into their lives and, for a season, both of these sons made no spiritual progress. Thank God, they finally broke their relationships with these friends, and now, they are both laboring in the fields God has called them to plow.

Lord, help me to be careful to fellowship with godly friends.

Daily Deposit: Pray for your loved ones today to be equally yoked.

September 4

Read: Ecclesiastes 7:1–9:18; 2 Corinthians 7:8–16; Psalm 48:1–14; Proverbs 22:17–19

What Causes Impatience?
Ecclesiastes 7:1–9:18

Even though the book of Ecclesiastes is extremely negative, we can find some exciting, powerful, positive nuggets throughout its pages. One such nugget is found in our reading today. Solomon wrote:

> The patient in spirit is better than the proud in spirit. Do not hasten in your spirit to be angry, for anger rests in the bosom of fools.
>
> —Ecclesiastes 7:8–9

Solomon also wrote that "by pride comes nothing but strife" (Prov. 13:10). Pride is the root of all contention. Pride first causes us to be impatient. Then we are frustrated. That frustration turns to anger and a root of bitterness and unforgiveness can grow in our hearts. This root can defile not only us, but all those around us. If we are bitter and angry, the only way we can be delivered from that tormenting state is to humble ourselves and confess our own pride.

We need to quit the blame game that always says, "I am angry at you because of what you did or said." Instead, we need to get at the root of our own anger. No one on this earth has the power to make us angry. We open the door to anger through our own pride. Anger does rest in the bosom of fools. When we give way to anger, we are nothing but prideful fools. We become disgusted with others for the way they have let us down, and then we become disgusting wretches bound by our own prideful anger.

You might ask, "What is positive and powerful about this nugget of truth?" When we know the truth about our own pride, we can humble ourselves in the sight of God and others, by confessing our own pride. Now there is not only power in confession, but there is also cleansing in confession. The positive note in this nugget of truth is that we can be delivered from our own pride when we confess it. So what are you waiting for? Join me as I make this confession.

> *Lord, I confess the many times my impatience has turned into frustration, and my frustration has turned into anger. Forgive me for being prideful, and help me to humble myself daily before You and also before those I have been angered against.*

Daily Deposit: Anger is a bedfellow we do not want to sleep with overnight. Do not let the sun go down on your anger. Admit your own faults to one another, so that you can be healed. When we forgive one another, our hearts will become tenderized, not tormented.

September 5

Joy and Poverty
2 Corinthians 8:1–15

It has been our privilege to travel to some of the poorest countries on earth. We have been to India, Mexico, and Jamaica, just to name a few. As I observed the people in these countries, I saw a correlation between joy and poverty. When we were in India, the Indian pastors we visited saved their wages for weeks to buy our mission team soft drinks. As we drank, we noticed the bright, white smiles on the dark faces surrounding us. They were so happy because we enjoyed their gifts to us.

In Mexico, we ministered in a camp meeting where all the pastors gathered to praise the Lord and to listen to our team, as we taught from the Bible. Some of the pastors came in with their flocks, and their flocks actually looked like sheep. They were covered with white, chalky dust. They had come from a dry, dusty area in Mexico where they do not have enough water to take baths. Yet, they were all filled with the bubbling waters of the Holy Spirit and they danced and gave God and us the gift of joyful worship.

In Jamaica, we had the opportunity to visit a small Mennonite church located on a high hill where there was no running water. The pastor and his wife glowed with joy when we gave them my first devotional book and several other books I had written. The pastor's wife excitedly related that she had had a dream two nights before. In the dream she saw people with white faces come to the church with wonderful food. She said, "This is an answer to my prayers and the manifestation of my dream. We are all hungry for the Word of God conveyed in these books." She shared how she also was a writer, and wanted me to see if I could duplicate some of her writings. She wanted the gift of her writings to be shared with many.

These people were joyful because they all were living in the kingdom of God. Paul wrote:

> For the kingdom of God is not eating and drinking, but righteousness and peace and joy in the Holy Spirit.
>
> —Romans 14:17

It did not matter to them that their dwellings were shacks with no running water. They were joyful in their poverty, because they were rich in the Spirit. Paul shared in our reading today how the churches of Macedonia, even in their great trials of affliction and deep poverty, abounded with joy because of their liberality. No matter how poor we may be, we always can give liberally. It is in the giving that we receive the joy that no man can steal from us.

Lord, help me to always be a giver.

Daily Deposit: Whenever we give to others on earth, we add to our bank account in heaven.

September 6

A Love Song
Song of Solomon 1:1–4:16

If I could choose a modern day portrayal of the same holy love conveyed in the Song of Solomon (Song of Songs), I would choose the love story between C.S. Lewis and his bride, a Jewish admirer who read his essays and fell in love with him. He was a professor who wrote many books on theology and the meaning of life. "Shadow Lands" was a movie made about this romance. There was one line in the movie I will never forget. Their wedding vows included this statement, "With my body I thee worship." This line best describes the love relationship God desires to have with us.

There are many sacrifices we can offer to Jesus Christ (our Bridegroom) to demonstrate the love we have for Him; however, there is only one sacrifice worthy of His love for us. This sacrifice is our whole being (body, soul, and spirit). Jesus, the Father, and Holy Spirit love our praise and worship, but praise and worship are just love messages to the Holy Trinity. God desires for our bodies to be lifted up to Him daily as a living sacrifice. This is the act of worship pleasing to Him. He wants us to enter a love relationship with Him comparable to the relationship between husband and wife. The intimate relationship between husband and wife produces fruit, and an intimate relationship with God also produces fruit.

The love story of C. S. Lewis conveys the progression we make as we grow in our intimacy with Jesus Christ. First, C. S. Lewis' Jewish admirer read all of his essays. She devoured their content. Our romance with Jesus begins by reading what God has said about Him in the Bible.

The Jewish admirer of C. S. Lewis finally got up enough courage to meet him in person, and she attended one of his lectures. As we read God's Word, a hunger develops in us and we want to know Jesus better.

C. S. Lewis began to meet with his admirer on a regular basis and their communication soon developed into communion with one another and, finally, marriage.

As we communicate with Jesus in prayer and also listen carefully to what He wants to share with us, we desire to be one with Him. We want His life to be our life. We become hidden with Jesus Christ in God, which is a union no man can put asunder.

The first chapter of the Song of Solomon expresses the desire for us to enjoy our romance with Jesus, His Son and our Bridegroom. The second chapter conveys God's provision and protection of us through His Son Jesus Christ. The third chapter reveals God's ability to hold us forever in His arms because of what Jesus Christ did on the cross.

The fourth chapter unveils God's admiration of our beauty, as He sees us through our Bridegoom's eyes. This survey of God's love expressed through Jesus Christ to us is worth much meditation. Read it slowly and devour its contents.

Father, thank You for giving me Jesus to be my beloved bridegroom.

Daily Deposit: The love letters from Jesus will be read to us again in heaven.

Intimacy—The Key to Successful Marriages
Song of Solomon 5:1–8:14

When my husband and I taught a marriage course in our church, the most difficult chapter we had to cover was the chapter on intimacy. Most people do not like to discuss the intimate aspects of their marriage. Of course, intimacy in marriage includes much more than just our sexual relationship. It also includes our ability to communicate our feelings to one another in a non-threatening way. After teaching this course, I learned several key points that are essential to establishing intimacy with my mate. These key points are discussed in the Song of Solomon.

Chapter 5 of this love song describes the friendship of the two lovers. *The best way to establish intimacy is to first develop a "giving friendship."* This chapter begins with these words, "I have come to my garden, my sister, my spouse." When we do not consider our spouse as someone to meet our needs, but as someone we can share life with, like brothers and sisters, we will begin to establish a good foundation for intimacy.

Chapter 6 describes the beauty that the two lovers see in one another. *Intimacy is based upon our image of one another.* How do we see one another? Do we see God's beauty in one another and draw this beauty to the forefront, or do we criticize and judge each other as we view only our partner's failings? We need to see one another through the eyes of Jesus. He sees us spotless, lovely, and clean.

Chapter 7 talks about the fruitfulness that comes through intimacy. The goal of marriage is more than just having children. Becoming co-laborers who bear much fruit in God's vineyard should be one of the chief goals of a Christian marriage. *One of the greatest ways to establish intimacy in a marriage is to have a common goal.* If our goal together is to glorify God in our marriage and to bear much fruit for Him, then our marriage will be both glorious and intimate.

Chapter 8 continues declaring God's love for us through Jesus Christ. *Intimacy in marriage will never be established until we as individuals have an intimate relationship with Jesus Christ.* We must first see ourselves as God's precious gift to Him. Then we must see one another as God's gift to each other. Granted, these gifts are not perfect by any means, but as they are opened through intimacy the beauty inside of our packaging (our outer man) will be discovered. If we marry with the intent to change one another or to draw out the potential we see in one another, we will be building on a shaky foundation.

Lord, help me to grow in my intimacy with You.

Daily Deposit: When we see Jesus face-to-face, we will know Him completely, and we will be known as He is known. Until that day, we can grow in the knowledge of His love for us as we spend intimate times with Him in His Word and in prayer.

September 8

What Are Our Spiritual Weapons?
2 Corinthians 10:1–18

Recently, our little granddaughter spent the night with us. Her quiet sleep was suddenly interrupted when she began to cry uncontrollably. My son and I spent over an hour trying to get her calmed down. Finally, we concluded we were not dealing with physical pain. The torment she was experiencing was probably caused by a fearful dream. Satan loves to attack us in the night, and children are often most vulnerable to his attacks. When we finally took authority in Jesus' name over the tormenting spirits, her body relaxed, and she was able to go back to sleep.

My son and I then began to talk about our spiritual weapons. I quoted 2 Corinthians 10:3–6, and we discussed it together. We cannot fight spiritual battles with carnal weapons. We must use our spiritual weapons, which are:

- The spoken name of Jesus
- The spoken blood of Jesus
- The spoken Word of God
- All kinds of spoken prayers (including praise and worship)
- The spoken keys to the kingdom—the authority we have to bind and loose
- The spoken power of agreement in prayer
- The spoken full armor of God (Ephesians 6)

I am sure there are more weapons, and it might be well for you to study more on this subject so that you can learn to skillfully employ these spiritual weapons. The battleground is our minds. We are coming against imaginations and prideful thoughts that exalt themselves against the knowledge of God. Only a renewed mind can come against imaginations and prideful thoughts. We can never expect to recognize satan's lies if we are not saturated with God's truths! However, we can use God's Word, spoken out loud, to do warfare for others who are not saturated with God's Word.

We have to recognize that the battle is the Lord's. We must give our disobedient thoughts and imaginations to Jesus, who then can give us the strength to obey His truths. It is most effective when we speak out loud these words, "Lord Jesus, I right now give you this vain imagination and thought. Take it captive and send me a righteous thought." We will then be ready to avenge every disobedient thought or imagination when we consistently do this.

Satan is the prince and power of the air; so we must penetrate his domain by speaking out loud. Silent warfare will never work. God teaches us to war not only for ourselves, but also for others. We never war alone. Jesus is the General of every battle.

Lord, help me to give Your Word voice so that the enemy will flee.

Daily Deposit: Angels and Jesus are waiting for you to speak God's Word on earth so they can come to your aid quickly in every spiritual battle you face!

September 9

One Husband
2 Corinthians 11:1–15

In previous devotionals this month we have discussed marriage (both physical and spiritual marriage). Paul begins this chapter with these words (v. 2):

> For I am jealous for you with godly jealousy. For I have betrothed you to one husband, that I may present you as a chaste virgin to Christ.

When we were in Peru, my husband and I had the opportunity to minister to many abused and brokenhearted women. We were with a team called "Daughters of Peru." The goal of every team sent to Peru under this name was to cooperate with Jesus, as He personally healed the hearts of many of these women and as He became to them the husband they never had. So many women in Peru have experienced physical and verbal abuse from their husbands. We learned quickly that Jesus is the only One who can heal broken hearts, and He also is the only husband that meets our every spiritual need.

To seal the ministry Jesus did during our many conferences and open air meetings, we gave silver rings to the women, to symbolize their marriage to Jesus. After two hundred women came forward in one of these meetings, my husband was overwhelmed with the women reaching towards him as he passed out these rings. Some of these women were definitely not virgins when they married. The good news is that when we are betrothed to Jesus, He is able to put our past under His blood and make us pure, chaste spiritual virgins through His covering of righteousness.

Paul expressed his fear that false teachers and apostles would seduce those newly betrothed to Jesus, to draw them away from the simple truths of the Gospel. Paul preached the Gospel free of charge, but evidently deceitful workers had transformed themselves into apostles of Christ, and they were charging for their preaching.

False teachers and apostles are still among us today. This is why we have to saturate ourselves with the Word of God so that we will not be deceived. The Gospel is simple. Anyone who tries to make it complicated is in deception. The Gospel is presented correctly when the preacher or teacher includes the following: the life, death, burial, resurrection, ascension, and present position of Jesus Christ who is our intercessor and who also is above every principality and power. The fact that Jesus Christ is God in the flesh who became the perfect sacrifice for our sins also must be clearly presented. A mixed Gospel is being preached today that presents Jesus as merely the babe in the manger and the great teacher, but not the King of kings and Lord of lords. Jesus has all power over the enemy and has given us that same power. He is able to present us clean and pure before God because we, as believers, have received His righteousness. The good news is great news if it is delivered in the power of God's anointing and in the clarity of His truth.

Lord, help me to present the Gospel correctly to others.

Daily Deposit: The true Gospel is the power of God unto salvation. Declare it!

September 10

Read: Isaiah 6:1–7:25; 2 Corinthians 11:16–33; Psalm 54:1–7; Proverbs 23:1–3

Battle Scars
2 Corinthians 11:16–33

We have been talking about spiritual union with Christ, who is not only our husband, but who is also our General in every battle that we face in this life. During my fifty and more years as a Christian, I have acquired quite a list of battle scars. But my list pales compared to Paul's list. Listen to Paul's list:

- I received forty minus one stripes from the Jews five times.
- I was beaten with rods three times.
- I was stoned once and left for dead.
- I was shipwrecked three times.
- I spent one night and day in the deep.
- I was in peril on the seas.
- I was in peril on land (perils by robbers and my own countrymen).
- I was in peril of the Gentiles.
- I was in peril in the city.
- I was in peril in the wilderness.
- I was in peril among false brethren.
- I was weary and often sleepless.
- I was often without food or water.
- I was often without the proper clothing to keep me warm.
- I often fasted.
- I had many concerns I had to deal with and pray about for all the churches.
- I was lifted in a basket to escape a whole garrison of soldiers.

This is quite a "Battle Scar" list. Paul, however, saw it differently. Paul called this list his "Boast List." He said, "If I must boast, I will boast in things which concern my infirmity" (v. 30). Through all of his afflictions and persecutions, Paul could boldly boast about the Lord's strength and deliverance. These perilous times caused Paul to be so weak that he had to depend completely upon the strength of the Lord. I doubt that many of us will ever go through the trials and persecutions Paul did. We can be assured, however, that Jesus will see us through every fiery trial if we depend upon His strength and His Word.

Lord, thank You for seeing me through so many trials.

Daily Deposit: When we are weak and depend upon Jesus, a victory shout is heard in heaven, and a victory page is added to our Book of Remembrance.

September 11

Read: Isaiah 8:1–9:21; 2 Corinthians 12:1–10; Psalm 55:1–23; Proverbs 23:4–5

What Should Make Us Boast?
2 Corinthians 12:1–10

Yesterday we talked about the battle scars Paul encountered. These battle scars gave Paul a reason to boast in the Lord because, when he was weak, the Lord showed Himself strong on Paul's behalf. Paul said he only boasted in his infirmities. Today's passage reinforces his stand about boasting. The passage begins with the description of a man's vision or actual visit to the third heaven. Paul shared:

> I know a man in Christ who fourteen years ago-whether in the body I do not know, or whether out of the body I do not know, God knows—such a one was caught up to the third heaven. And I know such a man—whether in the body or out of the body I do not know, God knows—how he was caught up into Paradise and heard inexpressible words, which it is not lawful for a man to utter. Of such a one I will boast; yet of myself I will not boast, except in my infirmities.
>
> —2 Corinthians 12:2–5

Many theologians believe Paul was speaking about himself. We do not know, but we do know that Paul consistently refused to boast in anything but the Lord or his own infirmities. He then shared about the thorn in the flesh God allowed to remain even though he asked for it to be removed. Theologians have their special interpretations of what this thorn was, but Paul told us exactly what this thorn was. He said (v. 7):

> A thorn in the flesh was given to me, a messenger of Satan to buffet me, lest I be exalted above measure.

Paul's thorn in the flesh was a messenger of satan sent to buffet him. I may be wrong, but I think this messenger was the spirit of pride that always harassed Paul. Paul was a brilliant man who had impressive credentials. Maybe he even had a personal encounter in the third heaven. He had a lot to boast about, and I believe a spirit of pride was always whispering in his ear, "Paul, take the glory!" Paul had to consistently resist this temptation. This is why he was careful only to boast in the Lord or in his own weaknesses. The psalmist David told us what we should boast in when he wrote, "My soul shall make its boast in the LORD" (Ps. 34:2). David also wrote, "In God we boast all day long" (Ps. 44:8).

Lord, help me to always boast in You.

Daily Deposit: Make a boast list for the Lord. Your list will be recorded in heaven!

September 12

What Should We Seek?
2 Corinthians 12:11–21

Throughout the Bible we see many things we should seek. We see in the Hebrew scriptures how God told us to seek His face. We see in the New Testament how Jesus told us to "Seek the Kingdom first and its righteousness" (Matt. 6:33). Today's passage shares about something Paul considered important for every Christian to seek. He said (vv. 14–15):

> I do not seek yours, but you. For the children ought not to lay up for the parents, but the parents for the children. And I will very gladly spend and be spent for your souls; though the more abundantly I love you, the less I am loved.

Although Paul was never married, he was the spiritual father of many. He always saw himself as a spiritual parent. He was planning to go the third time to Corinth. He wanted them to understand that he was not seeking their support, but he was seeking them. Too many ministries seek after financial support when their first priority should be to spiritually support the body of Christ. Paul did not want his spiritual children to lay up financial support for him. He was more interested in leaving a spiritual inheritance for them. He was willing to be spent for their souls. He was willing to spend hours teaching and training his spiritual children. However, his parenting skills sometimes were rejected by his children.

Sometimes parents have to no longer be the "nice guys," when it comes to disciplining their children. Paul spent much time disciplining his spiritual children through his letters, and some of his children did not like to be disciplined.

Parenting in the natural is similar, in some ways, to parenting in the spiritual realm. Both natural and spiritual parents have the responsibility to teach, train, and discipline their children. Sometimes I hear people say, "I am raising my children in the ways of the Lord." We do not raise children like a farmer raises cows or raises a crop. Both natural and spiritual children have to be taught, trained, and disciplined.

I can remember thinking that if I was too much of a disciplinarian, my children would reject me. I even had dreams about not being able to spank my children, because I feared their rejection. This fear was dealt with by the Lord when I had to keep a rebellious four-year-old for three weeks while his parents attended a three-week spiritual conference. I asked the parents if I had permission to spank their child. They said, "Yes." I noticed that when I had to spank their child, their child always curled up in my lap and hugged me after the spanking. I learned that discipline does not always bring rejection. Paul was more interested in his children's spiritual growth than their acceptance of him.

Lord, help me to be a good spiritual parent.

Daily Deposit: Pray for your spiritual children today.

September 13

Power and Weakness
2 Corinthians 13:1–14

The Kingdom of God is just the opposite of the world's system. Power in the world's system is usually displayed through political leaders or rich people who have the wealth to buy power. Those who are most powerful in the Kingdom of God are those who recognize their own weaknesses and who rely on the great strength they have in Jesus Christ. Paul was such a Christian.

Paul planned to visit Corinth for the third time. There had been sin in the camp and he had already addressed some of the issues concerning various sins in the Church at Corinth. Paul was quite aware of the many weaknesses of the flesh that the Church of Corinth was experiencing. He wanted them to understand, however, that in their weakest moments, they could depend upon Jesus to be strong on their behalf. He wrote (v. 4):

> For though He was crucified in weakness, yet He lives by the power of God. For we also are weak in Him, but we shall live with Him by the power of God toward you.

Paul was reminding the Church at Corinth that if they saw any strength in him, it came from the Lord's strength, not his own. He challenged the Church at Corinth to examine themselves and test their own faith. He wanted them to have complete assurance that their faith was not just a religion. They had a living faith based on the very person of Christ who lived, moved, and had His being within them. His prayer for the Church at Corinth was that they would be complete in Jesus Christ. He ended his letter to Corinth with these words (v.11):

> Become complete. Be of good comfort, be of one mind, live in peace; and the God of love and peace will be with you.

His salutation should become one of the key goals of our lives. We should recognize our own weaknesses and trust in the Holy Spirit to conform us to the image of Jesus Christ. We, however, do play a great part in this conformation. We are required to live in unity, peace, and love. When we live this way, we can expect the Holy Spirit to help us become complete. It is the power of Jesus Christ made perfect in our weakness that causes us to become complete in Him.

Lord, help me to live in unity, peace, and love.

Daily Deposit: Place all your faith in Jesus Christ today, and He will show Himself strong through you even at your weakest moments.

September 14

A Different Gospel
Galatians 1:1–24

Paul's letters were sent to various cities where there were problems in the body of Christ in that city. Paul began his letters with this usual greeting, "To the Church of God, which is at _____[a certain city]." The letter to the Galatians, however, is not addressed to one city. Instead it is addressed to an area that included several cities. Galatia was a northern, central region in Asia Minor, which included the towns of Antioch, Iconium, Lsytra, and Derbe. The name of the region originated in the third century B.C. when a tribe of people from Gaul migrated to the area.

After reading Paul's letters to the Church at Corinth, we see the major problem at Corinth was the people's vulnerability to their own lusts. Their focus often was more on themselves and filling their lustful desires, than on God. This was not the problem in the region of Galatia. Many of the churches of this region had reverted back to legalism.

Judaizers had taught that certain Old Testament laws were still binding upon Christians. The Judaizers taught that salvation by faith alone in Jesus Christ and the grace supplied to believers by the power of the Holy Spirit were inadequate. They wanted to add to faith the observance of the Law. These Judaizers tried to discredit Paul as an apostle. Paul spent time in this letter defending his apostleship.

This same perversion of the Gospel exists today. Legalism teaches that justification depends upon a person's own efforts. Such a belief denies the sufficiency of the cross. It is simply a different Gospel.

The focus of both the Church at Corinth and the churches in the region of Galatia was wrong. Both had lost sight of the amazing grace available to them through the cross of Jesus Christ. The Church at Corinth was self-centered which caused all kinds of sin. The churches in Galatia were also self-centered in their efforts to prove their own righteousness by their self-efforts.

Whenever we get our focus off of Jesus—His death and atonement for us, His burial and resurrection, His ascension, His position, and His ministry through us by the power of the Holy Spirit—we are in danger of either becoming legalistic or lustful in our belief and behavior.

Paul preached Christ crucified and Christ the power of God and the wisdom of God. This is the true Gospel. Help us all to be true to the true Gospel.

Lord, help me never to depend upon my own self-effort.

Daily Deposit: Focus on Jesus today. Think about His death that purchased liberation from the bondage of sin for you. Don't stop there. Think about how He is now in heaven, making constant intercession on your behalf. Your day will be a heavenly day, and your thoughts will be recorded in your Book of Remembrance in heaven.

September 15

Read: Isaiah 19:1–21:17; Galatians 2:1–16; Psalm 59:1–17; Proverbs 23:13–14

Spies of Liberty
Galatians 2:1–16

Paul called the Judaizers "spies of liberty" (v. 4). These legalists observed the liberty that grace had given to the churches, but their pride made them think that they could please God more by their own self-efforts as they attempted to keep the Law.

Their false belief that they could please God by their own works was based upon their wrong image of God. Somehow they saw God as a Father who shows favoritism to those who perform well in their Christian walk. Nothing could be further from the truth. The scriptures teach us that God is near to and blesses those who are of a contrite, humble spirit. He graces those who know that without faith and trust in Jesus and His finished work, they could do nothing.

Paul made it clear that God is not a respecter of persons. Paul wrote, "God shows personal favoritism to no man-for those who seemed to be something added nothing to me" (v. 6). To put it bluntly, "God has no pets."

So many people today are bound by performance. They feel that if they could just do one more "righteous thing," God will be pleased with them. For so long in my own life I believed God was making a list of my sins and a list of my righteous deeds. If my righteous deeds were longer than my list of sins then I was "okay" with God. This wrong belief was shattered completely when I had a life-changing experience by a lakeside.

I was at a retreat, and the retreat leader instructed us to sit by the lake, be quiet, ask God questions, and then wait for an answer. My prayer life before this experience was always a one-way conversation. I gave my prayer requests to God, and I never waited for Him to speak to me. On that day I sat on a log by the lake and asked God this question:

What is wrong with my life? Many Christians I observe are filled with joy, and I just don't have this joy. As I waited for the answer, I heard His still, quiet voice say:

> Linda, what is wrong with your life is that you have been trying to earn My love. My love is free. I gave it to you over 2,000 years ago on the cross. Receive My love, rest in My love, and quit trying to live for Me. Instead, let me live My life through you. If you did nothing but sit on that log the rest of your life, I would still love you.

Lord, help me to receive Your love daily.

Daily Deposit: Put your hands out right now and say, "Lord, I receive Your love; I rest in Your love, and I trust You to live Your life through me!"

September 16

Sons of Abraham
Galatians 2:17–3:7

The number of Jews who now believe in Jesus is increasing daily. Jewish leaders tell those who have made recent commitments to Christ, that they are no longer Jewish and that they have forsaken the house of Abraham forever. Nothing could be further from the truth. When a Jewish person becomes a believer in Jesus Christ, he does not lose his Jewish roots. In fact, for the first time, he fully understands his Jewish roots. The truth is that both Gentiles and Jewish believers are of the faith of Abraham and therefore are sons of Abraham. Gentiles have been adopted into the household of Abraham by faith.

The Jewish believers in Galatia were insisting that the Gentiles be circumcised and follow other Jewish laws. Paul made it clear to them that we are justified by faith, not our works. He wrote (Gal. 3:5–7):

> Therefore He who supplies the Spirit to you and works miracles among you, does He do it by the works of the law, or by the hearing of faith?—just as Abraham "believed God, and it was accounted to him for righteousness." Therefore know that only those who are of faith are sons of Abraham.

God promised Abraham that all nations would be blessed through him, and this surely has come to pass. Jesus was the Seed of Abraham, and now Gentile believers are from that same Seed simply because they have received Jesus and they have been born again by the Spirit of God.

Paul challenged the churches in Galatia to remember how they received the power of God to do miracles. He reminded them that they received this power through the hearing of the Word of God which brought faith to their hearts.

Nothing has changed, as far as our faith is concerned since the time Paul wrote these letters. Our faith is built on nothing less than Jesus Christ and His righteousness.

The faith to believe comes from hearing the Word of God. Are you sharing the Word of God with others so that they also can be members of the household of Abraham?

Lord, help me to be faithful to share Your Word with others.

Daily Deposit: We are where we are today in our faith because of Jewish men and women who were faithful to God. We have the scriptures, the prophets, the proverbs, and, most of all, Jesus Christ, because of the faithfulness of Jewish people. This fact should inspire us to share with grateful hearts our faith with Jewish people. Today, pray for the Jewish people you know to have their eyes opened to receive Jesus Christ.

September 17

The Cross and the Curse
Galatians 3:8–22

Our passage today says, "For it is written, 'Cursed is everyone who does not continue in all things which are written in the book of the law, to do them'" (v. 10). Not one of us is capable of keeping the law. Jesus fulfilled the law, and He told us that we only have to do two things to fulfill God's law today. We fulfill the law when we love the Lord with all of our hearts and when we love our neighbor as ourselves.

No man can ever be justified by the law, since it is impossible for anyone to be completely obedient to the law. We must put our faith in Jesus Christ. Only He has the power to fulfill the law through us. His perfect love within us is able to even give us the power to forgive those who have wronged and hurt us.

A recent movie called *The Passion* has caused quite a stir, especially among Jewish people. This movie portrays the last twelve hours of Jesus' life on earth. The scenes follow exactly the descriptions given in the Gospel accounts. When Pilate asked the crowds whether they wanted to release Jesus or Barabbas, many of the Jewish religious leaders cried out for Pilate to release Barabbas and to crucify Jesus. Some Jewish people in the crowds exclaimed, "His curse be on us and on our children!" In the original script, these words were included in the movie, but later the director decided to not emphasize these words.

This movie has raised this question, "Who killed Jesus?" The correct answer to this question is that no one killed Jesus. He willingly gave His life to redeem us all from every curse. He became a curse for us because it is written, "Cursed is every one that hangs on a tree" (v. 13). When the nails went into Jesus body on the cross, the curse of the law was also nailed to the cross. Our walk with the Lord now is a walk of faith, not a walk of works. When Jesus died for us, we were justified (just as if we had never sinned). We became the righteousness of God in Christ Jesus. We must believe these truths.

Many today are still trying to work their way to heaven. The road to heaven, however, is a road called *Faith*. By grace are we saved through faith, and even the faith we have to be saved is a gift from God. We no longer have to serve the law. All we have to do now is serve the Lord Jesus Christ.

Lord, thank You for delivering me from the curse of the law.

Daily Deposit: Today, commit all of your works to the Lord, and He will establish your thoughts and give you the power to accomplish His works today.

Read: Isaiah 28:14–30:11; Galatians 3:23–4:31; Psalm 62:1–12; Proverbs 23:19–21

The Cornerstone
Isaiah 28:14–30:11

We leave our study of Galatians briefly to dip into the Hebrew scriptures. Even though Isaiah had not experienced the power of the cross of Christ, he prophesied that the day would come when that power would be available to all those who believe. The book of Isaiah is one of my favorites because it contains so many prophetic scriptures about Jesus Christ. Today's reading is no exception. We hear these words written by Isaiah thousands of years before Christ:

> Therefore thus saith the LORD God, Behold I lay in Zion for a foundation a stone, a tried stone, a precious corner stone, a sure foundation: he that believeth shall not make haste. Judgment also will I lay to the line, and righteousness to the plummet.
> —ISAIAH 28:16–17, KJV

The members of our church built our first building with their own hands. I remember the lines being set for the foundation to be poured. Before the lines could be stretched, however, there had to be a cornerstone. All the lines would have to be drawn from that cornerstone so that the foundation would not be off center.

It is so easy to get off center in our Christian walk just as the churches in Galatia did. We enjoy the grace of God for a season, but before you know it, we become performance oriented again. When we really understand that Jesus Christ is the precious cornerstone from whom everything in our lives must be founded, we will begin to have victory over our fleshly lusts. Jesus was punished on the cross to purchase our redemption from sin with His own precious blood. To continue a life of sin would be to deny the power of the cross and to reject the precious Cornerstone of life and His finished work on the cross. Is your focus upon our Precious Cornerstone? Without Him your life will always be off center.

Lord, forgive me for taking the cross for granted. Help me to remember Your sacrifice for me daily.

Daily Deposit: Examine your life today and see if everything in your life is centered upon Jesus Christ. The Holy Spirit will help uncover where you got off center. Dealing with sin today will reap great rewards in heaven.

September 19

Read: Isaiah 30:12–33:12; Galatians 5:1–12; Psalm 63:1–11; Proverbs 23:22

The Yoke of Bondage
Galatians 5:1–12

In our September 3rd devotion, we talked about how important it is not to be unequally yoked. We learned that we are to select our friends and mates carefully, because if we select ungodly friends or mates, we can easily veer off course in our Christian walk. We learned that yoking is practiced when two oxen share the same wooden collar. All went well with the plowman if both oxen obeyed his commands. However, if one did not, the plowman would have difficulty accomplishing his work.

Today's passage speaks about another yoke–the yoke of bondage. There are many yokes of bondage spoken of in the scriptures. Some examples are the:

- Bondage of fear (Rom. 8:15)
- Bondage of corruption (Rom. 8:21)
- Bondage of slavery (Exod. 1:14)
- Bondage of the law (Gal. 2:4)
- Bondage of the fear of death (Heb. 2:15)
- Bondage of the world (2 Pet. 2:19–22)

Paul warned the Galatians not to be brought again into the bondage of the law. He exhorted them to stand fast in the liberty which Christ purchased for them on the cross. He said that anyone who attempted to be justified by law had fallen from grace. When we think of someone falling from grace, we often think of some backsliding Christian who returns to his old, worldly life style. We seldom think that we can fall from grace every time we try to justify our own actions by the law and not faith.

Paul made it clear that only faith can set us free from all bondage. The type of faith, however, that Paul spoke of is the faith that works through love (v. 6). The love chapter of Corinthians (1 Cor. 13) spoke of having the faith to remove mountains and how that faith avails nothing if we do not have love.

Faith operates through love only when our focus is upon God's extravagant love demonstrated for us on the cross. When we tap into just a small measure of that love, the chains of sin in our lives will begin to fall off. Christians who are rooted and grounded in the love of Jesus Christ will seldom fall from grace.

Lord, thank You for Your extravagant love. Help me to understand and abide in it every day.

Daily Deposit: Today and every day meditate on the love of Jesus Christ. Remember that the Father loves you with the same love that He loves Jesus, His only son.

Your meditations about the love of Christ will help you not to fall from grace; your thoughts about Christ will be recorded in your Book of Remembrance in heaven.

September 20

Read: Isaiah 33:13–36:22; Galatians 5:13–26; Psalm 64:1–10; Proverbs 23:23

The Law of Love
Galatians 5:13–26

As we draw closer to the end of our study of Galatians, we have a clearer picture of the one thing under which we are to be in bondage. That one thing is Jesus Christ who loves us with the same love the Father had for Him. Paul always saw himself as a slave to Jesus Christ. He, however, was a love slave, not a bondservant (a servant who is under the bondage of his master). The extravagant love of Jesus Christ does not force us to serve Him. His love is filled with grace, which is the power to serve Him. His love also extends to us the continual choice by our own free will to serve or not to serve Him.

We learned in our study of Leviticus that every seven years a master offered freedom to his slaves. It was their choice to remain in their master's service or to leave. The free will God extends to us is given so that we can choose to love Him. If we had no choice, we would just be puppets on strings.

Paul warned the Galatians not to become entangled again with the yoke of bondage. They were called to liberty by the grace of God, but they were warned never to use their liberty as an opportunity for the flesh. Through love, they were to serve one another (v. 13). Paul told the Galatians exactly the one law to which they were to be in bondage. He wrote (v. 14):

> For all the law is fulfilled in one word, even in this: "You shall love your neighbor as yourself."

When we are bound to the law of love, we will not fulfill the lusts of our own flesh. Paul continued with this exhortation (vv. 16–18):

> I say then: Walk in the Spirit, and you shall not fulfill the lust of the flesh. For the flesh lusts against the Spirit, and the Spirit against the flesh; and these are contrary to one another, so that you do not do the things that you wish. But if you are led by the Spirit, you are not under the law.

This passage ends with the list of the works of the flesh and the fruits of the Spirit. Examine your heart today in the light of this list and see if you are walking in the Spirit or in the flesh. When we are bound by love to Christ and to others, there will be little time for sin in our lives.

Lord, thank You for giving me the choice to become Your love slave.

Daily Deposit: Write down some ways you can express your love to others. Express your love to someone else in one of these ways today. Your deeds of love are recorded in your Book of Remembrance.

September 21

Sowing and Reaping
Galatians 6:1–18

We close out our study today of Galatians. It has been a joy for me to gain new insights with you. We have talked about the one law to which we are to be in "bondage." That law is the law of love. When we truly love one another, our love will be displayed by our words and our deeds. Paul talked about some of the ways we can sow love to one another. He also talked about what happens when we sow to our own flesh. Some of the ways we can sow love to one another are:

- Gently restore fellow Christians who have fallen into sin (v. 1).
- Bear one another's burdens (pray for those who are in bondage to sin) (v. 2).
- Bear your own load (examine your heart and deal with sin in your life) (v. 5).
- Sow to the spirit (v. 8)
- Don't grow weary in well-doing (v. 9).
- Do good to all, especially to those in the household of faith (v. 10).

If we faithfully concentrate on doing the above list, we will not have time to fulfill the lusts of our flesh. Paul warned us not to be deceived. Whatever we sow, we will also reap. Without question, there are seeds of love we can sow daily, and there are seeds of the flesh we can sow daily. If we sow to the flesh, we will reap corruption, but if we sow to the Spirit we will, of the Spirit, reap everlasting life. Which type of sowing appeals to you?

A good way to measure our sowing is to make a list of how we spend our time. Do we spend more time sowing to the flesh or to the Spirit? The fruits of our lives will be determined by how we spend our time. Another way to measure our sowing is to make a list of how we spend our money. Do we spend more money sowing into the works of the Kingdom of God or into our own pleasure and entertainment? We can also ask ourselves, "What is it that I think about all the time?" Our thought life will reveal whether or not we are sowing to the Spirit or to the flesh.

We are entering God's last great harvest when souls will be gathered throughout the earth into God's barn. Are you a laborer in this last day who is sowing more to the Spirit than to the flesh?

Lord, I want to sow to the Spirit and not to the flesh. Help me!

Daily Deposit: The good news is that the Holy Spirit can help us daily sow to the Spirit. Call upon His help today, and your day will be fruitful. Fruitful days are recorded in your Book of Remembrance.

September 22

Read: Isaiah 39:1—41:16; Ephesians 1:1—23; Psalm 66:1—20; Proverbs 23:26—28

Chosen for What?
Ephesians 1:1—23

We begin today another study of one of Paul's letters. I have always had a desire to visit the ruins of Ephesus, and I pray I will be able to do this before I die. Ephesus was a principal port on the west coast of Asia Minor, situated near present-day Izmir in Turkey. It was one of the seven churches Jesus addressed in Revelation. Paul ministered in Ephesus for over two years, and he established deep, lasting relationships with the believers in Ephesus. Paul wrote to the Ephesians when he was in prison in Rome. God's secret intention for the body of Christ (the Church) is revealed in this letter. I can't wait to see this secret unfolding as we read together this marvelous epistle.

Paul began this letter by reviewing how God had chosen them from the foundation of the earth. Theologians battle about predestination and election, but the truth is, God knew us before the foundations of the earth were formed. This fact is beyond my human comprehension, but by faith, I believe it. He knew us and chose us.

Why did God choose us, and what did he choose us for? The answers to these questions are given in our reading today. God chose us because He loved us. We are accepted and loved by Him. We are His beloved (v. 6).

God chose us to bless us with the following:

- Adoption (v. 4)
- Redemption (v. 7)
- Forgiveness (v. 7)
- Purpose (His purpose) (vs. 9)
- Inheritance (v. 11)
- Calling (His calling) (v. 11)
- Holiness (v. 4)
- Glory (v. 12)

He also chose us to play a part in the revelation of secret intention: to gather together in one all things in Christ, both which are in heaven and which are on earth—in Him (v. 10). We are partners with God to fulfill this purpose.

This passage ends with a prayer I pray for my family and loved ones. Join me as I pray:

I pray that the eyes of their understanding will be enlightened and that they might know what is the hope of their calling and that they experience all the riches of the glory of their inheritance in the saints. I pray that Christ will work within them, according to His mighty power. I pray that they might know their position in and with Christ who is far above all principalities, powers, might, and dominion.

Daily Deposit: Meditate on your position in Christ Jesus today.

September 23

Created for What?
Ephesians 2:1–22

Yesterday, we talked about when we were chosen and why we were chosen. Today's passage reveals why we were created. God created both Jew and Gentile to show forth His glory. We are His workmanship created to show the good works of Jesus Christ through us to others (v. 10).

As we read this passage, we see how Paul emphasized the oneness of the body of Christ. Christ died for Jewish and Gentile people, but God's goal, through the death of Christ, was to make both Jew and Gentile one new man (v. 15).

Through the cross, God intended to pave the way that all the walls of separation between Jews and Gentiles would be pulled down. When Jesus' flesh was torn on the cross, He also made provision for the enmity between the Jew and Gentile to be abolished. The cross provided a way in which all of our differences could be put to death, and we now can be reconciled to one another.

Satan hates reconciliation and he works tirelessly to keep it from happening. The provision for one new man was made on the cross, but the manifestation of the one man has yet to occur. Over the centuries since Christ died, satan has been able to keep a division between Jews and Gentiles. The moment a Jewish person becomes a believer in Jesus Christ, however, he no longer is at enmity with Gentiles. This is why satan battles feverishly to keep Jews and Gentiles separated.

We have had the opportunity to visit a Messianic congregation called Temple Beth Halel (House of Praise). I have noticed that the anointing at those services is powerful. I asked God why this is so. He answered that question and spoke to my heart these words:

> I am so delighted that Jews and Gentiles are worshiping together. This is why I have granted this congregation such a powerful anointing.

No matter whether we are Jewish or Gentile, we all have to enter the same door to be saved. That door is Jesus, and the handle to the door is called grace. Paul made it clear that it was by grace that we are saved through faith, and it has nothing to do with ourselves or our good works. Salvation is a gift from God. Both Jewish and Gentile believers become citizens of heaven, saints, and members of the household of God when they are born again. Together, we are building a dwelling place for God in the Spirit. Don't keep this good news to yourself!

Lord, thank You for all the good works You created me to do.

Daily Deposit: One of the greatest works you can do is to reach out to someone who is Jewish and share this good news with them. God is ready for His body to be completed, and the Jews are an important part of that body.

Read: Isaiah 43:14–45:10; Ephesians 3:1–21; Psalm 68:1–18; Proverbs 24:1–2

The Great Mystery
Ephesians 3:1–21

There is something about the word *mystery* that stirs our curiosity. Something inside of us begins to crave the solution to the mystery. Paul briefly touched on the "mystery" of Christ in our first passage in Ephesians, but now he is ready to share with the Ephesians both the mystery and how this mystery will be solved. The mystery was spelled out by Paul when he wrote:

> By revelation He made known to me the mystery (as I have briefly written already, by which, when you read, you may understand my knowledge in the mystery of Christ), which in other ages was not made known to the sons of men, as it has now been revealed by the Spirit to His holy apostles and prophets: *THAT THE GENTILES SHOULD BE FELLOW HEIRS, OF THE SAME BODY, AND PARTAKERS OF HIS PROMISE IN CHRIST THROUGH THE GOSPEL.*
>
> —EPHESIANS 3:3–6, EMPHASIS ADDED

Paul shared that this mystery now had been made known to the Church, to principalities, and powers in the heavenly places. I know satan trembled when this mystery was revealed to him. At that moment in history, he began to try to separate Jewish believers from Gentile believers. He was doing a pretty good job, as you might recall, in the region of Galatia.

There is no question that we are in a horrific battle in these last days. Satan is trying to cause division in the Church and division between Jews and Gentiles. He knows that mystery involves unity, and he is being successful right now in bringing disunity in the body of Christ.

We do not need to lose hope, however. We know that Jesus' prayer, that we may be one even as He and the father are one, will be answered. (See John 17:20-21.) We can join Jesus in agreement in this prayer, as we pray together the same prayer Paul prayed in this passage:

> That He would grant you, according to the riches of His glory, to be strengthened with might through His Spirit in the inner man, that Christ may dwell in your hearts through faith; that you, being rooted and grounded in love, may be able to comprehend with all the saints what is the width and length and depth and height—and to know the love of Christ which passes knowledge; that you may be filled with all the fullness of God.
>
> —EPHESIANS 3:16–19

Daily Deposit: Today, pray for unity in your own local church body, and then pray for the unity of the body of Christ all over the world.

September 25

The Perfect Man
Ephesians 4:1–16

It was Sunday afternoon, the time scheduled to unveil the painting in the foyer of our church. The new nursery, in honor of Rachel, an eighteen-month-old child who had died that year from a brain tumor, was completed. In honor of this dedication, a painting of Jesus with Rachel had been completed. The days before this completion were trying days for me. I had given money to hire a professional artist to paint over the first rendition. Some members were not excited about replacing the earlier portrayal of Rachel in a garden with Jesus. The artist seemed anointed and inspired to portray the glorified Jesus in His priestly garments. His hand held Rachel in his arms, like a shepherd holding a small lamb. The name *Rachel* means "little lamb."

The artist told me that he did not plan to paint the face of Jesus, because he did not feel qualified. The artist had painted many scenes with Jesus before, but he always was careful not to show his face. The grandmother of Rachel saw the picture the day before it was unveiled, and the artist asked her what she felt the picture needed. She replied, "That picture needs a face. Christ is the head of the Church, and the body of Christ you have portrayed has no face. This is not good." The artist saw her point, and later that day, he told me that he might have a surprise for me at the unveiling.

There was silence as the curtain hiding the painting was removed. When the curtain was dropped, a breathtaking awe filled the audience. The artist had painted the face of Jesus. His beauty and strength was pouring from the canvas.

Paul wrote that the perfect man, (the body of Christ) was becoming mature and would one day meet the measure of the stature of the fullness of Christ (v. 13). The artist (the Holy Spirit) is painting a picture now. His picture at the present time has Christ's head, but the body is not complete. However, it is now taking form. The response of the audience when the "perfect man" (the unified body of Christ) is unveiled will be the same as the breathtaking response of the audience that viewed the full painting of Christ (face and body). We can all look forward to that day.

We can hasten that day by speaking the truth in love to one another and by helping one another grow up in all things into Him who is the head—Christ (v. 15).

Our mandate today is to equip the saints of God for the work of the ministry for the edifying of the body of Christ. This challenges me to get to work!

Lord, thank You for anointing me to do my part in edifying the body of Christ.

Daily Deposit: If you have not found your place in the body of Christ yet, seek the Lord today and ask him what part of the body are you. Are you a hand, a foot, a voice, or what? He will tell you.

September 26

Poor Eyesight
Ephesians 4:17–32

As we grow older, our eyesight begins to fail. Solomon described this phenomena of aging when he wrote:

> And those that look through the windows grow dim.
>
> —ECCLESIASTES 12:3

The eyes of our bodies are the windows to our souls. Often these windows become dim because the filth of this world has clouded our view. Paul warned the Ephesians not to allow this to happen to them when he wrote (vv. 17–18):

> This I say, therefore, and testify in the Lord, that you should no longer walk as the rest of the Gentiles walk, in the futility of their mind, having their understanding darkened, being alienated from the life of God, because of the ignorance that is in them, because of the blindness of their heart; who, being past feeling, have given themselves over to lewdness, to work all uncleanness with greediness.

Paul was warning the Ephesians not to give in to the lust of the eyes (greedy longings, covetousness, vain imaginations, and fantasies in their minds). We all have this lust, and satan knows it. The eye of the mind is the imagination. The prince of darkness continually bombards our minds with worldly images. Sadly, he is having great success with pornography today, even with Christians. Satan blinds us and darkens our understanding.

Jesus said, "The lamp of the body is the eye. If therefore your eye is good, your whole body will be full of light" (Matt. 6:22). I know several men who are having a battle with pornography. The key to the victory over this degrading addiction is "focus."

They are vulnerable to this lust because they have lost their Godly focus. God created the imagination to aid us in our communion with Him. When we worship the Lord and close our eyes, we usually see heavenly images. Some people picture God on His throne and others may see Jesus walking along the Sea of Galilee. To overcome pornography, we have to place our focus once again upon Jesus through worship and praise.

Paul urged the Ephesians to put off the old man, which is corrupt because of deceitful lusts, and to be renewed in the spirit of their minds. The renewal of the mind through reading and declaring the scriptures out loud will also help break the bondage of pornography. One also has to confess his/her addiction and speak about it truthfully instead of covering it with lies.

Lord, help me to put on the new man daily.

Daily Deposit: Fill your day with worship and praise and you will not fulfill your lusts.

Children of the Light
Ephesians 5:1–33

We talked yesterday about our eyesight. Paul ended that passage by challenging the Ephesians to daily put on the new man. He told the Ephesians they could put off the old man when they:

- Renew their minds (Eph. 4:23).
- Renounce lying (Eph. 4:25).
- Refuse to give place to the devil through anger (Eph. 4:27).
- Refrain from stealing and do honest labor (Eph. 4:28).
- Renew their speech (only speak those things that edify) (Eph. 4:29).
- Renounce bitterness, wrath, anger, clamor, and evil speaking (Eph. 4:32).
- Respond with tenderness and forgiveness to others (Eph. 4:32).

Paul continued his list in our passage today when he challenged the Ephesians to be imitators of God. They were exhorted to put off the old man by doing the following:

- Refuse to fornicate (Eph. 5:3).
- Refuse to covet (Eph. 5:3).
- Refrain from filthiness, foolish talking, and coarse jesting (Eph. 5:4).
- Resist deception (Eph. 5:6).
- Refrain from fellowshiping with the unfruitful works of darkness (Eph. 5:11).
- Refuse to get drunk.

Paul challenged them to put on the new man by doing the following:

- Imitate Christ (Eph. 5:1).
- Increase in the fruits of the Spirit (Eph. 5:9).
- Invest their time wisely (redeem the time) (Eph. 5:16).
- Invest in being filled with the Spirit by speaking to one another in psalms and hymns and spiritual songs, singing and making melody in your heart to the Lord Jesus Christ, always giving thanks, and submitting to one another in love (Eph. 5:19–33).

I am challenged by this list, and I know I need the help of the Holy Spirit daily to put off the old man and to put on the new man. When the body of Christ faithfully does this, we will see His body reach the stature of the fullness of Jesus Christ.

Holy Spirit, help me daily to be filled with You.

Daily Deposit: Review this list today and daily for a week. Your life will be changed.

Walking in the Light
Ephesians 6:1–24

When we walk in the light, there is no room for darkness in our lives. John wrote: "But if we walk in the light as He is in the light, we have fellowship with one another, and the blood of Jesus Christ His Son cleanses us from all sin" (1 John 1:7).

We conclude the letter of Paul to the Ephesians today. Most of his letter presents effective ways in which the Ephesians, and all of us, can daily walk in the light. Our past passages listed some of these ways. Paul continued sharing these ways in today's passage. He exhorted the Ephesians and all of us to:

- Teach our children to obey and honor their parents (v.1).
- Train up our children in the admonition of the Lord and to not provoke them to wrath (v. 2).
- Trust the Lord to help us be good, sincere employees who work willingly to please the Lord (vv.5–8).
- Trust the Lord to help us be good employers who do not threaten, but who look after the welfare of our employees (v. 9).
- Trust the Lord to help us put on the full armor of God (vv. 10–18).

All of these exhortations are impossible to fulfill without the infilling of the Holy Spirit in our lives. We cannot trust in our own self-effort to meet the glorious expectation God has for us to be like Jesus Christ in all of our words and deeds. To daily walk in the light, we must daily put on our armor of light. Jesus is the light of the world, and when we put on the new man, we put on the armor of light. That armor includes:

- The girdle of truth (speak the truth in love to each other) (v. 24).
- The breastplate of righteousness (the Lord's righteousness) (v. 14).
- The shoes of the preparation of the gospel of peace (v. 15).
- The shield of faith (faith comes by hearing God's Word) (v. 16).
- The helmet of salvation (assurance of our salvation) (v. 17).
- The sword of the Spirit (declare the Word of God) (v. 18).
- The voice of God's Word through prayer (all kinds of prayer— praying in the Spirit, persevering prayer, and supplications) (v. 18).

The number *seven* means "complete." When we do these seven things listed above we will have our armor of light in place.

Lord, thank You for being my light.

Daily Deposit: Putting on the full armor means putting on the new man. Review the ways you can put off the old man and put on the new man, and pray for God's help.

September 29

Complete
Philippians 1:1–26

If you are like me, you sometimes have a hard time completing the things you start. The good news is that the Holy Spirit can help us complete all the things we start in our walk in the Spirit. Yesterday we ended our study of Paul's letter to the Ephesians. I was challenged by this letter to daily walk in the Spirit. Today, we begin studying Paul's letter to the Philippians.

Paul established the church in Philippi during his second missionary journey. He enjoyed a closer friendship with the Philippians than any of the other churches he established. He loved their missionary zeal. The letter itself is mainly a "thank you" note to the Philippians for a contribution they had sent to him by one of their members, Epaphroditus. Even though Paul wrote the letter from his prison cell in Rome, this letter is an expression of Paul's joy in the Lord. The letter is also filled with tenderness and love.

Paul's theme of the completion of the body of Christ continues in this letter. He wrote that he was confident of this one thing (v. 6):

> He who has begun a good work in you will complete it until the day of Jesus Christ.

As I write this devotional, I have this verse in a frame by my computer—"He who calls you is faithful, who also will do it" (1 Thess. 5:24). I know my weaknesses, and I know that only the Holy Spirit can give me the strength to finish what I begin. Paul's prayer for the Philippians is one we can pray for ourselves and others:

> I pray, that your love may abound still more and more in knowledge and all discernment, that you may approve the things that are excellent, that you may be sincere and without offense…being filled with the fruits of righteousness which are by Jesus Christ, to the glory and praise of God.
> —Philippians 1:9–11

Paul's priorities were right, and he expressed them when he wrote, "For to me, to live is Christ, and to die is gain" (v. 21). That statement I'm sure challenged the Philippians to walk in the light.

Lord, help me to be not only challenged by this letter, but also to allow You to complete every good work you have designed for me to do.

Daily Deposit: Each day is an opportunity to finish what we started yesterday. Ask the Holy Spirit to complete every work God begins in your life.

September 30

Oneness
Philippians 1:27–2:18

P aul knew that the body of Christ would never experience the fullness of the stature of Christ, if they were not unified. I fear what God is seeing today is a disjointed body. The only way to overcome this lack of unity is to be knitted together with one another in love. Today's passage gives us some of the ways unity can be accomplished.

Paul exhorted the Philippians to:

- Like mindedness, having the same love, being of one accord, of one mind (v.2).
- Let nothing be done from selfish ambition or conceit (v. 3).
- Let all things be done in lowliness of mind (v. 3).
- Let each esteem others better than themselves (v. 3).
- Let each of you look not only to his own interests, but also to the interest of others (v. 4).
- Let the mind of Christ be in them (vv. 5-11).
- Let God work within them both to will and to do of His good pleasure (v. 13).

My life verse is, "It is God who works in you both to will and to do for His good pleasure" (Phil. 2:13). Paul knew full well that his life was not his own. His life was the life of Jesus Christ, and his responsibility was to allow the life of Christ to shine through him continually. When our focus is off of ourselves and on to Jesus Christ and the work He has for us to do while we are still on earth, we will be able to walk in the light. We will be able to be "blameless and harmless, children of God without fault in the midst of a crooked and perverse generation (v. 15)." We are children of the light, and when we begin to walk in obedience to the above list, His light will shine through us, and men will see our good works and glorify our Heavenly Father. When each of us keeps our focus on the Lord, the body of Christ will experience oneness.

Lord, thank You for living Your life through me.

Daily Deposit: Review this list daily, and ask the Holy Spirit to help you walk in the light.

October 1

Where Is Your Confidence?
Philippians 2:19–3:3

When we were young, we were taught to have self-confidence. Our parents wanted us to do well in the world, and in order to do well, they wanted us to be confident in ourselves and our own abilities. This worldly way of thinking is exactly opposite of the way God thinks. One of the main goals our perfect parent, our Heavenly Father, has is for us to be confident in nothing else but Him. Paul wrote to the Philippians: "Rejoice in Christ Jesus, and have no confidence in the flesh" (Phil. 3:3).

God wants us to be completely dependent upon Him and His grace (His supernatural ability to work in us and through us). Paul had learned this principle. He never took credit for the things he did, but instead, he gave all the glory to God because he knew it was God who worked through him both to will and to do of His good pleasure. He knew that it was grace that labored through him. He was careful not to put any confidence in his own flesh because he knew if he did, he would be operating in the flesh and not the Spirit.

Paul was a brilliant man. He could easily have put confidence in his mental prowess, his spiritual and educational training, and his experiences as an apostle, but he refused to be confident in these things. He said he placed his confidence in only one thing and that thing was Jesus Christ and Him crucified.

He wrote:

> And I, brethren, when I came to you, did not come with excellence of speech or of wisdom declaring to you the testimony of God. For I determined not to know anything among you except Jesus Christ and Him crucified.
>
> —1 Corinthians 2:1–2

He said he did not want to persuade men with his human wisdom, but in demonstration of the Spirit and of power so that the faith of those who heard him would be based upon the power of God, not the wisdom of men (1 Cor. 2:3–5).

Paul knew the moment he put any confidence in his own flesh, he would lose the anointing of God. We also lose our anointing whenever we put our confidence in our own abilities, talents, training, or schooling. Whenever our focus is on ourselves rather than God, the light He wants to shine through us is blocked by our own flesh.

Lord, help me to always depend upon You and Your grace.

Daily Deposit: Today, allow grace to labor through you.

October 2

Read: Isaiah 66:1–24; Philippians 3:4–21; Psalm 74:1–23; Proverbs 24:15–16

Faith Is Gain
Philippians 3:4–21

When I was young, my parents enrolled my sisters and me in a multitude of classes that would help us gain confidence in our skills and in ourselves. We took piano lessons, sewing lessons, tailoring lessons, tennis lessons, swimming lessons, cooking lessons, dancing lessons, and we even took lessons on how to correctly put on our makeup. All of these lessons were good, but there truly was only one thing we needed to learn to equip us to live godly, righteous lives. We needed to learn how to increase in our faith. The godly life is the life that continually grows in faith. Paul told us in his letter to the Romans that "faith comes by hearing, and hearing by the word of God" (Rom. 10:17).

I am so thankful because our parents insisted that we regularly attend BTU (Baptist Training Union) every Sunday evening. The training we gained there helped us grow in faith, because the training was centered upon the Word of God. We had to memorize the Word, speak the Word in talks and learn where to find things in the Word of God. I remember having "sword drills" when we competed with the other students to find verses in the Bible. I can still hear the words of our BTU teacher when she gave us a verse to look up. She said, "Draw swords, ready, go!" We lifted our Bibles in unison and rapidly turned to the scripture given. The first student who read the scripture out loud won the competition.

There were no sword drills in Paul's day, but he knew the importance of God's Word. Paul reviewed all he had experienced that would qualify him as a righteous, religious Jew. His list involved his own righteousness, and then he wrote (vv. 8–10):

> Yet indeed I also count all things loss for the excellence of the knowledge of Christ Jesus my Lord, for whom I have suffered the loss of all things, and count them as rubbish, that I may gain Christ and be found in Him, not having my own righteousness, which is from the law, but that which is through faith in Christ, the righteousness which is from God by faith; that I may know Him and the power of His resurrection, and the fellowship of His sufferings, being conformed to His death.

Paul invited the Philippians to join in following his example of forgetting those things that are behind and pressing forward toward the goal for the prize of the upward call of God in Christ Jesus. Will you follow Paul's example?

Lord, help me to grow daily in faith as I hear Your Word.

Daily Deposit: The only diploma we will be given in heaven is the one that reads, "Finished With Faith." Take time to hear God's Word today.

October 3

He Can! We Cannot!
Jeremiah 1:1–2:30

We leave our study of Paul's letters to dip once again into the Hebrew scriptures. The last chapter of Philippians is presented in my first book, *Around the Word in 365 Days*. I called that devotional, "Pray About Everything; Worry About Nothing." Our reading today follows our theme about confidence.

When I was young, I remember my mother reading me the story about the little train that tried to climb a hill. The train kept saying, "I think I can, I think I can, I think I can!" The chugging chant of the little train changed, as he began to gain speed when he exclaimed, "I know I can, I know I can!" That was a story designed to help us have confidence in our own abilities. However, the moment we think we can do anything without the help of God; His grace will not be able to operate through us. Paul knew that where he was weak, God was strong. If we are truthful about our own abilities, compared to the supernatural power of God's grace, we know we cannot put any confidence in our own natural strengths and abilities.

When we peruse the Hebrew scriptures, we can conclude that God certainly chose the weak to confound the wise. Even though Abraham was a great man, God revealed His grace to Abraham when he experienced his weakest moment in the flesh. I imagine everything in Abraham's flesh was crying out, "Oh no!" when he was called to sacrifice his own son, Isaac. However, Abraham's faith won over his flesh and he said "Yes" by faith, in that moment when he was called to give the ultimate sacrifice. Moses gave excuses to God about why he could not fulfill what God had called him to do. He said he was slow of speech, but God supplied what Moses needed to deliver the children of Israel from their cruel bondage in Egypt.

In our passage today, Jeremiah also gave his excuse to God when God called him to be a prophet to warn Israel. Jeremiah said, "Ah, Lord God! Behold, I cannot speak, for I am a youth" (Jer. 1:6). God responded with these words (1:7-8):

> Do not say, "I am a youth," for you shall go to all to whom I send you, and whatever I command you, you shall speak. Do not be afraid of their faces, for I am with you to deliver you.

God was able to perform His Word through a man who had no confidence in himself. Is God performing His Word through you today?

Lord, help me not to give You excuses when You call me to do something.

Daily Deposit: Memorize this verse today, "Faithful is he that calleth you, who also will do it" (1 Thess. 5:24, KJV). When you speak this verse out loud, faith will spring up within you, and your words will be recorded in your Book of Remembrance.

October 4

Read: Jeremiah 2:31–4:18; Colossians 1:1–19; Psalm 76:1–12; Proverbs 24:21–22

What Is Your Attire?
Jeremiah 2:31–4:18

The world places so much emphasis on outward appearances. Any stocks invested in the clothing industry would probably be a good investment, since there will always be a need for clothing. I remember walking through the garment district of New York City and I was overwhelmed by the amounts of clothing that are manufactured.

One of my lusts is a lust for pretty clothing. Often I am more concerned about my outward appearance than I should be. I find myself thinking about what I am going to wear on certain occasions, even when I am in the middle of worship. I guess satan knows how to distract me. However, Jesus taught us to take no thought about what we would wear (Matt. 6:25–34). When the prophet, Samuel, had to choose a new king from the sons of Jesse, God warned him not to look on the outer appearance of Jesse's sons. When the sons passed before Samuel, Samuel wanted to pick Eliab because of his appearance, but God said:

> Do not look at his appearance or at his physical stature, because I have refused him. For the LORD does not see as man sees; for man looks at the outward appearance, but the LORD looks at the heart.
>
> —1 SAMUEL 16:7

In our passage today, God asked Israel this question, "Can a virgin forget her ornaments, or a bride her attire?" God sadly spoke these words, "Yet My people have forgotten Me days without number" (Jer. 2:32). Israel's worldly sin had blotted out their memory of the goodness of God.

The clothing we should think about daily is mentioned many times in the scriptures. The garments we will wear in heaven are the spotless white robes of righteousness. Jesus said:

> He who overcomes shall be clothed in white garments, and I will not blot out his name from the Book of Life; but I will confess his name before My Father and before His angels.
>
> —REVELATION 3:5

The good news is that we do not have to wait until we get to heaven to receive these beautiful garments. The moment we accept Jesus as our Lord and Savior, we are dressed in His robe of righteousness. As we allow the righteousness of Jesus Christ to be displayed on earth through us, threads are added to this garment. This thought should daily challenge us to stay on the path of righteousness. Jesus leads us in that path for His namesake so that our lives will glorify Him.

Lord, thank You for my beautiful bridal garment.

Daily Deposit: Pray for His righteousness to shine through your life today.

October 5

Read: Jeremiah 4:19–6:14; Colossians 1:20–2:7; Psalm 77:1–20; Proverbs 24:23–25

What Withholds Good?
Jeremiah 4:19–6:14

It is just about as hard to wade through the deep waters prophesied in Jeremiah as it was to wade through the traumatic experiences Job had. If Job and Jeremiah went to counseling today, the counselor would probably say that both of them have melancholy temperaments. We need melancholy temperaments in the body of Christ, however. If everyone in the body were sanguine, we would have a Pollyanna view of God.

The books of both Job and Jeremiah are not books you would want to read if you are experiencing depression. Even though neither book is very uplifting, both books have nuggets that could change our way of thinking and even change our lives. One of those nuggets is found in our passage today. Jeremiah spoke God's words when he said (5:23–25):

> But this people has a defiant and rebellious heart…they do not say in their heart,
> "Let us now fear the LORD our God, Who gives rain, both the former and latter, in
> its season. He reserves for us the appointed weeks of harvest."Your iniquities have
> turned these things away, and your sins have withheld good from you."

When things are not going right in our lives, our human natures want to blame someone. We may blame ourselves or others, but often we blame God. Granted, God does allow adversity in our lives to shape His character within us. The good that God always wants to give us, however, is often withheld because of our own rebellion and pride. God spoke through Jeremiah that the iniquities and sins of the people had withheld good from them. Iniquities are usually generational. The tendency to sin in certain areas is often passed down from generation to generation. The sin of spiritual idolatry can bring a curse to the third and fourth generation. The good news, however, is that we do have the power to break those generational iniquities and curses.

God wants to bless us all, and He wants to draw near to us daily. The wall of our own sins separates us from fellowship with God and from tasting and seeing that the Lord is good. Repentance is the only gateway through that wall. To fellowship with God, we must walk in the light, and this means we must be honest, confess, and repent of our sins.

God will always withhold His judgment when an individual or even a nation repents. Remember the story of Nineveh. A whole nation was spared because the people heard Jonah's warning of impending judgment and repented.

Do you feel like God is withholding good from you? Ask Him to shine a light on any sin that would separate you from having fellowship with Him.

Lord, search my heart and show me if I need to confess any sins.

Daily Deposit: Whenever we confess our sins, God not only forgives us, but He also cleanses us of all unrighteousness. Wait before the Lord today and let Him search your heart. He wants to daily have unhindered fellowship with you.

October 6

Who Robs God?

Jeremiah 6:15–8:7

M ost of us are familiar with the passage in Malachi that challenges us all to tithe our money to the Lord. Malachi asked this question (Mal. 3:8):

> Will a man rob God? Yet you have robbed Me! But you say, "In what way have we robbed You?" In tithes and offerings.

The thought that we could rob Almighty God (creator of the whole universe) of anything is almost unimaginable, but it is true. We rob God when we withhold our tithes and offerings, and we also rob God every time we willfully sin. When we willfully sin, God is robbed of the blessings that He wants to grant us.

In our passage today God said that his own house, His very temple had become a den of thieves (Jer. 7:11). They had robbed God because they had oppressed the fatherless and the widow, shed innocent blood, lied, and walked after other gods. Jesus referred to this very verse when he overthrew the tables in the temple and shouted:

> It is written, "My house shall be called a house of prayer," but you have made it a "den of thieves."
>
> —MATTHEW 21:13

I have never seen a church invitation or sign that said, "Come fellowship with a den of thieves." The response to such a negative invitation would not grow the crowds on Sunday. We must be honest, however, and admit that there are many thieves sitting next to us on Sunday mornings. If we really get honest, we could say that often we sit in church after we have spent a week robbing God with our own willful sinning.

Even though satan is called a thief and a robber, we join his ranks every time we rebel against God because of our own pride. Every day we go our own way is a day that we are led astray by our own lusts. On those days we have robbed God of the blessings and grace He wants to give us.

We casually say to people, "Have a blessed day!" when we have denied ourselves a blessed day by our own sinful pride. When we do not commit our works, our ways, and the members of our own body to be used for His glory during the day, we most likely will not experience a blessed day. We have robbed God of a day He could use for His glory. We have robbed God of a laborer who could be effectively used in this last great harvest.

Lord, forgive me for not taking time daily to commit my day and myself to You.

Daily Deposit: Whenever we humble ourselves and admit our own pride, the angels rejoice in heaven and satan trembles in fear. Think about that today!

October 7

Read: Jeremiah 8:8–9:26; Colossians 3:1–17; Psalm 78:26–58; Proverbs 24:27

What Can We Glory In?
Jeremiah 8:8–9:26

No one ever speaks of the glorious days Jeremiah experienced. Jeremiah prophesied to Judah during the reigns of Josiah, Jehoiakim, Jehoiachin, and Zedekiah. He was called around 626 B.C. and ministered until a short time after the fall of Jerusalem in 586 B.C. Jeremiah spent over forty years warning Judah to repent. More is known about Jeremiah's personal life than is known about any other Old Testament prophet. We see his melancholy temperament as he expresses his concerns and frustrations. Jeremiah was often called "the weeping prophet" because his laments were delivered with wailing and tears.

What kept Jeremiah going for those forty years? Certainly the response of the people did not encourage him at all. He continually was confronted by their lack of hearing, their stiff-necked wills, and their denials of their own sins.

Jeremiah was encouraged to keep on keeping on by only one thing. That one thing is also what will keep us keeping on in the midst of troubled times. Listen to God's words to Jeremiah (Jer. 9:23–24):

> "Let not the wise man glory in his wisdom, Let not the mighty man glory in his might, Nor let the rich man glory in his riches; but let him who glories glory in this, That he understands and knows me, That I am the LORD, exercising loving-kindness, judgment, and righteousness in the earth. For in these I delight," says the Lord.

Jeremiah spent time in God's presence. He experienced God's glory. A good definition of glory is the "manifest presence of God." When we spend time with God, and experience His presence, we begin to understand and know Him better. We begin to see that God is not out to get us. We come to know that His judgments are always met with mercy. His loving-kindness is forever to every generation. His mercies are new every morning and great is His faithfulness. Jeremiah was able to greet the next day with faith even though he saw no change in the people he was addressing. His faith was in God, not people, and he knew his message was what God wanted him to deliver. The gory days Jeremiah faced were filled with God's glory. Are your days filled with God's glory?

Lord, forgive me for the days I run out of the house without spending time with You.

Daily Deposit: Take time to absorb God's glory today.

October 8

Read: Jeremiah 10:1–11:23; Colossians 3:18–4:18; Psalm 78:59–72; Proverbs 24:28–29

What Do We Worship?
Jeremiah 10:1–11:23

Oh no, do you realize there are only a little over two months until Christmas? By now some of the department stores have their Christmas decorations on display. The Christmas train loaded with gifts and toys is about to roar down the tracks. I can just hear its whistle coming closer and closer. Panic! What will I buy the children and grandchildren?

Most of us face Christmas with more dread than delight. The reason for this is that our focus is on Christmas, not Christ. My sister was in a store buying early Christmas gifts. The cashier thought they were birthday gifts. Whose party are we having at Christmastime anyway, and what are the gifts we can give Him? These are the questions we need to ask ourselves in the days before Christmas.

After reading the passage today, we might even ask ourselves this question, "Should I have a Christmas tree? Listen to God's words to Jeremiah:

> For the customs of the peoples are futile; For one cuts a tree from the forest, the work of the hands of the workman, with an ax. They decorate it with silver and gold; They fasten it with nails and hammers so that it will not topple.
>
> —JEREMIAH 10:3–4

Was Jeremiah warning us not to have Christmas trees? We had a Christian tell us one time that it was an abomination to have a Christmas tree, and he directed our attention to these verses in Jeremiah. Now this is going a little too far. Some religions like Jehovah Witness do not allow their members to have Christmas trees. "Ba humbug!"

Are we not allowed to have any fun at Christmastime? Whose party is it anyway? Doesn't Jesus want us to enjoy His birthday?

These verses were not written about Christmas trees, even though the description seems to fit. When Jeremiah lived there was no Christmas and certainly there were no Christmas trees. Jeremiah was referring to the idols the Gentiles made out of trees. They carved trees into images, decorated them with silver and gold and fastened them up with nails to altars so they would not fall. Jeremiah was warning Judah not to become like the Gentiles in their idol worship.

Have you made an idol out of Christmas? Have you allowed the business of Christmas to rob you of the joy of the Lord? Whatever captures our thoughts can become an idol. Has Christmas captured your thoughts or has Christ captured them?

Lord, forgive me for becoming anxious over Christmas.

Daily Deposit: Let Jesus reign in your thoughts today.

October 9

A People of Renown
Jeremiah 12:1–14:10

When we were in Russia, we had the opportunity to visit the *Hermitage*. This museum, which was formerly a palace, was filled with priceless artwork. As I viewed various paintings, I thought, "These artists were all people of renown." People of renown are people who receive praise for their lives and works, even centuries after their deaths. If we were honest with ourselves, we would have to admit that we would like to be people of renown. Our passage today tells us exactly how we can become people of renown.

God had given Jeremiah some unusual instructions. He was to take a sash and hide it under a rock on the banks of the Euphrates. After many days passed, God told Jeremiah to go get the sash. When Jeremiah lifted the sash from under the rock, it was ruined and useless. God then spoke these words to Jeremiah:

> "For as the sash clings to the waist of a man, so I have caused the whole house of Israel and the whole house of Judah to cling to Me," says the Lord, "that they may become My people, for renown, for praise, and for glory; but they would not hear."
> —JEREMIAH 13:11

God's plan for Judah was to make them a people for renown, praise, and for His glory. They, however, would not hear or heed Jeremiah's warnings to repent. Jerusalem was later destroyed and the people went into captivity in Babylon.

God's plan for us is to make us a people of renown who will be to His praise and glory. The psalmist David wrote this about mankind:

> For you have made him a little lower than the angels, and You have crowned him with glory and honor.
> —PSALM 8:5

We were created for God's praise and glory. Our lives will not be useless if we will let the glory of God within us shine, so that men may see our good works and glorify God. Jesus exhorted us not to hide the light of the glory of God within us under a bushel (Matt. 5:15–16). We do not want our fate to be the same fate of that ruined sash that was hidden under the rock.

Lord, help me to allow Your glory to shine through me today.

Daily Deposit: There are works God wants you to walk in today. "For we are His workmanship, created in Christ Jesus for good works, which God prepared beforehand that we should walk in them" (Eph. 2:10).

October 10

Worthy Walking
1 Thessalonians 2:9–3:13

Yesterday we were challenged in our passage from Jeremiah not to hide God's glory within us, but to allow God to use us for His glory. Today's passage continues this theme when Paul exhorted the Thessalonians to:

> Walk worthy of God who calls you into His own kingdom and glory.
> —1 THESSALONIANS 2:12

We are all called as believers into God's kingdom and glory, and we are also called to walk worthy of this calling. We are not called, however, to walk this path by ourselves. One of my favorite songs when I was a teenager was called "You'll Never Walk Alone." I remember our high school chorus singing this song when I graduated from high school. Somehow this song brought comfort to my heart, because I knew my future would not be a lonely future. There would be people who would walk through life with me. I also knew that God would walk with me throughout my life. Jesus promised never to leave me or forsake me.

To meet the challenge of walking worthy of our calling, we need to have the body of Christ surrounding us and exhorting us, to keep walking the walk of faith. Paul's letter to the Thessalonians was filled with exhortation and comfort. Paul sent Timothy, a fellow laborer in the gospel of Christ, to the Thessalonians to encourage them concerning their faith. (See 1 Thess. 3:2.) Paul wanted them to know that he was praying for them and that, even though he could not be with them, he sent someone to hold their hands as they continued the walk of faith. Timothy was sent to them to encourage and establish them in their faith.

Paul prayed that the day would come when he would be able to see the Thessalonians once again, face-to-face, and perfect what might be lacking in their faith. He wanted their hearts to be blameless in holiness before God at the coming of the Lord Jesus Christ with all of His saints. (See 1 Thess. 3:10–13.)

As we draw near to the coming of Jesus Christ, we must exhort others in the body of Christ to walk worthy of their callings. Daily, we need to exhort someone in the body of Christ to love and good works. We are all "fellows in the same ship." Fellowship is essential in these last days. This is why the writer of Hebrews exhorted us not to forsake the assembling of ourselves together and so much the more as we see the Day of the Lord's return approaching. (See Heb. 10:25.)

Lord, help me to encourage those Christians I know to keep walking the "faith walk."

Daily Deposit: Ask the Lord to show you someone you can exhort today. Fellow laborers in this last day are only a telephone call or an e-mail away.

October 11

Trees of Righteousness
Jeremiah 16:16–18:23

If we are to walk worthy of our calling, we need to know what our calling is. I did a study one time on the various common callings we have as part of the body of Christ. I discovered nearly forty callings we all have in common. One of these callings is presented in today's reading in Jeremiah. Jeremiah wrote (Jer. 17:7–8):

> Blessed is the man who trusts in the LORD, and whose hope is the LORD. For he shall be like a tree planted by the waters, which spreads out its roots by the river, and will not fear when heat comes; but its leaf will be green, and will not be anxious in the year of drought, nor will cease from yielding fruit.

Similar words were written by King David in Psalm 1:3 when David compared the man who meditates on God's Word day and night as a man who:

> Shall be like a tree planted by the rivers of water, that brings forth its fruit in its season, whose leaf also shall not wither, and whatever he does shall prosper.

The message in both of these readings is that we are called to be trees of righteousness. The only way we can fulfill this calling is to be a people who meditate on God's Word day and night and who put their trust and hope in the Lord. God gave this same message to several of His prophets. Isaiah called us the plantings of the Lord.

In these last days, many Christians are experiencing fiery trials. The temperature of trials has been turned higher. Why would God allow such a thing? God is sifting His saints, and He knows the only way the character of Christ can be formed in us is to allow our faith to be tested and tried, even as gold is tested and tried. Peter even told us not to be amazed at the fiery trials we would experience. He exhorted us to rejoice, to the extent that we are made partakers of Christ's sufferings that, when His glory is revealed, we might also be glad with exceeding joy. (See 1 Pet. 4:12–13.)

It encourages me that God sees me as a tree of righteousness. It also challenges me to walk worthy of this calling. To survive the heat of the drought of these last days, I must meditate on God's Word day and night. God's Word will establish me in trust and hope, and the waters of His Word will satiate my soul during these days.

Lord, help me to walk worthy of this calling.

Daily Deposit: Spend time in God's Word today. Pick several verses to meditate on during the day.

October 12

Light the Fire
Jeremiah 19:1–21:14

Yesterday, we talked about going through fiery trials and how God has turned up the temperature of trials in these last days. We sing a song in our church called "Light the Fire Again." Whenever we pray for God to light the fire within us or to send His fire, we are praying for much more than just the power of His anointing to be ignited in our lives. We are saying to the Lord, "Whatever it takes God, let Your fire be stirred within me." The igniting and sustaining fire of God within us might mean persecution as it did for Jeremiah.

Jeremiah had become a reproach. He was in derision daily. He was placed in stocks. Things were going so badly for Jeremiah that he was tempted not to speak what the Lord gave him to speak to Judah. He did not give in to this temptation, and so he wrote:

> Then I said, "I will not make mention of Him, nor speak anymore in His name." But His word was in my heart like a burning fire shut up in my bones; I was weary of holding it back, and I could not.
>
> —JEREMIAH 20:9

All of Jeremiah's friends mocked him and watched for him to stumble. Jeremiah, however, knew he was not walking through those trials and persecutions alone. He wrote, "But the Lord is with me as a mighty, awesome One" (Jer. 20:11).

Jeremiah had not read the letters of Paul, James, or Peter that included God's purpose in allowing trials in our lives. Jeremiah did have access to the Book of Job; so maybe this gave him insight into what was happening to him. He wrote:

> But, O LORD of hosts, You who test the righteous, and see the mind of my heart.
>
> —JEREMIAH 20:12

Jeremiah knew he was being tested by God, and he also knew that God would one day avenge him of his enemies because he had pleaded his cause to Him. The last of the passage shows Jeremiah's vulnerability to his melancholy temperament. Suddenly, after writing, "Sing to the LORD! Praise the LORD!" (20:13), he sinks into the depths of despondency again. This is why we need the body of Christ to buoy our spirits when we are down. Jeremiah did not have the body of Christ to encourage Him.

Lord, help me to reach out to those I know need encouragement.

Daily Deposit: Write a note to someone who needs encouragement today.

October 13

Building Houses
Jeremiah 22:1–23:20

Judah's physical houses were abandoned when they went into captivity because they did not properly build their spiritual houses. Jeremiah wrote (22:13):

> Woe to him who builds his house by unrighteousness and his chambers by injustice.

Sometimes we spend more time building and caring for our physical houses than we do building and caring for our spiritual houses, which are the temples of the Holy Spirit. The scriptures instruct us how we should build our spiritual houses. Jesus exhorted us to build our houses upon the rock when He said:

> Therefore whoever hears these sayings of Mine, and does them, I will liken him to a wise man who built his house on the rock: and the rain descended, the floods came, and the winds blew and beat on that house; and it did not fall, for it was founded on the rock.
>
> —MATTHEW 7:24–25

If we hear and obey God's Word, our spiritual houses will be built on a rock-solid foundation. Peter compared the body of Christ to *living stones who are built up into a spiritual house to offer up spiritual sacrifices acceptable to God through Jesus Christ.* The cornerstone of this house is Jesus Christ. (See 1 Peter 2:5–6.) If we love one another and offer the spiritual sacrifices of our worship, praise, thanksgiving, and our very own bodies, we will be the living stones who will build a house for the Bridegroom.

Paul called himself a wise master builder who laid the foundation for others to build upon. He challenged the believers, however, to take heed how they built upon this foundation. He exhorted the Corinthians and other believers to build on the foundation with gold, silver, and precious stones, instead of wood, hay, and straw. It will not be until the Day of Judgment that our works will be revealed by fire. If our works endure, we will receive a reward. Paul asked the Corinthians if they knew they were the temple of God and he warned them against defiling that temple. (See 1 Corinthians 10–17.)

Solomon built a glorious temple for God, but he wrote about building our spiritual temples when he said, "Through wisdom a house is built, and by understanding it is established; by knowledge the rooms are filled with all precious and pleasant riches" (Prov. 24:3–4). The wisdom, understanding, and knowledge of Jesus are great building blocks for our spiritual houses.

Lord, help me build a proper home for You.

Daily Deposit: Offer some spiritual sacrifices today and add to your building.

October 14

Read: Jeremiah 23:21–25:38; 2 Thessalonians 2:1–17; Psalm 84:1–12; Proverbs 25:15

What's the Good Word?
Jeremiah 23:21–25:38

A common greeting we often give to our friends is, "What's the good word?" When we say this, we are telling them that we want to hear what is going on in their lives. We are also hoping that what they share with us will be good news. Our past readings in Jeremiah were filled with gloom and doom. Didn't God have anything to say to Judah that would encourage Judah? After all, aren't we exhorted in the scriptures to encourage one another? Our passage today does have a good word for Judah. Listen to these words:

> For I will set My eyes on them for good, and I will bring them back to this land; I will build them and not pull them down, and I will plant them and not pluck them up. Then I will give them a heart to know Me, that I am the LORD; and they shall be My people, and I will be their God, for they shall return to Me with their whole heart.

> —JEREMIAH 24:6–7

Now that was an encouraging word! God said he had allowed Judah to be carried away captive for their own good into the land of the Chaldeans (24:5). When Babylon invaded Judah, I am sure no one in Judah could agree with God that what they were experiencing was for their good. Such is the case for all of us today when we go through trials. It is hard for us to see any good when we go through any of the four "T's" (trouble, trials, temptations, and tribulation). It is hard for us to remember that God allows these four "T's" to conform us to the image of Jesus Christ. Certainly the image of Jesus Christ is more than good. It is great!

Adversity comes to some, even more than others, but through it all, God is working something for our good. We can be confident that if we love God and are called according to His purpose, He will work everything eventually for our good (Rom. 8:28, paraphrased).

Lord, thank You for working all things together for my good.

Daily Deposit: Write down some of the trials you have experienced to this date and record how God has already worked some them for your good. Your words will be recorded in your Book of Remembrance.

October 15

Worthy Work
2 Thessalonians 3:1–18

In past devotions, we have been talking about walking worthy of our calling in Christ Jesus. When we walk worthy of our calling, we will accomplish worthwhile works. We will be able to produce fruitful works that will survive the test of fire on that great day when we will receive our rewards in heaven. Only those works that we do through Christ will last, and all others will fade into the past.

Today is my birthday, and it is a good day to meditate on my past and also to look forward to the future. My prayer on this day is similar to the prayer Paul prayed as an introduction to our passage today. He prayed:

> Now may our Lord Jesus Christ Himself, and our God and Father, who has loved us and given us everlasting consolation and good hope by grace, comfort your hearts and establish you in every good word and work.
>
> —2 Thessalonians 2:16–17

On this birthday I pray that every good word and work I have done in the past and in the future will be eternally established.

Paul had confidence that the Thessalonians would do the things he had commanded them, and that the Lord would direct their hearts into the love of God and into the patience of Christ (3:5). I pray that God has that same confidence in me.

When you are my age, you really see the importance of redeeming the time and making every word and work count for the Lord. My prayer is that my last years on earth will be even more fruitful than my past sixty and more years. I want to leave this earth in a blaze of glory with the fire of the Lord and the light of His love still burning brightly through me.

Paul warned the Thessalonians not to become busybodies. We only become busybodies when we are not busy with the work of God's Kingdom. We need to work, for the night is coming soon when we can work no more. Paul exhorted the Thessalonians not to become weary in well doing.

There is a tendency for people who are retired to be content to play golf, read, and just pleasure themselves. If, however, we have the fire of the Lord ignited in our old bones, we will be enthusiastic laborers in this last harvest. Pleasuring ourselves will not be our top priority. Pleasing God will be first on our list. What is tops on your list?

Lord, let these last years of my life be gloriously fruitful.

Daily Deposit: Ask God to show you ways to expand the borders of your influence in God's Kingdom. Maybe he will tell you to write a book, like He instructed me.

October 16

Godly Edification
1 Timothy 1:1–20

We leave Jeremiah for this brief look into Timothy. The past letters of Paul we have studied had one major goal—to edify the body of Christ in the various cities Paul had established churches. *Webster's Dictionary* defines the word *edify* as the process of instructing morally and spiritually, with the goal to improve.

Paul's letters to Timothy were written to encourage and edify Timothy. Timothy was like a son to Paul. When Eunice, Timothy's mother, and Lois, Timothy's grandmother, were converted to Christ (probably during Paul's first trip to Lystra, a city in Lyconia), they wasted no time in giving Timothy good moral and spiritual instruction.

Paul reminded Timothy of the genuine faith his grandmother and mother had in his second letter to Timothy. (See 2 Timothy 1:5.) Eunice was married to a Gentile, and Timothy's father refused to have Timothy circumcised. Since Paul never mentions the faith of Timothy's father, we assume he had not been converted. This should encourage all those who live in a home where the spouse is not a believer. The believing spouse can do much towards the spiritual and moral training of their children.

Even though we know that generational spiritual idolatry can affect up to the fourth generation, Paul did not want Timothy to focus on past generations. (See Exodus 20:5, 34:7.) He instructed Timothy to give the believers the following warning:

> Charge some that they teach no other doctrine, nor give heed to fables and endless genealogies, which cause disputes rather than godly edification which is in faith.
> —1 Timothy 1:3–4

Paul knew the danger of people being defined by their past. When we become believers, all things become new. When Paul wrote to the Church at Philippi, he said:

> Brethren, I do not count myself to have apprehended; but one thing I do, forgetting those things which are behind and reaching forward to those things which are ahead, I press toward the goal for the prize of the upward call of God in Christ Jesus.
> —Philippians 3:13–14

Paul defined what godly edification is when he told Timothy that we are to build up the body of Christ by exhorting them and teaching them to love from a pure heart, from a good conscience, and from sincere faith (1 Tim. 4:5). Let this be your goal.

Lord, help me to be a godly edifier to the body of Christ.

Daily Deposit: Give thanks today for the godly influences of past generations in your life. Pray for the generations that will follow you to love God and others with a pure heart, to have sincere faith, and to walk in obedience to God's will.

October 17

The Gathering
Jeremiah 30:1–31:26

We sat with several Russian immigrants who had come from the north to Israel. We all were waiting to be admitted to the distribution area of an organization called "Friends of Israel." This organization provides clothes and household goods to help the thousands of Russian immigrants that are flooding into Israel daily. As we waited, I thought about Jeremiah's prophecy:

> Sing with gladness for Jacob, and shout among the chief of nations; proclaim, give praise, and say, "O Lord, save Your people, the remnant of Israel!" Behold, I will bring them from the north country, and gather them from the ends of the earth.
> —JEREMIAH 31:7–8

Well over a million Jewish immigrants have entered Israel in the past few years. Thousands of Jewish people have been gathered from Ethiopia and other nations. God is fulfilling His promise to raise up a remnant people in Israel. God also promises in this passage to "satiate the soul of the priests with abundance, And My people shall by satisfied with My goodness" (31:14). The Lord spoke these words: "There is hope in your future, says the LORD, [that your children] shall come back from the land of the enemy" (31:17).

Earlier the Lord spoke these words through Jeremiah:

> For I know the thoughts that I think toward you, says the LORD, thoughts of peace and not of evil, to give you a future and a hope. Then you will call upon Me and go and pray to Me, and I will listen to you. And you will seek Me and find Me, when you search for me with all your heart. I will be found by you, says the LORD, and I will bring you back from your captivity; I will gather you from all the nations and from all the places where I have driven you, says the LORD, and I will bring you to the place from which I cause you to be carried away captive.
> —JEREMIAH 29:11–14

These words were spoken to those who were in captivity in Babylon. God promised to release them from their captivity in the seventieth year of their captivity. Think about this. The Jews in Russia were under cruel communism for seventy years.

History has a way of repeating itself, and God is still faithful to His promises.

Lord, I pray for this last great ingathering of Your people to Israel.

Daily Deposit: What a joy it is to live in this day! Ask God today what your part is in this last great ingathering and harvest of souls.

October 18

A New Covenant
Jeremiah 31:27–32:44

L ast night we attended a Jewish Sabbath Service. Everything was in Hebrew, but we were able to follow the various chants because they were also written in English. The whole evening, I was thinking about the dedication these people had to honor God, even though they were not enjoying the new covenant God promised them. Our passage today speaks about this new covenant:

> Behold, the days are coming, says the LORD, when I will make a new covenant with the house of Israel and with the house of Judah—not according to the covenant that I made with their fathers in the day that I took them by the hand to lead them out of the land of Egypt, My covenant which they broke, though I was a husband to them, says the Lord. But this is the covenant that I will make with the house of Israel after those days, says the LORD: I will put My law in their minds, and write it on their hearts, and I will be their God, and they shall be My people. No more shall every man teach his neighbor, and every man his brother, saying, "Know the LORD," for they all shall know Me, from the least of them to the greatest of them, says the LORD. For I will forgive their iniquity, and their sin I will remember no more.
> —JEREMIAH 31:31–34

It is evident that this new covenant has yet to be established within the Jewish community. Until this date, Jewish people have had a veil over their eyes. God has permitted them to have a spirit of slumber and they have not yet awakened to their full inheritance. The day, however, is rapidly approaching when the above prophecy will be fulfilled. Even as I speak, thousands of Jewish people are having their eyes opened and they are accepting Jesus Christ as their Messiah.

God promised that as long as we have seasons of the year, sunlight by day, and moonlight by night, the seed of Israel shall never cease. (See Jeremiah 31:35–36.) God has kept His promise, and although Jewish people have been scattered among the nations, their faith and their seed still continues. Today God is restoring the land of Israel, and in the near future He will fulfill His promise to Israel to satiate their souls with the water of His Holy Spirit. God's spirit will be poured out upon all flesh, as Joel prophesied. Already there are over eighty Messianic congregations meeting in Israel.

Lord, thank You for being so faithful to Your chosen people.

Daily Deposit: Pray today for the peace of Jerusalem.

October 19

God's Telephone Number
Jeremiah 33:1–34:22

Aging has a way of creeping up on us. After my sixtieth birthday, I noticed that my memory is not what it used to be. I especially have trouble remembering telephone numbers. However, the telephone number given in today's passage is the one I never forget. Many call it God's telephone number. The word of the Lord came to Jeremiah when he was shut up in the court of the prison. The Lord said:

> Call to Me, and I will answer you, and show you great and mighty things, which you do not know.
>
> —JEREMIAH 33:3

Jeremiah needed that encouraging word. We all need it. Whenever we are in distress or just need God to speak to us, we need to remember His telephone number—JEREMIAH 33:3. I have called that number on a multitude of occasions in my life time.

The invitation to seek God and call upon Him is a golden thread that ties the Old Testament and New Testament together. Adam was given the invitation to come to God in the garden. God asked Adam, "Where are you?" God wanted Adam to come out of hiding after he had sinned, but Adam was afraid. (See Genesis 3:9.) Jesus said:

> Come to Me, all you who labor and are heavy laden, and I will give you rest. Take My yoke upon you, and learn from Me, for I am gentle and lowly in heart, and you will find rest for your souls. For My yoke is easy and My burden is light.
>
> —MATTHEW 11:28–30

Job longed to hear God's call when he wrote, "Then call, and I will answer; or let me speak, then You respond to me" (Job 13:22). Job was describing what we know as prayer. Prayer is simply responding to God's call to prayer and then having a conversation with Him. We can do this any day of our lives. In fact, God's telephone is never busy. He can't wait for us to dial JEREMIAH 33:3.

Do you know some people who seem to have a "hotline to heaven?" Such people simply have a willing and obedient heart to do and say whatever God tells them. They also call God's heavenly line many times every day. I don't think God has caller ID, but when we talk with Him daily, He can't wait to hear our voice. The only reason we would hesitate to talk with God is because we might be afraid of what He will tell us, as Adam was in the garden. Have you dialed God's phone number today?

Lord, help me to always know You are just a prayer away.

Daily Deposit: The first voice I want to hear every morning is God's voice. Have you heard His voice this morning? He is waiting for your call.

October 20

Hearing and Obeying
Jeremiah 35:1–36:32

"Can you hear me now?" This question is asked on a TV commercial for a cell phone company. As a man with the cell phone walks from place to place, he stops at each place and asks, "Can you hear me now?" Every time I see this commercial, I think about God and how often He must ask us the same question. But we are not listening!

Every day, God has things He wants us to hear, but too often we do not take time to listen. We talked earlier about God's telephone number (Jeremiah 33:3). The promise in this verse is that if we will call upon Him, He will hear and show us great and mighty things which we do not know. We may be faithful to call upon the Lord in prayer, but too often we fail to wait for an answer. After we have reeled off our prayer requests to God, we hang up that heavenly phone and go about the business of the day. If we did this to a friend who calls us on the phone, he most likely would think we were extremely rude!

Our passage is about hearing God's Word. Jeremiah was instructed by God to write a scroll containing all the words God had spoken to Him against all the nation—from the day of Josiah to the present day. Baruch assisted Jeremiah and read the scroll to the people in the Lord's house, since Jeremiah was confined and could not deliver the words himself. A fast was proclaimed and the scroll was read in the presence of the scribes and all the people. Fear fell upon the people and the princes asked Baruch to give them the scroll so they could read it to the king. They instructed Baruch to hide with Jeremiah before they read it to the king.

When the princes read the words to King Jehoiakim, he took the scroll from Baruch's hands, ripped it to pieces with a knife and threw it into the fire. He then ordered the princes to find Baruch and Jeremiah. When Jeremiah heard this news, he wrote another scroll and prophesied in that scroll the punishment that would come upon King Jehoiakim and his family because he refused to hear God's words of warning.

King Jehoiakim heard God's words, but he refused to listen and obey. God wants us both to hear and obey His Word. The way to live a blessed life is simple. Throughout the Bible, God blesses those who hear and obey His Word. Living a blessed life does not mean living a life without troubles. We will have tribulation, as Jesus promised, but we will be able to be of good cheer even though we experience persecution and trials. Paul was able to get through all of his trials, because he knew the secret of rejoicing in the Lord in the midst of great trials.

God is asking you today, "Can you hear me now?" Hear what He is saying to you today with an obedient heart that is willing to follow His instructions.

Lord, forgive me for the times I have talked to You, but I never waited to hear what You had to say to me.

Daily Deposit: When you pray today, pray with your Bible open and ask God to speak to you from His Word by His Holy Spirit.

October 21

Is It Well With Your Soul?
Jeremiah 37:1–38:28

One of my favorite songs is "It is Well With My Soul." We learned yesterday how we could live a blessed life. When we hear and obey God's Word, all will be well with our souls. As we see in our passage today, the circumstances in Jeremiah's life became more difficult when he obeyed God's words and delivered them to King Zedekiah, the son of Josiah. In fact, Jeremiah was thrown into a mud hole and left to die.

Obeying God's Word does not guarantee us a life without difficulties, but it does guarantee us a soul that will survive and be victorious even in the midst of great trials. Like Jeremiah, Jesus' life became more difficult when He obeyed God's word. When Jesus agonized in the Garden of Gethsemane, His soul experienced what our souls often experience when we face great trials. Jesus said, His soul was "exceedingly sorrowful, even to death" (Mark 14:34). The sorrow Jesus experienced on that dark evening when He was betrayed, however, was transformed into joy after He died on the cross and was resurrected.

As we read Paul's letters, and even the stories of the patriarchs in the Old Testament, we see how none of them were spared troubles. All of them, however, eventually experienced God's deliverance. All the apostles were martyred, but the joy of the Lord within them kept their souls from sinking into the mire. We see how Jeremiah was delivered out of his mud hole. God's Word tells us that "many are the afflictions of the righteous, but the LORD delivers [us] out of them all" (Ps. 34:19).

Jesus instructed us not to allow our souls to be troubled. Just after Jesus told Peter that he would deny him, Jesus said these words, "Let not your heart be troubled; you believe in God, believe also in me" (John 14:1).

When Jesus delivered these words, He knew the persecutions and even the martyrdom, His apostles would experience. He gave them the promise that He would prepare a place for them. Those words of comfort probably flashed through the minds of the apostles just before they were martyred. The heavens opened to Stephen while he was being stoned, and it was well with his soul.

A young boy was seriously injured when he rode his bike down his driveway and hit my car. It was not my fault, but his family sued me. The insurance company called me and advised me to get an additional lawyer because they were afraid I would face a messy trial. I responded, "I already have a lawyer." I hung up the phone and began to sing, "Joy is the flag flown from the castle of my heart when the King is in residence there." My lawyer was Jesus, and the lawsuit was settled out of court for $1,000. Throughout that great trial, when I didn't know whether this young boy would live or die, it was well with my soul because the King resided in my heart. Is it well with your soul today?

Lord, help me to keep my eyes focused on You when I experience trials.

Daily Deposit: Jesus is the Bishop of your soul and He will give you His joy to strengthen and comfort your soul through every trial.

October 22

Obedience
Jeremiah 39:2–42:18

" Now children, let's "OBEY!" Those words ring in my ears for days after we return from a visit with our son in Dothan, Alabama. He and his wife have four children. The oldest child is only five years old. Obedience certainly is not the top priority for these children, although it is top priority for their parents.

The frustration our son and his wife experience in trying to establish instant obedience in their children cannot be compared to the frustration and sorrow God experiences when he sees His children disobey. From the time of Adam and Eve's disobedience in the Garden of Eden, God has viewed the continual disobedience of His children.

God viewed what happened to Judah when many refused to heed Jeremiah's warnings. God had warned King Zedekiah and told him to remain in the city when the Babylonians invaded, but King Zedekiah fled in fear from Jerusalem. His disobedience cost him his eyesight and the life of all of his sons. (See Jeremiah 39:6–7.)

We will save ourselves a lot of misery if we will obey God's Word. God's Word is the rod of correction that will often spare us from trouble, if we will obey His instructions. God sees what will happen down the road if we refuse to heed his warnings and obey His Word. When we fail to read and heed "The Manufacturer's Handbook" (the Bible), we will experience failure, not faith, as we go through various trials.

The stories in the Bible are given to us as examples to help keep us from making the same mistakes the nation of Israel and others made through their disobedience. Paul wrote to the church at Corinth these words:

> Now these things [Paul was speaking of the wilderness experience of the Children of Israel] became our examples, to the intent that we should not lust after evil things as they also lusted.
>
> —1 Corinthians 10:6

Paul continued to share how the Children of Israel disobeyed God because they tempted God and complained to God. Paul said, "All these things happened to them as examples, and they were written for our admonition" (1 Cor. 10:11). Such examples should encourage us all to *obey*.

Lord, help me to OBEY.

Daily Deposit: Review some of the ways people in the Bible disobeyed God. The results and consequences of their disobedience affected not only them, but also the generations that followed.

October 23

Promises, Promises
Jeremiah 42:1–44:23

"Daddy, Daddy, I'll be good! I promise!" This is the cry heard from children just before they get a "time out" or a spanking. Suddenly, they want to OBEY. This cry is also heard after daddy enforces some kind of discipline. They exclaim, "Daddy, I promise never to do that again!" How many times has Abba, our Heavenly Daddy, heard the same promises from us? We hear this cry in our passage today.

Throughout the book of Jeremiah we saw how Judah and Israel did not do what God was telling them to do, and only a remnant of the people was left. The remnant asked Jeremiah to seek God for them and ask Him what they should do. They promised Jeremiah that they would obey God's instructions completely this time. Jeremiah promised them that he would seek the Lord for them. He told them he would tell them exactly what the Lord said, and he promised to hold nothing back from them (42:4). In response, the remnant said they would do everything God told Jeremiah to tell them. They said (42:6):

> Whether it is pleasing or displeasing, we will obey the voice of the LORD our God to whom we send you, that it may be well with us when we obey the voice of the LORD our God.

The remnant was in Bethlehem when they asked Jeremiah to petition the Lord for them. They were about to flee to Egypt because they feared the King of Babylon. After ten days, Jeremiah received a word from the Lord. He received a message exhorting the remnant to remain in the land. If they did this, God promised to plant them and not pluck them up. He told them not to be afraid of the King of Babylon, because He would be with them to deliver them from his hand. God warned them that if they fled to Egypt, things would not go well with them. God warned them that famine and the sword awaited them in Egypt if they disobeyed Him and fled there in fear.

God knew the hearts of the remnant in Judah. In fact, he called them *hypocrites* because they said they would obey whatever the Lord told Jeremiah. God knew they would not. Some even accused Jeremiah of speaking falsely. Because they did not follow God's instructions, God told them: "Behold, I will set My face against you for catastrophe and for cutting off all Judah" (44:11).

The results of not obeying the voice of God are never good. The remnant of Judah even began to worship other gods. They burned incense to the queen of heaven. They reverted back to idolatry because they felt things were better for them when they worshipped the queen of heaven (44:17–19). God told them that the very calamity they were experiencing came upon them because of their idolatry.

Lord, help me to obey Your voice.

Daily Deposit: Listen for God's voice today and obey His voice.

October 24

Does God Punish?
Jeremiah 44:24–47:7

"But we live in the age of grace, and Jesus bore our punishment or chastisement on the cross." I hear this often from fellow believers, and both statements are true. However, the writer of Hebrews makes it clear that even after the cross; God still chastens those He loves like a father chastens his own children. Listen to these words:

> My son, do not despise the chastening of the Lord. Nor be discouraged when you are rebuked by Him; for whom the Lord loves He chastens, and scourges every son whom He receives. If you endure chastening, God deals with you as with sons; for what son is there whom a father does not chasten? But if you are without chastening, of which all have become partakers, then you are illegitimate and not sons. Furthermore, we have had human fathers who corrected us, and we paid them respect. Shall we not much more readily be in subjection to the Father of spirits and live? For they indeed for a few days chastened us as seemed best to them, but He for our profit, that we may be partakers of His holiness.

The word *chasten* in Greek means "to train up a child, to discipline by punishment, to educate, to instruct, learn, and teach." God had heard enough of Judah's promises and it was now time for discipline. He told them, "Behold, I will watch over them for adversity and not for good" (Jer. 44:27).

He told them, through Jeremiah, that those who survived famine and sword would know whose words will stand, Mine or theirs. He said (44:29):

> "And this shall be a sign to you," says the LORD, "that I will punish you in this place, that you may know that My words will surely stand against you for adversity."

God had to punish Judah for two reasons: They trusted in their own works and their own treasures more than they trusted in Him. This was the lust, called the pride of life. (See Jeremiah 48:7.) Their willfulness had to be broken just as the willful rebellion of a child has to be broken by a loving father.

Lord, help me to receive Your rod of correction through Your Word, not circumstances.

Daily Deposit: Listen to God's Word today and obey His Word.

October 25

Woe Is Me!
Jeremiah 48:1–49:22

We have an expression in the South that reveals our deepest emotions when we are going through a hard time. The expression is "Woe is me!" As Jeremiah was describing the judgments that would happen to Israel because of their disobedience, many were crying out to God and saying, "Woe is me!"

Jeremiah declared the "woes" that would come upon Moab. The Moabites were known for their prideful ways. Their own pride would become their shame. The Moabites had exalted themselves against the Lord, and now God was bringing them low. God caused their wine to fail. Jeremiah wept when rejoicing and shouting was no longer heard in the land of Moab. God destroyed Moab with all of its riches.

Jeremiah wept over the destruction of the Ammonites and the Edomites. God takes no pleasure in the destruction of a rebellious people. God sent Jeremiah to warn them, but they all went their own willful way.

When we go our own willful way, the results that await us will always cause us to say, "Woe is me!" Many years ago I hit a little boy who rode his bicycle down his steep driveway right into my car. The boy was critically injured, but later recovered. His mother came running down the driveway and said, "I told Richey a million times not to ride his bike down the driveway into the street." God had warned Judah and Israel what seemed like a million times to obey His Word, so they could be spared the misery they now were encountering.

Jeremiah continued to declare God's judgments against Damascus, Kedar, and Elam. We all have times when we go our own willful ways. Our Abba, heavenly Father, weeps when He looks upon our rebellion because He knows the consequences of our rebellion. Proverbs tells us that "there is a way that seems right to a man, but its end is the way of death" (Prov. 14:12). "Pride goes before destruction" (Prov. 16:18). This challenges me to humble myself daily before the Lord.

Lord, help me to stay humble.

Daily Deposit: I know a man who throws his hands up in the air every morning and exclaims, "Lord, I humble myself before you." Try that this morning, and God will lift you up during the day.

October 26

The Resting Place
Jeremiah 49:23–50:46

Like sheep searching from mountain to mountain to find their resting place, Israel and Judah had lost their way. Their shepherds had led them astray (50:6). They had forgotten their resting place. Israel was like scattered sheep and the lions had driven them away. They first faced the king of Assyria who devoured them, and now it was Nebuchadnezzar king of Babylon that wounded them (50:17).

God often compares people to sheep. As believers, we are sheep of His pasture and He is our Good Shepherd. He leads us in paths of righteousness for His name's sake, and He sits us down by the still waters. His rod and staff protect us. (See Psalm 23.) Jesus is our Good Shepherd Who desires for us always to find rest in Him. If we will still our souls every morning we will hear His gentle invitation:

> Come to Me, all you who labor and are heavy laden, and I will give you rest. Take my yoke upon you and learn from Me, for I am gentle and lowly in heart, and you will find rest for your souls. For My yoke is easy and My burden is light.
> —MATTHEW 11:28–30

The only way we can find rest for our souls is to learn meekness and humility from Jesus. How can we do this? If we want to learn anything in the natural, we usually have to study and sit in the classroom while the instructor teaches us. Every morning when we awaken, Jesus invites us to His classroom. The textbook is the Bible. The Holy Spirit takes the things of Jesus Christ and shows them to us as we read the Bible. When we look into the Gospels, we see the meekness and lowliness that was always demonstrated through Jesus' acts of compassion. Jesus was always yoked to the Father by the Holy Spirit. He invites us daily to take that same yoke upon us.

Walking in the Spirit all day long will be much easier for us if we begin the day in this classroom. Meekness and humility are definitely not natural traits in our character. The only way to be humble of heart is to have Jesus rule in our hearts. Humility is seeing ourselves as God sees us, and in order to do that, we must receive the love of Jesus into our hearts. Humility is also the ability to cast all of our cares upon Jesus. We will not cast our cares upon Jesus if we do not trust Him to perfect everything that is a concern to us.

Although the book of Jeremiah is rather depressing because so much misery is described, there are hopeful notes in Jeremiah. Jeremiah prophesied of the day when Babylon would be destroyed and God would pardon Judah. Proud Babylon would grow feeble and the evil shepherds that withstood the Good Shepherd would be destroyed. Babylon's flocks would be destroyed. The resting place of Israel and Judah would be restored.

Lord, help me to daily enter Your classroom and find rest.

Daily Deposit: Spend time this morning in God's classroom.

October 27

A Battle-Ax
Jeremiah 51:1–53

Although the land of Judah was filled with sin against the Holy One of Israel, God did not forsake Israel or Judah. In fact, His plan was to soon use them as His battle-ax to come against Babylon. He said, "You are My battle-ax and weapons of war" (51:20).

The thought that God can use us as weapons of warfare is mind-boggling. However, every day we live we are called to be used as God's weapons against satan. The battleground is our minds. The weapons of our warfare are mighty through God. (See 2 Corinthians 10:4–5.) We are able to pull down every stronghold by coming against our own vain imaginations and every high thought that exalts itself against the knowledge of God. Then we bring our thoughts to Jesus so that He can imprison our rebellious, worldly thoughts and give us the victory.

Other prophets spoke of how God prepares us and uses us as weapons of warfare. Isaiah wrote (Isa. 41:14–16):

> "Fear not, you worm Jacob, You men of Israel! I will help you," says the LORD and your Redeemer, the Holy One of Israel. "Behold, I will make you into a new threshing sledge with sharp teeth; you shall thresh the mountains and beat them small, and make the hills like chaff. You shall winnow them, the wind shall carry them away, and the whirlwind shall scatter them; You shall rejoice in the LORD, and glory in the Holy One of Israel."

God said He would use Israel and Judah to break the nation of Babylon into pieces and to destroy kingdoms (51:20–24). God promised that every purpose of His would be performed against Babylon (51:29). The Lord compared Babylon to a threshing floor (51:33), and His sharp threshing instruments were ready to make Babylon chaff and blow them away. Judgment would come against the carved images in Babylon (51:47).

Truly the battle always belongs to the Lord, and He gives us the victory over all of our enemies. However, He has chosen us as His weapons to destroy the works of the devil. Listen to the words of Isaiah again:

> "Behold, I have created the blacksmith who blows the coals in the fire, Who brings forth an instrument for his work, and I have created the spoiler to destroy. No weapon formed against you shall prosper, and every tongue which rises against you in judgment you shall condemn. This is the heritage of the servants of the LORD, and their righteousness is from Me," says the LORD.
>
> —ISAIAH 54:16–17

Lord, use me as a weapon against satan today.

Daily Deposit: Ask God to sharpen you as His weapon today.

October 28

The Performance of God's Word
Jeremiah 51:54–52:34

We end our study of Jeremiah today. All the words Jeremiah prophesied came to pass. God's Word never returns void, it always performs what it is sent out to do. As we began our study of Jeremiah, God spoke these words to Jeremiah:

> Behold, I have put My words in your mouth. See, I have this day set you over the nations and over the kingdoms, to root out and to pull down, to destroy and to thrown down, to build and to plant.
>
> —JEREMIAH 1:9–10

God told Jeremiah that He would hasten to perform His Word. The major weapon we have against satan is God's Word. God's Word, spoken through our mouths has the power to throw down the enemy and to plant trees of righteousness in our land.

Words are building blocks. When we use God's Word skillfully we can destroy the condemning words satan has used to build his stronghold or fortress in our minds. We can condemn those words of judgment, criticism, and accusation. We can then use God's Word to renew our minds and to rebuild His sanctified Temple in our minds.

Words are also like bullets. Our tongues are weapons that can be used for good or for evil. Our mouths are like loaded guns. Our lips are the double barrel of this gun. The bullets the enemy loads into our guns are thoughts and imaginations. The triggers of our guns are our tongues. If we refrain from pulling the trigger and unloading the bullets of our thoughts and imaginations in the form of words, we can disarm the enemy.

We need to reflect before we speak and ask ourselves this question: "Will what I am about to say heal or hurt?" We need to reread words written in e-mails and letters with this question in mind before we send them to their destination. We need to give the urge to blast someone a chance to pass.

God was able to use Jeremiah's tongue to pull down and to plant. How is God using your tongue today?

Lord, help me to speak Your words to edify others.

Daily Deposit: Pray today for God to use your words for good, not for evil.

October 29

Effective Sharing
Philemon 1:1–25

Most churches have various sharing groups, or fellowship groups, where people share their hearts with one another and pray for one another. These groups can be effective, or they can be destructive. When we gather in such sharing groups, we have to be careful to not gossip or share negative reports. We need to esteem each person in the group higher than ourselves, and we must speak words that edify. Some of these sharing groups can turn into what I call "lemon squeezes." When I was a teenager, we used to have "lemon squeezes." They were terrible meetings when one person would be put in the middle of the circle, and those seated around them would tell what they did not like about that person. Those meetings were anything but edifying, but even some of our church sharing meetings can pull down people instead of build them up.

Our passage today gives us an important guideline about sharing. Paul wrote to Philemon and complimented him on his love and faith towards the Lord Jesus and toward all saints (v. 5). He prayed that the sharing of Philemon's faith would become effective by the acknowledgment of every good thing which is in you in Christ Jesus (v. 6). Whenever we share about the good things in our lives that the Lord has done, our sharing will be effective. No one likes to hear a laundry list of past sins from someone who is now walking with the Lord. When we hear testimonies that exalt Jesus and acknowledge His work of grace in the life of a person, our faith is stirred.

Lord, help me to share my faith effectively with others.

Daily Deposit: Write down some things God has done in your own life. Ask the Holy Spirit to help you prepare a three-minute testimony about all God has done in your life. When you give your testimony, your words will be recorded in your Book of Remembrance in heaven.

October 30

Read: Lamentations 2:22–3:66; Hebrews 1:1–14; Psalm 102:1–28; Proverbs 26:21–22

My Son
Hebrews 1:1–14

Hebrews is one of my favorite books of the Bible. We do not know who the author is, but whoever he was, he was able to clearly reveal Jesus as not only the Son of God, but also our High Priest. The author shows the supremacy of Christ over the prophets (Heb. 1:1–3), angels (1:4–2:18), Moses (3:1–19), Joshua (4:1–13), Aaron (4:4:14–7:18) and the whole ritual of Judaism (7:19–10:39).

Hebrews was written before the destruction of the Temple in A.D. 70. The author was either in Rome when he wrote Hebrews or he was writing to the Christians in Rome. The majority of the early Christians were Jewish. In my first devotional book, *Around The Word in 365 Days*, I highlighted Hebrews in most of the devotionals for November. I recommend that you reference *Around The Word In 365 Days*, as you do your readings in Hebrews in the month of November. The author of Hebrews first introduces Jesus to us as God's Son when he said:

> God, who at various times and in various ways spoke in time past to the fathers by the prophets, has in these last days spoken to us by His Son, whom He has appointed heir of all things, through whom also He made the worlds; who being the brightness of His glory and the express image of His person, and upholding all things by the word of His power, when He had by Himself purged our sins, sat down at the right hand of the Majesty on high, having become so much better than the angels, as He has by inheritance obtained a more excellent name than they.
> —Hebrews 1:1–4

The more excellent name Jesus had was *My Son*. The author of Hebrews made this point:

> For to which of the angels did He ever say: "You are My Son, Today I have begotten You"? And again: "I will be to Him a Father, And He shall be to Me a Son"?
> —Hebrews 1:5

My husband and I have three wonderful sons. Whenever I introduce any of them, I say, "I want you to meet my son." Something inside of me rejoices when I say those words, "my son." Throughout history our Abba, heavenly Father, has been saying to the world, "I want you to meet My Son." Pray for those who have not met Him yet.

Father, thank You for introducing me to Your Son, Jesus.

Daily Deposit: Introduce someone to God's Son today.

October 31

Valuable As Fine Gold
Lamentations 4:1–5:22

When two of my sons were into some worldly activities, I cried out to the Lord and prayed this prayer:

> *Oh Lord, please keep my sons from presumptuous sins, and don't allow them to do anything that they would be ashamed of when they meet You face-to-face.*

God answered my prayer with these words:

> Don't worry about your sons. I already see them as my three golden vessels, and they will be as fine gold on the day they meet Me face-to-face.

I held on to those encouraging words as I saw my two sons get deeper into the things of this world. God was faithful to His Word. Today, all three of our sons are serving the Lord and seeking His face.

Jeremiah wrote these words about the sons of Zion:

> How the gold has become dim! How changed the fine gold! The stones of the sanctuary are scattered at the head of every street. The precious sons of Zion, valuable as fine gold, how they are regarded as clay pots, the work of the hands of the potter!
>
> —Lamentations 4:1–2

These were sorrowful words, but God had not forsaken Judah and Israel. His plan was to raise up a remnant from the sons of Zion who would love and serve him. When we read God's Word we see how long-suffering God is. He never gives up on His people.

Yes, He may experience sorrow over their rebellious ways, but His plan always is to restore, redeem, and to raise up a holy remnant. His plan is to have many sons who will honor Him and who will do His will on this earth.

There is another prayer I prayed when two of my sons were not living for the Lord. You might want to join me as I pray this prayer for those you know who are in rebellion.

> *Lord, may the glitter of this world grow dim to them, and the glory of Your presence grow brighter.*

Daily Deposit: Ask God to lay on your heart today those who need His glory.

November 1

Ezekiel Saw the Wheel
Ezekiel 1:1–3:15

Today we will begin our dig into the treasures revealed in the book of Ezekiel. The name *Ezekiel* means "God strengthens." Ezekiel was a priest who was trained during the reign of king Jehoiakim in Judah. His wife died about the time of the destruction of Jerusalem in 586 B.C. Ezekiel was an ecstatic Jewish prophet who had a mystical, visionary connection with God. His spiritual experiences were a forerunner to the activities of the Holy Spirit described in the New Testament. Today we would label Ezekiel as a "charismatic." Ezekiel's message was directed toward those Jews who were in exile in Babylon. The book can be divided into three sections: Judah's judgment (chapters 4–24), the heathen nations' judgment (chapters 25–32), and the future blessings for God's covenant people (chapters 33–48).

There was an old spiritual song in the south called, "Ezekiel Saw the Wheel." The song describes in dramatic fashion what Ezekiel saw when he was captive in the land of the Chaldeans by the River Chebar. The descriptions of the chariot, the cherubim, the throne of God, and the form and glory of God in Ezekiel 1 are truly breathtaking. I know an artist who attempted to capture Ezekiel's vision on canvas, and he had to be anointed when he portrayed this.

God gave Ezekiel the same commission He gave to Jeremiah. God told Ezekiel to speak what He told Him to speak to Israel and Judah. God instructed Ezekiel to eat the scroll that contained His words. Like Jeremiah, Ezekiel was instructed not to be afraid of the faces of those in rebellion. God promised to make Ezekiel's face and forehead harder than flint (2:9). When Ezekiel received his commission, he was actually lifted up and taken away by the Spirit (2:14). Ezekiel was told to warn the wicked to turn from their wicked ways (3:18). If the wicked did not respond to his message, they would die, but Ezekiel's soul would be delivered (3:19).

As we study Ezekiel this month, there are many relevant lessons we can learn. We are challenged as individuals to live moral lives. Again, we see the nature of Abba, revealed in Ezekiel, just as it was revealed in Jeremiah. God is a loving Father who suffers long with His people and longs to show mercy and forgiveness to them. But the day comes when He must discipline, because He is a righteous and jealous God. The book of Ezekiel ends with the hopeful note that God wins in the end. Even Ezekiel, who prophesied years before Jesus was born, knew the rest of the story. At the end of the history of this earth, as we know it, we will see every knee bow and every tongue confess that Jesus Christ is Lord. Hallelujah!

Lord, help me to share the rest of the story with others.

Daily Deposit: Read the last page of the Bible today to see the rest of the story.

November 2

Watchman and Warnings
Ezekiel 3:16–6:14

The prophets of the Lord usually have the same calling. They are called to be watchmen, and they are called to warn the people. God required Jeremiah and Ezekiel to not only watch and warn, but also to do some very strange things. Jeremiah was told to bury a sash in the mud near the river.

Today, we read Ezekiel's assignment. Ezekiel was to portray exactly what had happened to Israel in a dramatic way. He was to lay a clay tablet before him. The tablet was to represent the city of Jerusalem. He was to lay siege to it, build a siege wall against it, and heap up a mound against it. He was to take an iron plate and set it as an iron wall between him and the city. He was told to lie on his left side for the iniquity of the house of Israel for 390 days. Then he was to lie on his right side, to bear the iniquity of Judah for 40 days. God said He would restrain Ezekiel, so he could not move.

God instructed Ezekiel to eat a special recipe of bread cooked in cow dung and to drink a certain amount of water to sustain him during this time. God told Ezekiel to cut off his hair, weigh it and then burn it. Ezekiel prophesied against Israel and Judah, and then he prophesied against the mountains of Israel. God told Ezekiel that he would destroy one-third by pestilence, one-third by the sword, and one-third of the people would be scattered to the wind. (See Ezekiel 5:12.)

During my lifetime, God has required me to do some strange things, but I have never had an assignment like Jeremiah's or Ezekiel's. Both of these prophets amaze me by their obedience. They followed God's instructions to the letter, without questioning Him.

Aren't you thankful that the Lord has never required such unusual things of you? However, God does still require the same two things of you that He required of Jeremiah and Ezekiel. God requires you to watch and pray and to warn both the wicked and the righteous who have rebelled against Him. Jesus gave us all some very important End Time instructions when He said:

> Take heed, watch and pray; for you do not know when the time is.…Watch therefore, for you do not know when the master of the house is coming.…and what I say to you, I say to all: Watch!
>
> —MARK 13:33–37

All of us have this urgent assignment—to watch and be prepared for the Lord's second coming. We are to warn those who are wicked and also to warn those righteous people who we know are in rebellion. We are to pray that they turn away from their rebellion. We do not want them to perish! Are you watching and warning?

Lord, help me to watch and pray.

Daily Deposit: Pray for your backsliding friends and family today!

November 3

Read: Ezekiel 7:1–9:11; Hebrews 5:1–14; Psalm 105:1–15; Proverbs 26:28

Sighing and Crying
Ezekiel 7:1–9:11

When a person is depressed, he or she usually sighs a lot. They also can be very weepy. Certainly Ezekiel and Jeremiah had every reason to be depressed. They both had the assignment to warn Judah and Israel of impending judgment if the people did not repent. They both faithfully delivered their messages, but after their warnings they had to watch all the destruction that came upon the land because their audience did not heed their warnings. The sighing and crying mentioned in our passage today, however, are not signs of depression. They are signs of deep intercession.

God gave instruction to the angels to mark with ink all those who sighed and cried for Israel and Judah. Those who wept over the idolatry and rebellion of Israel and Judah would be spared when destruction came upon their lands. (See Ezekiel 9:4.)

There are times in our own lives when we sigh and cry over the conditions that exist in our nation, our churches, and our families. As we lift our concerns to the Lord, we have confidence that He will perfect those things that are a concern to us. The psalmist David wrote:

> Though I walk in the midst of trouble, You will revive me; You will stretch out Your hand against the wrath of my enemies, and Your right hand will save me. The Lord will perfect that which concerns me; Your mercy, O LORD, endures forever; Do not forsake the works of Your hands.
>
> —PSALM 138:7–8

Ezekiel, Jeremiah, and a remnant of people received the burden of the Lord for their nation. They sighed and cried, and God heard their cries. Even though judgment did fall upon their land, God spared a remnant of faithful people who would hear and obey Him. The books of Jeremiah and Ezekiel both hold forth the promise of God's restoration and redemption.

We may not have weeping prophets like Jeremiah and Ezekiel today, but we do have a faithful remnant of people who intercede with tears for their nation, their families, and their churches. Are you a part of God's faithful remnant? "Those who sow in tears shall reap in joy" (Ps. 126:5).

Lord, help me to pray more effectively for my nation, my family, and my church.

Daily Deposit: Today, ask the Holy Spirit to pray (through you) the prayers that need to be prayed for your nation, your family, and your church. You may experience tears.

November 4

The Anchor of Hope
Hebrews 6:1–20

Hope deferred makes the heart sick. (See Proverbs 13:12.) We live in a day when there are many heartsick people because they have placed their hope in the security of earthly things. Our passage today tells about a steadfast hope that is eternally reliable. Hebrews 6:17–20 says:

> Thus God, determining to show more abundantly to the heirs of promise the immutability of His counsel, confirmed it by an oath, that by two immutable things, in which it is impossible for God to lie, we might have strong consolation, who have fled for refuge to lay hold of the hope set before us. This hope we have as an anchor of the soul, both sure and steadfast, and which enters the presence behind the veil, where the forerunner has entered for us, even Jesus, having become High Priest forever according to the order of Melchizedek.

I have two mental pictures as I review this passage. First, I see Jesus holding an anchor in His hand. Attached to the anchor is a long line, called *hope*. This line stretches around the globe. Jesus runs with this anchor into God's throne room. He sits down at the right hand of God the Father and lays the anchor at Abba's feet. He says, "It is finished!" I believe this actually happened when the veil of the temple was rent in two after Jesus gave His spirit into the hands of the Father.

Another mental picture I have portrays this line of hope attached to a pavilion of praise around every believer. God dwells in the midst of our praise, and as believers on earth remain in praise, they are attached to God's throne room with this line called *hope*.

Later, the writer of Hebrews tells us, "Now faith is the substance of things hoped for, the evidence of things not seen" (Heb. 11:1). The line of hope that is tethered from God's throne room to the place of refuge (the pavilion of praise) has verses of scripture entwining it. As we declare God's Word, the line of hope becomes stronger and more secure. Whenever we pray, we travel a highway paved with hope into God's throne room.

We live in a day when everything in life is tenuous. Our souls are vulnerable to sudden storms and we need this anchor of hope to keep us from being submerged under our circumstances. When we place our hope in God's written Word, the Bible, and God's living Word, Jesus Christ, our souls will be at peace and steady, even when the waves of adversity are beating against us.

Lord, help me to put all my trust in You and Your Word.

Daily Deposit: Memorize some promises today that will cause hope to spring eternal within your soul.

November 5

A Priest Forever
Hebrews 7:1–17

One of the first Bible studies I attended was a study on Hebrews. My husband was in the army and we had been invited to attend an Officers Christian Union Bible Study. The teacher was discussing Hebrews 7. He went on and on about the order of Melchizedek. I couldn't even pronounce that name! At the time, I had no understanding of this passage at all. I simply had to accept by faith what the teacher had said, with the hope that someday I would understand.

After almost forty years, I now have a better understanding of this passage. The author of Hebrews was proving that Jesus was a better High Priest than even Aaron. Aaron, the brother of Moses, was the first priest. His father was Levi, and all the priests, from that time forward, came from the tribe of Levi. When one priest died, his son took that position. The priesthood never departed from the Levitical line.

Jesus, however, was from the tribe of Judah. God saw to it that Jesus came from an eternal priestly line, not the line of Levi, which was temporal. In Genesis, we read the story of Abraham's encounter with Melchizedek. (See Genesis 14:18–20.) Melchizedek had no parents. (See Hebrews 7:3.) He was an eternal being who, at that time, was the priest of the Most High God. Melchizedek was also a king. He was called the *king of Salem. Salem* means "peace." Abraham gave tithes to Melchizedek.

Of necessity, God had to have another priesthood to prepare the way for Jesus. Melchizedek was God's provision for that priesthood. The perfection of the priesthood came through Jesus Christ, who is in the order of the eternal priesthood of Melchizedek.

David wrote about this divine order of priesthood years before Jesus was born. He wrote in Psalm 110:4, "The LORD has sworn and will not relent, 'You are a priest forever according to the order of Melchizedek.'"

What does all this mean to me today? This passage demonstrates how God is able to prepare the way for my future, just as He prepared the way for Jesus to belong to a divine order of priesthood. Jesus, as my High Priest, has gone before me, and because He was divine as well as human, He is an effective High Priest who can make perfect intercession for me, because He knows how I feel!

Lord, thank You for being my personal High Priest.

Daily Deposit: Write down some ways God has prepared you for future events.

November 6

Changeless Christ
Hebrews 7:18–28

We live in a world filled with change. It steadies my emotions, that are vulnerable to ups and downs, to know and believe in an unchanging Christ. I learned a song from my daughter-in-law that expresses how Jesus never changes. She sings this song to her four children as she puts them to bed. The chorus is, "He is the never changing Jesus, never changing, never changing. He is the never changing Jesus who lives forever more." This song rings in my ears for days after we visit our four grand children. What a comforting song to sing to children who will experience a life that will face constant change. I think of this song when I read these verses in Hebrews 7:23–24:

> Also there were many priests, because they were prevented by death from continuing. But He, because He continues forever, has an unchangeable priesthood.

The priesthood of Aaron was subject to change, because of death. The priesthood of Jesus is perfect because He is eternal. He is our perfect priest, and He also provided the perfect sacrifice that satisfied all of the Father's requirements for His righteousness to be established on this earth. Jesus is holy, harmless, undefiled, separate from sinners, and is higher than the heavens (v. 27). When He died on the cross, He dealt the final blow to sin. When He was raised from the dead, He overcame death and the grave. Because of Jesus' death and resurrection, we can look forward to receiving a new, changeless body that will be eternal. Until that day, we can be changed from glory to glory, as we daily commit our bodies to God as a living sacrifice. As our minds are renewed by the Word of God, we are transformed day by day to be more like Jesus.

The exciting fact about this unchanging priesthood is that we now are priests of the living God, who can intercede for others. Through our intercession, people can be established as trees of righteousness that will remain even when the winds of adversity blow against them.

In these end days, when troubles will be on the increase, we can depend upon two things that will never change—the Word of God and Jesus Christ. Jesus is the same yesterday, today, and forever, and He forever lives to make perfect intercession for the saints. What a comfort! (See Hebrews 13:8.)

Jesus, thank You for being both my perfect High Priest and the perfect sacrifice for my sins.

Daily Deposit: Meditate on this passage tonight before you go to bed. You will have a good night's sleep.

November 7

Like Mother, Like Daughter
Ezekiel 16:43–17:24

The familiar sayings, "like mother, like daughter" and "like father, like son," originate in the Bible. Ezekiel compared the lewdness and the abominations that Israel and Judah had committed to the same sinful conditions of their past generation (v. 45). History has a way of repeating itself.

God told Moses that the sins of the fathers are visited upon the children to the third and fourth generation. (See Exodus 20:5.) *Iniquities* are generational tendencies to sin that are passed from generation to generation. The good news is that history does not have to repeat itself. Jesus died on a tree to break all the generational curses that have come from our family trees. We, however, must possess this truth and declare it in order to be free from generational curses. I learned this principle when I prayed for my brother-in-law.

After praying for years for the salvation of my sister-in-law's husband, we finally had a breakthrough. My husband's sister came for a visit while her husband was on a hunting trip. On the first night of her visit, we decided to pray in agreement, once again, for her husband's salvation. I had recently heard about breaking ancestral ties and generational curses. That night I prayed the following prayer for her husband:

> *Father, in the name of Jesus Christ of Nazareth, God's only Son, I con-*
> *fess the sins of Bob's forefathers back to ten generations. I remit their*
> *sins of spiritual idolatry when they knowingly or ignorantly entered*
> *satan's realm of darkness through the occult or false religion. I break*
> *all generational curses and ancestral ties in Bob's family line. I release*
> *Bob from the influence of spirits that want to repeat family bondages. I*
> *declare that Bob's bloodline is now covered by the blood of Jesus.*

As I prayed this prayer, I had a vision. A block of wood over Bob's head was preventing a glorious light from heaven from shining on Bob. As we prayed, I saw that block of wood move, and the light was shining fully on Bob. I exclaimed excitedly, we have had a spiritual breakthrough.

On Sunday, Bob appeared early in the morning at our door to pick up his wife and child. He said, "I came early so we could make it to church this morning." Their boy asked, "Daddy, are you sick?" Until that day, Bob had never attended church with his family. Their church was in revival and on that following Thursday night, Bob was gloriously saved. The spirit of darkness that blinded Bob's eyes to salvation was defeated when we broke generational curses over Bob.

> *Lord, thank You for giving us all authority in Your name over the*
> *power of the prince of darkness.*

Daily Deposit: Pray for your loved ones today and break generational curses.

November 8

Precious Souls
Ezekiel 18:1–19:14

E very soul is precious to God. He declares to Ezekiel in this passage, "Behold, all souls are Mine" (Ezek. 18:4). God desires for no soul to perish, but the truth is, that the soul that sins will die. This is why God sent His only begotten Son into the world to be the perfect sacrifice for our sins when He died on the cross. The provision was made then to save the whole world, but sadly the whole world will not receive this great provision.

We talked yesterday about iniquities (the generational bent towards certain sins). Generational darkness, because of spiritual idolatry, can blind a person from God's spiritual truths. In this passage, however, God makes it clear to Ezekiel that each man is responsible for his own sin. If a father has sinned greatly, and a son refuses to go the same sinful way of his father, then the son's soul will be saved.

Sin always leads to death. The Bible even tells us that the man who commits adultery lacks understanding and destroys his own soul. (See Proverbs 6:32.) Whenever we repent of our sins, life takes the place of the death that was caused by that sin. We can even pray for others who we see sin, and God will grant them life. John wrote:

> He who has the Son has life; he who does not have the Son of God does not have life. These things I have written to you who believe in the name of the Son of God, that you may know that you have eternal life, and that you may continue to believe in the name of the Son of God.
>
> Now this is the confidence that we have in Him, that if we ask anything according to His will, He hears us. And if we know that He hears us, whatever we ask, we know that we have the petitions that we have asked of Him.
>
> If anyone sees his brother sinning a sin which does not lead to death, he will ask, and He will give him life for those who commit sin not leading to death. I do not say that he should pray about that.
>
> —1 John 5:12–16

What a privilege we have to be priests of the living God who can pray for others who sin.

Lord, thank You for making me a priest.

Daily Deposit: Make a list of people for whom you can pray for today. Life can be imparted to them through your prayers.

November 9

What Is That Smell?
Ezekiel 20:1–49

What is that smell? This is the question my husband asks often when we open the door of our home after a long trip away. It doesn't take us long to find the source of the smell. It usually is some rotting fruit or a sack of potatoes that has gone bad. The smell was probably in the house when we were home, but we didn't notice it. There were other smells that smothered the smell of something rotting. The house also was closed with no air circulating in it; so the smell was magnified.

Even though God is a Spirit, He has a keen sense of smell. Our spirits within us also have spiritual senses. The house of Israel had been closed to God for a long time.

In this passage, God reviews all the disobedience and rebellion of the house of Israel. The aroma of their drink offerings and burnt sacrifices had become a stench to Him, because they had hearts filled with idolatry. The hearts of Israel had been given to worship the gods of the Gentiles. Their hearts had been closed to the fresh breeze of the Holy Spirit for years.

Some elders had come to Ezekiel to inquire of the Lord. God's response was not what they were anticipating. God exclaimed:

> "Have you come to inquire of Me? As I live," says the LORD God, "I will not be inquired of by you."
>
> —EZEKIEL 20:3

God reminded them of how He had to take their forefathers into the wilderness because of their disobedience. He reminded them of the many times He was at the point of destroying them, but, for His name's sake, He did not make an end of them. He did not want His name profaned among the Gentiles who were watching God's dealings with the Children of Israel.

God promised to take them into a land flowing with milk and honey, and He kept His promises. The day came, however, when God pronounced the Children of Israel unclean because of their idolatry (v.26). They provoked God with their drink offerings to other gods, which smelled sweet to them. But to God, the aroma smelled like something rotting. The souls of His beloved children were rotting because of their idolatry.

With all of their idolatry, God did not give up on His children entirely. His plan was to raise up a faithful remnant. He would accept this remnant as a sweet aroma when He gathered them together out of the countries where He scattered them (v. 41). They would know He is God, the Lord of all, when He returned them to Israel. They would repent with godly sorrow and loathe themselves because of the evil they had committed.

Lord, may I always be a sweet aroma to You.

Daily Deposit: Today, ask the Holy Spirit to show you any sin in your life that would block the sweet aroma of His presence with you?

November 10

Read: Ezekiel 21:1–22:31; Hebrews 10:1–17; Psalm 108:1–13; Proverbs 27:12

The Sword
Ezekiel 21:1–22:31

As I sought the Lord about the name of the ministry He had given me, I heard these words, "Call it 'Voice of the Sword.'" Many years earlier I asked the Lord what part of the body I was. Was I a hand, a toe, a nose, or what? I was led to read about John the Baptist and how he was called "*a voice crying in the wilderness.*" I then knew what part of the body God had called me to be. He wanted me to be *His voice* in this earth to declare His Word (the Sword of the Spirit).

The prophets of old had similar callings. God put His words in their mouths, and they gave His Word voice on this earth. The message they delivered often was not received by the people, but this did not stop God's constant warnings through His chosen prophets.

The word of the Lord came to Ezekiel. In our passage today, God gives clear warning to Israel. God told Ezekiel to declare to the people that His sword was polished, sharpened, and drawn to bring judgment to the people if they did not repent. God appointed two ways for His sword to come against Israel. First, Babylon would come against Jerusalem, and then it would come against Rabbah of the Ammonites (21:20).

When we read the severe warning in this passage, we have to acknowledge that God still judges nations. He lifts up the humble and brings low the proud. The day would come when He would deal with Babylon and bring them low, but only after He had used them as a sword against Israel.

God uses nations for His purposes. He is sovereign. This passage makes me want to intercede more for my own nation. God has withheld His complete judgment from falling upon this land, because we still have faithful intercessors.

Lord, help me to pray daily for my nation and for the peace of Jerusalem.

Daily Deposit: As you pray for your nation's leaders today, pray that they will hear God's voice, and not the voice of false counselors.

November 11

Soul Ties
Ezekiel 23:1–49

We live in a day when sexual union is considered just an act that will fulfill our senses. Many are giving their bodies freely to one another, without the covering or commitment of marriage. The Bible says that the man who commits adultery lacks understanding. (See Proverbs 6:32.) He does not realize that, by this act, he can destroy his own soul. The Bible also tells us that if we join ourselves to a harlot, we become one with that harlot. Our spirits and souls are joined as one with that harlot. (See 1 Corinthians 6:15–16.)

Sexual union outside of marriage causes us to be tied to the soul of the one with whom we had sex. Whatever darkness was in the soul of the one we united ourselves with is able to invade our souls. That darkness has the potential to destroy our souls.

Israel had joined herself to many lovers. She had gone after the gods of other nations—the Babylonians, the Chaldeans, Pekod, Shoa, Koa, and the Assyrians. The gods of the nations looked so inviting, and Israel gave herself freely to those gods in a spiritual union that would soon backfire. The very nations to whom the Children of Israel joined themselves, through idolatry, would become their enemies, appointed by God to destroy them.

Adultery and idolatry, in God's eyes, are like twins. A person who commits adultery sins against his own body and gives the temple of his body to worship that person. Sex was created to be an act of worship. I loved the marriage vows in the movie about C. S. Lewis. He and his bride said, "I join myself to you in the act of worship to the Lord." Marriage is a holy union, and sex was created for a husband and wife to enjoy under the covenant of marriage.

Sex education in the schools today is not teaching the biblical facts about sex. We have a responsibility as parents to give these facts to our children. Our children will be spared much misery if we will teach them to be pure. We need also to pray daily for this generation, because seducing spirits are seeking to destroy the souls of our youth.

Lord, help me to speak Your spiritual truths about sex.

Daily Deposit: Pray for this generation. Cry out for God's mercy. Pray for parents to teach their children in the ways of the Lord.

November 12

Read: Ezekiel 24:1–26:21; Hebrews 11:1–16; Psalm 110:1–7; Proverbs 27:14

The Bread of Sorrow
Ezekiel 24:1–26:21

We have all eaten the "bread of sorrow" at times in our lives. God told Ezekiel that his wife would die, but He commanded Ezekiel not to mourn, weep, or even have tears. God commanded Ezekiel not to eat man's *bread of sorrow*. He told Ezekiel to sigh in silence. Then God gave the words He wanted Ezekiel to speak to Israel. Babylon would soon lay siege to Jerusalem and many of their children would die by the sword.

I think if I were Ezekiel, I would have just curled up under my covers and stayed in bed until it was all over. Ezekiel, however, was an obedient servant of the Lord. He never allowed himself to eat man's *bread of sorrow*. Ezekiel, however, many times did partake of God's sorrow. Godly sorrow always works repentance in our lives. Man's sorrow only is temporary and usually produces no change in either our attitude or our actions.

Paul wrote to the Corinthians about godly sorrow. He said:

> For even if I made you sorry with my letter, I do not regret it; though I did regret it. For I perceive that the same epistle made you sorry, though only for a while. Now I rejoice, not that you were made sorry, but that your sorrow led to repentance. For you were made sorry in a godly manner, that you might suffer loss from us in nothing. For godly sorrow produces repentance leading to salvation, not to be regretted; but the sorrow of the world produces death. For I observe this very thing, that you sorrowed in a godly manner: What diligence it produced in you, what clearing of yourselves, what indignation, what fear, what vehement desire, what zeal, what vindication! In all things you proved yourselves to be clear in this matter.
> —2 Corinthians 7:8-11

Godly sorrow not only produces repentance in us, but it also produces diligence, the clearing of our consciences from guilt, indignation against the sin we allowed in our lives, the fear of the Lord, a vehement desire to live righteous lives, great zeal to do the will of the Father, and total vindication in the sight of God and eventually others. If I had to choose between godly sorrow and worldly sorrow, I think I would choose godly sorrow.

Lord, help me to always experience godly sorrow when I sin.

Daily Deposit: Ask the Holy Spirit to help you uncover any unconfessed sins.

November 13

The King of Tyre
Ezekiel 27:1–28:26

Ezekiel began to lament over the city of Tyre. Then he told how the prince of Tyre would fall from his lofty seat of pride. Suddenly the lament changes to the king of Tyre. (See Ezekiel 27:11–19.) The description of this king has led some theologians to believe that the description is of satan before his fall and before the creation of man. Ezekiel wrote:

> You were the seal of perfection, full of wisdom and perfect in beauty. You were in Eden, the garden of God; every precious stone was your covering: the sardius, topaz, and diamond, beryl, onyx, and jasper, sapphire, turquoise, and emerald with gold. The workmanship of your timbrels and pipes was prepared for you on the day you were created. You were the anointed cherub who covers; I established you; You were on the holy mountain of God; you walked back and forth in the midst of fiery stones. You were perfect in your ways from the day you were created, till iniquity was found in you.
>
> —EZEKIEL 28:12

There is no question in my mind, after reading this, that Ezekiel was describing Lucifer. When Lucifer's heart was lifted up, God cast him to the ground. Lucifer's wisdom was corrupted because of his pride and beauty.

Pride was Lucifer's downfall, and it is the downfall of many who trust in riches, worldly wisdom and their own beauty, rather than trusting in the Lord. Lucifer was allowed to be next to God on His holy mountain. That, however, was not enough for Lucifer. He wanted more power. Pride always leads to a power play.

Ever since his fall, satan has tempted man to crave more power. He has tempted man to live independently of God. Pride always goes before a fall. Pride is the source of all contention. God resists the proud and gives grace to the humble. When we meditate on how Lucifer fell, we are challenged to humble ourselves daily before the Lord. A good prayer to pray is:

> *Lord, without You I can do nothing. I am totally dependent upon You today. I ask for Your grace to labor through me today. Keep me from being prideful, and give me a contrite, grateful heart.*

Daily Deposit: A great way to humble yourself today is to cast every care you have upon Jesus. Make a list of those things that concern you and then release them to the Lord.

November 14

Pride Is Possessive
Ezekiel 29:1–30:26

Yesterday, we learned what caused the fall of Lucifer. In Ephesians 6, we learn that we do not wrestle against flesh and blood, but we wrestle against principalities, against powers, against the rulers of darkness of this world, and against spiritual wickedness in heavenly places (Eph. 6:12). Many Christians live defeated lives because they do not understand that they are in a spiritual battle. We must employ spiritual weapons to fight this spiritual battle. Paul wrote in 2 Corinthians 10:4–5:

> For the weapons of our warfare are not carnal but mighty in God for pulling down strongholds, casting down arguments and every high thing that exalts itself against the knowledge of God, bringing every thought into captivity to the obedience of Christ.

Our spiritual weapons are the name of Jesus, the blood of Jesus, the Word of God and prayer (all kinds of prayer). If we look at what Paul wrote about strongholds, we see that pride is what causes us to have exalted thoughts that come against the knowledge of God. The door was open for pride to come into mankind when the serpent (satan) was able to put doubt in Eve's mind. Satan questioned, "Has God indeed said 'You shall not eat of every tree of the garden?'" (Gen. 3:1). Eve received the doubt, and then satan pushed the door of Eve's heart wide open for pride to enter when he said these words:

> You will not surely die. For God knows that in the day you eat of it your eyes will be opened, and you will be like God, knowing good and evil.
>
> —GENESIS 3:4–5

Eve felt like God was withholding something good from her. The doubt planted in her mind expanded to lack of trust in God, believing satan's lie, a craving for more knowledge and finally a desire for more power to be as gods. Satan was offering Eve the opportunity to open the door to his kingdom of darkness. Eve wanted to possess something she did not have. The door to satan's kingdom is always pride.

In our reading today, Ezekiel proclaims the downfall of Pharaoh because he said, "The River is mine, and I have made it." Pharaoh actually believed that the river belonged to him. Any time we feel like something belongs to us, we have opened the door to pride, and that pride will lead to destruction. Pharaoh had a thought that exalted itself against the knowledge of God. In reality we possess nothing. We are only stewards of God's possessions on this earth. God is the possessor of all things.

Lord, keep me from the snare of pride.

Daily Deposit: Trust your day to the Lord. It truly belongs to Him, not you.

November 15

Read: Ezekiel 31:1–32:32; Hebrews 12:14–29; Psalm 113:1–114:8; Proverbs 27:18–20

Trees of Righteousness
Ezekiel 31:1–32:32

We had the opportunity, on our first visit to Israel in 1977, to plant trees on the hillsides of Jerusalem. Years of neglect and war had taken its toll on the trees in Israel. It was not until Israel became a state in 1948 that the replanting of trees began. Our last trip to Israel was in 2000, and the hillsides of all Israel are now covered with trees. Trees are a symbol of life to Israelis. They are also a symbol of life to God. We see in the scriptures, many times, when we are called trees of righteousness, the plantings of the Lord.

In the garden there were two trees—the tree of life and the tree of the knowledge of good and evil. As we saw yesterday, Eve gave in to the serpent's temptation to eat the fruit from the tree of knowledge of good and evil. When she and Adam received the knowledge of good and evil, God had to place cherubim with flaming swords around the tree of life to prevent Adam and Eve from partaking of that tree. (See Gen. 3:24.) The kingdom of darkness had entered Adam and Eve, and God did not want that kingdom to be eternal. The good news is that all those who believe in Jesus Christ will live eternally in God's kingdom of light. Jesus died on a tree so that we might be delivered from sin and all curses. He is the tree of life that we can partake of daily to live righteous lives.

God compared the pride of Pharaoh and his multitudes to the trees of Lebanon with their thick boughs that seemed to reach to heaven. Their height was exalted above all the trees of the field, and their boughs multiplied. Under their shadow, great nations made their home. These great cedar trees were in the garden of God, and their excellence and beauty exceeded every tree that was in the garden, with the exception of the Tree of Life. Because Pharaoh had lifted his heart up in pride like the height of the trees of Lebanon, Pharaoh and his multitudes would be destroyed. Babylon would invade Egypt and destroy it. God asks the question of Pharaoh, "To which of the trees in Eden will you then be likened in glory and greatness?" (Ezek. 31:18).

God planned to use the sword of Babylon to plunder the pomp of Pharaoh and his multitudes (Ezek. 32:12). God resists the proud and gives grace to the humble. When we are in pride we have two enemies—satan and God. Satan seeks to destroy us through pride; while God plans to resist us, until we humble ourselves and seek Him.

Lord, I come to You to learn meekness and lowliness of heart.

Daily Deposit: Look up scriptures today on meekness. God has a lot to say about this fruit of the spirit, and we all need to learn more.

November 16

Pine Trees
Ezekiel 33:1–34:31

Pine trees are abundant in the southern states. These trees are extremely tall, but their roots are shallow. When we have ice or wind storms, pine trees are the first to topple. We have lost many pine trees in our own yard over the years, but the deeper rooted deciduous trees still remain. I was reminded of the nature of pine trees when I read this verse of scripture from our passage today:

> Therefore, you, O son of man, say to the house of Israel: "Thus you say 'If our transgressions and our sins lie upon us, and we pine away in them, how can we then live?'"
>
> —EZEKIEL 33:10

The expression "pine away" was also mentioned in Ezekiel 24:23 which says:

> You shall pine away in your iniquities and mourn with one another.

The verb *pine* in *Webster's New World Dictionary* means "to waste away through grief, pain or hunger or to have an intense longing or desire." *Pining away* over our own transgressions and sins will only produce death, not life. Life comes when we stop pining away (wallowing in regret and grief) over our sins and repent of our sins.

We learned, earlier, that godly sorrow produces repentance. Israel was sorry for its sins. Its people never heeded Ezekiel's warnings to repent. They were trusting in their own righteousness and they refused to turn away from their sin to God, who is all righteousness. God desired for Israel to be trees of righteousness that would not topple when the winds of adversity blew upon them. Sadly, Israel was like the pine trees that fall quickly, due to their shallow roots of self-righteousness.

Another interesting fact about pine trees is that their wood does not make good firewood. We have tried to burn some of the pine trees that toppled in our yard, but the pine simply does not catch fire easily. People who trust in their own righteousness do not catch fire easily either. The fire of the Holy Spirit cannot be kindled in the hearts of the self-righteous because pride shields their hearts from being anointed by the Holy Spirit.

Lord, help me never to trust in my own righteousness.

Daily Deposit: Pray for your loved ones who are not saved, due to their still trusting in their own righteousness.

Jealousy
Ezekiel 35:1–36:38

This month, we have talked much about pride. Pride and jealousy are like twin brothers. They are two principalities that cause contention and strife. Pride and jealousy are the powers that cause war. Pride causes us to want more power and possessions, and jealousy causes us to be envious of those who have more than we do. We see in our passage today that jealousy also will lead to destruction.

God gave instructions to Ezekiel to prophesy against Mt. Seir. Mt. Seir is where the Edomites (the descendants of Esau) lived. Esau lost both his birthright and his blessing, because he was a man controlled by his fleshly lusts. His god was his belly.

He sold his birthright to Jacob for a mass of pottage (lentil soup). Esau was jealous of his brother, Jacob, because Jacob was favored by his mother. Jacob usurped the birthright and blessing that belonged to him. This made Esau furious. The roots of jealousy and anger that developed in Esau became generational principalities that had power over the offspring that followed Esau.

Jealousy and anger were still operative in the Edomites, when Jerusalem fell. The Edomites turned the fugitives over to the Babylonians to be killed. They looted Judah's ruined towns. They were jealous because Judah had more than they did. Edom wanted to possess the possessions of Judah and Israel. Ezekiel spoke God's words to Edom and said (Ezek. 35:11):

> I will do according to your anger and according to the envy which you showed in your hatred against them; and I will make Myself known among them when I judge you.

God promised to make Mt. Seir desolate, because the Edomites had boasted with their mouths against the Lord. God was jealous against Edom and all the nations that wanted to possess Israel (36:5). Israel belonged to God, and He would never let them be completely destroyed. We serve an unchanging God who still will not allow Israel to be destroyed completely. God promised to restore Israel and cause them to be fruitful once again. The nations that had come against Israel would be put to shame.

The same God who was jealous over Israel because Israel was His precious possession is jealous over us. The jealousy of God is a good jealousy because it causes Him to destroy our idolatrous ways. He wants us to have no other God's before Him, because we belong to Him. The purpose of all of God's warnings through Ezekiel to Israel was to urge them to repent and turn from their idolatrous ways. They did not repent, but God would eventually have a people who would serve Him with all of their hearts.

Lord, thank You for speaking to me about the idols in my life.

Daily Deposit: Ask the Holy Spirit to show you if you still have idols.

November 18

Dry Bones
Ezekiel 37:1–38:23

After the invasion of Babylon, all seemed lost in Israel. Israel said, "Our bones are dry, our hope is lost, and we ourselves are cut off!" (37:11). Have you ever felt that way? We all go though dry times in our lives when God seems distant, and sometimes we even feel cut off. The truth, however, is that Jesus has promised never to leave us or forsake us. I believe God allows these dry times in our lives to make us hunger and thirst for more of Him. We often do not appreciate and delight in His presence as we should. Satan would love for us to begin complaining and murmuring just as the Children of Israel did when they were without water. God, however, wants us to pour out our complaints to Him. He is never put off when we express our feelings to Him. David was a man after God's own heart because he poured out his heart to the Lord.

Proverbs tells us that a broken spirit dries the bones, but a merry heart does good like medicine. (See Proverbs 17:22.) Israel was broken in spirit. It appeared as if all were lost. God had not forsaken them, however. He planned to restore Israel, and our passage today reveals God's plan.

Ezekiel was lifted in the spirit to behold a valley of dry bones. God asked him, "Can these bones live?" (37:4). Then God told Ezekiel to speak life to those dry bones. The moment he spoke life to them, muscles, tissue, and sinew began to come on those dry bones. Then Ezekiel was commanded to say to the four winds to breathe on those who were slain so they might live (v. 9). The bones became a great army. God then gave this glorious prophecy about Israel (Ezek. 37:14):

> "I will put My Spirit in you, and you shall live, and I will place you in your own land. Then you shall know that I, the LORD, have spoken it and performed it," says the LORD.

Ezekiel was instructed to take a stick and write on it *Judah*. He was told to take another stick and write on it *Ephraim*. He was told to join them together into one stick. I believe the two sticks formed a cross when they were joined. God explained to Ezekiel that the house of Ephraim, Joseph's son by his Gentile Egyptian wife, and Judah, the son of Israel, would become one. Paul tells us that God has broken down the wall of enmity between Gentiles and Jews through the cross. He wrote, "For He Himself is our peace, who has made both one, and has broken down the middle wall of separation" (Eph. 2:14).

Ezekiel's actions, to speak to the dry bones and to join the two sticks together, revealed God's plan to reconcile both Jew and Gentile to Himself, through the cross of Jesus. Restoration and redemption are promised to all who will believe in Jesus.

Lord, thank You for Your great plan.

Daily Deposit: Pray for God to unveil the eyes of your Jewish friends.

November 19

Who Is Gog?
Ezekiel 39:1–40:27

As we study prophets like Isaiah, Jeremiah, and Ezekiel, we see how often their focus shifts from their present day to what will happen in the End Times. Such is the case in our passage today. Most of the chapters beginning today will be prophecies about the last days.

Ezekiel was told to prophesy against the prince of Gog. Gog is the spiritual chief prince over the principality of all Islam. His territory includes Magog, or the southern Islamic nations in the dissolved Soviet Union. It also includes Meshech and Tubal. Meshech and Tubal were two of the sons of Japheth, the son of Noah. These two sons were the forefathers of the European nations. In the End Times, some of the European nations will side with the Islamic nations to come against Israel. These nations will be destroyed as they try to descend upon Israel from the Golan Heights.

This war, predicted in Ezekiel 39, will be so great that it will take Israel seven months to bury the dead (39:12). The birds of prey will multiply to eat the flesh of those who are slain. After this "great war," the Gentiles will know that God's plan from the beginning was to gather His people into His promised land, to sanctify them or set them apart for His glory. God promises to pour out His Spirit on the house of Israel.

My heart pounds every time I read these chapters, because I believe the time is drawing near when these prophesies will be fulfilled. My heart is not pounding in fear, but in great anticipation of the Lord's soon return.

Lord, You will fulfill all You have promised. Help me to be faithful to receive Your promises.

Daily Deposit: Pray for the peace of Jerusalem. Every time you pray this prayer, you are also praying for the soon Second Coming of Jesus Christ. There will be no peace in Jerusalem until He comes.

Where Do Wars Originate?

James 4:1–17

Yesterday, we discussed the future war that will come during the last days when Islam will come against Israel. We leave our survey of Ezekiel briefly to discover the reasons for all wars in this passage. This chapter in James begins with the question, "Where do wars and fights *come* from among you?" (v. 1).

James answers this question by listing the following reasons we experience war:

- A desire for pleasure (the lust of the flesh)
- Covetousness (the lust of the eyes)
- Trusting in the world's system rather than trusting in God (the lust of the pride of life)

Every war that has ever been, or will be, is caused by the very lusts that war within our own members. Whether we like it or not, we are stuck with the lust of the flesh (seeking to fulfill our own senses in an addictive way), the lust of the eyes (vain imaginations, fantasies, covetousness, and greedy longings in our minds), and the lust of the pride of life (trusting in ourselves and our own resources more than we trust in God). (See 1 John 2:16.)

Our study of Ezekiel clearly reveals these three lusts—as we have seen pride, jealousy, covetousness, idolatry, and rebellion displayed, not only by Israel and Judah, but also by every nation that came against them.

We learned this month how pride opens the door of our hearts to the kingdom of darkness, and how God resists the proud for this very reason. James exhorts us all to submit ourselves to God and resist the devil as he knocks on the door of our hearts. (See James 4:7.) Out of our hearts proceed all of these lusts. All satan has to do is get us to take his bait when he appeals to one of these lusts. When we say, "I will seek pleasure; I will entertain idolatrous thoughts, and I will trust in my own efforts," we have opened the door to satan's dark kingdom through our own pride. God help us all!

God beckons us to draw near to Him; because it is only in that position that we will be able to be successful in winning over our own lusts. We must call upon Jesus to fight this spiritual battle for us, as we employ our spiritual weapons.

We open the door to pride even when we say, "Tomorrow we will go to such and such a city, spend a year there, buy and sell, and make a profit" (v. 13). There may be no tomorrow. We cannot boast about tomorrow or anything, but the Lord. We can boast that through the shed blood of Jesus, His name, and His Word we can have the victory over succumbing to our own lusts.

Lord, thank You for giving me spiritual weapons to resist the devil.

Daily Deposit: Declare today, that the battle is the Lord's and the victory is yours.

November 21

Restoration of the Temple
Ezekiel 42:1–43:27

Not only does God plan to restore Israel, but He also plans to restore His temple in the end days. Exact measurements of the third temple are given to Ezekiel in the next few chapters. The service of the priests is described and, in today's reading, we see the most exciting element of the temple's restoration. Ezekiel wrote (vv. 43:1–3):

> Afterward he brought me to the gate, the gate that faces toward the east. And behold, the glory of the God of Israel came from the way of the east. His voice *was* like the sound of many waters; and the earth shone with His glory. It was like the appearance of the vision which I saw—like the vision which I saw when I came to destroy the city. The visions were like the vision which I saw by the River Chebar; and I fell on my face.

All of the events in the Bible, from Genesis to Revelation, express one goal–to restore completely the broken relationship between man and God that occurred in the garden of Eden. To accomplish this goal, God would have to sanctify a people unto Himself, immerse them with His Spirit and allow His glory to shine through them. God has already provided the way for this to happen when He sent Jesus to die for our sins. Jesus truly is the way for God's glory to be revealed on earth. What a plan and what a privilege we have to be part of that plan. Just as surely as He lives, all the earth will one day be filled with the glory of the Lord. (See Num.14:21.)

Lord, thank You for including me in Your great plan.

Daily Deposit: Ask the Holy Spirit to show you ways you can glorify Jesus today.

The Temple
Ezekiel 44:1–45:12

Every time we visit Israel we always go to the *Temple Institute*. After we step down some narrow stairs, our guide shows us a film about the work the Institute is doing. It is exciting to see all the preparations that are being made to make ready for the Temple to be restored in Israel. There is much controversy over whether or not the Temple will be restored, but as we read these last chapters of Ezekiel, we cannot help but believe that God is giving measurements for a physical temple, not a spiritual temple.

After the film, we are shown the priestly garments, the menorah, the altar of incense, the table of showbread, and many other items that will be used in the Temple.

Years of research have gone into producing the exact replicas of these items.

We met a man in Israel who comes to the states to gather monies for this Temple. Again, many do not feel this Temple is a physical temple since we are now the temple of the Holy Spirit. Others feel like the Temple must be restored before the antichrist is revealed. The abomination of desolation in Daniel does present the need for some type of restoration before the antichrist does away with the daily sacrifices. Daniel spoke of the activities of the antichrist when he wrote:

> And forces shall be mustered by him, and they shall defile the sanctuary fortress; then they shall take away the daily sacrifices, and place there the abomination of desolation. Those who do wickedly against the covenant he shall corrupt with flattery; but the people who know their God shall be strong, and carry out great exploits.
>
> —DANIEL 11:31–32

Jesus spoke of this abomination of desolation when He described what would happen in the End Times:

> And this gospel of the kingdom will be preached in all the world as a witness to all the nations, and then the end will come. Therefore when you see the 'abomination of desolation,' spoken of by Daniel the prophet, standing in the holy place, then let those who are in Judea flee to the mountains.
>
> —MATTHEW 24:16

All of this challenges me to be ready for Christ's Second Coming because the time truly is short.

Lord, help me to daily be prepared for Your Second Coming.

Daily Deposit: Pray for those who are not prepared for His *soon* coming!

November 23

Restoration of the Sacrificial System
Ezekiel 45:13–46:24

When we were at the Temple Institute, we saw all the articles that will be used when the sacrificial system is restored in the Temple. There is a controversy among theologians about the sacrificial system being restored. However, it is evident that Ezekiel is prophesying of the last days. In our passage today, God gives Ezekiel great details about how the sacrifices are to be performed.

The question asked by many theologians is, "Why would there be any need for restoration of the sacrifices since Jesus is our perfect sacrifice?" The original sacrificial system, detailed in Leviticus, was instituted so that God's people would have a covering for their sins. This covering of blood was a shadow of the true payment which would be made when Jesus died on the cross to remove our sins, transgressions, and iniquities.

The restoration of the temple and the sacrificial system, I believe, is to herald the Second Coming of Jesus Christ, when He will rule from His temple in Jerusalem. Zechariah prophesied that Jesus would build the temple of the Lord when He comes again:

> Behold, the Man whose name is the BRANCH! From His place He shall branch out.
> And He shall build the temple of the LORD; Yes, He shall build the temple of the
> LORD. He shall bear the glory, And shall sit and rule on His throne; So He shall be a
> priest on His throne, And the counsel of peace shall be between them both.
> —ZECHARIAH 6:12

The Jewish people have no sacrificial system today. The sacrificial system ceased when the temple was destroyed in 70 A.D. Ezekiel's temple, described in these passages, along with the sacrificial system that is reinstated, are necessary, in order for the Jewish people to recognize Jesus as the perfect sacrifice, the lamb without blemish. The recognition of Jesus as their perfect sacrifice is also described in Zechariah when he prophesied:

> And I will pour on the house of David and on the inhabitants of Jerusalem the
> Spirit of grace and supplication; then they will look on Me whom they pierced. Yes,
> they will mourn for Him as one mourns for his only son, and grieve for Him as
> one grieves for a firstborn.
> —ZECHARIAH 12:10

Lord, thank You for Your preparations for Your Second Coming.

Daily Deposit: Pray for your Jewish friends today to have their eyes opened.

November 24

The River of Life
Ezekiel 47:1–48:35

We finish our survey of Ezekiel today. The visions revealed to Ezekiel, when he was caught up in the Spirit, are magnificent. Every time I read them, I stand in awe of God's might, power, and wisdom. I feel I need to bow and say, "Holy, Holy, Holy is the Lord. Power and glory and honor to the lamb who was slain from the foundation of the earth!" God's plan to redeem and restore His people is breathtaking. We cannot understand all of the things revealed in Ezekiel with our natural mind. God must interpret them to us by His Spirit.

There is a great Day of Atonement coming for the remnant that is left in Israel. Ezekiel spoke of this in our passage today. Zechariah even described it in greater detail. Zechariah spoke of this Day of Atonement when he said:

> In that day a fountain shall be opened for the house of David and for the inhabitants of Jerusalem, for sin and for uncleanness.

On that day the Jewish people will ask Jesus (their revealed Messiah), "'What are these wounds between your arms?' Then he will answer, 'Those with which I was wounded in the house of my friends.'" (Zech. 13:6).

Ezekiel spoke of water that flowed under the threshold of the temple toward the east towards the sea (Ezek. 47:1). When it reached the sea, its waters were healed. Wherever the river flowed, every living thing that moves will live. Along the banks of this river were all kinds of trees used for food. The leaves on these trees did not wither, their fruit never failed, and the leaves were used for medicine (Ezek. 47:8–9, 12). John spoke of this river when he wrote:

> And he showed me a pure river of water of life, clear as crystal, proceeding out of the throne of God and of the Lamb. In the midst of the street of it, and on either side of the river, was there a tree of life, which bare twelve manner of fruits, and yielded her fruit every month: and the leaves of the tree were for the healing of the nations.
>
> —Revelation 22:1–2, KJV

Paul also spoke about that Day of Atonement when he wrote:

> And so all Israel shall be saved: as it is written, There shall come out of Sion the Deliverer, and shall turn away ungodliness from Jacob.
>
> —Romans 11:26

Lord, thank You for being faithful to fulfill Your great plans.

Daily Deposit: Read Revelation 22 today and be blessed.

November 25

An Excellent Spirit
Daniel 1:1–2:23

One of my constant prayers as a mother was for all three of my boys to have the same excellent spirit Daniel had. Daniel was a young man, gifted with wisdom, knowledge and understanding. But it was Daniel's excellent spirit that caused him to use his wisdom, knowledge, and understanding to accomplish God's purposes in his life.

Daniel was deported as a teenager, in 605 B.C., to Babylon where he lived over sixty years. Daniel was a trainee in Nebuchadnezzar's court. He gained such favor with those in authority that he eventually became an advisor to foreign kings.

The name *Daniel* means "God is my Judge." God judged Daniel, along with three other young men, to be worthy to represent him in a pagan culture. Three Hebrew young men also trained with Daniel in Babylon. These men were renamed *Shadrach, Meshach*, and *Abed-Nego*. These men made the decision not to defile their bodily temples with the king's dainties. They must have read Proverbs 23:1–3 which says:

> When you sit down to eat with a ruler, consider carefully what is before you; and put a knife to your throat if you are a man given to appetite. Do not desire his delicacies, for they are deceptive food.

Daniel challenged the chief steward to give his friends and himself only vegetables to eat and water to drink. At the end of ten days, they were to examine the four to see if their appearance was more excellent than the men who ate the king's delicacies. At the end of ten days, the four young men were healthier in appearance than their counterparts. These young men were not only healthier than their counterparts, but they also were ten times wiser. They were filled with knowledge and understanding.

Daniel was also skilled in the interpretation of dreams. Like Joseph, God had given Daniel this special gift and it was used to gain favor with the king. After having a dream that none of his wise men could interpret, the king threatened to kill all the wise men, including Daniel and his friends. Daniel asked the king to give him time to interpret the dream. Then Daniel asked for his friends to pray for him as he sought the Lord for the interpretation. God was faithful to hear their prayers, and the secret of the dream was revealed to Daniel in a night vision.

We will see later in Daniel how this beautiful theme of standing up for one's beliefs in God always brings ultimate victory. Every teenager should read this book. It will encourage them to stand up for their faith in their schools and jobs.

Lord, may this next generation be bold to stand up for their beliefs.

Daily Deposit: Pray for the Christian youth in our schools to have the same excellent spirit as Daniel.

A Revealer of Secrets
Daniel 2:24–3:30

Years ago there was a TV show called "I've Got a Secret." The guest would usually be a well-known star who had a secret. A panel of famous people would try to guess the secret of the guest star. There is something mystical and exciting about secrets.

However, we fool ourselves if we think we can keep anything a secret from God. When Jesus walked on earth, He was able to discern even the deepest secrets of the people He met. Remember the woman at the well? Jesus told her she had been married five times, and the man she was with at the present time was not her husband. Jesus' revelation of that secret opened the door for her home-town to believe in Him. (See John 4.)

In our passage today, we see how Daniel's interpretation of King Nebuchadnezzar's dream convinced the king that Daniel's "God is the God of gods, the Lord of kings, and a revealer of secrets" (Dan. 2:47). Daniel's revelation gained Daniel such favor that the king made him ruler over the whole province of Babylon and chief administrator over all the wise men.

Shortly after his dream was interpreted, Nebuchadnezzar made an image of himself, and at the sound of the king's symphony, everyone was ordered to fall down and worship the gold image. Daniel's friends, Shadrach, Meshach, and Abed-Nego, refused to bow down. When the king discovered this, he threatened to throw them into a fiery furnace if they still refused to bow down before him.

Shadrach, Meshach and Abed-Nego, however, had a great secret that the king would soon know. These three friends of Daniel knew that their God had the power to deliver them from the fire. When they told this secret to Nebuchadnezzar, he was furious and threw them into the fiery furnace that was seven times hotter than normal.

Daniel's friends knew God had the power to deliver them, but even if He chose not to deliver them, they would never bow down and worship the king's image. As the fire raged, suddenly the king and all those present saw four men in the fire, not just three. The fourth had the appearance like the Son of God. Daniel's friends were delivered. The fire had no power over them, the hair on their heads was not even singed and their garments did not even smell like smoke.

Many years ago, God told me a secret. Just six months before I had a tragic accident when my car hit an eight-year-old boy riding on his bike, I heard the following words while I took communion in my church: "*Linda, you are going to go through a fiery trial, but just like Daniels' friends you will be delivered and you will not even have the smell of smoke on you.*" I told the secret that day to my husband, and six months letter I faced this fiery trial. That secret word from the Lord kept my faith from failing during the months of this boy's recovery when he almost died. God is faithful to keep both His promises and His secrets. The boy was healed and I led him to the Lord.

Lord, thank You for knowing all the secrets of my future.

Daily Deposit: Give your future to the Lord today and trust Him with it.

November 27

Shout It From the Rooftops
Daniel 4:1–37

There is a secret every believer has in common. This secret, however, is not to be kept. We are called to shout this secret to the whole world. Paul told about this mysterious secret when he said:

> I became a minister according to the stewardship from God which was given to me for you, to fulfill the word of God, the mystery which has been hidden from ages and from generations, but now has been revealed to His saints. To them God willed to make known what are the riches of the glory of this mystery among the Gentiles: which is Christ in you, the hope of glory.
>
> —COLOSSIANS 1:25–27

God had revealed to King Nebuchadnezzar, His very own Son, who was with Daniel's friends in the fire. Jesus had not come in bodily form yet to earth, but He was with God from the beginning, and He was with Daniel's friends to deliver them.

Nebuchadnezzar was so excited about this revelation that he promoted Daniel's friends and made an astounding declaration to all the peoples, nations, and languages that dwell in all the earth. He declared:

> How great are His signs, and how mighty His wonders! His Kingdom is an everlasting kingdom, and His dominion is from generation to generation.
>
> —DANIEL 4:3

If a pagan king, who was still bound by pride, could make such a declaration, how much more should we shout this great news from the rooftops of our neighborhoods. If we do not declare the Gospel, we will not fulfill the high calling every believer has to be a witness on this earth.

Nebuchadnezzar's pride was brought low when he became insane and looked and lived like a wild beast for a season. When his understanding returned, he blessed the Most High and praised and honored Him who lives forever. After this season, Nebuchadnezzar proclaimed:

> Now I, Nebuchadnezzar, praise and extol and honor the King of heaven, all of whose works are truth, and His ways justice. And those who walk in pride He is able to put down.
>
> —DANIEL 4:37

What keeps us from shouting the great mystery and secret of the Gospel to others is simply our own pride.

Lord, deliver me from pride.

Daily Deposit: Tell someone today this good news.

November 28

Read: Daniel 5:1–31; 2 Peter 2:1–22; Psalm 119:113–131; Proverbs 28:19–20

The Handwriting Is On the Wall
Daniel 5:1–31

"The handwriting is on the wall" is an expression that many use often; however, few know this expression comes straight from the Scriptures. This expression came from today's passage. When we say "the handwriting is on the wall," we usually mean something has been declared that will occur in the future. That is exactly what happened when Daniel interpreted the handwriting on the wall of King Belshazzar's banquet hall.

King Belshazzar was the son of Nebuchadnezzar. He did not accept his father's own faith in God. Where was Belshazzar when Daniel interpreted his father's dreams and when Daniel's friends were delivered from the fiery furnace? Belshazzar didn't even know Daniel existed.

The same spirit of pride and idolatry that bound King Nebuchadnezzar for the first part of his life was passed on to his son. The Scriptures tell us that spiritual idolatry can be passed to the third and fourth generation. The sins of the father can be visited upon the children. (See Exodus 20:5.)

King Belshazzar ordered all the vessels his father had taken from God's Temple to be brought to him. These vessels were distributed to the people at his banquet. They toasted the gods of sliver and gold with these holy goblets. Suddenly, the fingers of a man's hand appeared and wrote opposite the lamp stand on the plaster of the wall, and the king saw part of the hand that wrote. The king began to tremble and he cried aloud for the astrologers and soothsayers. When they were gathered, he told them:

> Whoever reads this writing, and tells me the interpretation, shall be clothed with purple and have a chain of gold around his neck; and he shall be the third ruler in the kingdom.
>
> —DANIEL 5:7

When the queen was summoned to the banquet hall, she told her husband about Daniel who had the Holy Spirit of God in him and who had great wisdom and understanding. When Daniel was brought to the room, the king told Daniel what he would receive if he interpreted the writings. Daniel refused the gifts and rewards, and then he reviewed Nebuchadnezzar's life to his son. He told how Nebuchadnezzar's pride was brought low when he became like a beast, until he finally acknowledged that Daniel's God was the one true God. Daniel's interpretation of the handwriting declared the end of Belshazzar's kingdom, which would be divided and given to the Persians. That very night, Belshazzar was slain and Darius the Mede received the kingdom.

The handwriting will be on the wall for us if we refuse to humble ourselves before the Lord. We will be brought low, even as Nebuchadnezzar and Belshazzar were.

Lord, help me to humble myself before you daily.

Daily Deposit: Today, humble yourself and trust God to take care of your future.

November 29

The Handwriting of the Prophets
2 Peter 3:1–18

We temporarily leave Daniel to search for treasures in the New Testament. The second letter Peter wrote was written towards the end of his life just before he was martyred. Peter warned believers to beware of false teachers. He wrote:

> Be mindful of the words which were spoken before by the holy prophets, and of the commandment of us, the apostles of the Lord and Savior, knowing this first: that scoffers will come in the last days, walking according to their own lusts, and saying, "Where is the promise of His coming? For since the fathers fell asleep, all things continue as they were from the beginning of creation."
>
> —2 PETER 3:2–4

Peter said that such scoffers willfully forgot that the heavens and earth were created by the Word of God. Peter urged his audience to always remember that "one day is as a thousand years, and a thousand years as one day" (v. 8).

We have studied many of the prophets of old in this devotional book. Most of these prophets had something to say about the last days. We do need to review these prophetic scriptures so that we will be able to be faithful watchman who watch and pray in these End Times.

Peter warned that the day of the Lord will come as a thief in the night; the heavens will pass away with a great noise, and the elements will melt with fervent heat. The earth will be consumed. The prophets of old wrote on the walls of our hearts when they prophesied about that great final day of the Lord.

We should not tremble with fear like Belshazzar did when he saw the handwriting on the wall. Peter challenged us all to look forward to a new heaven and earth and to be found blameless and spotless on the day of the Lord.

Knowing what will happen in the future should cause us to remain steadfast and not to be led astray by scoffers and false teachers. We can grow in the grace and the knowledge of the Lord Jesus Christ, as we faithfully read the Bible through each year.

Reading the prophetic words about the End Times causes me to give thanks to the Lord, because He has chosen me to be a declarer of His Word in these End Times. What a great privilege! As I read Jesus' prophetic words about the last days, I want to pray more diligently for those who are lost. Jesus is coming soon! The handwriting is on the wall!

Lord, help me to prepare others for Your soon coming.

Daily Deposit: Pray for your lost friends and loved ones today.

A Faithful Watchman
Daniel 7:1–28

Daniel was a faithful watchman who interceded for his nation. Even though he was persecuted, Daniel prospered under four rulers—Nebuchadnezzar, Belshazzar, Darius, and Cyrus. During Darius's reign, Daniel was thrown into the lions' den because the governors and satraps were jealous of Daniel, and they set a trap for him. They got Darius to decree that no one could petition any god or man for thirty days, except the king. If anyone broke this decree, they would be thrown into the lion's den.

When Daniel heard this decree, he continued his usual times of prayer. He even opened his windows and knelt towards Jerusalem three times on the very day this decree was given. Darius was forced to throw Daniel into the lions den, but just as God rescued Daniel's friends, He also rescued Daniel from the lions.

During the rule of Belshazzar, Daniel dreamed about four beasts. His dream included a revelation of the last days and what would happen in heaven during these days. As Daniel watched in the night visions, he saw One like the Son of Man coming with the clouds of heaven. This One came to the Ancient of Days who gave Him dominion and glory and a kingdom of all peoples, nations and languages who would serve Him forever.

Daniel asked for the interpretation of this dream, and he received it. The great beasts represented four kings who would arise on the earth. Their dominion would be taken away.

Daniel was especially interested in the fourth beast that had ten horns on his head, teeth of iron and nails of bronze. This beast trampled the residue of the earth with its feet. The interpretation came. Daniel understood that the fourth beast represented a kingdom that would devour the whole earth, trample it down, and break it to pieces. This beastly ruler would speak pompous words against God, and he would persecute the saints. He would try to change the times and the law. The saints would be given over to him for a time, and times, and half a time. His dominion would eventually be taken away, and the saints would have an everlasting kingdom, and all dominions would serve the Lord.

Theologians all agree that this fourth beast represents the Antichrist. We do not need to fear these last days described in Daniel's dream, because we know we belong to Jesus Christ. Whether the Antichrist is revealed while we are still living remains to be seen. We must, however, be ready for the Lord's return every day that we live. Like Daniel, we should be faithful watchman on the wall who pray, day and night, for laborers to labor in the fields that are white for harvest and souls to be gathered. What a privilege to be alive during this last great harvest! Watch and pray!

Lord, I want to be a faithful watchman like Daniel.

Daily Deposit: Pray for all the laborers you know who are gathering God's harvest.

December 1

End Times
Daniel 8:1–27

As we finish our yearly readings, it is fitting that we will close our readings with the Minor Prophets and the Book of Revelation. I will not even attempt to interpret the scriptures we will read in the month of December. Instead, I will try to relay the meaning these scriptures have for us today. We can have our theological discussions and interpretations of these final books of the Bible, but we do not live in the future. We live in the now, and faith is now. Jesus gave us this charge:

> Seek first the kingdom of God and His righteousness, and all these things shall be added to you. Therefore do not worry about tomorrow, for tomorrow will worry about its own things. Sufficient for the day is its own trouble.
> —MATTHEW 6:33–34

We will be looking at some future troubled times as we read these last books of the Bible, but we can be of good cheer because we know the rest of the story. We know who wins in the end.

Daniel knew who wins in the end. God unveiled his eyes to see the time of the Antichrist. The interpretation of the dream of the four beasts revealed exactly what the Antichrist would do in the last days. During the reign of Belshazzar, Daniel had another vision of beasts. He saw a ram that overpowers the world. It was defeated by a goat with one great horn. This great horn was broken off and replaced by four horns. From one of these horns came another horn which set itself up as "prince of the host" and desolated God's people.

When Daniel was seeking the meaning of all of this, Gabriel appeared to him and interpreted the vision. The two-horned ram represented the kings of Media and Persia. The male goat represented the king of Greece. History tells us that Alexander died suddenly and was replaced by four Hellenic kingdoms. A stern-faced king would arise from one of these kingdoms.

Where do we fit in this vision? Right now we are living in the times of the Gentiles that precede the revelation of the Antichrist. The confederation of the European states with the currency of the *Euro* is a precursor to the four kingdoms that will produce the Antichrist. We are truly living in the last of the last days.

Lord, help me to live each day as if it were my last day on earth.

Daily Deposit: Don't waste time today. Redeem every minute and use it wisely. Ask God what part you have in ushering in these last days.

335

December 2

Understanding the Times
Daniel 9:1–10:21

In these last days, we need to be like the citizens of Berea. When Paul and Silas preached in the synagogue of the Jews, in Berea, their words were received with all readiness, and they searched the scriptures daily to find out whether these things were so. Many of them believed and even some of the Greeks became believers. (See Acts 17:11–12.)

As we read about the last days, we need to search out the scriptures to discover for ourselves exactly what God is saying to each of us. Our faith should be deepened as we hear and study God's Word.

Daniel was a student of the scriptures. He had read the prophets many times. He was familiar with Jeremiah's prophecy:

> And this whole land shall be a desolation and an astonishment, and these nations shall serve the king of Babylon seventy years.
> —JEREMIAH 25:11

When Daniel reread this prophecy, he understood that the seventy-year period spoken of by Jeremiah was about to be completed. Knowing that these seventy years were about to be fulfilled, he set his face toward the Lord God and began to supplicate and make his requests known to the Lord. Daniel could have been anxious about what would happen after Israel was no longer in bondage to Babylon. But instead, he made his requests known to the Lord, through supplication with thanksgiving. Daniel did not have Paul's letters to read, but he had the same excellent spirit Paul had when he wrote:

> Be anxious for nothing, but in everything by prayer and supplication, with thanksgiving, let your requests be made known to God; and the peace of God, which surpasses all understanding, will guard your hearts and minds through Christ Jesus.
> —PHILIPPIANS 4:6–7

Daniel began to confess his own sins and the sins of his people. Confession of our own sins is a great way to begin our prayer times with the Lord. We need to use the "ABCD" approach to prayer.

A—Approach God with thanksgiving and praise.

B—Base our prayers on the scriptures.

C—Confess our sins before the Lord.

D—Declare God's Word with faith in prayer. Daniel's prayer in our passage was so powerful that Gabriel appeared to him and assured Daniel that God heard him. He set things in motion in the spirit realm immediately, as a response to Daniel's effective prayers.

Lord, help me to pray effectively like Daniel.

Daily Deposit: Ask the Holy Spirit to give you the prayers He wants you to pray today.

December 3

Read: Daniel 11:1–34; 1 John 3:7–24; Psalm 122:1–9; Proverbs 29:1

Wars and Wars
Daniel 11:1–34

From the moment Daniel began his intercession for his nation, wars were being fought in the second heaven where Satan dwells. In Daniel 10, we learned that from the first day Daniel set his heart to understand, and to humble himself, his words were heard in the third heaven where God dwells. The assignment was given to an angelic being at that moment to come to interpret the visions Daniel experienced. The prince of the kingdom of Persia withstood this angel for twenty-one days and then Michael, one of the chief princes, came to help him do battle.

The visions Daniel had about future wars spoke of physical wars and physical kingdoms. However, behind every physical leader and kingdom and every physical war there are spiritual princes (angels—both good and bad) who are battling in the second heaven. Paul told us that we are not fighting a flesh and blood battle on earth. The true battle we face everyday is with principalities and powers, rulers of darkness and wickedness in heavenly places. (See Ephesians 6:12.)

Both good and evil angels are organized in ranks and have the power to influence earthly national events and individuals. Daniel's prayers activated the battle in the second heaven. David revealed in Psalm 103 that angels are activated when they hear God's Word spoken on earth:

> Bless the LORD, you His angels, Who excel in strength, who do His Word, heeding the voice of His word.
>
> —PSALM 103:20

We learn in our passage today that the angelic being who spoke to Daniel actually strengthened Darius the Mede. (See Daniel 11:1.) This angel also revealed to Daniel many things that would happen in the future. Great detail was given about the kings who would war and the kingdoms that would be uprooted. This angel reviewed the same pattern of wars that were revealed to Daniel earlier. All of these wars would lead up to the revelation of the Antichrist on earth.

If Daniel were alive today, he could write a book on the End Times, and it would make a million. Isn't it a blessing that we do not have to read a multitude of books on the End Times to get the one message God wants us to receive? That message is, "Be ready at all times to meet Jesus face-to-face." That day could be today. Are you ready?

Lord, thank You for creating angels to assist me in this life.

Daily Deposit: Give your moments to the Lord today. Each minute counts because the clock is ticking, and the last chime heralding Jesus' coming could occur today.

December 4

The Appointed Time
Daniel 11:36–12:13

A multitude of time lines and dates have been projected, based on the facts in Daniel. Sometimes I think God smiles from heaven at our feeble efforts to understand His timing. We just learned that one day is as a thousand years and a thousand years is as a day to Him. Needless to say, God does not march to the drumbeat of our timetables and calendars. He has an appointed time for everything. We learned in our passage yesterday that the time of the end is for an appointed time. (See Daniel 11:35.)

At the time appointed, Michael, the angel assigned to watch over Israel, will stand up. He will watch over Israel during their great time of trouble called "Jacob's troubles."

This will be the great tribulation period Jesus spoke about, in Matthew 24:15–28. Just after the tribulation, the sun will be darkened, and the moon will not give light, the stars will fall from heaven, and the powers of the heavens will be shaken. (See Matthew 24:29.) Then the Son of Man will appear in heaven, and He will come on the clouds of heaven with power and great glory. (See Matthew 24:30.) At that appointed time, angels will be assigned to gather together His elect from the four winds, from one end of heaven to the other. (See Matthew 24:31.)

Jesus said that not even He knows the day or the hour of this event (Matt. 24:36). Only the Father knows when it is time for the Bridegroom to come. In the early days in Israel, the bridegroom went away for usually a year to prepare a home for his bride to be. When he completed the house, the father of the bridegroom inspected it. The bridegroom could not go to receive his bride until his father checked out every detail of the house and approved it for occupation. Only the father could give the final word that all the preparations for the house were completed.

We live in the day when our Heavenly Father is inspecting the home of His Son and His bride. The finishing touches are being made, and when our Heavenly Father gives the word to His Son, the appointed time will be manifested on earth.

Daniel was instructed to seal the words of the book. At the appointed time when the house is ready, the Holy Father will give the word to the Lamb of God (His only Son) to open the book. At that appointed time, Daniel and all the saints before him and after him will receive their inheritance. We have a lot to look forward to. I feel like shouting, "Come, Lord Jesus!"

Lord, thank You for being faithful to fulfill Your appointments on time.

Daily Deposit: Pray that God will help you be on time for every divine appointment He has for you today and in the days ahead.

December 5

The Hedge of Thorns
Hosea 1:1–3:5

The prophets Hosea, Joel, and Amos unfold God's extravagant, everlasting love to us. God is love and the essence of His power is love. The authority He has over nations, His divine sovereignty, and His righteous judgments are all channeled through His great love for mankind. Hosea, Joel, and Amos received a glimpse of that love. Now it is our pleasure to peruse their prophecies and to discover for ourselves the measureless, endless, and unchanging love of God.

As we studied the Major Prophets, we saw how God often used their personal experiences to illustrate His prophetic message through them. God uses that same method with the Minor Prophets. Hosea's personal experiences especially express God's message to Israel.

The name *Hosea* means "Salvation" or "Deliverance." He prophesied around 715 B.C. The book of Hosea is about a people who needed to understand the love of God. We have a better understanding of God's love, as we see Hosea's life and read his prophecies. We also see the great responsibility of every believer to display the love of God to the world in these last days.

God instructed Hosea to marry a harlot. Hosea obeyed and took Gomer to be his wife, and she had a son by him. The son was named *Jezreel* which means "God will sow." God would soon sow destruction to the house of Israel in the Valley of Jezreel. She later had a daughter who was named *Lo-Ruhamah* which means "unloved or not pitied." God would no longer have pity upon Israel. He would utterly take them away.

The adultery of Gomer illustrated the sin of Israel. Her children represented God's plan to judge Israel for her spiritual adultery. After the birth of her children, Gomer left Hosea, to live with other men. Finally, she had to sell herself as a bondservant. Hosea purchased Gomer from her master and brought her home, where she remained faithful for a season.

God placed a hedge of thorns around Gomer, who represented Israel, to keep her from finding her lovers (2:6–7). The day would come when she would return to her first husband (the God of Israel). I have used this passage about the hedge of thorns to pray for my children during the times when they were not walking in God's ways. You might want to join me in this prayer for all the prodigals you know who need to return home.

> In the Name of Jesus Christ of Nazareth, I ask You, Father, to place a hedge of thorns around _____, to keep them from going the way of seducing spirits who seek to entice them and lead them astray by their own worldly lusts.

Daily Deposit: Pray today for this generation to remain faithful to God.

December 6

Unconditional Love
Hosea 4:1–5:15

L aced through the prophecies of God's severe judgments upon Israel, are many prophetic messages that cause hope to spring in the hearts of all those who are in despair.
Yesterday's reading was filled with hope. Even though God would take away the grain, the
new wine, and the linen and cause the mirth to cease, the day would come when He would
allure Israel back to Himself. At that time, He would comfort her, give her vineyards, and
a door of hope would spring up in the Valley of Achor (despair). Israel would sing and
rejoice, as in the days of her youth. In that day, Israel will call the Lord her husband. God
will betroth Israel forever under a new covenant. He will betroth Israel in righteousness,
justice, loving-kindness, and mercy.

The life of Hosea explodes with God's unconditional love. God instructed Hosea to buy
back Gomer, who had left him for other lovers. Gomer would remain faithful to Hosea for
many days. In the latter days, God will gather Israel to Himself, and they will know His
goodness.

When we visit Israel, we often are taken into the rooms behind the Western Wall. There
we see men dressed in black sitting at tables studying the scriptures. When I see this scene,
I am reminded of Jesus' words to the Pharisees and scribes (John 5:39):

> You search the Scriptures, for in them you think you have eternal life; and these
> are they which testify of Me. But you are not willing to come to Me that you may
> have life.

Less than 2 percent of Israel believes in God. Our son had the opportunity to live in a
kibbutz for a summer, and he was shocked at the unbelief and worldliness of those with him
in the kibbutz. Those who do believe in God are like the Pharisees and scribes. They have
no idea how much God loves them. They try to prove their devotion to God through their
religious observances.

The cry of God is the same cry He had when He said through Hosea the prophet: "My
people are destroyed for lack of knowledge" (Hosea 4:6). At the time of Hosea, "harlotry,
wine, and new wine enslave[d] the heart[s] of the people" (Hosea 4:11). Israel was like a
stubborn calf, like a lamb who left the flock and was lost in the open country. (See Hosea
4:16.) Nothing much has changed over the centuries.

Throughout the scriptures God gives the invitation to come to Him, to know Him, and
to receive His unconditional love. God bought us back from the slave market of sin with the
precious blood of His only begotten Son. The way to come to Him has been paved. How can
people continue to refuse such unconditional love?

Lord, thank You for Your unconditional love.

Daily Deposit: Pray for the lost to receive His unconditional love.

December 7

The Third Day
Hosea 6:1–9:17

We live in exciting times. We are living in the third day that Hosea prophesied about when he said:

> Come, and let us return to the LORD; For He has torn, but He will heal us; He has stricken, but He will bind us up. After two days He will revive us; On the third day He will raise us up, that we may live in His sight.
>
> —HOSEA 6:1–2

When we celebrated the birth of a new millennium, we were celebrating much more than just the introduction of another 1,000 years. Few realize that in the year 2000, we entered the third day when Jesus will return and our bodies will be resurrected. We learned earlier that a day is as a thousand years, and a thousand years is as a day. It has been 2000 years since the birth of Jesus. His active ministry on earth lasted for a period of three years. At the end of three years, Jesus was crucified. He died on the cross, and on the third day He rose again. We are privileged to be living in the day prophesied by Hosea when God will heal and revive us so we may live forever in His sight.

Wow! What a privilege it is to be living in this day. We do not know the day nor the hour of the Lord's return, but we do know, without a doubt, that we are in the season of His return. Hosea spoke these words: "He will come to us like the rain, like the latter and former rain to the earth" (Hos. 6:3).

Recently, I had a supernatural experience. I was setting our patio table for breakfast, when I looked up and saw a shocking sight. It was a gorgeous day. The sky was like an October sky with not a cloud in it. Suddenly, I heard the sound of rain. I looked up, and rain was pouring from a cloudless sky. The rain only covered an opening of about ten yards. I looked heavenward to see if there was a cloud above the rain, and there was none. Only the sun was beaming down on the raindrops causing them to look like sparkling diamonds as they fell to the ground.

I asked the Lord what all of this meant, and He said,

> This is one sign of the latter rain. The latter rain will saturate the earth in the end days and there will be a great harvest of souls.

What a privilege it is to be a laborer in this last great harvest.

Lord, help me to gather many unto You in this season of the latter rain.

Daily Deposit: Pray for more laborers during this harvest time.

December 8

Read: Hosea 10:1–14:9; Jude 1:1–25; Psalm 127:1–5; Proverb s 29:15–17

Fallow Ground
Hosea 10:1–14:9

Gardening is not my favorite task because it is a lot of work. First, the soil has to be prepared. The rocks and roots have to be removed, and then the soil has to be broken by a plow, spade, or hoe to make it fit to receive the seeds. If the rocks and roots are not removed, the seed will not have room to take root.

As I write this, I'm looking at our flower boxes. The pansies are drooping over the sides of the boxes, and none of them look like they will make it through the winter. I know why they look so distressed. We were in a hurry when we planted them. We did not take the time to prepare the soil properly. None of the pansies had room to take root sufficiently, and now they are all undernourished. There is no way we can rescue them now because the cold has taken it toll on the shallow roots.

Hosea shared how Israel, Ephraim, and Samaria had plowed wickedness instead of preparing their hearts to receive God's love:

> You have plowed wickedness; you have reaped iniquity. You have eaten the fruit of lies, because you trusted in your own way.
> —HOSEA 10:13

> Sow for yourselves righteousness; reap in mercy; break up your fallow ground, For it is time to seek the LORD, till He comes and rains righteousness on you.
> —HOSEA 10:12

Israel, Ephraim, and Samaria had been drawn by the gentle bands of God's love and were fed by Him, but now they had become bent on backsliding. Only Judah remained faithful to God. God reminded them how He knew them in the wilderness, but now they had forgotten Him.

God cried out for Israel, Ephraim, and Samaria to break up the fallow ground of their hearts to receive His Word once again. God, however, did not give up on them. He promised to heal their backsliding. He promised to lengthen their shallow roots and spread their branches.

Why do people backslide? The answer is revealed in this passage. People who backslide have not been rooted and grounded in the love of Jesus Christ. They have not known the ways of God. They received the Word, but they never grew in faith. The roots of bitterness and unforgiveness and the rocks of idolatry and lust prevented their roots from going deep into God's love. The Master Gardner, however, can take the tender plants that never grew and replant them in prepared soil. He is doing this today, so that many will receive the rains of righteousness that are pouring down on this last harvest.

Lord, help me to always keep my heart soft to receive Your Word.

Daily Deposit: Pray for those you know who have backslidden.

December 9

Read: Joel 1:1–3:21; Revelation 1:1–20; Psalm 128:1–6; Proverbs 29:18

When All Seems Lost
Joel 1:1–3:21

A s we learned in Hosea, God does redeem and restore. This message is also conveyed in Joel. Joel prophesied in a day when all seemed to be lost in Judah. A mammoth plague of locusts denuded the vegetation and even stripped the bark off the fig trees. In only a few hours, what was lush and green was turned into a wasteland.

Famine and drought resulted, and Joel knew God had allowed this destruction as a judgment upon the land.

It was time to cry out to the Lord. Joel spoke the words of the Lord (2:12):

> "Now, therefore," says the LORD, "Turn to Me with all your heart, with fasting, with weeping, and with mourning."

Like Isaiah, Joel was exhorting the people to rend their hearts, not just their garments. God was calling them to repent, and if they did, He promised to take pity upon them. God would restore their grain, wine and oil, and they would no longer be a reproach among the nations. God would give them the former and latter rains.

Joel's prophecies traveled the highway of time to the last days when God would pour out His Spirit upon all flesh. Just after this outpouring, the day of the Lord would come, and on that day whoever called on the name of the Lord would be saved.

Joel prophesied the End-Day war, when all the nations will be gathered in the Valley of Jehoshaphat, to be judged. He also prophesied the Day of the Lord would come when the heavens would shake and the stars, moon, and sun would grow dark. The Lord would set up His kingdom in Jerusalem, and a fountain would flow from God's throne, and Judah would abide forever.

In the midst of desolation, God promised to restore all the years the locusts had eaten. Spiritual locusts have laid bare many fruitful trees of righteousness in this last day. These spiritual locusts are coming in waves now, to destroy God's people. Paul warned Timothy that, in the last days, seducing spirits would lead many astray. The love of many will wax cold in these End Times, but many will receive the outpouring of God's Spirit, and broken hearts and lives will be healed. Their fruitfulness will be restored.

At Pentecost, when the Holy Spirit was poured out upon the 120 believers in the upper room, things were set in motion for the greatest outpouring of God's Spirit at the End Times. Peter quoted from Joel, when the people accused the believers of being drunk because they were speaking with other tongues. (See Acts 2:17–21.) The outpouring Peter and the people experienced at Pentecost pales in the light of the outpouring of God's Spirit that we will see just before Jesus comes again.

Lord, keep me filled and anointed by Your Spirit.

Daily Deposit: Pray for the latter rain to fall in your neighborhood and community.

December 10

Agreement
Amos 1:1–3:15

A mos was a shepherd in the small town of Tekoa in the Judean hills. God does not always choose the most educated and trained people to deliver His message. The name *Amos* means "Burden Bearer." God always gives His message to those whose hearts grieve when they see their people living in rebellion against Him. A true prophet of the Lord does not just deliver God's warnings and exhortations. God's chosen prophets were men who were willing to bear the burden of their people. They were willing to weep over the spiritual condition of their lands.

Amos prophesied during the reigns of Uzziah of Judah (792–740 B.C.) and Jeroboam II of Israel (793–753 B.C.). Both Judah and Israel were experiencing great prosperity at the time Amos prophesied, but they were impoverished spiritually. Everyone seemed to agree that their prosperity was a sign of God's blessings. They continued in their immorality and idolatry, without fear of judgment.

Amos was given the assignment to give a wake-up call to Israel and its seven neighbors, including Judah. A spirit of slumber had desensitized these people to their true spiritual condition. The judgments given in the Book of Amos should be a wake-up call for all of us.

Amos listed the specific sins of Damascus (1:3–5), Gaza (1:6–8), Tyre (1:9–10), Edom (1:11–12), Ammon (1:13–15), Moab (2:1–3), Judah (2:4–5) and Israel (2:6–16). The justice system was corrupt and the rich were oppressing the poor. The punishment of Israel was detailed (3:11–15).

The major sin of Israel and its neighbors was that of not obeying God's commandments. Their agreement with God's covenant had been broken. Amos asked Israel, "Can two walk together, unless they are agreed?" (v. 3:3). Israel and the surrounding neighbors walked away from God's Holy Covenant. They were traveling the road to destruction, and they did not even know it. Like many today, they felt like God was no longer in the judgment business. They convinced themselves that God would let their sins go unpunished.

Amos had not been lulled to sleep by deception. He knew the truth. He said (v.3:7):

> Surely the LORD God does nothing, unless He reveals His secret to His servants and prophets.

The day of reckoning was at hand. The spiritual conditions described in Amos are similar to the condition of our own land. When 9/11 occurred, many began to seek the Lord, and some truly repented. However, we have not experienced the repentance necessary to bring revival to this country. It is time for us to turn from the path of rebellion, to walk once again in agreement with God.

Lord, forgive me for the times I have gone my own way.

Daily Deposit: Pray for your nation, and especially lift up the judicial system.

December 11

Hard Hearts
Amos 4:1–6:14

When we were in Israel just after Desert Storm, we walked along the beaches of Netanya and collected heart-shaped pebbles that had washed up on the shore. Many on our tour took these hearts home with them to remind them to pray for Israel. God promised that one day He would turn the hearts of stone in Israel to hearts of flesh. He would write His law on their hearts. Jeremiah declared the words of the Lord concerning that day:

> But this is the covenant that I will make with the house of Israel after those days, says the LORD: I will put My law in their minds, and write it on their hearts; and I will be their God, and they shall be My people.
>
> —JEREMIAH 31:33

That day has yet to come. During the time of Amos, Israel had become hardened. Even though they had experienced many disciplinary judgments of God upon their people and their land, they remained unresponsive and unrepentant. Amos warned them to prepare to meet their God, but they did not heed His warning. The repentance God desired was not a return to the rituals of feasts and sacrifices. God's call for repentance was the same call Samuel delivered to rebellious Saul. Samuel told Saul that obedience was better than sacrifice. (See 1 Samuel 15:22.)

God wanted a people who would obey Him, because they loved Him. True repentance includes a change of heart that is confirmed by a change in behavior. Israel continued in their idolatry. They sat in luxury, while they neglected the poor.

Amos was prophesying to a complacent people who had no desire to seek the Lord. Their needs were being met. They were satisfied. There was no hunger or thirst for righteousness. Sin had become a comfortable bed partner, and they were unwilling to wake up to see the monster sleeping next to them.

Israel was lifted up in pride. They soon would be brought low. Pride will always put a shell around the hearts of men. When we become self-sufficient and comfortable with our lives the way they are, we no longer humble ourselves to seek the Lord. God is near to those who have a contrite heart. Those who realize their spiritual poverty are those God seeks to help.

One of the greatest gifts God can give us is the gift of helplessness. Israel was about to receive the gift of helplessness through the judgments that would come upon their land and their people. They would soon recognize that they were a needy people.

Lord, may I always hunger for Your presence.

Daily Deposit: Pray for those you know who feel they do not need God in their lives.

December 12

Sifted Saints

Amos 7:1–9:15

When I was in high school, I took home economics. I remember our teacher showing us how to sift ingredients for a cake. She said the whole purpose of sifting is to get all the lumps out and to blend the ingredients, so when the liquid is added, the batter will be smooth. She said well sifted ingredients will produce a beautifully textured cake when it comes out of the oven. The Lord was about to sift Israel. Amos proclaimed:

> For surely I…will sift the house of Israel among all nations, as grain is sifted in a sieve; yet not the smallest grain shall fall to the ground.
>
> —Amos 9:9

The message the Lord gave Amos to deliver to Israel was so unpopular that Amaziah, the priest of Bethel, accused Amos of conspiracy against the house of Israel.

Amaziah said, "The land is not able to bear all his words" (Amos 7:10). The words Amos had to deliver included all the severe judgments God would send to Israel if they did not repent. Some of these judgments included locusts, fire, famine, and the sword. Amazaiah was so upset by these declarations of judgment that he exclaimed to Amos:

> Go, you seer! Flee to the land of Judah. There eat bread, and there prophesy. But never again prophesy at Bethel.
>
> —Amos 7:12

Judgment did fall on Israel, just as Amos prophesied. However, the book of Amos ends on a positive note. Amos saw down the isle of time to the altar where the bride (all true believers) and Bridegroom (Jesus Christ) would be joined together.

He prophesied about a great harvest coming before this wedding takes place:

> "Behold, the days are coming," says the Lord, "when the plowman shall overtake the reaper, and the treader of grapes him who sows seed; the mountains shall drip with sweet wine, and all the hills shall flow with it."
>
> —Amos 9:13

God promised to leave a remnant in Israel. He promised to plant them in their land and never pull them up again. (See Amos 9:15.) We live in this time prophesied by Amos. God is sifting His saints. Just as He had to get the hard lumps of pride out of the hearts of His beloved Israel, God is now sifting the saints. All that is not wholly surrendered to Him will be sifted. Jesus is coming for a bride who will have soft, contrite hearts. Have you experienced any sifting lately? I know I have.

Lord, soften my heart.

Daily Deposit: Pray for those you know who need their hearts softened.

December 13

Watching Without Praying
Obadiah 1:1–21

My husband and I like to watch movies. I refuse to watch a movie unless it has a happy ending. The drama on the pages of the Bible is much more exciting than any movie I have ever seen. I love reading the Bible, because I know the rest of the story. I have read the last chapter and I know the last scene of the drama.

Even though the Minor Prophets declared judgments upon Israel and Judah, they usually ended on a positive note. We will be looking into the drama prophesied by Obadiah, Jonah, and Micah who spoke God's words between 753 and 586 B.C. The judgments declared by these prophets were horrendous, but the hope projected revealed God's mercy.

As we watch the drama unfold in the days of the Minor Prophets, we must understand that we as believers are also on the stage of time. We forget that with God there is no time or space. He lives in a multitude of dimensions, and He is eternal. His message to His beloved, however, does not change. The message is:

> Humble Yourselves before Me. Repent and allow Me to redeem and restore. My mercy is everlasting and it extends from generation to generation. Turn from your pride and selfish ways and find life.

The prophecies throughout the Bible should cause us to pray more. Daniel stopped everything and set his heart to fast and pray when he reviewed the prophecies of Jeremiah who predicted the Babylonian captivity of Israel would end in the seventieth year. We have to remember that God's Word must be given voice on earth to affect changes in the spiritual realm. Watching the drama, without praying for ourselves and those who do not yet know the Lord, is not what Jesus commissioned us to do in the last days. He said, "Watch and pray."

Obadiah declared a scorching judgment upon Edom. Edom watched and did nothing when they saw Israel in distress. Just as Esau (the father of the descendents in Edom) gave up his birthright to Jacob, Edom would now lose everything. The house of Jacob would possess their possessions. Obadiah prophesied that the house of Jacob and Joseph would catch fire with the zeal of the Lord, but the house of Esau would be as stubble (vv. 17–18). The mountains of Esau would be judged.

We cannot stand idly by and watch the wicked be destroyed without praying for souls. It is harvest time. The laborers are few. The seed is the Word of God and the labor is prayer.

Lord, help me to watch and pray in these End Times.

Daily Deposit: Pray for more laborers in this last great harvest.

December 14

God's Inclusive Love
Jonah 1:1—4:11

Have you ever doubted that God could love wicked men as much as He loves you? Think about the tragedy of 9/11. Do you really think God had the same love for the terrorists who died, as He did for those who died in the Twin Towers? This is hard for us to comprehend, but the truth is "God so loved the world that He gave His only begotten Son, that whoever believes in Him should not perish but have everlasting life" (John 3:16).

God is concerned about all the earth's inhabitants. Jonah doubted that God could love pagan Nineveh. When Jonah was given orders by God to go and cry out against the wickedness in Nineveh, Jonah fled from the presence of the Lord.

It is impossible for us to flee from the presence of the Lord, and Jonah soon discovered this. Jonah was first in the belly of the boat going to Tarshish and later in the belly of a great fish God had prepared to swallow Jonah. Jonah was sound asleep in the belly of the boat when a great storm arose. The storm was a wake-up call, to remind Jonah of his disobedience which he soon confessed to the men on the boat. He told them to throw him overboard so that the storm would cease, because he knew God was angry with Him.

Jonah was in the belly of the fish for three days and three nights. God was with Jonah in both of these "belly" experiences. Jonah gave up trying to flee God's presence; so he decided, instead, to seek God's presence. The belly of the fish became a holy sanctuary where Jonah began to praise and give thanks to the Lord. The Lord heard Jonah's praise and spoke to the fish. The fish vomited up Jonah.

When Jonah reached the shores of Nineveh, he probably looked like a supernatural being. I'm sure the acid in the belly of the fish's stomach had turned his skin and his clothes white as snow. The message God gave to Jonah to deliver to Nineveh was simple: "Yet forty days, and Nineveh shall be overthrown!" (Jon. 3:4).

Nineveh believed and heeded the warning. The leaders proclaimed a fast and the people and even the beasts were dressed in sackcloth. When God saw their repentant hearts, He released Nineveh from His planned judgment. Jonah resented the fact that God could show mercy on such a rebellious, wicked people who deserved His judgment.

While Jonah was pouting under his little man-made shelter, God prepared a shade plant to cover him from the sun. Jonah was so grateful for God's mercy towards him. However, God prepared a worm to eat the plant, and when the sun was beating upon Jonah's head, he wished he could die. Jonah pitied the destroyed plant more than he pitied Nineveh. God rebuked Jonah for his lack of pity.

Whenever we sit in judgment of people whom we think deserve God's wrath, we run the risk of being judged by God ourselves. God may allow several *belly experiences* for us, until we repent of our lack of love and mercy towards others.

Lord, thank You for Your mercy.

Daily Deposit: Share God's all-inclusive love with someone today.

December 15

The Rest of the Story
Revelation 6:1–17

We leave the Minor Prophets to see the rest of the story, as revealed in Revelation. Revelation is a series of visions recorded by the apostle John, during a time of great persecution of Christians. It was written before the destruction of the Temple in A.D. 70.

Yesterday, we talked about God's all-inclusive love. Truly, God's desire is that none perish, but that all come to the knowledge of His dear Son. Many, however, will reject His all-inclusive invitation of, "Whosoever will, may come." Those who reject God's gift of salvation will experience God's judgment and wrath.

Today's passage describes the six seals the Lamb of God will break at the end of days. As each seal is broken, great disasters will come upon the earth. John is told to look and see what happens as each seal is broken. When the first seal was broken, John saw a white horse. A crowned rider with a bow in His hand sat on this horse, and he was sent out to conquer. The second seal revealed a red horse sent out to make war. The third seal revealed a black horse sent out to cause famine, and the fourth seal revealed a pale horse sent out to cause death.

The fifth seal revealed the souls who had been slain for the Word of God, and the sixth seal revealed a great earthquake, when the sun became black as sackcloth and the moon became as blood.

Jesus spoke of all these disasters in His description of the last days in Matthew 24. He warned of wars and rumors of wars, famines, pestilences, and earthquakes in various places. He spoke of how many will be betrayed, persecuted, and killed for His names' sake. He spoke of the great tribulation period that will be followed by the signs in the heavens. The sun will be darkened, the moon will give no light, and the stars will fall from heaven, and the powers of the heavens will be shaken. (See Matthew 24:6–29.)

There will be one great day when the wrath of the Lamb will come upon the earth. This, however, is not the end of the story. Jesus said that after that great day of wrath, He will appear in heaven with great power and glory, and He will gather His elect from the four winds, from one end of heaven to the other. (See Matthew 24:31.) Jesus made it clear that not even He knows the day or the hour of His coming. (See Matthew 24:36.) Only His Father knows this information.

Jesus ended His dramatic presentation (the times John described in Revelation) with the parable of the faithful servant who is always ready for His master's return—who faithfully distributes food to the master's household in due season (Matt. 24:44-46). The rest of the story is that Jesus conquers every foe, the wicked are destroyed and the righteous live forever with Him. The part we play in the rest of the story is simply to be faithful servants who distribute God's Word. Jesus said, "Heaven and earth will pass away, but My words will by no means pass away" (Matt. 24:35).

Lord, help me to remain faithful.

Daily Deposit: Feed on God's Word today, and be ready to share your food.

December 16

The Ruler and Remnant
Micah 5:1–7:20

The treasure chest of the book of Micah is filled with brilliant jewels that shine revelation light into our hearts. Micah prophesied at the time of Isaiah. The name *Micah* means "He Who Is Like Yahweh." We all want to be more like Jesus, and the prophetic book of Micah challenges us to allow the Holy Spirit to change us from glory to glory, into the image of Jesus Christ. The word pictures and poetry in the book of Micah provide more than just interesting reading. The words have the power to change our hearts. The birth and the birthplace of Jesus are prophesied in our passage today:

> But you, Bethlehem Ephrathah, though you are little among the thousands of Judah, yet out of you shall come forth to Me the One to be Ruler in Israel, Whose goings forth are from of old, from everlasting.
>
> —MICAH 5:2

Micah spoke of a remnant that would return to Israel. The Ruler would be as a shepherd, to feed the flock, and "this One shall be peace." Let that phrase sink into your heart. Jesus (this One) is peace. There truly is no peace without Jesus. He is the Prince of Peace who wants to invade your life with a peace that passes your understanding.

Other rulers invade territory to destroy, but Jesus invades the land of your soul to bring peace. To experience that peace, however, we must be willing to destroy the strongholds in our souls by taking every thought captive to the obedience of Jesus Christ. (See 2 Corinthians 10:4–7.)

When we daily give every thought that exalts itself against the knowledge of God to Jesus, we are then ready to accomplish His will on earth by doing what He requires us to do. God's requirements are:

- To do justly
- To love mercy
- To walk humbly with your God (Micah 6:8)

Before you make your "To Do List" for the day, pray this prayer:

> *Lord, help me to do justly today by esteeming others higher than myself. Help me to obtain mercy by showing mercy to others. Help me to humble myself before You by casting all my cares upon You.*

Daily Deposit: Remind yourself and others that Jesus is our peace; Jesus is the One Who justifies us because He is just, and Jesus is the merciful One Who humbled Himself to become like you, so that you can become like Him.

December 17

Repentance and Retribution
Nahum 1:1–3:19

"Can this be the same Nineveh that repented when Jonah warned them?" This is the question I asked myself as I read the pages of Nahum. I soon discovered that even though Nineveh repented for a season, they later returned to their wickedness. Nineveh had experienced God's great mercy. God relented of the judgment He planned for Nineveh when He saw their repentant hearts. However, the grace and mercy God had shown to Nineveh was about to be withdrawn because they had returned to their wickedness. Nahum declared God's judgment that would bring retribution to Nineveh, even though He had delivered them earlier from His wrath.

God's long-suffering does have limits. God continually extends His grace and mercy to us, but our own sin can separate us from receiving His mercy and grace. When we do not confess our sins to God and to one another, and we no longer fellowship with others in the light, we run the risk of hardening our own hearts. The darkness sin brings into our lives can block God's glory light from shining on us and through us. We will not experience God's grace and glory again, until we recognize our need to repent. Repentance opens the gates of our hearts to receive God's glory and grace once again.

How could Nineveh return to their wickedness when they had experienced God's great deliverance? How can a person who received God's great gift of salvation go back to a life of sin? I believe the cycle of sin can begin again in our lives if we have ungrateful hearts that take God's grace for granted. Paul wrote about this cycle of sin in Romans 1. He described the downward spiral of sin that people who even know God can experience if they refuse to repent by confessing their sins and turning away from them. Such people:

- Did not glorify God.
- Did not thank God.
- Did not take their thoughts captive to the obedience of Jesus Christ.
- Opened their hearts to idolatry.
- Exchanged the truth for a lie.
- Worshipped the creature more than the creator.
- Did not desire to retain God in their knowledge.
- Forgot that God is a righteous judge who will judge their words and deeds.

We open the door to the devil's deception when we take God's grace for granted. Nineveh took God's grace for granted, and God's judgment came upon them.

Lord, help me to always have an attitude of gratitude.

Daily Deposit: Pray for those you know who have backslidden.

December 18

Read: Habakkuk 1:1–3:19; Revelation 9:1–21; Psalm 137:1–9; Proverbs 30:10

No Repentance
Revelation 9:1–21

The warnings of the Minor Prophets were given to exhort the people to repent. Nineveh repented and was spared the judgment of God, but later, they went back to their old wicked ways and God's judgment came upon them.

The judgment described in our Revelation passage today is horrific. As I read it, a cold chill goes up my spine. First, the bottomless pit is opened and the smoke ascending out of the pit darkens the sun and the air. Demonic creatures that look like locusts are released to torment the people left on earth, for five months. Their torment is like the torment of a scorpion when it strikes a man. Stings are in their tails, and they are given the power to hurt people. After this torment, a 200 million army is released. Out of the mouths of the horses come fire, smoke, and brimstone.

In the days of this torment, people will seek death and will not find it. The shocking part of this passage is that no one repents in response to these judgments. They stay in their immorality and idolatry and refuse to repent of their murders or their sorceries and thefts.

It is hard for me to imagine such a time on earth when people become so hardened that they refuse to repent. Surely the Holy Spirit is not present at this time. The Holy Spirit is more powerful than any seducing spirit. He has the power to convict people of sin. He has the power to woo people back from their backsliding. The love of God is shed abroad in our hearts by the Holy Spirit. The scene described in this chapter reveals that the people left on the earth at this time are void of love and void of conviction.

I know that no one, who has received Jesus Christ as their Lord and Savior, will be on earth at this time in history. This knowledge causes me to share the love of Jesus Christ and the Gospel message with as many people as I can now, while there is still time. A time is coming on the earth when there will be no messengers of God's kingdom on earth. A time is coming when the labor of the harvest ceases. The harvest will be gathered, and then all hell will break loose. I cannot bear the thought that any of my loved ones would be left on earth to face such terror as described in this passage.

We do not know the day or the hour of the coming of Jesus Christ, but we must work now for the night is coming when no man can work. Jesus said:

> I must work the works of Him who sent Me while it is day; the night is coming when no one can work. As long as I am in the world, I am the light of the world.
>
> —JOHN 9:4–5

Lord, help me to be an effective laborer in this last great harvest.

Daily Deposit: Pray for the Holy Spirit to lead you to the people whose hearts are ready to be translated from the kingdom of darkness to the kingdom of God's dear Son.

December 19

Hidden in Christ
Zephaniah 1:1–3:20

Yesterday, we talked about a time of darkness on earth, when no man will repent. Zephaniah reaches far into the future and speaks about the very time described in Revelation 9. When the fullness of God's wrath is released on earth and all hell breaks loose, those who have upheld God's justice will be hidden from the Lord's anger.

Zephaniah's name means "The Lord Has Hidden." Zephaniah's cry was (Zeph. 2:1–2):

> Gather yourselves…Before the decree is issued, or the day passes like chaff, before the LORD's fierce anger comes upon you, Before the day of the Lord's anger comes upon you!

Zephaniah warned that "the great day of the LORD is near" (Zeph. 1:14). He described that day as a day of distress, devastation, darkness, and desolation. (See Zephaniah 1:15–16.)

Zephaniah exhorted the meek on earth to seek the Lord and to seek humility and righteousness. It sounds like Zephaniah read some of Micah's words, where Micah wrote that the Lord requires us to do justly, seek mercy, and walk humbly with our God.

I feel such comfort in my soul, because I know my loved ones will be spared this great day of God's wrath. They have received Jesus Christ as their Lord and Savior and they are already in that secret hiding place David described in Psalm 91. They are in the hiding place described by Paul in Colossians 3:2–3:

> Set your mind on things above, not on things on the earth. For you died, and your life is hidden with Christ in God.

My comfort is changed to challenge as I think about the millions of people who have not yet entered this secret hiding place. When I think about the terror they will face if they do not discover this hiding place, my heart is grieved. I am challenged to share the Gospel with as many as I can, while it is still day.

Hope springs within my soul, as I read the last chapter of Zephaniah. He spoke of the day of restoration that will come after the great and terrible day of the Lord. In that day, no man will be ashamed of his deeds, and those who have received Him will be a meek and humble people, because they have trusted in the name of the Lord. There will no longer be any fear. Don't you want everyone you know to experience this restoration?

Lord, increase my burden for souls.

Daily Deposit: Pray for lost souls to be gathered together into this hiding place.

December 20

Restoration
Haggai 1:1—2:23

Every day for a whole week, I went out to my carport where I worked laboriously on a piece of furniture that was in horrible condition. This was my first attempt to restore a piece of furniture. If I had known it took so much labor, I don't think I would have even started the project. First, I had to take off all the old paint; then I had to sand it down, and finally I was ready to put several layers of new varnish on this old piece of furniture. After the sanding, I realized how beautiful the wood was. It had been hidden under thick layers of paint.

Restoration is hard work. Haggai challenged the people to begin restoration on the temple. The name *Haggai* means "Festive." Haggai was a contemporary of Zechariah. He was an exhorter par excellence, and his message was needed to bring a discouraged band of people together to rebuild the temple. Haggai faced the monumental task of taking a people from a place of disinterest, discouragement, and dissatisfaction to a place of delight. Every pastor can identify with Haggai's task.

The people had returned from exile and all they were interested in was survival. They were interested only in rebuilding their personal lives and dwelling places. God tried to wake them from their apathy. God described the fruitlessness of their self efforts. We only become fruitful when we yield ourselves to the Lord and allow Him to labor through us.

In response to God's words through Haggai, some interest was finally shown, and a few made a feeble start to rebuild the temple. However, they soon were discouraged. Every day they went to work on the temple they faced the mocking and criticisms of those who were against this project. Some of the older ones who had seen the glory of the first temple criticized and judged their efforts because they did not see how the restored temple could ever be as beautiful as the one they knew. The workers yielded to discouragement and stopped building the temple. Haggai had to encourage them and assure them that their efforts, along with the strength of the Lord, would produce a glorious temple that would be filled with the glory of God.

Once the restoration was underway, the people became dissatisfied. They expected the work of three months to undo the neglect of sixteen years. To counter this dissatisfaction, Haggai delivered God's blessing upon the people.

The problems we encounter as we undergo the Lord's restoration of our own souls are similar to the problems Haggai had to overcome in the restoration of the temple. We forget that we cannot undo in a moment of time the years we neglected feeding our souls the Bread of Life and drinking from the wells of Salvation. We may become discouraged, but we must not yield to discouragement. Only as we yield ourselves to the Lord in the restoration process of our souls will we be able to overcome all disinterest, discouragement, and dissatisfaction. The future glory is worth the waiting.

Lord, thank You for restoring my soul.

Daily Deposit: Ask the Lord if there are more areas in your soul that need restoring.

December 21

Christmas Feast
Revelation 12:1–17

There are only four more days until Christmas. Every Christmas I love to play *The Messiah* while I prepare food for our Christmas dinner. Today is the day I usually begin cooking for that feast with our family. It takes four days to prepare the meal and only one half hour to eat it. It is worth the hours of preparation, however, to see the delighted looks on the faces of my family as they gobble down the gobbler and devour the dressing.

Throughout the Christmas season these words from *The Messiah* ring in my spirit:

> The kingdoms of this world have become the kingdoms of our Lord and of His Christ, and He shall reign forever and ever!
>
> —Revelation 11:15

The good news proclaimed in our Revelation reading today is that the great dragon, that old serpent, the devil, will be cast down. A loud voice from heaven will declare:

> Now salvation, and strength, and the kingdom of our God, and the power of His Christ has come, for the accuser of our brethren, who accused them before our God day and night, has been cast down.
>
> —Revelation 12:10

The drama accelerates, as the dragon knows his time is short and as he comes against Israel with great force. The time spoken of here is the time Jesus spoke of when He shared about the last days, the days of Jacob's troubles, when the Antichrist will come against Israel. (See Matthew 24.) God, however, has prepared a refuge for Israel in the caves of Petra in Jordan. The believers will overcome satan by the blood of the Lamb and the word of their testimony, and they will not love their lives to the death (v. 11).

The next few chapters of Revelation describe more trouble in the earth, because of the Antichrist, but we know the rest of the story. We know who wins!

Our Christmas feasts will pale in comparison to the wedding feast in heaven when we will celebrate with our victorious Bridegroom. Until that time, we prepare for the feast by watching and praying, witnessing and winning souls. At this great feast, I believe we will be seated next to all the souls we witnessed to while on earth. The greeting at this feast will not be, "Merry Christmas." Instead, our greeting will be "Jesus reigns forever and ever," and we will toast the Lord of lords and King of kings!

Lord, help me to invite many to that great wedding feast

Daily Deposit: Ask the Holy Spirit to give you some names to invite to the wedding feast.

December 22

Invite Your Friends and Neighbors
Zechariah 2:1–3:10

We usually invite additional people to join our family at our Christmas feast. We like to invite people who have no other place to go because their families live far away. These guests usually seem warmed, not only by our fire, but also by the Lord who is always our guest of honor.

An invitation is issued in our reading today. The Lord, through the mouth of Zechariah, exhorts everyone to invite his neighbor to come under the vine and under the fig tree (Zech. 3:10). The fig tree represents the nation, Israel, and the vine is Jesus Christ.

The invitation spoken of in this passage is to be extended when all Israel will be saved in a day. The remnant spared during Jacob's troubles will see the coming of the Lord. Later, Zechariah speaks of how the remnant will go into their homes and mourn as families after they look upon the One they have pierced. Just as Joseph revealed himself to his brothers, Jesus will reveal Himself to His Jewish brethren.

Zechariah was a contemporary of Haggai who shared Haggai's assignment to arouse the Jews to complete the task of reconstructing the temple. His prophesies are the most Messianic of any of the other minor prophets. Zechariah experienced eight visions that were shared with the Jews to confirm God's great love for them. Zechariah's name means "Yahweh Remembers." God will never forget His beloved Chosen People. He has a great plan for their redemption, restoration, and resurrection.

One vision described in our passage today was of a man with a measuring line. He was measuring God's city. Zechariah prophesied that the day would come when there would be no need for walls in Jerusalem, because God Himself would be a wall of fire all around her, and He would be the glory in the midst of her (Zech. 2:5).

Zechariah had another vision in which he saw the high priest, Joshua, dressed in filthy clothing. Joshua was standing before the Angel of the Lord. As Zechariah watched, the filthy clothes were removed, and Joshua was dressed in rich garments (Zech. 2:1–5). Joshua then was given this charge (Zech. 3:7):

> If you will walk in My ways, and if you will keep My command, then you shall also judge My house, and likewise have charge of My courts; I will give you places to walk among these who stand Here.

These two visions unveil God's great plan for His Chosen People. After the Lord reveals Himself to His Chosen, a fountain of cleansing will be opened, and Israel will be cleansed and saved in a day. Many nations will then be invited to come and dwell in Israel where Jesus will sit on His throne during the 1,000 year reign. What a day that will be!

Lord, thank You for Your great plan to gather all to Yourself.

Daily Deposit: Pray for the peace of Jerusalem today.

December 23

Read: Zechariah 4:1–5:11; Revelation 14:1–20; Psalm 142:1–7; Proverbs 30:21–23

The Lamb on the Mountain
Revelation 14:1–20

We spoke yesterday about the day when Jesus will reveal Himself to His Jewish brethren. On that day He will set His feet down on the Mount of Olives and the mountain will be split in half. One of my favorite spots in Jerusalem is the Mount of Olives. I love standing on this mountain that provides a great panoramic view of Jerusalem. I also enjoy meditating in the Church of All Nations, located at the foot of the mountain. Next to the Church of All Nations is the garden of Gethsemane. It is fitting that our Lord would return to this place. As I sat on the steps of the Church of All Nations and looked at the golden gate where Jesus will again make a triumphant entry into Jerusalem, I realized the very place I was sitting would one day be rubble when the Mount of Olives is split in two.

Our passage today in Revelation speaks about the Lamb who will stand on Mount Zion with the 144,000 who have remained faithful during the great tribulation. A new song was sung in heaven and only the 144,000 could learn the song. These 144,000 were very special people. They were all virgin men who were without fault and who had no deceit in their mouths.

Just as Zechariah had many visions, John the revelator also described a multitude of visions in the book of Revelation. He saw an angel flying in the midst of heaven who had the everlasting Gospel to preach to all those on the earth–to every tribe, nation, tongue, and people. The message he gave was, "Fear God and give glory to Him, for the hour of His judgment has come; and worship Him who made heaven and earth, the sea and springs of water" (v. 7). This was God's provision to gather the last soul that was written in the Lamb's Book of Life before He judged the earth for the last time.

The angels were to reap the harvest and then gather the wicked to throw them into the great winepress of the wrath of God.

As I read this chapter of Revelation, I am moved by God's great mercy. His desire that none perish was expressed when He gave the assignment to the angel to fly over the earth with the Gospel message. Today, we have a satellite called *Sky Angel* that transmits the Gospel message to every nation. I believe this is a forerunner to God's special angel who will deliver the last Gospel message on earth.

We have a responsibility to declare this Gospel message to as many as we can today. This Christmas season affords a great opportunity to have doors of witness opened for us to share the gospel with others. Look for those opportunities.

Lord, thank You for choosing me to spread Your Gospel.

Daily Deposit: Pray for open doors today to share the greatest story every told.

December 24

Read: Zechariah 6:1–7:14; Revelation 15:1–8; Psalm 143:1–12; Proverbs 30:24–28

King and Priest
Zechariah 6:1–7:14

On Christmas Eve we usually read Luke's account of Jesus' birth. I always have a hard time imagining that my Lord and King, who is now my high priest, came as a helpless babe. We now have eight grandchildren, and when I look at the vulnerability of these little ones just after they are born, I cannot imagine that Jesus, the King of kings and Lord of lords, was willing to be a vulnerable baby who was dependent totally upon His parents care to survive.

On our trips to Bethlehem, we have had the opportunity many times to bow down and touch the actual spot where they believe Jesus was born. The Church of the Nativity is filled with people of all nations and denominations who come at Christmastime to remember the birth of Jesus. Zechariah prophesied about Jesus' role as king and priest. He said:

> Behold, the Man whose name is the BRANCH! From His place He shall branch out, and He shall build the Temple of the LORD; Yes, He shall build the temple of the LORD. He shall bear the glory, and shall sit and rule on His throne; So He shall be a priest on His throne, and the counsel of peace shall be between them both.
> —ZECHARIAH 6:12–13

The message the angels delivered to the shepherds when Jesus was born in Bethlehem was, "Glory to God in the highest, And on earth peace, goodwill toward men!" (Luke 2:14). God's great plan to have the perfect priest who could perfectly intercede for His beloved people was set in motion with the birth of Jesus. As a man, Jesus was touched with all the feelings of our weaknesses. This qualified Him to become our perfect intercessor. Jesus now sits on the right hand of God the Father. From that throne room, Jesus is making constant and perfect intercession for us. The counsel of peace is between the Father and the Son, because the Prince of Peace pulled down the wall of separation between the Holy Father and us. When Jesus shed His blood on the cross, He gained for us the confident entrance into God's throne room to find grace when we are in times of need. Even before we know our needs, Jesus is making intercession for what we will face in the future. Isn't that good news! Go tell it on the mountain that Jesus Christ is born and that He ever lives to make intercession for us. He is not only the Prince of Peace, but He is also Lord of lords and King of kings.

Lord, thank You for becoming a baby and ruling now as King.

Daily Deposit: Share the Christmas story with someone who has not yet met King Jesus.

December 25

The Holy Mountain
Zechariah 8:1–23

"We're Marching to Zion" is one of my favorite hymns. Yesterday we were challenged to go tell the Gospel on the mountain. As we near the close of this year, sharing the Gospel with others should be our number one goal for the next year. The day Zechariah prophesied about is coming soon. He spoke of the time when the Lord would return to Zion and dwell in the midst of Jerusalem. Jerusalem would be called the "City of Truth, the Mountain of the LORD of hosts, the Holy Mountain" (8:3).

The description that Zechariah gave of Jerusalem after the Lord's return fills me with Christmas joy. Listen to some of his words:

> Old men and old women shall again sit in the streets of Jerusalem, each one with his staff in his hand because of great age. The streets of the city shall be full of boys and girls playing in the streets.
>
> —ZECHARIAH 8:4–5

> For the seed shall be prosperous. The vine shall give its fruit, The ground shall give her increase, and the heavens shall give their dew—I will cause the remnant of this people to possess all of these.
>
> —ZECHARIAH 8:12

> Yes, many peoples and strong nations shall come to seek the LORD of hosts in Jerusalem, and to pray before the LORD.
>
> —ZECHARIAH 8:22

> In those days ten men from every language of the nations shall grasp the sleeve of a Jewish man, saying, "Let us go with you, for we have heard that God is with you."
>
> —ZECHARIAH 8:23

The birth of our Lord paved the way for the gathering of both Gentiles and Jews in this last great harvest. The day will come when nations will not gather in Bethlehem and Jerusalem to remember the birth of Jesus. Instead, they will gather in Jerusalem to see the King of kings and Lord of lords seated on His throne in Zion! The march to Zion will be a victory march!

Lord, thank You for a day to remember Your birth. Thank You also for a day to meditate on Your return to Zion.

Daily Deposit: Take time out of this busy day to spend time in the presence of the Lord. He has a special Christmas message for you. Take time to listen.

December 26

Jewels in His Crown
Zechariah 9:1–17

Forty-five years ago I received a special glory crown. That special glory crown was my wonderful husband. On our wedding day, my husband became the head who would crown me as his glory. The Bible says that the wife is the glory of her husband, and the man is the image and glory of God. (See 1 Corinthians 11:7.) Zechariah spoke of a day that would come when our Bridegroom, Jesus, would make us as jewels in His crown. He prophesied:

> The LORD their God will save them in that day, as a flock of His people. For they shall be like the jewels of a crown, lifted like a banner over His land—For how great is its goodness and how great its beauty!
>
> —ZECHARIAH 9:16–17

As we celebrate our anniversary, my husband and I look forward to the time we will celebrate at that great wedding feast with Jesus. Our wedding reception was very simple, but I have attended many elaborate sit-down dinners after weddings. We will all sit down at a table that has been prepared for us from the foundation of the earth. Jesus will take care of every detail, and the feast will be beyond description. We will soon read in Malachi how Jesus will claim His Bride:

> "They shall be Mine," says the LORD of hosts, "on the day I make them My jewels."
>
> —MALACHI 3:17

We will be as jewels to our Bridegroom, Jesus, when we see Him face-to-face. Until that day, we need to express to others what precious jewels they are to the Lord. Many broken-hearted people, who have experienced rejection, have a hard time seeing themselves as precious jewels. It was my joy, when my husband and I ministered in Ukraine, to pray for those precious people who attended our family seminar. As Tom and I laid our hands on each individual and prayed for them, the Lord revealed the special jewel each individual was to Him. Some were diamonds, and many were rubies. As I spoke out the jewel they represented to Jesus, there were many tears, because the jewel Jesus saw them as had special meaning to them. Do you know you are the Bridegroom's precious jewel?

Lord, thank You for seeing me as Your precious jewel.

Daily Deposit: Tell someone today how precious they are to the Lord.

December 27

Whistle While You Work
Zechariah 10:1–11:17

Most of us are familiar with the movie, *Snow White*. One of the songs in that movie is "Whistle While You Work." I can still picture the seven dwarfs whistling away while they did their work. Did you know that God loves whistling, and the devil hates it? The other day when I was having a hard time taking my thoughts captive because I was beginning to worry about something, I heard these instructions:

"Start whistling. The devil hates whistling." I believe those instructions came from the Lord, and today's reading confirmed this. As Zechariah was prophesying about the last days, the LORD told him this:

> I will whistle for them and gather them, for I will redeem them; and they shall increase as they once increased. I will sow them among the peoples, and they shall remember Me in far countries; They shall live, together with their children, and they shall return.
>
> —ZECHARIAH 10:8–9

When God gathers His children from the far corners of the earth, He will whistle for them. The King James Version says that God will "hiss for them." I much prefer the New King James Version. Isaiah prophesied this event when he also said:

> He will lift up a banner to the nations from afar, and will whistle to them from the end of the earth; Surely they shall come with speed, swiftly.
>
> —ISAIAH 5:26

I always wished I could do that great whistle people use when they put their fingers on the inside of the sides of their mouths and blow a whistle that can be heard for miles. I never could perfect that whistle. I could have used it to call my boys home at dinnertime. They were usually scattered throughout the neighborhood.

One of my happiest memories from my childhood was hearing my mother whistle in the kitchen while she prepared our meals. She had a great whistle, and she often whistled hymns. When I was attending a church in California, a man did a solo I'll never forget it. He did not sing his solo. He whistled his solo, and it was glorious.

There is something joyful about whistling, and the joy of the Lord is our strength. If you are having a hard time keeping your thoughts from wandering off into worry, you might try the weapon of whistling. If you whistle while you work during the day, I believe your spirit will be lifted.

Lord, thank You for showing me another weapon of warfare.

Daily Deposit: – Whenever you become anxious or worried, pray and whistle today! You'll be surprised at how you will be strengthened in the spirit.

December 28

Are You Ready?
Revelation 19:1–21

John recorded these joyful words he heard as he had a vision of heaven:

> "Let us be glad and rejoice and give Him glory, for the marriage of the Lamb has come, and His wife [bride] has made herself ready" And to her it was granted to be arrayed in fine linen, clean and bright, for the fine linen is the righteous acts of the saints. Then he said to me, "Write: Blessed are those who are called to the marriage supper of the Lamb!" And he said to me, "These are the true sayings of God."
> —REVELATION 19:7–9

As I write this devotional, my precious adopted daughter in the Lord, Misha, is preparing to be married next weekend. The date of the wedding is February 21, 2004. I am excited about her wedding and also thrilled that I will finish writing these devotionals a week before she is married. I know the week before the wedding will be truly busy.

Our daughter in the Lord came to us when she needed a place to live. She has lived in our little apartment adjacent to our home for almost five years. Since I never had a daughter, it has been a joy to observe her and all her activities as the wedding draws closer. The smile on her fiancé's face grows bigger every day. The joy we all are experiencing now, however, pales in comparison to the joy our Heavenly Father and our Bridegroom (Jesus), are experiencing as they watch the activities of the bride (the church) in these last days, as she prepares herself for the wedding in heaven.

The preparations Misha has made for the wedding are extensive. Every day she checks her "To Do List" to be sure she doesn't forget a thing.

It might be time for us to check our "To Do List" in preparation for our marriage with our wonderful Bridegroom. Our wedding garments will be made of our righteous acts. (See Revelation 19:8.) Most of these righteous acts can be found in Romans 12. Daily, we need to: present our bodies as a living sacrifice to the Lord; to renew our minds by speaking and reading God's Word; to humble ourselves before the Lord and learn meekness and lowliness of heart; to use our spiritual gifts; to exhort one another to love and good works; to give with liberality; lead with diligence; show mercy with cheerfulness; love without hypocrisy, hate evil, cling to what is good; be kind and affectionate to one another, esteem others higher than ourselves; stay fervent in the spirit, rejoice in hope, be patient in tribulation; distribute to the saints; be hospitable; bless those who persecute us, rejoice with those who rejoice; weep with those who weep; set our minds on things above; do not be proud; repay evil with blessing; think about good things; do not avenge yourself, and live peaceably with all men. If you do these things your wedding garment will be gorgeous.

Lord, help me daily to prepare myself for Your coming.

Daily Deposit: Fill your day today with these righteous acts.

December 29

The Devil's Workshop
Revelation 20:1–15

You have probably heard the expression, "An idle mind is the devil's workshop." Truly, our minds are the battlegrounds where we fight all of our spiritual battles with the devil. The devil has the power to put thoughts into our minds, even though he cannot read our minds. Our thoughts are what control the rest of our activities. The devil loves to give us vain imaginations and fantasies. He uses imagery as a weapon. In today's passage we see the major tool the enemy uses against us. Before we discover that tool, however, I would like to list some of the other tools the devil uses daily in our lives to try to take us captive to his thoughts. Here are just a few of his tools: distraction, depression, dissimulation, degradation, disruption, division, dread and fear, despair, disturbance, destruction, doubt and anxiety, and delay and procrastination.

You can probably add to the list of "D" words the devil uses as tools against us. However, his major tool is revealed in our passage today:

> He laid hold of the dragon, that serpent of old, who is the devil and satan, and bound him for a thousand years; and he cast him into the bottomless pit, and shut him up, and set a seal on him, so that he should not *deceive* the nations no more till the thousand years were finished. But after these things he must be released for a little while.
>
> —REVELATION 20:2–3, EMPHASIS ADDED

Deception is the major tool of the devil. When we recognize that the thoughts he gives us daily are all lies, we will be in a better position to resist him. The only way we can recognize his lies is to fill our minds with God's truths. The data in the computer of our minds need to be so filled with God's truth, that the computer of our minds will almost automatically reject every thought that does not line up with God's Word. The problem with many saints, however, is that they have believed the devil's lies because they have not disciplined themselves to read God's word daily.

As we draw to the close of this year and the end of this devotional book, we all should dedicate ourselves to reading God's Word every day. Dedication and discipline are two "D" words the devil hates. Will you dedicate yourself to read the Bible through again next year?

Lord, with Your help I dedicate myself to reading the Bible through again next year and every year until You come.

Daily Deposit: Challenge someone you love to read the Bible through next year!

December 30

God Hates Divorce
Malachi 1:1–2:17

Malachi is the last of the Minor Prophets we will read this year. Malachi was a contemporary of Nehemiah. The book of Malachi was most likely written in 450 B.C. As the last of the twelve Minor Prophets, Malachi's book is filled with vital words that lead us into the tremendous treasures found in the New Testament. There was a great spiritual decline in his land when Malachi prophesied. Malachi addressed the disregard of God and the lack of love for the Lord that he saw in his people. They had divorced themselves from God and were unable to receive His love, His life changing power, and His support because sin had separated them from God. Malachi wrote:

> The Lord has been witness between you and the wife of your youth, with whom you have dealt treacherously; Yet she is your companion and your wife by covenant. But did He not make them one, having a remnant of the Spirit? And why one? He seeks godly offspring. Therefore take heed to your spirit, and let none deal treacherously with the wife of his youth. For the LORD God of Israel says that He hates divorce.
>
> —MALACHI 2:14–16

The divorce spoken of in this passage illustrated the divorce that happened between a covenant-keeping God and a people who disregarded His covenant. God was grieved over their neglect and their lack of love for Him.

We live in a time when divorces between married couples are just as prevalent in the church as they are in the world. I heard that over 50 percent of all marriages end in divorce. We also live in an age where sin has caused a treacherous divorce between God and believers. If you feel like God has forsaken you, guess who moved! God always keeps His covenant, but so many today have disregarded that covenant and moved away from God's presence. They love their sin more than they love God.

We just recently went through the tragedy of seeing one of our sons experience a divorce. The grief this divorce brought me was nothing to be compared to the grief God experiences when we choose to leave Him for other lovers. One of my major sorrows has been the separation between our family and our former daughter-in-law. We long to be reconciled to her, but she has not responded to our outreaches of love to her.

God reaches out to us in love daily. Have you responded to that love, or are you too busy to take time to return His love?

Lord, forgive me for not taking time to receive Your love.

Daily Deposit: Keep reaching out to those who have rejected your love. Love never fails.

December 31

The Rest of the Story
Revelation 22:1–21

We have traveled through the Bible and heard the words of the Major and Minor Prophets. Now we finish our readings for this year with the glorious last chapter of Revelation, which reveals the rest of the story. John described a pure river of water of life. It was clear as crystal and proceeded from the throne of God and of the Lamb. The river was lined with trees that bore twelve kinds of fruit. The leaves of these trees were for the healing of the nations. The description of this lovely scene was interrupted by this statement by Jesus to John (22:7):

> Behold, I am coming quickly! Blessed is he who keeps the words of the prophecy of this book.

John continued describing his heavenly vision. He saw the glory of God lighting the New Jerusalem. The curse of darkness had been removed completely. Again Jesus interrupted John's heavenly vision with these words (22:12–13):

> And behold, I am coming quickly, and My reward is with Me, to give to every one according to his work. I am the Alpha and the Omega, the Beginning and the End, the First and the Last.

Jesus identified Himself as the "Root and the Offspring of David, the Bright and Morning Star" (22:16). His last words to John were, "Surely I am coming quickly" (22:20).

One of the things I love to do in the morning is to walk out to get the paper, just before the sunrise. There, in the distance, I can see this one bright star shining brightly in the darkness, just before the dawn. I think about Jesus and how He called Himself the Bright and Morning star. I think of Jesus, the light of the world, who lights every man who comes into the world. I think of the many who have chosen darkness rather than receive His glorious light. Then I think about the souls I want to reach, who have yet to be translated from the kingdom of darkness into the kingdom of the light of Jesus Christ. My mind travels to the New Jerusalem, where there will be no need for light because the Son will be the light of that great city. My heart is moved to return to my quiet place where I read His Word and pray for those I know who have never received His love and His light.

Lord, help me to watch and pray because You are coming quickly. Even so Lord come!

Daily Deposit: Make a list of those you know who need the Lord, and be diligent to pray for them in this next year.

To Contact the Author:

Linda Sommer
6716 Wright Road
Atlanta, GA 30328
(404) 252-3187

trsommer@aol.com